THE RANDOM HOUSE
PRO BASEBALL DICTIONARY

THE RANDOM HOUSE
PRO BASEBALL DICTIONARY

Stephen Weinstein

RANDOM HOUSE
NEW YORK

To my mother and father who stayed up
late in order to give me the score.

Manufactured in the United States of America
First Edition

ISBN: 0-679-75074-6

New York   Toronto   London   Sydney   Auckland

Acknowledgments

The statistics used in this book have come from a variety of sources. My thanks to the public relations staffs of the Atlanta Braves, Los Angeles Dodgers, Minnesota Twins, New York Yankees, and Pittsburgh Pirates, and to the Baseball Hall of Fame Library, Cooperstown, New York. I have relied on the *The Baseball Encyclopedia, Ninth Edition* (New York: Macmillan Publishing Company, 1993), *Total Baseball: The Ultimate Encyclopedia of Baseball,* Edited by John Thorn and Pete Palmer, Third Edition (New York: HarperPerennial, 1993), *The Sporting News Official Baseball Register,* 1993 Edition (St. Louis, 1993), and *The Sporting News Baseball Guide,* 1993 Edition (St. Louis, 1993). Essential to my understanding of baseball history has been the three volume work by Dr. Harold Seymour, *Baseball: The Early Years* (New York: Oxford University Press, 1960), *Baseball: The Golden Age* (New York: Oxford University Press, 1971), and *Baseball: the People's Game* (New York: Oxford University Press, 1990). For more on 19th century ballplayers see *Nineteenth Century Stars,* Edited by Robert Tiemann and Mark Rucker (Society for American Baseball Research, 1989). My thanks also to Dr. Irene Tichenor, Head Librarian of the Brooklyn Historical Society, for access to the society's collection of 19th century baseball scorecards and ephemera, and to Alan Gardner for sharing his vast knowledge of baseball history.

Note on Statistics

Statistics for 19th century and early 20th century ballplayers are being revised continuously due to the ongoing research by members of the Society for American Baseball Research (SABR). I have tried to include the most accurate information available. Statistics for Negro Leaguers are incomplete and clearly do not reflect their full accomplishments. Men who played in both the Negro Leagues and the major leagues show their statistics for their major league years only. An exception is Satchel Paige, whose statistics do not include his major league totals. Nicknames have been provided for Negro League teams because they played in various leagues and barnstormed regularly.

Space limitations for this book necessitated including only those positions players who played in at least 1,500 games and those pitchers who hurled at least 1,750 innings. Exceptions were made for relief pitchers, and for men like Cookie Lavagetto, who achieved notable feats, and Jim Bouton, who made news for his book on life in baseball, titled *Ball Four*. This book has included outstanding, but perhaps little remembered, players of the late 19th and early 20th centuries, at the expense of more familiar, although less talented, players and managers of the last 20 years.

Team Nicknames and Franchise Shifts

American Association (1882–91)

Baltimore Orioles (1882–91)
Boston Reds (1891)
Brooklyn Trolley Dodgers (1884–88)
Brooklyn Bridegrooms (1889)
Cincinnati Red Stockings (1882–89)
Cincinnati Kellys (1891)
Cleveland Blues (1887–88)
Columbus Buckeyes (1883–84, 1989–91)
Kansas City Cowboys (1888–89)
Louisville Eclipse (1882–84)
Louisville Colonels (1885–91)
New York Metropolitans (1882–87)
Philadelphia Athletics (1882–91)
Pittsburgh Alleghenys (1882–86)
Richmond Hop-Bitters (1884)
St. Louis Browns (1882–91)
Toledo Blue Stockings (1884)
Washington Nationals (1884)

Players League (1890)

Boston Reds
Brooklyn Wonders
Buffalo Bisons
Chicago Pirates
Cleveland Infants
New York Giants
Philadelphia Quakers
Pittsburgh Burghers

Federal League (1914–15)

Baltimore Terrapins
Brooklyn Tip-Tops
Buffalo Buffeds (1914)
Buffalo Blues (1915)
Chicago Chi-Feds (1914)
Chicago Whales (1915)

Indianapolis Hoosiers
Kansas City Packers
Newark Peppers
St. Louis Terriers

American League (1901–)

Baltimore Orioles (1901–02), New York
  Highlanders (1903–12), Yankees (1913–)
Boston Somersets (1901–02), Pilgrims (1903–06),
  Red Sox (1907–)
Chicago White Stockings (1901–03), White Sox
  (1904–)
Cleveland Blues (1901–04), Naps (1905–14),
  Indians (1915–)
Detroit Tigers (1901–)
Kansas City Royals (1969–)
Los Angeles Angels (1961–64), California Angels
  (1965–)
Milwaukee Brewers (1901), St. Louis Browns
  (1902–53), Baltimore Orioles (1954–)
Philadelphia Athletics (1901–54), Kansas City
  Athletics (1955–67), Oakland Athletics (1968–)
Seattle Pilots (1969), Milwaukee Brewers (1970–)
Seattle Mariners (1977–)
Toronto Blue Jays (1977–)
Washington Senators (1901–60), Minnesota Twins
  (1961–)
Washington Senators (1961–71), Texas Rangers
  (1972–)

National League (1876–)

Baltimore Orioles (1892–99)
Boston Red Caps (1876–82), Beaneaters
  (1883–1906), Doves (1907–10), Rustlers
  (1911), Braves (1912–35), Bees (1936–40),
  Braves (1941–52), Milwaukee Braves
  (1953–65), Atlanta Braves (1966–)
Brooklyn Bridegrooms (1890–98), Superbas
  (1899–1910), Dodgers (1911–13), Robins

(1914–31), Dodgers (1932–57), Los Angeles
    Dodgers (1958–)
Buffalo Bisons (1879–85)
Chicago White Stockings (1876–89), Colts
    (1890–97), Orphans (1898–1901), Cubs
    (1902–)
Cincinnati Red Stockings (1876–77), Reds
    (1878–80)
Cincinnati Reds (1890–1952), Redlegs (1953–58),
    Reds (1959–)
Cleveland Blues (1879–84), Spiders (1889–99)
Colorado Rockies (1993–)
Florida Marlins (1993–)
Hartford Dark Blues (1876–77)
Houston Colt .45s (1962–64), Astros (1965–)
Indianapolis Hoosiers (1887–89)
Kansas City Cowboys (1886)
Louisville Grays (1876–77)
Louisville Colonels (1892–99)
Montreal Expos (1969–)
New York Mutuals (1876)
New York Gothams (1883–84), Giants
    (1885–1957), San Francisco Giants (1958–)
New York Mets (1962–)
Philadelphia Quakers (1883–89), Phillies
    (1890–1943), Blue Jays (1944–45), Phillies
    (1946–)
Pittsburgh Alleghenys (1887–90), Pirates (1891–)
Providence Grays (1878–85)
St. Louis Brown Stockings (1876–77)
St. Louis Maroons (1885–86)
St. Louis Browns (1892–98), Perfectos (1899),
    Cardinals (1900–)
San Diego Padres (1969–)
Troy Trojans (1879–82)
Washington Statesmen (1886–89)
Washington Senators (1892–99)
Worcester Ruby Legs (1880–82)

Position Abbreviations

1B	First Base
2B	Second Base
3B	Third Base
SS	Shortstop
OF	Outfield
P	Pitcher
MGR	Manager

League Abbreviations

AA	American Association
FL	Federal League
NL	National League
PL	Players League
UA	Union Association

World Series Results

Year	Winner	Loser
1884	Providence (NL)-3	New York (AA)-0
1885	Chicago (NL)-3	St. Louis (AA)-3; 1 tie
1886	St. Louis (AA)-4	Chicago (NL)-2
1887	Detroit (NL)-10	St. Louis (AA)-5
1888	New York (NL)-6	St. Louis (AA)-4
1889	New York (NL)-6	Brooklyn (AA)-3
1890	Brooklyn (NL)-3	Louisville (AA)-3; 1 tie
1892	Boston (NL)-5	Cleveland (NL)-0; 1 tie
1894	New York (NL)-4	Baltimore (NL)-0
1895	Cleveland (NL)-4	Baltimore (NL)-1
1896	Baltimore (NL)-4	Cleveland (NL)-0
1897	Baltimore (NL)-4	Boston (NL)-1
1900	Brooklyn (NL)-3	Pittsburgh (NL)-1
1903	Boston (AL)-5	Pittsburgh (NL)-3
1905	New York (NL)-4	Philadelphia (AL)-1
1906	Chicago (AL)-4	Chicago (NL)-2
1907	Chicago (NL)-4	Detroit (AL)-0; 1 tie
1908	Chicago (NL)-4	Detroit (AL)-1
1909	Pittsburgh (NL)-4	Detroit (AL)-3
1910	Philadelphia (AL)-4	Chicago (NL)-1
1911	Philadelphia (AL)-4	New York (NL)-2
1912	Boston (AL)-4	New York (NL)-3; 1 tie
1913	Philadelphia (AL)-4	New York (NL)-1
1914	Boston (NL)-4	Philadelphia (AL)-0
1915	Boston (AL)-4	Philadelphia (NL)-1
1916	Boston (AL)-4	Brooklyn (NL)-1
1917	Chicago (AL)-4	New York (NL)-2
1918	Boston (AL)-4	Chicago (NL)-2
1919	Cincinnati (NL)-5	Chicago (AL)-3
1920	Cleveland (AL)-5	Brooklyn (NL)-2
1921	New York (NL)-5	New York (AL)-3

1922	New York (NL)-4	New York (AL)-0; 1 tie
1923	New York (AL)-4	New York (NL)-2
1924	Washington (AL)-4	New York (NL)-3
1925	Pittsburgh (NL)-4	Washington (AL)-3
1926	St. Louis (NL)-4	New York (AL)-3
1927	New York (AL)-4	Pittsburgh (NL)-0
1928	New York (AL)-4	St. Louis (NL)-0
1929	Philadelphia (AL)-4	Chicago (NL)-1
1930	Philadelphia (AL)-4	St. Louis (NL)-2
1931	St. Louis (NL)-4	Philadelphia (AL)-3
1932	New York (AL)-4	Chicago (NL)-0
1933	New York (NL)-4	Washington (AL)-1
1934	St. Louis (NL)-4	Detroit (AL)-3
1935	Detroit (AL)-4	Chicago (NL)-2
1936	New York (AL)-4	New York (NL)-2
1937	New York (AL)-4	New York (NL)-1
1938	New York (AL)-4	Chicago (NL)-0
1939	New York (AL)-4	Cincinnati (NL)-0
1940	Cincinnati (NL)-4	Detroit (AL)-3
1941	New York (AL)-4	Brooklyn (NL)-1
1942	St. Louis (NL)-4	New York (AL)-1
1943	New York (AL)-4	St. Louis (NL)-1
1944	St. Louis (NL)-4	St. Louis (AL)-2
1945	Detroit (AL)-4	Chicago (NL)-3
1946	St. Louis (NL)-4	Boston (AL)-3
1947	New York (AL)-4	Brooklyn (NL)-3
1948	Cleveland (AL)-4	Boston (NL)-2
1949	New York (AL)-4	Brooklyn (NL)-1
1950	New York (AL)-4	Philadelphia (NL)-0
1951	New York (AL)-4	New York (NL)-2
1952	New York (AL)-4	Brooklyn (NL)-3
1953	New York (AL)-4	Brooklyn (NL)-2
1954	New York (NL)-4	Cleveland (AL)-0
1955	Brooklyn (NL)-4	New York (AL)-3
1956	New York (AL)-4	Brooklyn (NL)-3
1957	Milwaukee (NL)-4	New York (AL)-3
1958	New York (AL)-4	Milwaukee (NL)-3
1959	Los Angeles (NL)-4	Chicago (AL)-2

1960	Pittsburgh (NL)-4	New York (AL)-3
1961	New York (AL)-4	Cincinnati (NL)-1
1962	New York (AL)-4	San Francisco (NL)-3
1963	Los Angeles (NL)-4	New York (AL)-0
1964	St. Louis (NL)-4	New York (AL)-3
1965	Los Angeles (NL)-4	Minnesota (AL)-3
1966	Baltimore (AL)-4	Los Angeles (NL)-0
1967	St. Louis (NL)-4	Boston (AL)-3
1968	Detroit (AL)-4	St. Louis (NL)-3
1969	New York (NL)-4	Baltimore (AL)-1
1970	Baltimore (AL)-4	Cincinnati (NL)-1
1971	Pittsburgh (NL)-4	Baltimore (AL)-3
1972	Oakland (AL)-4	Cincinnati (NL)-3
1973	Oakland (AL)-4	New York (NL)-3
1974	Oakland (AL)-4	Los Angeles (NL)-1
1975	Cincinnati (NL)-4	Boston (AL)-3
1976	Cincinnati (NL)-4	New York (AL)-0
1977	New York (AL)-4	Los Angeles (NL)-2
1978	New York (AL)-4	Los Angeles (NL)-2
1979	Pittsburgh (NL)-4	Baltimore (AL)-3
1980	Philadelphia (NL)-4	Kansas City (AL)-2
1981	Los Angeles (NL)-4	New York (AL)-2
1982	St. Louis (NL)-4	Milwaukee (AL)-3
1983	Baltimore (AL)-4	Philadelphia (NL)-1
1984	Detroit (AL)-4	San Diego (NL)-1
1985	Kansas City (AL)-4	St. Louis (NL)-3
1986	New York (NL)-4	Boston (AL)-3
1987	Minnesota (AL)-4	St. Louis (NL)-3
1988	Los Angeles (NL)-4	Oakland (AL)-1
1989	Oakland (AL)-4	San Francisco (NL)-0
1990	Cincinnati (NL)-4	Oakland (AL)-0
1991	Minnesota (AL)-4	Atlanta (NL)-3
1992	Toronto (AL)-4	Atlanta (NL)-2
1993	Toronto (AL)-4	Philadelphia (NL)-2

Baseball's All-Time Statistical Leaders

	Games
Pete Rose	3,562
Carl Yastrzemski	3,308
Hank Aaron	3,298
Ty Cobb	3,035
Stan Musial	3,026
Willie Mays	2,992
Rusty Staub	2,951
Brooks Robinson	2,896
Robin Yount*	2,856
Dave Winfield*	2,850
Al Kaline	2,834
Eddie Collins	2,826
Reggie Jackson	2,820
Frank Robinson	2,808
Honus Wagner	2,792
Tris Speaker	2,789
Tony Perez	2,777
Mel Ott	2,730
George Brett	2,707
Graig Nettles	2,700
Darrell Evans	2,687
Rabbit Maranville	2,670
Joe Morgan	2,649
Lou Brock	2,616
Dwight Evans	2,606

	Hits
Pete Rose	4,256
Ty Cobb	4,189
Hank Aaron	3,771
Stan Musial	3,630
Tris Speaker	3,514
Carl Yastrzemski	3,419
Honus Wagner	3,415
Eddie Collins	3,312

*Active

Willie Mays	3,283
Nap Lajoie	3,242
George Brett	3,154
Paul Waner	3,152
Robin Yount*	3,142
Rod Carew	3,053
Lou Brock	3,023
Dave Winfield*	3,014
Al Kaline	3,007
Roberto Clemente	3,000
Cap Anson	2,995
Sam Rice	2,987
Sam Crawford	2,961
Frank Robinson	2,943
Willie Keeler	2,932
Jake Beckley	2,930
Rogers Hornsby	2,930

Home Runs

Hank Aaron	755
Babe Ruth	714
Willie Mays	660
Frank Robinson	586
Harmon Killebrew	573
Reggie Jackson	563
Mike Schmidt	548
Mickey Mantle	536
Jimmie Foxx	534
Willie McCovey	521
Ted Williams	521
Ernie Banks	512
Eddie Mathews	512
Mel Ott	511
Lou Gehrig	493
Stan Musial	475
Willie Stargell	475
Dave Winfield*	453
Carl Yastrzemski	452

*Active

Dave Kingman	442
Eddie Murray*	441
Billy Williams	426
Darrell Evans	414
Andre Dawson*	412
Duke Snider	407

Runs Batted In

Hank Aaron	2,297
Babe Ruth	2,213
Lou Gehrig	1,995
Stan Musial	1,951
Ty Cobb	1,937
Jimmie Foxx	1,922
Willie Mays	1,903
Cap Anson	1,879
Mel Ott	1,860
Carl Yastrzemski	1,844
Ted Williams	1,839
Al Simmons	1,827
Frank Robinson	1,812
Dave Winfield*	1,786
Honus Wagner	1,732
Reggie Jackson	1,702
Eddie Murray*	1,662
Tony Perez	1,652
Ernie Banks	1,636
Goose Goslin	1,609
Nap Lajoie	1,599
Mike Schmidt	1,595
George Brett	1,595
Rogers Hornsby	1,584
Harmon Killebrew	1,584

Batting Average

Ty Cobb	.366
Rogers Hornsby	.358
Joe Jackson	.356

*Active

Ed Delahanty	.346
Tris Speaker	.345
Ted Williams	.344
Billy Hamilton	.344
Dan Brouthers	.342
Babe Ruth	.342
Harry Heilmann	.342
Pete Browning	.341
Willie Keeler	.341
Bill Terry	.341
George Sisler	.340
Lou Gehrig	.340
Jesse Burkett	.338
Nap Lajoie	.338
Riggs Stephenson	.336
Wade Boggs*	.335
Al Simmons	.334
John McGraw	.334
Paul Waner	.333
Eddie Collins	.333
Mike Donlin	.333
Stan Musial	.331

Stolen Bases

Rickey Henderson*	1,095
Lou Brock	938
Billy Hamilton	912
Ty Cobb	891
Tim Raines*	751
Eddie Collins	744
Arlie Latham	739
Max Carey	738
Honus Wagner	722
Joe Morgan	689
Willie Wilson*	667
Tom Brown	657
Bert Campaneris	649
Vince Coleman*	648

*Active

George Davis	616
Dummy Hoy	594
Maury Wills	586
George Van Haltren	583
Hugh Duffy	574
Bid McPhee	568
Ozzie Smith*	563
Davey Lopes	557
Cesar Cedeno	550
Bill Dahlen	547
John Ward	540
	Wins
Cy Young	511
Walter Johnson	417
Pete Alexander	373
Christy Mathewson	373
Warren Spahn	363
Kid Nichols	361
Jim Galvin	360
Tim Keefe	342
Steve Carlton	329
John Clarkson	328
Eddie Plank	326
Don Sutton	324
Nolan Ryan	324
Phil Niekro	318
Gaylord Perry	314
Tom Seaver	311
Charles Radbourn	309
Mickey Welch	307
Lefty Grove	300
Early Wynn	300
Tommy John	288
Bert Blyleven	287
Robin Roberts	286
Ferguson Jenkins	284
Tony Mullane	284

*Active

	Innings Pitched
Cy Young	7,354
Jim Galvin	5,941
Walter Johnson	5,923
Phil Niekro	5,404
Nolan Ryan	5,385
Gaylord Perry	5,350
Don Sutton	5,282
Warren Spahn	5,243
Steve Carlton	5,217
Pete Alexander	5,189
Kid Nichols	5,056
Tim Keefe	5,047
Bert Blyleven	4,970
Mickey Welch	4,802
Tom Seaver	4,782
Christy Mathewson	4,780
Tommy John	4,710
Robin Roberts	4,688
Early Wynn	4,564
John Clarkson	4,536
Charles Radbourn	4,535
Tony Mullane	4,531
Jim Kaat	4,530
Ferguson Jenkins	4,500
Eddie Plank	4,495

	Strikeouts (Pitchers)
Nolan Ryan	5,714
Steve Carlton	4,136
Bert Blyleven	3,701
Tom Seaver	3,640
Don Sutton	3,574
Gaylord Perry	3,534
Walter Johnson	3,509
Phil Niekro	3,342
Ferguson Jenkins	3,192
Bob Gibson	3,117
Jim Bunning	2,855

Mickey Lolich	2,832
Cy Young	2,800
Frank Tanana	2,773
Warren Spahn	2,583
Bob Feller	2,581
Jerry Koosman	2,556
Tim Keefe	2,545
Christy Mathewson	2,502
Don Drysdale	2,486
Jim Kaat	2,461
Sam McDowell	2,453
Luis Tiant	2,416
Sandy Koufax	2,396
Jack Morris	2,378

	Earned Run Average
Ed Walsh	1.82
Addie Joss	1.89
Mordecai Brown	2.06
John Ward	2.10
Christy Mathewson	2.13
Walter Johnson	2.16
Rube Waddell	2.16
Orval Overall	2.23
Tommy Bond	2.25
Ed Ruelbach	2.28
Will White	2.28
Jim Scott	2.30
Eddie Plank	2.35
Larry Corcoran	2.36
Eddie Cicotte	2.38
Ed Killian	2.38
George McQuillan	2.38
Doc White	2.39
Nap Rucker	2.42
Terry Larkin	2.43
Jim McCormick	2.43
Jeff Tesreau	2.43
Chief Bender	2.46

Sam Leever	2.47
Lefty Leifeld	2.47
Hooks Wiltse	2.47
	Saves
Lee Smith*	401
Jeff Reardon*	365
Rollie Fingers	341
Rich Gossage*	308
Bruce Sutter	300
Dennis Eckersley*	275
Tom Henke*	260
Dave Righetti*	252
Dan Quisenberry	244
Sparky Lyle	238
John Franco*	236
Hoyt Wilhelm	227
Gene Garber	218
Dave Smith	216
Bobby Thigpen*	201
Roy Face	193
Doug Jones*	190
Mike Marshall	188
Mitch Williams*	186
Steve Bedrosian*	184
Kent Tekulve	184
Randy Myers*	184
Tug McGraw	180
Ron Perranoski	179
Lindy McDaniel	172

*Active

A

Aaron, Hank (Hammerin' Hank)
1934–
Indianapolis Clowns (1952), Milwaukee (NL 1954–65), Atlanta (NL 1966–74), Milwaukee (AL 1975–76)   OF, 1B, DH   BR/TR

3,298 games	.305 ba
3,771 hits	755 hr
2,297 rbi	240 sb

Baseball's all-time home run leader (755), Aaron also holds the major league record for games played, at bats, total bases, and RBI. His career epitomized consistency—13 consecutive seasons of scoring at least 100 runs, 20 consecutive seasons with at least 20 home runs, 11 seasons with more than 100 RBI, and a record 21 All-Star Games. He was the prototypical wrist hitter, staying back until the absolute last moment and then swinging the bat with a flick of his wrists. Overlooked in all of his offensive achievements was his sterling defensive play and his base-running ability. The NL's MVP in 1957, Aaron had his uniform number 44 retired by both the Braves and the Brewers. He was inducted into the Hall of Fame in 1982.

Abbott, Jim
1967–
California (AL 1989–92), New York (AL 1993 Active)   P   LHP

157 games	1061 innings
58-66 W–L	3.66 ERA
603 k's	

Born without a right hand, Abbott developed into one of the most promising lefties in the game, relying on a cut fastball and slider. He is adept at fielding ground balls, and batters long ago stopped trying to bunt for base hits against him. In 1991, Abbott won 18 games with a smart ERA of 2.89. He pitched a no-hitter in 1993, but otherwise stumbled through an 11–14 season.

Abernathy, Ted

1933–
Washington (AL 1955–57, 1960), Cleveland (AL 1963–64), Chicago (NL 1965–66, 1969–70), Atlanta (NL 1966), Cincinnati (NL 1967–68), St. Louis (NL 1970), Kansas City (AL 1970–72)   P
BR/RHP

681 games	1147 innings
63-69 W–L	3.46 ERA
765 k's	148 saves

A two-time Fireman of the Year, Abernathy was one of the best submarine pitchers in modern history. He didn't hit his stride until 1965, when he led the NL in game appearances (84) and saves (31). Abernathy found it difficult to put consecutive good seasons together.

Adams, Charles (Babe)

1882–1968
St. Louis (NL 1906), Pittsburgh (NL 1907, 1909–26)   P   BL/RHP

482 games	2,995 innings
194-140 W–L	2.76 ERA
1,036 k's	15 saves

Adams might have been the best purchase the Pirates ever made. As a rookie in 1909, he established a record 1.11 ERA and won three games in the World Series, including the decisive seventh game (8–0). He currently ranks first in Pirates history in shutouts (44) and third in wins. A control artist, Adams has the second-best ratio of walks to innings pitched in major league history.

Adcock, Joe

1927–

Cincinnati (NL 1950–52), Milwaukee (NL 1953–62), Cleveland (AL 1963), Los Angeles (AL 1964), California (AL 1965–66)   1B   BR/TR

1,959 games	.277 ba
1,832 hits	336 hr
1,122 rbi	20 sb

On any other team, Adcock would have been the leading slugger, but on the Milwaukee squads of the 1950s, he took a back seat to Hank Aaron and Eddie Mathews. Still, he belted 38 homers in 1956 and 35 more in 1961. Cozy Ebbets Field was the scene of Adcock's greatest game in 1954, when he cracked four home runs in one game.

Aguilera, Rick (Aggie)

1961–

New York (NL 1985–89), Minnesota (AL 1989–93 Active)   P   BR/RHP

373 games	822 innings
55-49 W–L	3.27 ERA
641 k's	156 saves

A fifth starter on the pitching-rich Mets, Aguilera began relieving during the 1989 season following an arm injury. He immediately took to bullpen duty, striking out 80 men in 69 innings. Ironically, Aguilera's success made him appealing to the Twins, who acquired him in a trade for Frank Viola midway through the 1989 season. He has gone on to record seasons of 32, 42, 41, and 34 saves since then. Aguilera's best pitch is his slider, and he also has an explosive fastball. One thing he misses in the AL is the chance to take his swings at the plate, for he is an outstanding batter.

Alexander, Doyle

1950–

Los Angeles (NL 1971), Baltimore (AL 1972–76),
New York (AL 1976, 1982–83), Texas (AL
1977–79), Atlanta (NL 1980, 1986–87), San
Francisco (NL 1981), Toronto (AL 1983–86),
Detroit (AL 1987–89)   P   BR/RHP

561 games	3,367 innings
194-174 W–L	3.76 ERA
1,528 k's	3 saves

Alexander was the epitome of the cagey veteran, relying on a herky-jerky motion, precise control, and the ability to change speeds on all his pitches. He salvaged his career on more than one occasion when it appeared he was washed up, but none was more surprising than the revival after his trade from the Yankees in 1983. He went on to win 17 games twice for Toronto and helped Detroit to the AL East crown in 1987 by winning nine consecutive decisions in a Tigers uniform.

Alexander, Grover (Pete)

1887–1950

Philadelphia (NL 1911–17, 1930), Chicago (NL
1918–26), St. Louis (NL 1926–29)   P
BR/RHP

696 games	5,189 innings
373-208 W–L	2.56 ERA
2,198 k's	32 saves

Pitching in Philadelphia's tiny Baker Bowl in 1916, Alexander tossed a major league record 16 shutouts, while leading the NL in wins (33), ERA (1.55), complete games (38), and strikeouts (167). He threw the ball hard and had the best change-up of his era, plus he had pinpoint control. An epileptic, Alexander also struggled with alcoholism later in his career. His 90 career shutouts are an NL record that more than warranted his induction into the Hall of Fame in 1938.

Allen, Johnny

1905–1959

New York (AL 1932–35), Cleveland (AL 1936–40),
St. Louis (AL 1941), Brooklyn (NL 1941–43), New
York (NL 1943–44)   P   BR/RHP

352 games	1,950 innings
142-75 W–L	3.75 ERA
1,070 k's	18 saves

Allen was one of the most successful pitchers in baseball history. Some skeptics might have attributed his
record to his tenure with the powerful Yankees, where
he had successive seasons of 17–4, 15–7, 5–2, and
13–6; but the argumentative Allen proved his worth
following a trade to Cleveland in 1936, when he went
20–10, followed by a remarkable 15–1 in 1937. His
best pitch was a moving fastball.

Allen, Newton (Newt, Colt)

1901–1988

All Nations (1922), Kansas City Monarchs (NLL
1922–31, 1932, 1935–44), St. Louis Stars (NLL
1931), Detroit Wolves (NLL 1932), Homestead
Grays (1932)   2B   BB/TR

792 games	.296 ba
961 hits	20 hr

Aggressive on the bases and unequaled at turning the
double play, Allen was the best second baseman in the
Negro Leagues during his era. No one had a better infield arm.

Allen, Richard (Dick)

1942–

Philadelphia (NL 1963–69, 1975–76), St. Louis (NL
1970), Los Angeles (NL 1971), Chicago (AL
1972–74), Oakland (AL 1977)   1B, 3B, OF
BR/TR

1,749 games	.292 ba
1,848 hits	351 hr
1,119 rbi	133 sb

Occasionally moody and controversial, Dick Allen was a feared slugger who still holds the NL record for total bases by a rookie. That year he batted .318 with 38 doubles, 13 triples, 29 home runs, and a league-best 125 runs scored. He went on to lead his league in slugging percentage three times. Although he spent the majority of his career in Philadelphia, Allen found contentment in Chicago under the gentle tutelage of eternal optimist Chuck Tanner.

Allison, Bob

1934–
Washington (AL 1958–60), Minnesota (AL 1961–70) **OF** **BR/TR**

1,541 games	.255 ba
1,281 hits	256 hr
796 rbi	84 sb

A strong right-handed slugger and a fine defensive outfielder, Allison formed part of a potent Twins attack that featured Harmon Killebrew. He hit 30 or more homers three times and twice knocked in over 100 runs.

Alomar, Roberto

1968–
San Diego (NL 1988–91), Toronto (AL 1992–93 Active) **2B** **BB/TR**

914 games	.297 ba
1,054 hits	56 hr
395 rbi	247 sb

Widely acclaimed as the best all-around player in the AL, Alomar can hit, hit with power, run, and field brilliantly. He has improved each year and in 1993 batted .326 with 109 runs scored and 93 RBI. Defensively, he has great range to either side. Above all, Alomar loves the game and plays hard every day.

Alou, Felipe

1935–

San Francisco (NL 1958–63), Milwaukee (NL 1964–65), Atlanta (NL 1966–69), Oakland (AL 1970–71), New York (AL 1971–73), Montreal (NL 1973), Milwaukee (AL 1974); MGR—Montreal (NL 1992–93 Active)   **OF, MGR**   **BR/TR**

2,082 games	.286 ba
2,101 hits	206 hr
852 rbi	107 sb

Alou came into the major leagues hitting line drives and never stopped until he retired 17 years later. He batted over .300 three times, but his best year came in 1966 when he hit .327 with 31 homers and 74 RBI while batting leadoff. That year he led the NL with 218 hits and 122 runs scored. When his brothers Matty and Jesus joined him in the Giants outfield during one game against the Mets, baseball history was made. In 1966, his brother Matty led the NL in batting (.342) and he finished second (.327), making them the only brother combination ever to finish one-two in the batting race.

Alou, Matty

1938–

San Francisco (NL 1960–65), Pittsburgh (NL 1966–70), St. Louis (NL 1971–72, 1973), Oakland (AL 1972), New York (AL 1973), San Diego (NL 1974)   **OF**   **BL/TL**

1,667 games	.307 ba
1,777 hits	31 hr
427 rbi	156 sb

The smallest of the three Alou brothers to play in the major leagues, Matty learned the art of hitting from Harry ("the Hat") Walker and began slapping the ball past the infield for base hit after base hit. He is the last NL'er to hit .330 or better four years in a row (1966–69). He led the NL in batting in his first attempt at this new style (.342 in 1966) and also led the league with 231 hits and 41 doubles in 1969.

Alston, Walter (Smokey)
1911–1984
MGR—Brooklyn (NL 1954–57), Los Angeles (NL 1958–76) MGR

The soft-spoken but strong-willed manager of the Dodgers, Alston worked on a succession of one-year contracts throughout his 23-year tenure. When the Dodgers hired him in 1954, the New York *Daily News* headlined him as "Walter Who?", but Alston went on to earn Brooklyn its only World Series crown in 1955. He skippered the Dodgers to three additional titles in Los Angeles in 1959, 1963, and 1965.

Ames, Leon (Red)
1882–1936
New York (NL 1903–13), Cincinnati (NL 1913–15), St. Louis (NL 1915–19), Philadelphia (NL 1919) P BB/RHP

533 games	3,198 innings
183-167 W–L	2.63 ERA
1,702 k's	36 saves

Ames was a dependable starter for John McGraw's Giants, winning 22 games for the 1905 World Series winners and 15 games in 1909. On opening day in 1909, he pitched a nine-inning no-hitter against the Dodgers, only to lose the game in the 13th inning 3–0.

Anderson, George (Sparky)
1934–
Philadelphia (NL 1959); MGR—Cincinnati (NL 1970–78), Detroit (AL 1979–93 Active) MGR, 2B
BR/TR

152 games	.218 ba
104 hits	34 rbi
6 sb	

At times, Sparky Anderson appears to be the living reincarnation of Casey Stengel, managing teams successfully year after year while regaling sportswriters with a mouthful of imponderable verbiage. In 1993, he surpassed Walter Alston to become the third winningest manager in major league history with 2,081 wins. Anderson has won World Series in the NL with Cincinnati in 1975 and 1976 and in the AL with Detroit in 1984, making him the only manager to win titles in both leagues.

Andujar, Joaquin

1952–
Houston (NL 1976–81, 1988), St. Louis (NL 1981–85), Oakland (AL 1986–87)　P
BB/RHP

405 games	2,153 innings
127-118 W–L	3.58 ERA
1,032 k's	9 saves

The self-proclaimed "One Tough Dominican," Andujar sometimes let his macho attitude get the best of his on-field performance, most particularly in the 1985 World Series against Kansas City. He won 20 games in 1984 and 21 in 1985 but surpassed 12 victories in only one other season. Andujar was a fierce competitor who relied on precise control of his pitches to keep batters off-stride.

Anson, Adrian (Cap)

1852–1922
Chicago (NL 1876–97); MGR—Chicago (NL 1879–97), New York (NL 1898)　1B, MGR
BR/TR

2,276 games	.329 ba
2,995 hits	97 hr
1,879 rbi	247 sb

Considered by many experts to have been the best player of the 19th century, Anson towered over most opponents on the diamond, both in size and bluster. At the plate, he had a peculiar wide-open stance and belted the ball with power to all fields. Defensively, Anson excelled at first base. And as a foul-mouthed, umpire-baiting manager, he led Chicago to five pennants.

Antonelli, Johnny

1930–

Boston (NL 1948–50), Milwaukee (NL 1953, 1961), New York (NL 1954–57), San Francisco (NL 1958–60), Cleveland (AL 1961)   P   BL/LHP

377 games	1,992 innings
126-110 W–L	3.34 ERA
1,162 k's	21 saves

A victim of the bonus baby system, Antonelli was lost on the Braves bench prior to his trade to the Giants for the ever-popular Bobby Thomson. He proved his value immediately upon his arrival at the Polo Grounds by going 21–7 in 1954 with a league-best 2.30 ERA and six shutouts. Antonelli went on to win once in the Giants' World Series sweep of Cleveland and reached the 20-victory plateau again in 1956.

Aparicio, Luis (Little Louie)

1934–

Chicago (AL 1956–62, 1968–70), Baltimore (AL 1963–67), Boston (AL 1971–73)   SS   BR/TR

2,599 games	.262 ba
2,677 hits	83 hr
791 rbi	506 sb

Aparicio helped bring the stolen base back into baseball in the 1950s. Considered a relic of the dead ball era, the stolen base was a lost art in the age of the slugger. Little Louie led the AL in steals a record nine consecutive seasons (1956–64), and he sparked many rallies for the Go-Go White Sox, the pennant winners in 1959. At shortstop, he had great range and one of the most powerful throwing arms of any period. He was inducted into the Hall of Fame in 1984.

Appier, Kevin
1967–
Kansas City (AL 1989–93 Active)   P   RHP

136 games	862 innings
59–38 W–L	2.95 ERA
631 k's	

Appier outlasted all the reputed aces of the Royals pitching staff, including Danny Jackson, Brett Saberhagen, and David Cone, to emerge as the real stopper. Improving with each season, he won 15 games in 1992 and 18 the following year when he led the AL in ERA (2.56). Appier relies on a moving fastball and a sharp slider.

Appling, Luke (Old Aches and Pains)
1909–1991
Chicago (AL 1930–50); MGR—Kansas City (AL 1967) SS, MGR   BR/TR

2,422 games	.310 ba
2,749 hits	45 hr
1,116 rbi	179 sb

A superb fielder who could also wield the sapling, Appling led the AL in batting in 1936 (.388) and in 1943 (.328). He was the first AL shortstop to lead the league in hitting. Expert at fouling off pitches not to his liking, he rarely struck out. The White Sox retired his uniform number 4, and he was inducted into the Hall of Fame in 1964.

Ashburn, Richie (Whitey)

1927–

Philadelphia (NL 1948–59), Chicago (NL 1960–61),
New York (NL 1962)   **OF**   **BL/TR**

2,189 games	.308 ba
2,574 hits	29 hr
586 rbi	234 sb

Philadelphians still ask, Why isn't Ashburn in the Hall
of Fame? He collected the most hits in the NL during
the fifties and fielded brilliantly, although he did not
have a strong throwing arm. Ashburn led the NL in
hits three times, as well as in batting in both 1955
(.338) and 1958 (.350). He hit over .300 nine times,
including his final season in the majors with the inept
1962 Mets.

Auker, Eldon (Big Six)

1910–

Detroit (AL 1933–38), Boston (AL 1939), St. Louis
(AL 1940–42)   **P**   **BR/RHP**

333 games	1,963 innings
130-101 W–L	4.42 ERA
594 k's	2 saves

The submarining right-handed Auker joined Schoolboy Rowe and Tommy Bridges to pitch the Tigers to
consecutive pennants in 1934–35. In 1934, he won 15
games but lost the decisive seventh game of the World
Series to St. Louis. The following year, he led the AL in
winning percentage (.720) when he went 18–7. Never
a strikeout pitcher, Auker made batters beat the ball
into the ground.

Averill, Earl

1902–1983

Cleveland (AL 1929–1939), Detroit (AL 1939–40),
Boston (NL 1941)   **OF**   **BL/TR**

1,668 games	.318 ba
2,019 hits	238 hr
1,164 rbi	70 sb

Averill is the only Hall of Famer (inducted in 1975) to hit a home run in his first time at bat in the big leagues, on opening day at that. A powerful hitter despite his small frame, he hit .300 or better eight times, including a career-best .378 in 1936 when he belted a league-high 232 hits. Averill slammed more than 30 home runs in three seasons and knocked in over 100 runs five times. The Indians retired his uniform number 3.

Avery, Steve
1970–
Atlanta (NL 1990–93 Active)   P   BL/LHP

| 126 games | 50-36 W–L |
| 3.49 ERA | 466 k's |

Avery is one of the top young left-handers in baseball today. He has great stuff and throws an assortment of fastballs, curves, and sliders. His breakthrough season came in 1991 when he went 18–8.

B

Baerga, Carlos
1968–
Cleveland (1990–93 Active)   2B   BB/TR

581 games	.301 ba
657 hits	59 hr
335 rbi	28 sb

In 1992, Baerga became the only second baseman in the history of the American League to hit .300, while racking up 20 home runs, 100 RBI, and 200 hits in one season. The following year he duplicated the feat and also slammed home runs from each side of the plate in the same inning. It's remarkable to think that

San Diego traded two second basemen the quality of Carlos Baerga and Roberto Alomar.

Bagby, Jim (Sarge)

1889–1954

Cincinnati (NL 1912), Cleveland (AL 1916–22),
Pittsburgh (NL 1923)   P   BB/RHP

316 games	1,821 innings
127-88 W–L	3.11 ERA
450 k's	29 saves

In 1920, Bagby had a dream season, leading the AL in wins (31), winning percentage (.721), game appearances (48), complete games (30), and innings pitched (339) as the Indians won the World Series. That fall, he became the first pitcher to hit a home run in the fall classic by connecting against Brooklyn. Bagby threw an effective change-up along with his fastball and curve.

Bagwell, Jeff

1968–

Houston (NL 1991–93 Active)   1B   BR/TR

460 games	.295 ba
494 hits	53 hr
266 rbi	30 sb

Bagwell has emerged as one of the top young hitters in the game. A pull hitter, he has a quick bat and takes a short stroke. In only three years with Houston, he has established a franchise record for consecutive games played. Named the NL Rookie of the Year in 1991, when he hit .294, Bagwell batted .320 in 1993.

Baines, Harold

1959–

Chicago (AL 1980–89), Texas (AL 1989–90),
Oakland (AL 1990–92), Baltimore (AL 1993 Active)
OF, DH   BL/TL

1,962 games	.288 ba
2,060 hits	261 hr
1,144 rbi	30 sb

This native of the Maryland Eastern Shore finally returned home in 1993 to play for the Baltimore Orioles. Baines spent his best seasons with the White Sox; following his trade to Texas, Chicago retired his uniform number 3. Although not a major power figure, he remains second in career home runs for the White Sox (186). Baines is a consistent, clutch hitter who hit between .271 and .321 every year from 1981 to 1991. He is one of the few left-handed batters who hits left-handed pitching well enough not to be platooned.

Baker, Frank (Home Run)

1886–1963

Philadelphia (AL 1908–14), New York (AL 1916–22)   **3B**   **BL/TR**

1,575 games	.307 ba
1,838 hits	96 hr
1,013 rbi	235 sb

The third baseman in Connie Mack's $100,000 infield, "Home Run" Baker earned his nickname by belting two game-winning home runs in the 1911 World Series. Swinging a heavy 52-ounce bat, he led the AL in homers for four consecutive years (1911–14). The chief slugger of the dead ball era, Baker was inducted into the Hall of Fame in 1955.

Baker, Johnnie (Dusty)

1949–

Atlanta (NL 1968–75), Los Angeles (NL 1976–83), San Francisco (NL 1984), Oakland (AL 1985–86); MGR—San Francisco (NL 1993 Active)   **OF, MGR**   **BR/TR**

2,039 games	.278 ba
1,981 hits	242 hr
1,013 rbi	137 sb

Baker was a rare hitter who could hit for both average and power. He finished third in the NL in batting in 1972 (.321) and 1981 (.320), and he slammed 30 homers in 1977. Baker excelled in postseason play, hitting .371 in 17 NLCS matches and .292 in the 1977 World Series. In 1993, he managed the Giants to 103 victories, but finished second in a stirring race with the Braves.

Bancroft, Dave (Beauty)
1891–1972
Philadelphia (NL 1915–20), New York (NL 1920–23, 1930), Boston (NL 1924–27), Brooklyn (NL 1928–29); MGR—Boston (NL 1924–27)   SS, MGR   BB/TR

1,913 games	.279 ba
2,004 hits	32 hr
591 rbi	145 sb

Bancroft was a scrappy, holler guy on the infield who played on four pennant winners in his career, including the Phillies' first flag in 1915. Outstanding defensively, he also hit over .300 five times. He was inducted into the Hall of Fame in 1971.

Bando, Sal
1944–
Kansas City (AL 1966–67), Oakland (AL 1968–76), Milwaukee (AL 1977–81)   3B   BR/TR

2,019 games	.254 ba
1,790 hits	242 hr
1,039 rbi	75 sb

Bando's statistics never reflected his true value to the Athletics' outstanding clubs of the 1970s. Although he batted below .250 as frequently as he did above it, he drew many walks and delivered in the clutch. From 1969 to 1978, Bando drove in at least 75 runs each year while fielding his position smartly.

Banks, Ernie

1931–

Kansas City Monarchs (1950–53), Chicago (NL 1953–71)　**1B, SS**　**BR/TR**

2,528 games	.274 ba
2,583 hits	512 hr
1,636 rbi	50 sb

An ebullient figure on the ballfield, Banks greeted each day with the cry "Let's Play Two!" The most popular Cub in the history of the franchise, he generated tremendous power from a narrow frame. No shortstop since Honus Wagner packed the wallop that Banks did. He belted over 40 homers five times and was named the NL MVP in both 1958 and 1959. In 1958, he batted .313 with 47 homers and 129 RBI; the following year, he hit .304 with 45 home runs and 143 RBI. Knee injuries forced his move to first base, but he continued to slam the ball. Banks was inducted into the Hall of Fame in 1977, and the Cubs retired his uniform number 14.

Bannister, Floyd

1955–

Houston (NL 1977–78), Seattle (AL 1979–82), Chicago (AL 1983–87), Kansas City (AL 1988–89), California (AL 1991), Texas (AL 1992)　**P**
BL/LHP

431 games	2,388 innings
134–143 W–L	4.06 ERA
1,723 k's	

Bannister had great stuff but never became a consistent winner in the big leagues. He won 16 games for the White Sox in both 1983 and 1987, but most seasons found him below the .500 mark. In 1982, he led the AL in strikeouts (209).

Barber, Steve
1939–
Baltimore (AL 1960–67), New York (AL 1967–68),
Seattle (AL 1969), Chicago (NL 1970), Atlanta (NL
1970–72), California (AL 1972–73), San Francisco
(NL 1974)   P   BL/LHP

466 games	1,999 innings
121-106 W–L	3.36 ERA
1,309 k's	13 saves

The leading member of the Baby Birds pitching staff
nurtured by Paul Richards, Barber won 18 games in
1961 and 20 games in 1963, but he was troubled by
elbow problems and poor control throughout his career. Some nights it seemed that Barber would either
strike out or walk half the lineup. Indeed, he pitched
8.2 innings of an eventual no-hitter against Detroit in
1967 only to lose the game because he surrendered 10
free passes.

Barnes, Jesse (Nubby)
1892–1961
Boston (NL 1915–17, 1923–25), New York (NL
1918–23), Brooklyn (NL 1926–27)   P
BL/RHP

422 games	2,569 innings
152-150 W–L	3.22 ERA
653 k's	13 saves

A change-up artist, Barnes emerged as a star following
a trade to the Giants for Buck Herzog. He led the NL
in victories in 1919 (25) and won 20 the following
year. Jesse and his brother, pitcher and occasional
teammate Virgil Barnes, were the first siblings to op-
pose each other as starters in a 1927 match.

Bartell, Dick (Rowdy Richard)

1907–

Pittsburgh (NL 1927–30), Philadelphia (NL
1931–34), New York (NL 1935–38, 1941–43,
1946), Chicago (NL 1939), Detroit (AL 1940–41)
SS   BR/TR

2,016 games	.284 ba
2,165 hits	79 hr
710 rbi	109 sb

Bartell was a fierce competitor who battled opponents
with all his energy and was a willing participant in on-
field brawls. At bat, he stood right on top of the plate
and dared pitchers to hit him. He was a good clutch
hitter who played on two pennant winners in New
York and one in Detroit. In 1932, he batted .308 while
scoring 118 runs. Smart defensively, he had good range
but occasionally displayed a scatter arm.

Bauer, Hank

1922–

New York (AL 1948–59), Kansas City (AL
1960–61); MGR—Kansas City (AL 1961–62),
Baltimore (AL 1964–68), Oakland (AL 1969)   OF,
MGR   BR/TR

1,544 games	.277 ba
1,424 hits	164 hr
703 rbi	50 sb

Bauer personified the Yankees style during the fifties—tough, hustling, perfectionist, and willing to sacrifice individual glory for team success. A World War
II hero who fought on Okinawa, he brought a fierce
determination to the field. Fast afoot with good power,
Bauer often batted leadoff for the Yanks. Twice a .300
hitter, he platooned in the outfield with Gene Woodling. Given an opportunity to play regularly in 1955
and 1956, he belted a total of 46 homers and scored
193 runs. In World Series play, Bauer hit safely in a
record 18 consecutive games. Managing Baltimore in

1966, he brought the city its first modern World Series title.

Baylor, Don (Groove)
1949–
Baltimore (AL 1970–75), Oakland (AL 1976, 1988), California (AL 1977–82), New York (AL 1983–85), Boston (AL 1986–87), Minnesota (AL 1987); MGR—Colorado (NL 1993 Active)   DH, OF, MGR   BR/TR

2,292 games	.260 ba
2,135 hits	338 hr
1,276 rbi	285 sb

Wherever he played Baylor was acclaimed for his leadership qualities, so it was inevitable that he would one day manage in the majors. A feared slugger with good running speed, he became a good luck charm late in his career, appearing in three consecutive World Series with three different teams in 1986–88. In 1979, Baylor won the AL MVP award when he batted .296 with 36 home runs and 139 RBI. A dead-pull hitter, many of whose best drives curved foul at the last moment, Baylor never shied away from the inside pitch and was plunked 267 times. In the field, Baylor had a notoriously weak throwing arm that hastened his transition to designated hitter.

Beaumont, Clarence (Ginger)
1876–1956
Pittsburgh (NL 1899–1906), Boston (NL 1907–09), Chicago (NL 1910)   OF   BL/TR

1,463 games	.311 ba
1,759 hits	39 hr
617 rbi	254 sb

As a rookie in 1899, the fleet-footed, red-haired Beaumont batted .352. He led the NL in batting in 1902 (.357). Sparkplug of the dominant Pirates teams of the early 1900s, Beaumont was the first batter in the first modern World Series game, played in 1903.

Beckert, Glenn

1940–

Chicago (NL 1965–73), San Diego (NL 1974–75)

2B   **BR/TR**

1,320 games	.283 ba
1,473 hits	22 hr
360 rbi	49 sb

Beckert teamed with shortstop Don Kessinger to provide the Cubs with airtight inner defense for close to a decade. Smart at the plate, he was the ideal number-two batter in the lineup and could slap the ball to the opposite field. Extremely tough to whiff, Beckert fanned only 243 times in his career.

Beckley, Jacob (Jake, Old Eagle Eye)

1867–1918

Pittsburgh (NL 1888–89, 1891–96), Pittsburgh (PL 1890), New York (NL 1896–97), Cincinnati (NL 1897–1903), St. Louis (NL 1904–07)   **1B**

BL/TL

2,386 games	.308 ba
2,930 hits	88 hr
1,575 rbi	315 sb

Although he is little remembered today, Beckley played more games at first base than any man in major league history until Eddie Murray tied his mark in 1993. In the field, he was only average, with a notoriously weak arm, but at the plate he terrorized the opposition. Beckley batted over .300 13 times and slugged the ball with the best of his contemporaries. Beckley was inducted into the Hall of Fame in 1971.

Bedrosian, Steve (Bedrock)

1957–

Atlanta (NL 1981–85, 1993 Active), Philadelphia
(NL 1986–89), San Francisco (NL 1989–90),
Minnesota (AL 1991)   P   BR/RHP

657 games	1,116 innings
75-75 W–L	3.31 ERA
856 k's	184 saves

The NL's Rookie Pitcher of the Year in 1982 when he
went 8–6 with 11 saves, Bedrosian fell into disfavor in
Atlanta and was traded to Philadelphia, where he resurrected his career in 1987. Proving the bullpen's impor-
tance, he won the 1987 Cy Young Award when he
saved 40 games. Bedrosian relies on his fastball and
slider to make the tough outs.

Belanger, Mark (Blade)

1944–

Baltimore (AL 1965–81), Los Angeles (NL 1982)
SS   BR/TR

2,016 games	.228 ba
1,316 hits	20 hr
389 rbi	167 sb

The outstanding defensive shortstop of his generation,
Belanger teamed with third baseman Brooks Robinson
to make the left side of the Orioles infield impregnable.
A notoriously weak hitter, he was the epitome of the
good-field, no-hit player. Belanger is currently an executive with the Major League Baseball Players Association.

Bell, Buddy

1951–

Cleveland (AL 1972–78), Texas (AL 1979–85,
1989), Cincinnati (NL 1985–88), Houston (NL
1988)   3B   BR/TR

2,405 games	.279 ba
2,514 hits	201 hr
1,106 rbi	55 sb

Between 1979 and 1984, Bell won six consecutive Gold Gloves as the best-fielding third baseman in the AL. At the plate, he was a steady if not outstanding hitter who reached career highs of 101 RBI in 1979, a .329 average in 1980, and 20 homers in 1986.

Bell, George

1959–

Toronto (AL 1981–90), Chicago (NL 1991–92), Chicago (AL 1993)   **OF   BR/TR**

1,587 games	.278 ba
1,702 hits	265 hr
1,002 rbi	67 sb

Bell is at home with a bat in his hands. Few batters are as dangerous in the clutch. He chased home an AL-best 134 runs in 1987 and knocked in at least 100 runs in three seasons. Bell remains the only person who thinks he is still a good outfielder.

Bell, Gus

1928–

Pittsburgh (NL 1950–52), Cincinnati (NL 1953–61), New York (NL 1962), Milwaukee (NL 1962–64)   **OF   BL/TR**

1,741 games	.281 ba
1,823 hits	206 hr
942 rbi	30 sb

Gus and his son Buddy combined for the most hits by a father-son duo in major league history (4,337). Bell put together some powerful seasons for Cincinnati; in 1953–55, he hit .300, .299, and .308 and drove in a total of 310 runs with the aid of 74 homers.

Bell, James (Cool Papa)
1903–1991

St. Louis Stars (1922–31), Detroit Wolves (1932),
Kansas City Monarchs (1932), Pittsburgh Crawfords
(1933–36), Chicago American Giants (1942),
Homestead Grays (1943–46)   OF   BB/TL

919 games	.338 ba
1,335 hits	56 hr

Inducted into the Hall of Fame in 1972, Bell was possibly the fastest man to ever don a uniform. On one
occasion, he scored all the way from first on a bunt
down the third baseline. An outstanding center fielder,
he could outrun nearly any ball hit over his head.

Bell, Jay
1965–

Cleveland (AL 1986–88), Pittsburgh (NL 1989–93
Active) SS   BR/TR

823 games	.267 ba
814 hits	48 hr
290 rbi	54 sb

Misused by the Indians, Bell became one of the premier NL shortstops upon his arrival in Pittsburgh. Excellent defensively, he has hit better than expected,
homering 16 times and driving in 67 runs in 1991, and
batting .310 in 1993.

Belle, Albert
1966–

Cleveland (AL 1989–93 Active)   OF   BR/TR

506 games	.270 ba
507 hits	108 hr
376 rbi	36 sb

A recovering alcoholic, Belle has become one of the
most feared sluggers in the AL today. In 1992, he
slammed 34 roundtrippers and knocked home 112
runs, and in 1993 he led the league with 129 RBI.

Bench, Johnny

1947–

Cincinnati (NL 1967–83)   C   BR/TR

2,158 games	.267 ba
2,048 hits	389 hr
1,376 rbi	68 sb

Baseball experts regard Bench as the greatest catcher in the game's history. Superb defensively, he popularized catching the ball one-handed to avoid getting his meat hand injured. Bench could block balls in the dirt and rifle the ball to second base to erase potential base stealers. No catcher ever generated more power at the plate. His 389 home runs rank number one among catchers, and he belted at least 25 homers seven years in succession (1969–75). In 1970, Bench had a dream season, winning the NL MVP award while batting .293 with a league-high 45 home runs and 148 RBI. He won his second MVP award in 1972 when he knocked out 40 homers and chased home 125 runs. Bench was inducted into the Hall of Fame in 1989.

Bender, Charles (Chief)

1884–1954

Philadelphia (AL 1903–14), Baltimore (FL 1915), Philadelphia (NL 1916–17), Chicago (AL 1925)   P   BR/RHP

459 games	3,017 innings
212-127 W–L	2.46 ERA
1,711 k's	34 saves

Part Chippewa, Bender led Philadelphia to five pennants and three World Series titles in the early 1900s. Steady of nerve, he tossed a no-hitter in 1910 against Cleveland. However, after going 17–3 for the 1914 Athletics, Bender jumped to the Federal League, where he suffered through a 4–16 campaign. Bender was inducted into the Hall of Fame in 1953.

Benes, Andy

1967–

San Diego (NL 1989–93 Active) P BR/RHP

143 games	944 innings
59-54 W–L	3.44 ERA
721 k's	

An imposing presence on the mound, the 6-foot, 6-inch Benes throws extremely hard and deals a sharp slider as well. He won 15 times in 1991 and in 1993.

Bennett, Charlie

1854–1927

Milwaukee (NL 1878), Worcester (NL 1880), Detroit (NL 1881–88), Boston (NL 1889–93) C BR/TR

1,062 games	.256 ba
978 hits	55 hr
533 rbi	42 sb

One of the first catchers to wear an outside chest protector, Bennett was a popular player for Detroit in the 1880s. An outstanding defensive backstop, he batted .300 in his first three seasons in Detroit. After Bennett lost both his legs in a train accident in 1894, the Wolverines named their home field in his honor.

Berg, Morris (Moe)

1902–1972

Brooklyn (NL 1923), Chicago (AL 1926–30), Cleveland (AL 1931, 1934), Washington (AL 1932–34), Boston (AL 1935–39) C BR/TR

663 games	.243 ba
441 hits	6 hr
206 rbi	11 sb

A graduate of Princeton and recipient of a law degree from Columbia, Berg spoke 12 languages and was probably the most intelligent man ever to play the game. His photographs of Tokyo, taken during a major league tour of Japan in 1933, helped the United

States identify targets during WW II. On the field, he was a weak hitter but a sound defensive catcher, and he was very popular with his teammates. A baseball fan to the end, his last words were "How did the Mets do today?"

Berger, Wally

1905–1988
Boston (NL 1930–37), New York (NL 1937–38), Cincinnati (NL 1938–40), Philadelphia (NL 1940)
OF   BR/TR

1,350 games	.300 ba
1,550 hits	242 hr
898 rbi	36 sb

The only starting player in the 1934 All-Star Game not currently in the Hall of Fame, Berger set an NL rookie home run record in 1930 (38) and led the NL with 34 home runs and 130 RBI in 1935. Unfortunately, he went hitless in 18 at-bats in World Series play.

Berra, Lawrence (Yogi)

1925–
New York (AL 1946–63), New York (NL 1965); MGR—New York (AL 1964, 1984–85), New York (NL 1972–75)   C, OF, MGR   BL/TR

2,120 games	.285 ba
2,150 hits	358 hr
1,430 rbi	30 sb

A notorious bad-ball hitter, Berra's strike zone stretched to any pitch he could reach. A clutch hitter without equal, he played on 14 pennant winners and 10 world champion Yankees teams. Defensively, he improved greatly to become one of the best. Berra's value was recognized by three MVP awards. Of course, Yogi also became one of the most recognizable men in America for his maladroit use of the English language to express simple truths about life. Berra was inducted into the Hall of Fame in 1972.

Biggio, Craig

1965–

Houston (NL 1988–93 Active)　　2B, C　　BR/TR

800 games	.276 ba
799 hits	51 hr
256 rbi	124 sb

Until Biggio successfully completed the move, no other catcher had ever made a successful transition to centerfield and then to second base. An agile athlete with good running speed, he starred defensively at each position. At the plate, he sprayed the ball to all fields.

Billingham, Jack

1943–

Los Angeles (NL 1968), Houston (NL 1969–71), Cincinnati (NL 1972–77), Detroit (AL 1978–80), Boston (AL 1980)　　P　　BR/RHP

476 games	2,230 innings
145-113 W–L	3.83 ERA
1,141 k's	15 saves

Moved from the bullpen in 1970 by the Astros, Billingham became a strong, consistent starter in the NL for nearly a decade. During the years of the Big Red Machine, Billingham's sinker made him the team's most dependable starter, winning 19 games in 1973 and 1974 and 15 games in 1975. In 1973, he led the NL in innings pitched (293) and shutouts (7).

Blackwell, Ewell (The Whip)

1922–

Cincinnati (NL 1942, 1946–52), New York (AL 1952–53), Kansas City (AL 1955)　　P　　BR/RHP

236 games	1,321 innings
82-78 W–L	3.30 ERA
839 k's	10 saves

In the immediate postwar years, Ewell Blackwell struck fear into the hearts of right-handed batters in the National League by stepping toward third base before unleashing his blazing fastball. In 1947, he won 16 consecutive games, led the NL with 193 strikeouts, and nearly pitched back-to-back no-hitters.

Blair, Paul (Motormouth)
1944–

Baltimore (AL 1964–76), New York (AL 1977–79, 1980), Cincinnati (AL 1979)   OF   BR/TR

1,947 games	.250 ba
1,513 hits	134 hr
620 rbi	171 sb

One of the outstanding defensive center fielders in the history of the game, Blair played shallow to cut off bloops and low-liners but had the speed to race back and catch long drives. At the plate, he was a streaky hitter who hit .293 in 1967 and belted 26 home runs and knocked home 76 runs in 1969, but he had a tendency to step in the bucket after being beaned early in his career. Blair played in six World Series.

Blass, Steve
1942–

Pittsburgh (NL 1964, 1966–74)   P   BR/RHP

282 games	1,597 innings
103-76 W–L	3.63 ERA
896 k's	2 saves

Blass's career came to a bizarre end when he developed an inability to throw strikes in 1973. The pitching star in the 1971 World Series, winning twice, he won 18 games in 1968 and 19 in 1972 with an ERA under 2.50 each year. In 1972, Blass walked 84 men in 249 innings; the following year, he walked 84 in only 89 innings. In 1974, he was out of baseball after only one appearance.

Blue, Vida

1949–

Oakland (AL 1969–77), San Francisco (NL 1978–81, 1985–86), Kansas City (AL 1982–83) P

BB/LHP

502 games	3,343 innings
209-161 W–L	3.27 ERA
2,175 k's	2 saves

Blue burst upon America's consciousness in 1971, winning 24 games with a scintillating 1.82 ERA and 301 strikeouts. Fans across the nation flocked to see Blue pitch and he rarely disappointed them. He utilized a high leg kick in his delivery and generated tremendous speed and movement on his fastball. Blue later won 20 games in 1973 and 22 in 1975; after being traded to the Giants, he won 18 games in 1978.

Bluege, Oswald (Ossie)

1900–1985

Washington (AL 1922–39); MGR—Washington (AL 1943–47) 3B, MGR   BR/TR

1,867 games	.272 ba
1,751 hits	43 hr
848 rbi	140 sb

The stalwart third baseman for an entire generation of Senators fans, Bluege was one of the best defensive third basemen in the history of the game. Fast afoot, he slapped the ball to all fields.

Blyleven, Bert

1951–

Minnesota (AL 1970–76, 1986–88), Texas (AL 1976–77), Pittsburgh (NL 1978–80), Cleveland (AL 1981–85), California (AL 1989–90, 1992) P

BR/RHP

692 games	4,970 innings
287-250 W–L	3.31 ERA
3,701 k's	

Blyleven was one of only two major league pitchers to win a game before the age of 20 and past the age of 40. Longevity and consistency were the keynotes of his career. Blyleven threw one of the biggest breaking curve balls of his generation and a more than adequate fastball. He constantly challenged hitters and as a result surrendered more than his share of home runs, setting a major league record in 1986 when he allowed 50 taters. An unheralded strikeout artist, Blyleven currently ranks third in career Ks behind Nolan Ryan and Steve Carlton.

Boddicker, Mike

1957–
Baltimore (AL 1980–88), Boston (AL 1988–90), Kansas City (AL 1991–92), Milwaukee (AL 1993)
P   RHP

342 games	2,123 innings
134-116 W–L	3.80 ERA
1,330 k's	3 saves

When Boddicker burst upon the AL in 1983, he showed a great curve ball and won 16 games; he also pitched shutouts in the ALCS, against Chicago with 14 strikeouts, and in the World Series, stopping the Phillies on three hits. The next year, he led the AL with 20 wins and a 2.79 ERA, but he never fulfilled his early promise. Arm ailments hindered his career and he retired during the 1993 season.

Boggs, Wade

1958–
Boston (AL 1982–92), New York (AL 1993 Active)
3B   BL/TR

1,768 games	.335 ba
2,267 hits	87 hr
746 rbi	16 sb

The most superstitious player in the major leagues in recent memory, Boggs not only eats chicken every day but also follows the identical routine before each game during batting and fielding practice. It must work, because he has led the AL in batting six times, hitting a career-best .366 in 1988. Swinging from a closed stance, Boggs hits the vast majority of his balls to center and left for singles and doubles. He has improved his fielding and he has a strong arm.

Bonds, Barry

1964–

Pittsburgh (NL 1986–92), San Francisco (NL 1993 Active) **OF** BL/TR

1,169 games	.283 ba
1,165 hits	222 hr
679 rbi	280 sb

Widely acclaimed as the best all-around player in the game today, Bonds is an outstanding defensive player and a dangerous batter with excellent speed. The son of former major league star Bobby Bonds, Barry did not enjoy immediate success with Pittsburgh, batting only .223 as a rookie in 1986. After four years of less than superstar production, Bonds put together four sterling seasons, batting over .300 three times and knocking in at least 100 runs all four years. In left field, he covers an enormous amount of territory, and he has one of the strongest and most accurate throwing arms in the game. Signed to a $43-million multiyear contract by the Giants prior to the 1993 season, Bonds delivered beyond anyone's wildest expectations, batting .336 with 46 homers and 123 RBI to earn his third NL MVP award.

Bonds, Bobby

1946–

San Francisco (NL 1968–74), New York (AL 1975), California (AL 1976–77), Chicago (AL 1978), Texas (AL 1978), Cleveland (AL 1979), St. Louis (NL 1980), Chicago (NL 1981) **OF**   BR/TR

1,849 games	.268 ba
1,886 hits	332 hr
1,024 rbi	461 sb

Baseball's first publicized 30–30 man, Bonds combined great speed and power. A free swinger, he struck out 189 times for a major league record in 1970 and fanned at least 120 times in 10 seasons. Bonds was a streak hitter who could carry a team for a two-week span. Of course, he also endured stretches where he struck out 15 times in one week. His best season was in 1970 when he batted .302 with 200 hits, 26 homers, 134 runs scored, and 48 stolen bases. Defensively, he had few equals, and when he played alongside Garry Maddox and Gary Mathews in the Giants outfield, he formed part of one of the fastest trios in history.

Bonham, Ernie (Tiny)
1913–1949
New York (AL 1940–46), Pittsburgh (NL 1947–49)
P   BR/RHP

231 games	1,551 innings
103-72 W–L	3.06 ERA
478 k's	9 saves

A control artist, Bonham walked only 24 men in 226 innings in 1942 when he went 21–5 with a 2.27 ERA. A big bear of a man, Tiny was traded to Pittsburgh after WW II, but he died from appendicitis during the 1949 season.

Bonilla, Bobby (Bobby Bo)
1963–
Chicago (AL 1986), Pittsburgh (NL 1986–91), New York (NL 1992–93 Active)   **3B, OF   BB/TR**

1,185 games	.277 ba
1,173 hits	169 hr
683 rbi	35 sb

The jury is still out on whether the Mets made a disastrous mistake in signing Bonilla to a $29-million multiyear contract prior to the 1992 season. Following two .300-plus batting averages and four seasons of more than 100 RBI, in Pittsburgh, Bonilla seemed primed to return to his hometown. Unfortunately, his characteristic smile did not last through his initial season in New York, as he was beset by injuries and poor play. Although his performance improved in 1993, the team collapsed to a level not seen since the inept early days of the franchise.

Boone, Bob
1947–
Philadelphia (NL 1972–81), California (AL 1982–88), Kansas City (AL 1989–90)   C
BR/TR

2,264 games	.254 ba
1,838 hits	105 hr
826 rbi	38 sb

A thinking man's catcher, the Stanford-educated Boone proved his critics wrong by outlasting all rivals for his job. Traded by the Phillies after a subpar 1981 season when he batted .211, Boone improved with age and batted a career-high .295 at the age of 41. Sound defensively, he established a career mark for games played by a catcher that has since been broken by Carlton Fisk.

Bottomley, Jim (Sunny Jim)
1900–1959
St. Louis (NL 1922–32), Cincinnati (NL 1933–35), St. Louis (AL 1936–37)   1B   BL/TL

1,991 games	.310 ba
2,313 hits	219 hr
1,422 rbi	58 sb

Sunny Jim had a great personality and was liked by everyone in baseball. A strong, clutch hitter, he enjoyed one of the greatest days in major league history when he drove home 12 runs at Ebbets Field against Brooklyn in 1924. Bottomley knocked in more than 100 runs in six consecutive years (1924–29), leading the NL in 1926 and in 1928. He won the MVP award in 1928 and was inducted into the Hall of Fame in 1974.

Boudreau, Lou

1917–

Cleveland (AL 1938–50), Boston (AL 1951–52); MGR—Cleveland (AL 1942–50), Boston (AL 1952–54), Kansas City (AL 1955–57), Chicago (NL 1960)   **SS, MGR   BR/TR**

1,646 games	.295 ba
1,779 hits	68 hr
789 rbi	51 sb

A boy wonder, Boudreau became player-manager of Cleveland at the age of 24. In the field, he had good range and a strong arm. He devised the famous "Williams Shift," which placed three infielders between first and second to counter Boston slugger Ted Williams's propensity to pull the ball. In 1948, Boudreau won the MVP award, leading the Indians to the pennant by batting .355 with a career-best 18 homers and 106 RBI. The Indians retired his uniform number 5, and he was inducted into the Hall of Fame in 1970.

Bouton, Jim (Bulldog)

1939–

New York (AL 1962–68), Seattle (AL 1969), Houston (NL 1969–70), Atlanta (NL 1978)   **P
BR/RHP**

304 games	1,238 innings
62-63 W–L	3.57 ERA
720 k's	6 saves

When Bouton emerged as the Yankees right-handed ace in 1963, the team's dynasty appeared secure for the foreseeable future. He went 21–7 with a 2.53 ERA in 1963 and won 18 games plus two in the World Series the following year. Bouton exerted so much energy

when he threw that his cap flew off his head after each
of his overhand deliveries. In 1965, however, he hurt
his arm and began the slow drift downward that cul-
minated in a desperate attempt to throw a knuckleball
at age 39. In 1970, Bouton shocked baseball's hierar-
chy with his personal account of the 1969 season, *Ball
Four*.

Bowa, Larry

1945–
Philadelphia (NL 1970–81), Chicago (NL 1982–85),
New York (NL 1985); MGR—San Diego (NL
1987–88)   SS, MGR   BB/TR

2,247 games	.260 ba
2,191 hits	15 hr
525 rbi	318 sb

Bowa was a fierce competitor who made himself into a
major league hitter. In the field, he had few equals. His
tremendous range and sure hands produced the major
league's highest lifetime fielding percentage for a shortstop (.980).

Boyer, Cletis (Clete)

1937–
Kansas City (AL 1955–57), New York (AL
1959–66), Atlanta (NL 1967–71)   3B   BR/TR

1,725 games	.242 ba
1,396 hits	162 hr
654 rbi	41 sb

A magician with the glove at third base, Boyer could
dive to either side, snare balls, and rifle the ball to first
from his knees. His power at the plate was overshadowed by the rest of the power-laden Yankees lineup.
Traded to the Braves, Boyer launched 26 home runs
with 96 RBI in the homer haven down south.

Boyer, Ken

1931–1982

St. Louis (NL 1955–65), New York (NL 1966–67),
Chicago (AL 1967–68), Los Angeles (NL 1968–69);
MGR—St. Louis (NL 1978–80)   **3B, MGR**
BR/TR

2,034 games	.287 ba
2,143 hits	282 hr
1,141 rbi	105 sb

The best third baseman in Cardinals history, Boyer was
underrated throughout his career in St. Louis, primarily because he lacked flair and made everything look so
easy on the field. In 1964, he won the NL's MVP
award after batting .295 with 24 home runs and a
league-high 119 RBI, as well as fielding brilliantly. The
older brother of Yankees third baseman Clete Boyer,
Ken belted a grand-slam homer in game four of the
1964 World Series at Yankee Stadium. The Cardinals
retired his uniform number 14.

Branca, Ralph

1926–

Brooklyn (NL 1944–53, 1956), Detroit (AL
1953–54), New York (AL 1954)   **P**   **BR/RHP**

322 games	1,484 innings
88-68 W–L	3.79 ERA
829 k's	19 saves

A hard-throwing righty, Branca's name will forever be
associated with the fateful moment on October 3,
1951, when Bobby Thomson slammed a Branca fastball that got too much of the plate for a three-run
home run to win the National League pennant. Branca
went 21–12 in 1947 as the youthful ace of the Dodger
staff, but arm miseries hampered his career.

Brecheen, Harry (The Cat)

1914–

St. Louis (NL 1940, 1943–52), St. Louis (AL 1953)

P   BL/LHP

318 games	1,907 innings
133-92 W–L	2.92 ERA
901 k's	18 saves

During a six-year span in the forties, Brecheen was the top lefty in the NL, accumulating 96 victories against only 53 losses. He led the NL in winning percentage in both 1945 (.789) and 1948 (.741). In 1948, his 2.24 ERA, seven shutouts, and 149 strikeouts were also the best in the league. In the 1946 World Series against the Red Sox, Brecheen won three times, including games six and seven. An outstanding fielder, Brecheen later became a highly respected pitching coach for Baltimore in 1954–67.

Bresnahan, Roger (The Duke of Tralee)

1879–1944

Washington (NL 1897), Chicago (NL 1900), Baltimore (AL 1901–02), New York (NL 1902–08), St. Louis (NL 1909–12), Chicago (NL 1913–15); MGR—St. Louis (NL 1909–12), Chicago (NL 1915)   C, MGR   BR/TR

1,446 games	.279 ba
1,252 hits	26 hr
530 rbi	212 sb

Bresnahan began his career as a pitcher before moving behind the plate in 1901. A patient hitter who drew a high number of walks, and a fast runner too, he occasionally batted leadoff for McGraw's Giants. In 1907, Bresnahan introduced the use of cricket-style shin guards to protect against the hazards of catching. He was inducted into the Hall of Fame in 1945.

Brett, George
1953–

Kansas City (AL 1973–93)   3B   BL/TR

2,707 games	.305 ba
3,154 hits	317 hr
1,595 rbi	201 sb

A certain Hall of Famer, Brett joined Stan Musial in 1993 as the only major leaguers to rack up career totals of 3,000 hits, 300 homers, 600 doubles, and 100 triples. Brett usually swung from a slightly closed stance and lined the ball to all fields. Although not a slugger, he did belt at least 20 homers in eight seasons and clubbed a dramatic home run off Goose Gossage at Yankee Stadium to clinch the Royals' first pennant in 1980. Three years later, he hit another dramatic homer off Gossage in New York while using a bat coated with pine tar, precipitating one of the wildest scenes on any ballfield. In 1980, Brett flirted with the magical .400 mark but settled for .390. Defensively, he was not spectacular but he could make the plays.

Brewer, Chester (Chet)
1907–

Kansas City Monarch (1925–35, 1937, 1941), Washington Pilots (1932), New York Cubans (1936), Chicago American Giants (1946), Cleveland Buckeyes (1946–47)   P   BL/RHP

1,110 innings	89-63 W–L
552 k's	3 saves

Brewer threw a full assortment of pitches—fastball, curve, and emery ball. In 1929, he went 16–3 and in the following year earned 30 victories.

Brewer, Jim
1937–1987

Chicago (NL 1960–63), Los Angeles (NL 1964–75), California (AL 1975–76)   P   BL/LHP

584 games	1,040 innings
69-65 W–L	3.07 ERA
810 k's	132 saves

A screwball artist, Brewer was rescued by the Dodgers from the Cubs and became one of the top lefty relievers in the sixties. In Chicago, his claim to fame was getting slugged by Billy Martin in an on-field brawl and then successfully suing him for damages. Brewer saved at least 20 games in four out of five seasons between 1969 and 1973.

Bridges, Tommy

1906–1968
Detroit (AL 1930–43, 1945–46)   P   BR/RHP

424 games	2,826 innings
194-138 W–L	3.57 ERA
1,674 k's	10 saves

Though small in stature, Bridges threw a good fastball, but his fame rests on his curve ball, one of the best in major league history. He won 22, 21, and 23 games in 1934–36 and led the AL in strikeouts in the last two years. Tough in the clutch, Bridges won four World Series games for the Tigers. He still ranks in the top ten in all major pitching categories for the Tigers.

Briles, Nellie

1943–
St. Louis (NL 1965–70), Pittsburgh (NL 1971–73),
Kansas City (AL 1974–75), Texas (AL 1976–77),
Baltimore (AL 1977–78)   P   BR/RHP

454 games	2,111 innings
129-112 W–L	3.44 ERA
1,163 k's	22 saves

A fastball, slider pitcher, Briles was a tough competitor who was at his best in clutch situations. He went 14–5 for the 1967 world champion Cardinals and won 19 games the following year for the repeat pennant winners. In 1971, he pitched a two-hit victory for the Pirates in the World Series.

Brock, Lou

1939–
Chicago (NL 1961–64), St. Louis (NL 1964–79)
OF   BL/TL

2,616 games	.293 ba
3,023 hits	149 hr
900 rbi	938 sb

When the Cardinals acquired Brock for 20-game-winner Ernie Broglio midway through the 1964 season, many fans believed that Chicago had gotten the best of the deal. Brock had been an inconsistent batter with great speed and a propensity to strike out prior to his arrival in the Mound City. Batting .348, he went on to spark St. Louis to the pennant and the World Series title. A scientific base runner, Brock established a new record for career stolen bases (938). He also possessed remarkable power for a man his size and was one of only three men ever to hit a homer into the centerfield bleachers at the Polo Grounds. His .391 average in three World Series ranks second all-time, and he single-handedly intimidated the Red Sox in 1967 with his stolen bases. Brock entered the Hall of Fame in 1985.

Brosnan, Jim (Professor)

1929–
Chicago (NL 1954, 1956–58), St. Louis (NL 1958–59), Cincinnati (NL 1959–63), Chicago (AL 1963)   P   BR/RHP

385 games	831 innings
55-47 W–L	3.54 ERA
507 k's	67 saves

While still an active pitcher, Brosnan authored two chronicles of life in the National League. Refreshing for their humor and candor, *The Long Season* and *The Pennant Race* brought fans inside baseball. In 1961,

Brosnan enjoyed his best season, throwing his slider past all the teams in the league, with the notable exception of the Cubs, on his way to the World Series.

Brouthers, Dan (Big Dan)
1858–1932

Troy (NL 1879–80), Buffalo (NL 1881–85), Detroit (NL 1886–88), Boston (NL 1889), Boston (PL 1890), Boston (AA 1891), Brooklyn (NL 1892–93), Baltimore (NL 1894–95), Louisville (NL 1895), Philadelphia (NL 1896), New York (NL 1904) 1B
BL/TL

1,673 games	.342 ba
2,296 hits	106 hr
1,296 rbi	256 sb

In appearance, Brouthers typified the 19th-century ballplayer with his generous mustache. Sold by Buffalo to Detroit in 1885 in one of the biggest transactions up to that time, he was possibly the greatest slugger of the 19th century. Brouthers batted over .300 in 16 consecutive seasons from 1881 to 1896. He led his league five times in batting, and twice in home runs, and he knocked in over 100 RBI five times. At his retirement, Brouthers ranked number one in homers and RBI. He was inducted into the Hall of Fame in 1945.

Brown, Kevin
1965–

Texas (AL 1986, 1988–93 Active) P

161 games	1,108 innings
71-55 W–L	3.65 ERA
619 k's	

In 1992, the hard-throwing Brown emerged as one of the top hurlers in the AL, going 21–11. He has an excellent sinker and gets a high number of ground-ball outs.

Brown, Larry
1905–1972

Indianapolis ABC's (1923), Memphis Red Sox (1923–26, 1927–29, 1931, 1938–48), Chicago American Giants (1927, 1929, 1932–35,), New York Lincoln Giants (1930–31), Philadelphia Stars (1936–37)   **C, MGR   BR/TR**

767 games	.259 ba
620 hits	32 hr
13 sb	

Equipped with a rifle for an arm, Brown ranks with the best defensive catchers of all time. Although he was not a lusty hitter, he did bat .294 in 1928. Brown served as player-manager of the Memphis Red Sox in 1939–48.

Brown, Mordecai (Three-Finger)
1876–1948

St. Louis (NL 1903), Chicago (NL 1904–12, 1916), Cincinnati (NL 1913), St. Louis (FL 1914), Brooklyn (FL 1914), Chicago (FL 1915); MGR—St. Louis (FL 1914)   **P, MGR   BB/RHP**

481 games	3,172 innings
239-130 W–L	2.06 ERA
1,375 k's	48 saves

"Three-Finger" Brown lost much of his index finger and the use of his pinky on his pitching hand in a farming accident as a youth. Actually, the injury improved his sinker and curve. He won 20 games in six consecutive seasons, and in a series of storied matches with the great Christy Mathewson, he invariably came out the victor. His 2.06 career ERA ranks third in major league history. Brown was inducted into the Hall of Fame in 1949.

Brown, Willard
1911–

Kansas City Monarchs (1935–43, 1946–49), St. Louis (AL 1947)   **OF   BR/TR**

382 games	.355 ba
635 hits	62 hr
43 sb	

An outstanding slugger in the Negro Leagues, Brown starred in the mid-forties and was signed by the St. Louis Browns in 1947. He hit the first home run by a black in the AL that year but later left the team that year to rejoin the Monarchs.

Browning, Louis (Pete, The Gladiator)

1861–1905

Louisville (AA 1882–89), Cleveland (PL 1890), Pittsburgh (NL 1891), Cincinnati (NL 1891–92), Louisville (NL 1892–93), St. Louis (NL 1894), Brooklyn (NL 1894)   **OF**   **BR/TR**

1,183 games	.341 ba
1,646 hits	46 hr
353 rbi	258 sb

The biggest star in the American Association, Browning was a great hitter but a rather poor outfielder. As a rookie in Louisville, he batted a league-high .378 in 1882, and he later led the AA in 1885 (.362) and the Players League (.373) in 1890, its only year of existence. While toiling for Louisville in 1884, Browning had his bats custom-made by Hillerich and Company, thereby giving birth to the famous Louisville Slugger. Although his lifetime batting average ranks third among right-handed batters, he was never inducted into the Hall of Fame.

Browning, Tom

1960–

Cincinnati (NL 1984–93 Active)   **P**   **BL/LHP**

293 games	1,870 innings
120-87 W–L	3.91 ERA
975 k's	

The owner of a perfect game, pitched against the Dodgers in 1988, Browning had a string of seven seasons with double digits in victories snapped in 1992 due to a severe knee injury that incapacitated him for much of the year. He still has a bit of fan in him, as evidenced by his 1993 uniformed appearance atop a house on Sheffield Avenue across the street from Wrigley Field to watch a Cubs-Reds game with the fans who regularly congregate there.

Brunansky, Tom (Bruno)

1960–
California (AL 1981), Minnesota (AL 1982–88), St. Louis (NL 1988–90), Boston (AL 1990–92), Milwaukee (AL 1993 Active)   OF   BR/TR

1,736 games	.246 ba
1,495 hits	261 hr
885 rbi	69 sb

This power-hitting outfielder slammed at least 20 homers every year between 1982 and 1989, but his numbers have dropped in the last four seasons. Brunansky is an underrated outfielder.

Bruton, Bill

1925–
Milwaukee (NL 1953–60), Detroit (AL 1961–64)
OF   BL/TR

1,610 games	.273 ba
1,651 hits	94 hr
545 rbi	207 sb

Bruton led the NL in stolen bases in his first three years in the majors. Smart defensively, he was also a consistent batter who hit below .272 only three times.

Buckner, Bill (Billy Bucks)

1949–
Los Angeles (NL 1969–76), Chicago (NL 1977–84), Boston (AL 1984–87, 1990), California (AL 1987–88), Kansas City (AL 1988–89)   1B, OF
BL/TL

2,517 games	.289 ba
2,715 hits	174 hr
1,208 rbi	183 sb

Buckner was a great hitter who bounced back from a severely broken ankle to have a productive offensive career. Prior to his injury, he had good speed, but it diminished as his career progressed. Primarily a gap hitter, he hit at least 30 doubles eight times in his career. Buckner led the NL in hitting in 1980 (.324). Two of his best seasons came with the Red Sox in 1985 and 1986, when he knocked in 110 and 102 runs, but he will always be remembered for letting Mookie Wilson's slowly hit grounder roll through his legs in the 10th inning of the sixth game of the 1986 World Series against the Mets. His error allowed the winning run to score and kept Boston's record of World Series futility intact. Defensively, his high total of assists reflects his inability to run to first himself rather than great range.

Buffinton, Charlie

1861–1907
Boston (NL 1882–86), Philadelphia (NL 1887–89), Philadelphia (PL 1890), Boston (AA 1891), Baltimore (NL 1892); MGR—Philadelphia (PL 1890)   **P, MGR   BR/RHP**

414 games	3,404 innings
233-152 W–L	2.96 ERA
1,700 k's	3 saves

The pride of Fall River, Massachusetts, Buffinton starred for the nearby Boston Beaneaters in the 1880s. After his phenomenal 1884 season, when he pitched 587 innings and won 48 games, he hurt his arm and was dealt to Philadelphia, where he won more than 20 games three more times. Buffinton's best pitch was a sharp, downward-breaking curve ball.

Buford, Don

1937–

Chicago (AL 1963–67), Baltimore (AL 1968–72)

OF, 2B, 3B   BB/TR

1,286 games	.264 ba
1,203 hits	93 hr
418 rbi	200 sb

A pesky leadoff hitter, Buford hit a home run to start off the Orioles in the 1969 World Series and reportedly shouted to the Mets, "You ain't seen nothing yet!" Ironically, that turned out to be the series highlight for Baltimore. Excellent speed in the outfield but a poor throwing arm made Buford an average fielder. Yet he found a way to get on base and score runs, tallying 99 runs in three successive seasons (1969–71).

Buhl, Bob

1928–

Milwaukee (NL 1953–62), Chicago (NL 1962–66), Philadelphia (NL 1966–67)   P   BB/RHP

457 games	2,587 innings
166-132 W-L	3.55 ERA
1,268 k's	6 saves

In 1962, Buhl went the entire season—70 at-bats—without getting a single hit. Unfortunately, his hitting woes distracted fans from his fine pitching, which included two consecutive 18-game victory seasons (1956–57) and 10 years of double-digit success.

Bunning, Jim

1931–

Detroit (AL 1955–63), Philadelphia (NL 1964–67, 1970–71), Pittsburgh (NL 1968–69), Los Angeles (NL 1969)   P   BR/RHP

591 games	3,760 innings
224-184 W-L	3.27 ERA
2,855 k's	16 saves

On Father's Day in 1964, everything came up roses for this father of six, as Bunning pitched a perfect game against the Mets in New York. He became the first 20th-century pitcher to pitch a no-hitter in both leagues, having previously blanked the Red Sox in 1958. A wicked sidearm fastball was Bunning's best pitch. He twice led the AL in strikeouts and fanned over 200 men six times in his career. A 20-game winner in 1957, Bunning currently represents Kentucky in the U.S. House of Representatives.

Burdette, Lew
1926–
New York (AL 1950), Boston (NL 1951–52), Milwaukee (NL 1953–63), St. Louis (NL 1963–64), Chicago (NL 1964–65), Philadelphia (NL 1965), California (AL 1966–67)   P   BR/RHP

626 games	3,067 innings
203-144 W–L	3.66 ERA
1,074 k's	31 saves

Owner of the best spitball in the fifties, this former Yankee farmhand came back to haunt New York in the 1957 World Series, winning three games in Milwaukee's shocking victory over the lordly Yanks. Everyone knew Burdette threw the illegal pitch but it could never be proven, so he went on to shackle NL batters year after year. A consistent big winner for the Braves, he topped .600 five times and won 20 games twice.

Burgess, Forrest (Smokey)
1927–1991
Chicago (NL 1949, 1951), Philadelphia (NL 1952–55), Cincinnati (NL 1955–58), Pittsburgh (NL 1959–64), Chicago (AL 1964–67)   C
BL/TR

1,691 games	.295 ba
1,318 hits	126 hr
673 rbi	13 sb

It was said of Burgess that he could grab a bat in the dead of winter, step to the plate, and slam a base hit. His sweet swing produced a .368 average in part-time play for Philadelphia in 1954. But it was as a pinch hitter that he made his mark. He currently ranks second in career pinch hits with 145 and with 16 career pinch homers, is tied for third. Opposing managers dreaded his appearance late in the ballgame because of his uncanny clutch hitting.

Burkett, Jesse (Crab)

1868–1953
New York (NL 1890), Cleveland (NL 1891–98), St. Louis (NL 1899–1901), St. Louis (AL 1902–04), Boston (AL 1905)   OF   BL/TL

2,070 games	.339 ba
2,853 hits	75 hr
952 rbi	389 sb

One of the legendary players of the 19th century, Burkett had a serious disposition that led to his being nicknamed "Crab." Though he stood 5-feet, 8-inches and weighed only 155 pounds, he led the NL in batting average and hits in 1895 (.409, 225), 1896 (.410, 240), and again in 1901 (.376, 226). An expert bunter, Burkett later owned a minor league team and served as a coach under John McGraw. He was inducted into the Hall of Fame in 1946.

Burkett, John

1964–
San Francisco (NL 1987, 1990–93 Active)   P
BR/RHP

138 games	838 innings
61-34 W–L	3.87 ERA
506 k's	1 save

Prior to 1993, Burkett had never won more than 14 games in a season, compiling 39 victories in his first three full seasons. As famous for his bowling career as his mound work, Burkett took center stage in 1993 when he won 22 games for the Giants.

Burleson, Rick (Rooster)

1951–

Boston (AL 1974–80), California (AL 1981–84, 1986), Baltimore (AL 1987)   SS   BR/TR

1,346 games	.273 ba
1,401 hits	50 hr
449 rbi	72 sb

An aggressive, win-at-all-costs ballplayer, Burleson wore down his body playing seven years at Fenway Park. His value to the team cannot be measured by statistics alone, for he brought all the intangibles that go into winning baseball. After signing a free agent contract with the Angels, he suffered a succession of injuries. He played only sporadically for the last six years of his career.

Burns, George (Tioga George)

1893–1978

Detroit (AL 1914–17), Philadelphia (AL 1918–20, 1929), Cleveland (AL 1920–21, 1924–28), Boston (AL 1922–23), New York (AL 1928–29)   1B
BR/TR

1,866 games	.307 ba
2,018 hits	72 hr
951 rbi	153 sb

A slick first baseman and a contact hitter who neither walked nor fanned very often, Burns played for several AL teams but enjoyed his greatest success in Cleveland. In 1922, when he hit safely in 23 consecutive games for the Red Sox, he was in the midst of a seven-year span (1921–27) when he batted over .300 each year.

Burns's best year was 1926, when he hit .358 with a league-leading 216 hits and 64 doubles.

Burns, George
1889–1966
New York (NL 1911–21), Cincinnati (NL 1922–24), Philadelphia (NL 1925)   **OF**
BR/TR

1,853 games	.287 ba
2,077 hits	41 hr
611 rbi	383 sb

Standing upright at the plate, Burns hit the ball to all fields, collecting at least 20 doubles in 11 straight seasons. Fast afield, he covered the ground in the spacious Polo Grounds outfield and stole home 27 times in his career. Burns led the NL in steals in 1914 (62) and 1919 (40). He had a fine eye at the plate and also led the NL in walks five times.

Burns, Thomas (Oyster)
1864–1928
Wilmington (UA 1884), Baltimore (AA 1884–88), Brooklyn (AA 1888–89), Brooklyn (NL 1890–95), New York Giants (NL 1895)   **OF, SS**   **BR/TR**

1,187 games	.300 ba
1,389 hits	65 hr
673 rbi	263 sb

When the 1889 AA pennant-winning Brooklyn Bridegrooms jumped to the NL for the 1890 season, they retained their star right fielder and leading batsman Oyster Burns. After knocking in 100 runs in 1889, he celebrated Brooklyn's entrance to the NL in 1890 by leading the league with 128 RBI and ranking second with 13 home runs for the repeat pennant winners. In 1894, he batted a career-high .359.

Burroughs, Jeff

1951–

Washington (AL 1970–71), Texas (AL 1972–76), Atlanta (NL 1977–80), Seattle (AL 1981), Oakland (AL 1982–84), Toronto (AL 1985)   **OF, DH**
BR/TR

1,689 games	.261 ba
1,443 hits	240 hr
882 rbi	16 sb

In 1974, Burroughs appeared to be on his way to stardom when he won the AL MVP award at the tender age of 23. That year, he batted .301 with 25 home runs and a league-leading 118 RBI. He batted .226 and .237 in the following seasons and was sent packing to Atlanta's launching pad, where he revived with 41 homers and 114 RBI. But it was all downhill for the strikeout-prone slugger thereafter. In 1992, he resurfaced as the manager of the winning team in the Little League World Series.

Bush, Guy (The Mississippi Mudcat)

1901–1985

Chicago (NL 1923–34), Pittsburgh (NL 1935–36), Boston (NL 1936–37), St. Louis (NL 1938), Cincinnati (NL 1945)   **P   BR/RHP**

542 games	2,722 innings
176-136 W–L	3.86 ERA
850 k's	34 saves

Bush was known as a tough competitor and superior bench jockey who was not opposed to brushing batters off the plate. Hurling for the Cubs during their golden age in the thirties, he won 15 or more games in seven consecutive seasons (1928–34). Along with the usual assortment of pitches, Bush threw an effective screwball.

Bush, Joe (Bullet Joe)
1892–1974

Philadelphia (AL 1912–17, 1928), Boston (AL 1918–21), New York (AL 1922–24), St. Louis (AL 1925), Washington (AL 1926), Pittsburgh (NL 1926–27), New York (NL 1927)   **P**   **BR/RHP**

489 games	3,087 innings
195-183 W–L	3.51 ERA
1,319 k's	20 saves

Signed and nurtured by Connie Mack, Bush joined the Red Sox and eventually found his way on the shuttle to the Yankees in 1922. He led the AL in winning percentage (26–7, .788) his first year in pinstripes. Although a small man, Bush threw a hard fastball and an effective forkball.

Butler, Brett
1957–

Atlanta (NL 1981–83), Cleveland (AL 1984–87), San Francisco (NL 1988–90), Los Angeles (NL 1991–93 Active)   **OF**   **BL/TL**

1,834 games	.289 ba
1,958 hits	45 hr
481 rbi	476 sb

The best bunter in the majors today, Butler has batted over .300 three times in his career. Using an open stance, he has the knack of slicing singles to left field. A speedy base runner, he nevertheless has led his league three times in failed attempts to steal. Defensively, Butler covers a great deal of real estate, but he has only an average arm.

C

Caldwell, Mike

1949–

San Diego (NL 1971–73), San Francisco (NL 1974–76), Cincinnati (NL 1977), Milwaukee (AL 1977–84) P BR/LHP

475 games	2,408 innings
137-130 W–L	3.81 ERA
939 k's	18 saves

Some called it a spitter, Caldwell himself said it was a sinker, but after he began throwing it, he went 22–9 in 1978 and 16–6 in 1979. A durable hurler, he completed an AL-best 23 games in 1978 while pitching 293 innings. In the 1982 World Series, he won two games for Milwaukee. Caldwell had particular success against the Yankees; in one memorable incident, he hit Reggie Jackson with a pitch, precipitating a brawl.

Callison, Johnny

1939–

Chicago (AL 1958–59), Philadelphia (NL 1960–69), Chicago (NL 1970–71), New York (AL 1972–73)
OF   BL/TR

1,886 games	.264 ba
1,757 hits	226 hr
840 rbi	74 sb

Long the laughingstock of the National League, the Phillies seemed to be living a fantasy during the 1964 season. They were already comfortably ahead in the pennant race when Callison, their star outfielder, hit a dramatic ninth-inning home run against the invincible Dick Radatz at Shea Stadium to win the All-Star Game. Unfortunately, it all fell apart for the Phils in the last weeks of the season. That year was the highlight of Callison's career; he racked up a .274 average with 31 homers and 104 RBI. Sound defensively, he possessed a strong throwing arm in right field.

Camilli, Dolph

1907–
Chicago (NL 1933–34), Philadelphia (NL 1934–37), Brooklyn (NL 1938–43), Boston (NL 1945)　**1B**
BL/TL

1,490 games	.277 ba
1,482 hits	239 hr
950 rbi	60 sb

One of Larry MacPhail's first moves upon taking over the Dodgers in 1938 was his purchase of Camilli (then a holdout from the Phillies) for a reported $75,000. Camilli continued his lusty hitting in Flatbush, leading the Dodgers to the pennant in 1941, when he hit 34 homers and had 120 RBI, both league highs. Fine defensively, Camilli had enormous hands that enabled him to scoop low throws out of the dirt. After playing six years during the heated rivalry between the Dodgers and Giants, Camilli was traded to the enemy; rather than report to the hated Giants, he retired.

Camnitz, Howie (Red)

1881–1960
Pittsburgh (NL 1904, 1906–13), Philadelphia (NL 1913), Pittsburgh (FL 1914–15)　**P**　BR/RHP

326 games	2,085 innings
133-106 W-L	2.75 ERA
915 k's	15 saves

Camnitz was one of the pitching stars for Pittsburgh during the first decade of the 20th century. In 1909, he compiled one of the greatest seasons ever by a pitcher, going 25–6 with a 1.62 ERA. Three times a 20-game winner, he also lost 20 in 1913 after winning 22 the season before. Fairly typical of players of his era, Camnitz was a heavy drinker, and Pirates owner Barney

Dreyfuss withheld part of his salary in an attempt to keep him sober.

Campanella, Roy (Campy)

1921–1993

Baltimore Elite Giants (1937–42, 1944–45),
Brooklyn (NL 1948–57)   C   **BR/TR**

1,215 games	.276 ba
1,161 hits	242 hr
856 rbi	25 sb

Campanella loved baseball and his play exuded joy. The greatest catcher in Dodgers history, his quick reflexes behind the plate, strong throwing arm, and firm handling of pitchers warranted his three NL MVP awards. He revolutionized the art of catching by moving closer to home plate while awaiting each pitch. Short and stocky, he was a feared slugger who spread his feet wide apart in the batter's box and held his bat high above his head. He belted more than 30 home runs four times and knocked in at least 100 runs in three seasons. In 1953, Campy batted .312 with 41 homers and 142 RBI—remarkable figures for a catcher. A tragic auto accident after the 1957 season left the congenial Campanella a paraplegic and he became a symbol of courage. The Dodgers retired his uniform number 39, and he was inducted into the Hall of Fame in 1969.

Campaneris, Bert (Campy)

1942–

Kansas City (AL 1964–67), Oakland (AL 1968–76),
Texas (AL 1977–79), California (AL 1979–81), New
York (AL 1983)   SS   **BR/TR**

2,328 games	.259 ba
2,249 hits	79 hr
646 rbi	649 sb

Campaneris homered twice in his first major league game but thereafter hit more than eight home runs in a season only once in his 19-year career. He made his mark as the sparkplug of the Athletics dynasty of the early seventies—getting on, stealing a base, and scooping up every ball on the left side of the infield. Campy led the AL in stolen bases six times.

Campbell, Bill
1948–

Minnesota (AL 1973–76), Boston (AL 1977–81), Chicago (NL 1982–83), Philadelphia (NL 1984), St. Louis (NL 1985), Detroit (AL 1986), Montreal (NL 1987)   P   BR/RHP

700 games	1,229 innings
83-68 W–L	3.54 ERA
864 k's	126 saves

An effective sinker made Campbell one of the early big-money free agents following his 17–5 season in 1976. He went 13–9 with 31 saves for Boston in 1978 but hurt his arm and never put up big numbers again.

Candelaria, John (The Candy Man)
1953–

Pittsburgh (NL 1975–85, 1993), California (AL 1985–87), New York (NL 1987), New York (AL 1988–89), Montreal (NL 1989), Minnesota (AL 1990), Toronto (AL 1990), Los Angeles (NL 1991–92)   P   BR/LHP

600 games	2,526 innings
177-122 W–L	3.33 ERA
1,673 k's	29 saves

Pinpoint control of a wicked fastball and sharp-breaking curve made the 6-foot, 7-inch Candelaria a big winner from the start of his career. He won 16 games in 1976 and went 20–5 with an NL-best 2.34 ERA in 1977. Candelaria pitched a no-hitter against the Dodgers in 1976. The owner of a rubber arm who is still highly effective against left-handed batters, he became a reliever late in his career.

Candiotti, Tom

1957–

Milwaukee (AL 1983–84), Cleveland (AL 1986–91),
Toronto (AL 1991), Los Angeles (NL 1992–93
Active) P BR/RHP

278 games	1,822 innings
103-103 W–L	3.41 ERA
1,185 k's	

Once Candiotti gained control of his knuckleball and
had the confidence to throw it a majority of the time,
he became a big winner in the majors, surpassing 10
victories in five consecutive seasons. In 1986, he won
16 games for Cleveland and led the AL with 17 complete games. Prior to the 1992 season, he signed a lu-
crative free agent contract with the Dodgers.

Canseco, Jose

1964–

Oakland (AL 1985–92), Texas (AL 1992–93 Active)
OF BR/TR

1,032 games	.266 ba
1,033 hits	245 hr
780 rbi	134 sb

A legend in his own mind, Canseco is a strong power
hitter with good speed who cashed in on the fame that
followed his 40–40 season in 1988. That year, he hit
.307 with 42 homers, 124 RBI, and 40 stolen bases.
Traded by the Athletics because of his poor attitude,
Canseco is trying to resurrect his career in Texas. Defensively, Canseco turns many fly balls into an adven-
ture; in 1993, one fly ball hit his head and skipped over
the wall for a home run.

Cardenal, Jose

1943–

San Francisco (NL 1963–64), California (AL
1965–67), Cleveland (AL 1968–69), St. Louis (NL
1970–71), Milwaukee (AL 1971), Chicago (NL
1972–77), Philadelphia (NL 1978–79), New York
(NL 1979–80), Kansas City (AL 1980)   OF
BR/TR

2,017 games	.275 ba
1,913 hits	138 hr
775 rbi	329 sb

Cardenal bounced around five franchises before find-
ing a home at Wrigley Field, where he batted between
.291 and .317 from 1972 to 1976. Fast on the base
paths, he stole more than 20 bases 10 times. Yet for all
his accomplishments, he received scant recognition
during his playing years.

Carew, Rod

1945–

Minnesota (1967–78), California (1979–85)   1B,
2B   BL/TR

2,469 games	.328 ba
3,053 hits	92 hr
1,015 rbi	353 sb

A master batsman, Carew had the most relaxed stance
and swing of any major leaguer of his era. Born in Pan-
ama and raised in New York City, Carew won seven
AL batting titles and threatened to hit .400 in 1977
before settling for a .388 average. Dangerous on the
bases, he stole home seven times in 1969 alone and a
total of 16 times in his career. Only a lack of home run
power and an average throwing arm prevented Carew
from being hailed as the greatest player of the past 50
years. In recognition of his many qualities on and off
the diamond, both the Twins and the Angels retired
his uniform number 29, and the Hall of Fame inducted him in 1991.

Carey, Max (Scoops)

1890–1976

Pittsburgh (NL 1910–26), Brooklyn (NL 1926–29)

OF   BB/TR

2,476 games	.285 ba
2,665 hits	70 hr
800 rbi	738 sb

The outstanding ball hawk of his era, Carey utilized his great speed to track down fly balls in Forbes Field's expansive outfield. A smart base runner as well, he led the NL in steals 10 times, and in 1922 he stole 51 bases in 53 attempts. At the age of 35, he hit .458 for the champion Pirates in the 1925 World Series. Carey entered the Hall of Fame in 1961.

Carlton, Steve (Lefty)

1944–

St. Louis (NL 1965–71), Philadelphia (NL 1972–86), San Francisco (NL 1986), Chicago (AL 1986), Cleveland (AL 1987), Minnesota (AL 1987–88)   P   BL/LHP

741 games	5,217 innings
329-244 W–L	3.22 ERA
4,136 k's	2 saves

Owner of the sharpest-breaking slider in major league history, Carlton is the only pitcher ever to have won four Cy Young Awards. Traded by the Cardinals due to a contract hassle, he won 27 games—including 15 in a row—for a horrible Phillies team in 1972 that won only 32 other games all season. He started 14 opening day games for the Phillies and currently ranks second to Nolan Ryan in career strikeouts. Quotes by Carlton in the daily press were rare because he refused to talk to the media for most of his career.

Carroll, Clay (Hawk)

1941–

Milwaukee (NL 1964–65), Atlanta (NL 1966–68), Cincinnati (NL 1968–75), Chicago (AL 1976–77), St. Louis (NL 1977), Pittsburgh (NL 1978)   P

BR/RHP

731 games	1,353 innings
96-73 W–L	2.94 ERA
681 k's	143 saves

A tireless reliever, Carroll twice led the NL in appearances—in 1966 (73) and 1972 (65). Over a 10-year span in 1966–75, he averaged 61 games per year. In 1972, pitching for Sparky Anderson (alias "Captain Hook"), he saved a career-best 37 games and the Reds won the NL pennant. He pitched in three World Series for Cincinnati.

Carter, Gary (Kid)

1954–

Montreal (NL 1974–84, 1992), New York (NL 1985–89), Los Angeles (NL 1990), San Francisco (NL 1991)   C   BR/TR

2,296 games	.262 ba
2,092 hits	324 hr
1,225 rbi	39 sb

An 11-time All-Star and certain Hall of Famer, Carter brought a boyish enthusiasm to the game. Ever the optimist, his rah-rah attitude occasionally rubbed teammates the wrong way, but he was a fan favorite wherever he played. A pull hitter with excellent power, Carter slammed more than 20 home runs nine times and knocked in at least 100 runs on four occasions. His record of 298 homers as a catcher ranks second in NL history. Defensively, he had few equals, particularly when it came to blocking balls in the dirt. The Expos retired his uniform number 8.

Carter, Joe

1960–

Chicago (NL 1983), Cleveland (AL 1984–89), San Diego (NL 1990), Toronto (AL 1991–93 Active)

OF   BR/TR

1,499 games	.262 ba
1,523 hits	275 hr
994 rbi	189 sb

Strong wrists and a quick bat have made Carter one of the top clutch hitters in the game today. In seven of the last eight years, he has knocked in at least 105 runs; in the only year he missed, he had 98 RBI. Although Carter's average has fluctuated between .302 and .232, he has been a consistent power hitter and run producer. His ninth inning home run in Game Six of the 1993 World Series made Toronto champions for the second consecutive season.

Cartwright, Alexander

1820–1892

Executive

Generally credited with establishing the ground rules for the game of baseball as we know it today, Alexander Cartwright formed the Knickerbocker Baseball Club in 1845. He and his cohorts set the distance between bases at 90 feet, permitted nine fielders to a side, and prohibited the practice of throwing the ball at runners to put them out. The so-called Knickerbocker Rules spread throughout the nation. Cartwright was inducted into the Hall of Fame in 1938.

Carty, Rico

1939–

Milwaukee (NL 1963–65), Atlanta (NL 1966–72), Texas (AL 1973), Chicago (NL 1973), Oakland (AL 1973, 1978), Cleveland (AL 1974–77), Toronto (AL 1978, 1979)   OF, DH   BR/TR

1,651 games	.299 ba
1,677 hits	204 hr
890 rbi	21 sb

Carty was born to hit. After joining the Braves as a full-time outfielder in 1964, he hit well over .300 in five of the next six years, leading the NL in 1970 (.366). That year was his best as a run producer; he slammed 25 home runs and pushed across 101 runs. After a series of serious knee injuries limited Carty's playing time, he became a designated hitter in the American League.

Caruthers, Bob (Parisian Bob)
1864–1911
St. Louis (AA 1884–87), Brooklyn (AA 1888–89), Brooklyn (NL 1890–91), St. Louis (NL 1892)   **P**
BL/RHP

340 games	2,828 innings
218-99 W–L	2.83 ERA
900 k's	3 saves

After winning 40 games against only 13 losses for St. Louis in 1885, Caruthers vacationed in Paris that winter. When he threatened not to report unless his contract demands were met, he earned the nickname "Parisian Bob." He returned to St. Louis to win 30 games in 1886 and 29 more in 1887, but Browns owner Chris Von der Ahe tired of his demands and sold him to Brooklyn, where he continued his outstanding hurling. In 1889, he won 40 games again, as the Bridegrooms captured the AA pennant. Caruthers currently ranks third in career winning percentage, but he has not been inducted into the Hall of Fame.

Cash, Norm
1934–1986
Chicago (AL 1958–59), Detroit (AL 1960–74)   **1B**
BL/TL

2,089 games	.271 ba
1,820 hits	377 hr
1,103 rbi	43 sb

Cash won the AL batting crown in 1961 (.361) but never hit the .300 mark in any other season. His achievements that season were largely lost in the publicity surrounding Maris and Mantle's home run race—he also knocked out 41 homers, had 132 RBI, scored 119 runs, and walked 124 times. Cash did hit 39 homers in 1962, 30 in 1965, 32 in 1966, and 32 in 1971, so his power was unquestioned. A fun-loving guy, he was also one of the most popular players in Tigers history.

Cavarretta, Phil

1916–

Chicago (NL 1934–53), Chicago (AL 1954–55); MGR—Chicago (NL 1951–53)   **1B, OF, MGR BL/TL**

2,030 games	.293 ba
1,977 hits	95 hr
920 rbi	65 sb

A sharp-hitting first baseman, Cavarretta enjoyed his most productive years during WW II. He led the NL in batting in 1945 (.355); in 1944, he collected a league-best 197 hits and batted .321.

Cedeño, Cesar

1951–

Houston (NL 1970–81), Cincinnati (NL 1982–85), St. Louis (NL 1985), Los Angeles (NL 1986)   **OF, 1B   BR/TR**

2,006 games	.285 ba
2,087 hits	199 hr
976 rbi	550 sb

Cedeño had all the skills to excel. His Houston manager Leo Durocher even thought he had a chance to be the next Willie Mays. Although he showed flashes of brilliance—leading the league in doubles in 1971 and 1972, hitting 26 home runs with 102 RBI in 1974, stealing at least 50 bases in six consecutive seasons (1972–77), and fielding expertly—Cedeño never combined his talents consistently.

Cepeda, Orlando (The Baby Bull, Cha-Cha)

1937–

San Francisco (NL 1958–66), St. Louis (NL 1966–68), Atlanta (NL 1969–72), Oakland (AL 1972), Boston (AL 1973), Kansas City (AL 1974)

1B, OF   **BR/TR**

2,124 games	.297 ba
2,351 hits	379 hr
1,365 rbi	142 sb

When the Giants moved west to San Francisco in 1958, Cepeda became an immediate favorite with the fans, even surpassing Willie Mays in the eyes of the faithful. He hit .312 as a rookie, with 25 homers and 96 RBI in the first of seven outstanding seasons out west. In 1961, Cepeda belted 46 home runs and chased home 142 runs, both league-leading figures. A colorful player on the field and a team leader in the clubhouse, Cepeda reenergized his career following a trade to St. Louis in 1966. In 1967, he led El Birdos to the pennant when he hit .325 with 25 dingers and 111 RBI.

Cey, Ron (Penguin)

1948–

Los Angeles (NL 1971–82), Chicago (NL 1983–86), Oakland (AL 1987)   **3B**   **BR/TR**

2,073 games	.261 ba
1,868 hits	316 hr
1,139 rbi	24 sb

Nicknamed for his short limbs and penguin-like walk, Cey was a clutch hitter and an underrated defensive player at third. He formed part of one of the Dodgers' greatest infields in team history along with Bill Russell, Davey Lopes, and Steve Garvey. Cey hit at least 22 homers in 11 of 12 years, missing out only in the strike-shortened 1981 season.

Chadwick, Henry
1824–1908
Writer

The British-born Chadwick moved with his family as a youth to Brooklyn, where he fell in love with the game of baseball. As a young sportswriter in the late 1850s, he developed the box score; he later edited the *Spalding Guide* from 1881 to 1908. Throughout his career, Chadwick worked diligently to rid the game of immoral elements of gambling. Often called "the Father of Baseball," he was inducted into the Hall of Fame in 1938.

Chambliss, Chris
1948–
Cleveland (AL 1971–74), New York (AL 1974–79, 1988), Atlanta (NL 1980–86)   **1B**   **BL/TR**

2,173 games	.279 ba
2,109 hits	185 hr
972 rbi	40 sb

A quiet, consistent first baseman, Chambliss thrust himself into the limelight by belting one of the most significant homers in Yankees history. His ninth inning blast in the decisive game of the 1976 AL championship series gave New York its first pennant since 1964. He batted .524 in that series and .313 in the ensuing World Series. A good clutch hitter, Chambliss drove home 96, 90, and 90 runs in 1976–78.

Chance, Dean

1941–

Los Angeles (AL 1961–64), California (AL 1965–66), Minnesota (AL 1967–69), Cleveland (AL 1970), New York (NL 1970), Detroit (AL 1971)   P
BR/RHP

406 games	2,147 innings
128-115 W–L	2.92 ERA
1,534 k's	23 saves

For a seven-year span from 1962 to 1968, Chance was possibly the top right-hander in the AL. At his best in 1964, pitching on the high mound at Chavez Ravine, he went 20–9 with 11 shutouts and a minuscule 1.65 ERA. Chance also won 20 games for the Twins in 1967, but he hurt his arm in 1969 and was never the same thereafter. In his career, he won 13 games 1–0, the sixth most in major league history. Chance was one of the worst-hitting pitchers of all time, collecting only 44 hits for an average of .066.

Chance, Frank (The Peerless Leader)

1877–1924

Chicago (NL 1898–1912), New York (AL 1913–14); MGR—Chicago (NL 1905–12), New York (AL 1913–14), Boston (AL 1923)   1B, MGR
BR/TR

1,287 games	.296 ba
1,273 hits	20 hr
596 rbi	401 sb

As player-manager, "the Peerless Leader" brought the Cubs a degree of success that has not been matched in over 80 years. The salty-tongued manager won four pennants in five years (1906–10), as well as the Cubs' last championship in 1908. The 1906 squad won a major league record 116 games. Chance entered the Hall of Fame in 1946.

Chandler, Spurgeon (Spud)

1907–1990

New York (AL 1937–47)   P   BR/RHP

211 games	1,485 innings
109-43 W–L	2.84 ERA
614 k's	6 saves

When Chandler took the mound, the Yanks expected to win. He never had a losing season and produced records of 14–5 in 1938, 16–5 in 1942, 20–4 in 1943, and 20–8 in 1946. He also led the AL in 1943 with an ERA of 1.64.

Chapman, Ben

1908–1993

New York (AL 1930–36), Washington (AL 1936–37, 1941), Boston (AL 1937–38), Cleveland (AL 1939–40), Chicago (AL 1941), Brooklyn (NL 1944–45), Philadelphia (NL 1945–46); MGR—Philadelphia (NL 1945–48)   OF, MGR
BR/TR

1,716 games	.302 ba
1,958 hits	90 hr
977 rbi	287 sb

A hard-nosed ballplayer with outstanding running speed, Chapman led the AL in stolen bases in 1931–33 and in 1937. Strong defensively in centerfield, he wielded a sharp, nasty tongue on the diamond. As manager of the Phillies, he used racist language to attack Jackie Robinson in 1947.

Chapman, Ray

1891–1920

Cleveland (AL 1912–20)   SS   BR/TR

1,051 games	.278 ba
1,053 hits	17 hr
364 rbi	233 sb

Ray Chapman was the glue of the Indians infield and probably the most popular player on the team. In

1920, he was struck on the head by a pitched ball at the Polo Grounds in New York; tragically, he died the next day. He was a very fast runner and an excellent bunter.

Charleston, Oscar
1896–1954

Indianapolis ABC's (1915, 1920, 1922–23), Detroit Stars (1919), Chicago American Giants (1919, 1934), Harrisburg Giants (1924–27), Philadelphia Hilldales (1928–29), Homestead Grays (1930–31), Pittsburgh Crawfords (1932–34, 1935–38), Toledo Crawfords (1940–41) **OF, 1B**   **BL/TL**

821 games	.357 ba
1,069 hits	151 hr

Inducted into the Hall of Fame in 1976, Charleston was a legendary player who had the power of a Babe Ruth, the batting ability of a Ty Cobb, and the defensive skills of a Tris Speaker. Fast afoot, he played a shallow centerfield and could outrun any ball hit in his direction. Charleston was a feared base runner who would slide into bases with his spikes high. He was known for his explosive temper and instigated some memorable brawls on the diamond.

Chase, Hal (Prince Hal)
1883–1947

New York (AL 1905–13), Chicago (AL 1913–14), Buffalo (FL 1914–15), Cincinnati (NL 1916–18), New York (NL 1919); MGR—New York (AL 1910–11) **1B, MGR**   **BR/TL**

1,919 games	.291 ba
2,158 hits	57 hr
941 rbi	363 sb

Chase was intensely disliked by opposing players and teammates alike because of his lackluster play and his betting on games. Nevertheless, he has been rated one of the top fielding first basemen in baseball history and a pretty fair hitter as well. In 1916, he led the NL in batting (.339).

Chesbro, Jack (Happy Jack)
1874–1931
Pittsburgh (NL 1899–1902), New York (AL 1903–09), Boston (AL 1909)   P   BR/RHP

392 games	2,896 innings
198-132 W–L	2.68 ERA
1,265 k's	5 saves

A reknowned spitballer, Chesbro's 1904 season in New York ranks with the best in baseball history; he completed 48 of 51 starts, gaining 41 victories and pitching 454 innings. The dour hurler twice led the National League in winning percentage, an achievement he repeated in the junior circuit in 1904. He was inducted into the Hall of Fame in 1946.

Childs, Clarence (Cupid)
1867–1912
Philadelphia (NL 1888), Syracuse (AA 1890), Cleveland (NL 1891–98), St. Louis (NL 1899), Chicago (NL 1900–01)   2B   BL/TR

1,456 games	.306 ba
1,720 hits	20 hr
654 rbi	269 sb

An effective leadoff batter for Cleveland's fine squads in the 1890s, Childs was a patient batsman who walked more than 100 times in four of the five seasons between 1892 and 1896. He scored at least 105 runs in every year but one between 1890 and 1897. A fine fielder, he also batted a career-high .355 in 1896.

Cicotte, Eddie
1884–1969
Detroit (AL 1905), Boston (AL 1908–12), Chicago (AL 1912–20)   P   BB/RHP

502 games	3,223 innings
208-149 W–L	2.38 ERA
1,374 k's	25 saves

A wizard of the shine ball, Cicotte was the ace of the White Sox staff during the 1910s. He led the AL in wins in 1917 (28) and 1919 (29) but conspired with seven of his teammates to throw the 1919 World Series. As the starting pitcher in game one, Cicotte hit the Cincinnati leadoff batter to signal that the fix was in.

Clark, Jack (The Ripper)

1955–
San Francisco (NL 1975–84), St. Louis (1985–87), New York (AL 1988), San Diego (NL 1989–90), Boston (1991–92) **OF, 1B, DH** **BR/TR**

1,994 games	.267 ba
1,826 hits	340 hr
1,180 rbi	77 sb

Clark was a rebel who frequently defended his lesser-known teammates in battles against team management. Fans in the stands always paid attention when Clark batted because he could homer on any swing. Always a big swinger, as his career progressed, he became an extremely patient batter and his walk and strikeout totals rose dramatically. He led his league three times in drawing walks, and he fanned more than 133 times four times in the five years from 1987 to 1991. When healthy, Clark was one of the most feared sluggers in the game, slamming more than 20 homers 11 times in his career. In 1985 and 1987, Clark provided the only power for the pennant-winning Cardinals.

Clark, Will (The Natural, The Thrill)

1964–
San Francisco (NL 1986–93), Texas (AL 1994 Active) **1B** **BL/TL**

1,160 games	.299 ba
1,278 hits	176 hr
709 rbi	52 sb

A sweet swing marked Clark as a can't-miss star in his rookie season with the Giants. He didn't disappoint; in his first big league at-bat, against Nolan Ryan, Clark homered. In 1989, his best year, he batted .333 with 111 RBI, as the Giants won the pennant. Defensively, Clark has few peers.

Clarke, Fred (Cap)

1872–1960

Louisville (NL 1894–99), Pittsburgh (NL 1900–1, 1911, 1913–15); MGR—Louisville (NL 1897–99), Pittsburgh (NL 1900–15)   **OF, MGR**   **BL/TR**

2,242 games	.312 ba
2,672 hits	67 hr
1,015 rbi	506 sb

Though he was an outstanding defensive outfielder and strong hitter, Clarke's real fame rests on his managing the Pirates to glory in the first decade of the 20th century. He captured three consecutive pennants from 1901 to 1903 and won the World Series in 1909. Clarke entered the Hall of Fame in 1945.

Clarkson, John

1861–1909

Worcester (NL 1882), Chicago (NL 1884–87), Boston (NL 1888–92), Cleveland (NL 1892–94)   **P**
BR/RHP

531 games	4,536 innings
328-178 W–L	2.81 ERA
1,978 k's	5 saves

In the age of two-man pitching staffs, Clarkson twice hurled over 600 innings in a single season. Sold to Boston in 1887 for the then-astronomical sum of $10,000, he won 33, 49, 26, and 33 games for the Beaneaters. A moody and sensitive man, he died mysteriously at the age of 47. Clarkson was inducted into the Hall of Fame in 1963.

Clemens, Roger (Rocket Man)

1962–

Boston (AL 1984–93 Active)   P   RHP

302 games	2,222 innings
163-86 W–L	2.94 ERA
2,033 k's	

Simply the best pitcher in the game today, Clemens throws an outstanding fastball, has pinpoint control, changes speeds effectively with his breaking stuff, and has an intense desire to win. A three-time recipient of the Cy Young Award (1986, 1987, 1991), Clemens led the AL in ERA four times, in shutouts five times, and in winning percentage twice. He established the all-time strikeout record for a nine-inning game when he fanned 20 Mariners in 1986.

Clemente, Roberto (Bob)

1934–1972

Pittsburgh (NL 1955–72)   OF   BR/TR

2,433 games	.317 ba
3,000 hits	240 hr
1,305 rbi	83 sb

A brilliant batter, Clemente stood deep in the batter's box far from the plate and frequently slammed the pitch to the opposite field. He was an excellent right-fielder whose throwing arm commanded the respect of all base runners. Despite a wide variety of aches and pains, Clemente seemed to play better the more he complained. An inspirational player, he led the Pirates to World Series titles in 1960 and 1971. He died tragically after the 1972 season in a plane crash while carrying relief supplies to Nicaraguan earthquake victims. The Pirates retired his uniform number 21, and he was inducted into the Hall of Fame in 1973.

Clendenon, Donn

1935–

Pittsburgh (NL 1961–68), Montreal (NL 1969),
New York (NL 1969–71), St. Louis (NL 1972)   **1B**
BR/TR

1,362 games	.274 ba
1,273 hits	159 hr
682 rbi	90 sb

Acquired by the Mets midway through the 1969 season, Clendenon represented their first true power hitter, and he commanded respect around the league. In the Mets shocking five-game triumph in the 1969 World Series, he batted .357 and belted three home runs. Tall and slender, Clendenon took a long, looping swing at the ball from a deep crouch. As a result, he was prone to striking out. During his tenure with the free-swinging Bucs, he led the NL in fanning twice, including a whopping 163 times in 1968.

Clift, Harlond (Darkie)

1912–1992

St. Louis (AL 1934–43), Washington (AL 1943–45)
3B   BR/TR

1,582 games	.272 ba
1,558 hits	178 hr
829 rbi	69 sb

Clift was a star lost in the depths of the perennial second-division St. Louis Browns. Third base had historically been a position with few power hitters, and Clift's 29 roundtrippers in 1937 was a major league record. He surpassed his own mark the next season, when he belted 34 homers. Defensively, Clift was among the best; his 1937 records for one-season double plays and assists stood for nearly 35 years.

Cobb, Ty (The Georgia Peach)

1886–1961

Detroit (AL 1905–26), Philadelphia (AL 1927–28);
MGR—Detroit (AL 1921–26)   OF, MGR
BL/TR

3,035 games	.366 ba
4,189 hits	117 hr
1,937 rbi	891 sb

Baseball has never seen a competitor as fierce as Ty
Cobb. Driven to win, he antagonized opponents by
sliding with spikes high into any man who attempted
to apply a tag. Aloof from most of his teammates, he
considered each game a test of will. At the plate, he
stood upright, applying a peculiar split grip on the bat
with his hands. Extremely confident in his ability, he
won the AL batting title 10 times and retains the majors' highest lifetime average to this day. Cobb was an
inaugural member of the Hall of Fame in 1936.

Cochrane, Gordon (Mickey, Black Mike)

1903–1962

Philadelphia (AL 1925–33), Detroit (AL 1934–37);
MGR—Detroit (AL 1934–38)   C, MGR
BL/TR

1,482 games	.320 ba
1,652 hits	119 hr
832 rbi	64 sb

Cochrane was an erudite catcher who attended Boston
University. A fierce competitor and inspirational team
player, he sparked the Athletics to three consecutive
pennants from 1929 to 1931, and as player-manager
he led Detroit into the World Series in 1934 and 1935.
Unfortunately, a beaning in 1937 brought his career to
a premature close. He was inducted into the Hall of
Fame in 1947.

Colavito, Rocco (Rocky)

1933–

Cleveland (AL 1955–59, 1965–67), Detroit (AL 1960–63), Kansas City (AL 1964), Chicago (AL 1967), Los Angeles (NL 1968), New York (AL 1968)

OF   BR/TR

1,841 games	.266 ba
1,730 hits	374 hr
1,159 rbi	19 sb

Cleveland went into mourning when Frank ("Trader") Lane traded Colavito to Detroit for the 1959 AL batting champ Harvey Kuenn just before the start of the 1960 season. Fans loved his power, his accurate rifle-like arm, but above all his style. While getting settled in the batter's box, for instance, he pointed his bat in a menacing gesture at the pitcher. Although he produced some big years in Detroit, such as 45 home runs and 140 RBI in 1961, he never recaptured the glory of his days in Cleveland. At his retirement, his 374 homers ranked 15th on the all-time list.

Coleman, Joe

1947–

Washington (AL 1965–70), Detroit (AL 1971–76), Chicago (NL 1976), Oakland (AL 1977–78), Toronto (AL 1978), San Francisco (NL 1979), Pittsburgh (NL 1979)   **P   BR/RHP**

484 games	2,569 innings
142-135 W–L	3.70 ERA
1,728 k's	7 saves

The son of major league hurler Joe Coleman, Sr., Coleman benefited from his trade to Detroit for Denny McLain in 1971. He won 20 games his first year in Motown, 19 in 1972, and 23 in 1973. After his retirement, Coleman became a pitching coach for several organizations.

Coleman, Vince

1960–
St. Louis (NL 1985–90), New York (NL 1991–93)
OF   BB/TR

1,113 games	.266 ba
1,175 hits	20 hr
280 rbi	648 sb

An extremely fast runner who built his career on the hard Astroturf in St. Louis, Coleman made an ill-considered move to the grass field of Shea Stadium in 1991. During his tenure with the Cardinals, he led the NL in stolen bases his first six seasons in the majors, including three consecutive years with more than 100 steals. At one point, he stole 50 consecutive bases without being thrown out. After moving to the Mets, he suffered a series of hamstring and other leg injuries and incurred the wrath of Mets fans and management. For a leadoff batter, Coleman has a disappointingly low on-base average, due to his inability to draw walks. Defensively, his skills are only average; his speed barely outweighs his poor throwing arm. In 1993 Coleman was indicted for tossing a firecracker at a crowd of people following a game at Dodger Stadium and his baseball future is in doubt.

Collins, Eddie (Cocky)

1887–1951
Philadelphia (AL 1906–14, 1927–30), Chicago (AL 1915–26); MGR—Chicago (AL 1924–26)   2B,
MGR   BL/TR

2,826 games	.333 ba
3,312 hits	47 hr
1,300 rbi	744 sb

Confident if not cocky on the field, Collins was a leading member of Connie Mack's $100,000 infield of the early 20th century. He stood erect at the plate and sprayed the ball to all fields. A fast runner, he batted over .300 10 times. Defensively, he had no peers. Collins entered the Hall of Fame in 1945.

Collins, Jimmy

1870–1943

Boston (NL 1895, 1896–1900), Louisville (NL 1895), Boston (AL 1901–07), Philadelphia (AL 1907–08); MGR—Boston (AL 1901–06)   **3B, MGR   BR/TR**

1,726 games	.294 ba
2,000 hits	65 hr
983 rbi	194 sb

Collins was the best third baseman of the early 20th century, a magician in the field who perfected the off-balance throw on bunted balls. He batted a career-high .346 in 1897 for the Beaneaters. Collins entered the Hall of Fame in 1945.

Combs, Earle (The Kentucky Colonel)

1899–1976

New York (AL 1924–35)   **OF   BL/TR**

1,455 games	.325 ba
1,866 hits	58 hr
632 rbi	96 sb

The speedy leadoff hitter on the great Yankees teams of the 1920s, Combs was a spectacular center fielder whose only weakness was a poor throwing arm. In 1925, he overcame a badly broken leg to bat .342 and collect 203 hits. DiMaggio was the only other Yank to stroke more than 200 hits as a rookie. Combs led the AL in triples in 1927, 1928, and 1930. His career ended prematurely after a severe injury incurred when he crashed into the outfield wall in St. Louis in 1934. Combs was inducted into the Hall of Fame in 1970.

Comiskey, Charles (Commy, The Old Roman)

1859–1931

St. Louis (AA 1882–89, 1891), Chicago (PL 1890), Cincinnati (NL 1892–94) MGR—St. Louis (AA 1883–89, 1891), Chicago (PL 1890), Cincinnati (NL 1892–94) **1B, MGR** **BR/TR**

1,390 games	.264 ba
1,531 hits	29 hr
467 rbi	378 sb

Generally regarded as the first player on defense to stray off first base and throw to second to force runners, Comiskey is best remembered as the parsimonious owner of the White Sox, whose duplicitous penny-pinching drove his players to fix the 1919 World Series. He owned the White Sox franchise from its inception in 1901 until 1931.

Concepcion, Dave

1948–

Cincinnati (NL 1970–88) **SS** **BR/TR**

2,488 games	.267 ba
2,326 hits	101 hr
950 rbi	321 sb

Concepcion's great offensive talents kept him a step ahead of all the other shortstops in the NL. A consistent .270 hitter with extra-base power, he collected at least 22 doubles in 11 consecutive seasons; in 1979, he hit .281 with 16 home runs and 84 RBI. Defensively, he popularized the one-bounce throw on artificial turf from deep short to first base. A five-time Gold Glove winner, Concepcion is a potential Hall of Famer.

Cone, David (Coney)

1963–

Kansas City (AL 1986, 1993 Active), New York (NL 1987–92), Toronto (AL 1992) **P** **BL/RHP**

235 games	1,521 innings
95-65 W–L	3.14 ERA
1,418 k's	1 save

Sometimes Cone thinks too much on the mound. He throws a full assortment of pitches from a variety of angles when a fastball would do as well. His favorite pitch is a splitter, although he thinks he can still fool batters by throwing a two-strike Laredo (sidearm or south of the border) slider. The Mets stole Cone from the Royals in a 1986 trade, and he rewarded them by going 20–3 in 1988. After winning 14 games for three consecutive seasons, he won 17 in 1992 while pitching for both the Mets and Blue Jays. Cone led the NL in strikeouts in 1990 and 1991 and would have repeated in 1992 but for the trade to the AL. Don't let his boyish appearance fool you—he is one tough competitor.

Conigliaro, Tony (Tony C)

1945–1990
Boston (AL 1964–70, 1975), California (AL 1971)
OF   BR/TR

876 games	.264 ba
849 hits	166 hr
516 rbi	20 sb

Conigliaro had the perfect swing for Fenway Park. He appeared to be on his way to a fabulous career for the Red Sox until a Jack Hamilton fastball crushed his head in a 1967 game. As a 19-year-old rookie, "Tony C" belted 24 homers; the following year, he led the AL with 32 taters. Although he later hit 36 home runs with 116 RBI in a 1970 comeback, he was unable to fully regain his vision.

Connor, Roger

1857–1931

Troy (NL 1880–82), New York (NL 1883–89, 1891, 1893–94), New York (PL 1890), Philadelphia (NL 1892), St. Louis (NL 1894–97); MGR—St. Louis (NL 1896) **1B, MGR** **BL/TL**

1,997 games	.317 ba
2,467 hits	138 hr
1,322 rbi	244 sb

The home run king of the dead ball era, Connor crushed 138 career homers for a major league record that stood until 1921, when it was broken by Babe Ruth. A low-ball hitter, he batted over .300 12 times. Connor utilized his fine speed both on the bases and on defense. In 1890, he was one of the leading organizers of the Players League and also played for the New York franchise. Connor was inducted into the Hall of Fame in 1976.

Coombs, Jack (Cy, Colby Jack)

1882–1957

Philadelphia (AL 1906–14), Brooklyn (NL 1915–18), Detroit (AL 1920); MGR—Philadelphia (NL 1919) **P, MGR** **BB/RHP**

354 games	2,320 innings
158-110 W–L	2.78 ERA
1,052 k's	8 saves

Nicknamed for his attendance at Colby College, Coombs and Chief Bender were the only pitchers to appear in the 1910 World Series for the Athletics. Coombs won three games in that series. In 1910, he went 31–9 with an AL-record 13 shutouts and an ERA of 1.30. The next year, he won 28 games. In all, he won five World Series games without a loss.

Cooper, Cecil

1949–

Boston (AL 1971–76), Milwaukee (AL 1977–87)

1B, DH   BL/TL

1,896 games	.298 ba
2,192 hits	241 hr
1,125 rbi	89 sb

The Red Sox thought they were securing the AL pennant when they reacquired George Scott and Bernie Carbo in 1977 in exchange for Cecil Cooper. Trades like that have kept the Sox without a World Series championship since 1918. Cooper went on to hit .300 his first seven seasons in Milwaukee. He knocked in more than 100 runs four times, including league-leading marks of 122 in 1980 and 126 in 1983. A great low-ball hitter, Cooper never received the acclaim his performances warranted.

Cooper, Mort

1913–1958

St. Louis (NL 1938–45), Boston (NL 1945–47), New York (NL 1947), Chicago (NL 1949)   P

BR/RHP

295 games	1,840 innings
128-75 W–L	2.97 ERA
913 k's	14 saves

Cooper was a talkative and superstitious star for the Cardinals during the team's glory days in the early forties. In 1942, he switched uniform numbers for each game he pitched to match the victory he was shooting for. Cooper won 22 games that year. The following year, he led the NL again with 21 wins. Cooper and his brother Walker formed the Cardinals battery and the best brother combo in team history.

Cooper, Walker

1915–1991

St. Louis (NL 1940–45, 1956–57), New York (NL 1946–49), Cincinnati (NL 1949–50), Boston (NL 1950–52), Milwaukee (NL 1953), Pittsburgh (NL 1954), Chicago (NL 1954–55)   C   BR/TR

1,473 games	.285 ba
1,341 hits	173 hr
812 rbi	18 sb

Cooper was a heavy-hitting catcher of great strength and quiet demeanor. After teaming with his brother Mort for St. Louis, in 1945, he was sold to the Giants for $175,000—the largest cash-only transaction up to that time. He prospered at the Polo Grounds, slamming 35 homers with 122 RBI and a batting average of .305 in 1947.

Cooper, Wilbur

1892–1973

Pittsburgh (NL 1912–24), Chicago (NL 1925–26), Detroit (AL 1926)   P   BR/LHP

517 games	3,480 innings
216-178 W–L	2.89 ERA
1,252 k's	14 saves

One of the top hurlers not inducted into the Hall of Fame, Cooper remains the leader in career victories for the Pittsburgh franchise with 202. He won at least 17 games in eight consecutive years between 1917 and 1924. A workhorse, he completed 68 percent of his starts.

Coveleski, Stan

1889–1984

Philadelphia (AL 1912), Cleveland (AL 1916–24), Washington (AL 1925–27), New York (AL 1928)
P   BR/RHP

450 games	3,082 innings
215-142 W–L	2.89 ERA
981 k's	21 saves

Coveleski broke the hearts of Brooklyn fans in the 1920 World Series when he defeated the Robins three times while yielding only two runs. He had complete control over his favorite pitch, the spitball, and he would wet his fingers before every pitch to deceive batters. Five times a 20-game winner, he won 13 consecutive games in 1925. Coveleski was inducted into the Hall of Fame in 1969.

Cox, Billy
1919–1978
Pittsburgh (NL 1941, 1946–47), Brooklyn (NL 1948–54), Baltimore (AL 1955)   3B, SS
BR/TR

1,058 games	.262 ba
974 hits	66 hr
351 rbi	42 sb

Never a mighty slugger, Cox earned his fame on defense as the finest third baseman of his generation. His quick, catlike reflexes and rifle arm snuffed out many rallies against the Dodgers. At the plate, his best year was 1953, when he hit .291 with 10 homers.

Craig, Roger
1930–
Brooklyn (NL 1955–57), Los Angeles (NL 1958–61), New York (NL 1962–63), St. Louis (NL 1964), Cincinnati (NL 1965), Philadelphia (NL 1966); MGR—San Diego (NL 1978–79), San Francisco (NL 1985–92)   P, MGR   BR/RHP

368 games	1,536 innings
74-98 W–L	3.83 ERA
803 k's	19 saves

Craig's career in the majors resembled a ride on a roller coaster. He joined the Dodgers in 1955 in time for their first World Series title and worked as an occasional starter for the next six years. Picked up by the Mets in the 1962 expansion draft, he became the league's biggest loser, dropping 24 games in 1962 and 22 in 1963. Saved by a trade to St. Louis, he starred in the Cardinals' World Series victory that fall. After retiring, he became a pitching coach (the acknowledged master of the splitter) in Detroit, and a manager San Diego, and San Francisco. As he aged, Craig came to bear an uncanny resemblance to President Lyndon Johnson.

Cramer, Roger (Doc, Flit)
1905–1990

Philadelphia (AL 1929–35), Boston (AL 1936–40), Washington (AL 1941), Detroit (AL 1942–48)   **OF BL/TR**

2,239 games	.296 ba
2,705 hits	37 hr
842 rbi	62 sb

Probably the least-remembered 2,700-hit man in major league history, Cramer has stats superior to many Hall of Famers. He hit as high as .336 for the Athletics in 1932, and he collected over 200 hits three times, including a league-best 200 in 1940. He had little home run sock and drove home few runs, although he scored more than 90 runs in nine consecutive seasons. Defensively, he was an outstanding ball hawk with a strong arm.

Crandall, Del
1930–

Boston (NL 1949–50), Milwaukee (NL 1953–63), San Francisco (NL 1964), Pittsburgh (NL 1965), Cleveland (AL 1966); MGR—Milwaukee (AL 1972–75), Seattle (AL 1983–84)   **C, MGR BR/TR**

1,573 games	.254 ba
1,276 hits	179 hr
657 rbi	26 sb

Crandall, the semi-official manager for the Braves throughout most of his career, had value far beyond his yearly batting average. Thus, when he batted .294 in 1960 with 19 home runs and 77 RBI, he was the most valuable catcher in the NL.

Cravath, Clifford (Gavvy, Cactus)
1881–1963

Boston (AL 1908), Chicago (AL 1909), Washington (AL 1909), Philadelphia (NL 1912–20); MGR— Philadelphia (NL 1919–20) OF, MGR
BR/TR

1,220 games	.287 ba
1,134 hits	119 hr
719 rbi	89 sb

Baseball's all-time leading 20th century home run hitter prior to Babe Ruth with 119, Cravath led the NL six times and slammed 24 homers in the Phillies' 1915 pennant-winning season. A free-swinger in an era of slap hitters, he also struck out a league-high 89 times in 1916.

Crawford, Sam (Wahoo Sam)
1880–1968

Cincinnati (NL 1899–1902), Detroit (AL 1903–17)
OF BL/TL

2,517 games	.309 ba
2,961 hits	97 hr
1,525 rbi	367 sb

One of the outstanding sluggers of the dead ball era, Wahoo Sam belted a major league record 309 triples in his career. An independent thinker, he was one of the best-liked players of his generation. Crawford was elected to the Hall of Fame in 1957.

Cronin, Joe

1906–1984

Pittsburgh (NL 1926–27), Washington (AL 1928–34), Boston (AL 1935–45); MGR— Washington (AL 1933–34), Boston (AL 1935–47)

SS, MGR   BR/TR

2,124 games	.301 ba
2,285 hits	170 hr
1,424 rbi	87 sb

A strategist on the field, Cronin became player-manager of the Senators at the age of 27. A perennial AL All-Star, he reached career highs in 1930 in batting average (.346), hits (203), runs scored (127), and RBI (126). Cronin knocked in more than 100 runs eight times. In recognition of his career achievements, the Red Sox retired his uniform number 4. He was elected to the Hall of Fame in 1956.

Cross, Lafayette (Lave)

1866–1927

Louisville (AA 1887–88), Philadelphia (AA 1889, 1891), Philadelphia (PL 1890), Philadelphia (NL 1892–97), St. Louis (NL 1898, 1899–1900), Cleveland (NL 1899), Brooklyn (NL 1900), Philadelphia (AL 1901–05), Washington (AL 1906–07); MGR—Cleveland (NL 1899)   3B, C,

MGR   BR/TR

2,275 games	.292 ba
2,645 hits	47 hr
1,345 rbi	301 sb

The peripatetic Cross played for four different Philadelphia franchises, but he enjoyed his greatest success with the Athletics after jumping to the upstart AL team from Brooklyn in 1901. Primarily a third baseman, he batted .386 for the Phillies in 1894 with 125 RBI and .342 with 108 RBI for the Athletics in 1902. In 1899, he managed the inept Cleveland Spiders to a record of 8–30—a great deal better than Joe Quinn's 12–104.

Crowder, Alvin (General)

1899–1972

Washington (AL 1926–27, 1930–34), St. Louis (AL
1927–30), Detroit (AL 1934–36)   P   **BL/RHP**

402 games	2,344 innings
167-115 W–L	4.12 ERA
799 k's	22 saves

The name of the other General Crowder, the WW I
boss of the draft, evoked mixed memories for the youth
of America. This Crowder pitched effectively on some
of the best teams ever produced by the Browns and
Senators. He went 21–5 for St. Louis in 1928. Following a trade to Washington, he led the AL in wins in
both 1932 (26) and 1933 (24). The Senators won a
rare pennant in 1933.

Cruz, Jose (Cheo)

1947–

St. Louis (NL 1970–74), Houston (NL 1975–87),
New York (AL 1988)   OF   **BL/TL**

2,353 games	.284 ba
2,251 hits	165 hr
1,077 rbi	317 sb

When Jose Cruz stepped to the plate in the Astrodome,
Houston's fans weren't booing, they were chanting
Cruuuuz. Possibly the most popular position player in
Astros history, Cruz was a model of consistent excel-
lence, batting .300 six times, driving in at least 85 runs
four times, and stealing 30 bases five times. In the field,
he had sure hands if a less than powerful arm. The Astros retired his uniform number 25.

Cuccinello, Tony (Chick)

1907–

Cincinnati (NL 1930–31), Brooklyn (NL 1932–35),
Boston (NL 1936–40, 1942–43), New York (NL
1940), Chicago (AL 1943–45)   **2B, 3B**   **BR/TR**

1,704 games	.280 ba
1,729 hits	94 hr
884 rbi	42 sb

One of the fastest men in the National League during the thirties, Cuccinello was a smart player who excelled at the hit-and-run. A New York native, he batted .281 with 12 home runs and 77 RBI while playing every game for Brooklyn in 1932 and enjoyed four years with at least 80 RBI.

Cuellar, Mike

1937–

Cincinnati (NL 1959), St. Louis (NL 1964), Houston (NL 1965–68), Baltimore (AL 1969–76), California (AL 1977)   P   BL/LHP

453 games	2,808 innings
185-130 W-L	3.14 ERA
1,632 k's	11 saves

After spending five seasons in the NL with mixed success, Cuellar joined the Orioles at the age of 32, with his career hanging in the balance. In his first six seasons in Baltimore, the screwballing lefty made the Orioles front office men look like geniuses when he won 125 games, including 24 in 1970. From 1969 to 1975, Cuellar pitched at least 248 innings a year.

Cuppy, George (Nig)

1869–1922

Cleveland (NL 1892–98), St. Louis (NL 1899), Boston (NL 1900), Boston (AL 1901)   P
BR/RHP

302 games	2,284 innings
162-98 W-L	3.48 ERA
504 k's	5 saves

When Cleveland was a contender for NL supremacy in the 1890s, their leading hurler was Cuppy, a 20-game winner four times in the decade. Between 1892 and 1897, his lowest winning percentage was a nifty .615.

Cuyler, Hazen (Kiki)

1889–1950

Pittsburgh (NL 1921–27), Chicago (NL 1928–35), Cincinnati (NL 1935–37), Brooklyn (NL 1938)

OF   BR/TR

1,879 games	.321 ba
2,299 hits	128 hr
1,065 rbi	328 sb

A tremendous ball hawk with one of the strongest and most accurate throwing arms in big league history, Cuyler stung the ball hard enough to bat more than .300 10 times. His great speed also enabled him to lead the NL in stolen bases four times. He played on three pennant winners, driving in the winning run in the 1925 World Series for Pittsburgh. In 1927, Cuyler was entangled in controversy when a dispute with manager Donie Bush led to his being benched for the entire World Series, even though Pirates fans changed "We want Cuyler" again and again. Cuyler was inducted into the Hall of Fame in 1968.

D

Dahlen, Bill (Bad Bill)

1870–1950

Chicago (NL 1891–98), Brooklyn (NL 1899–1903, 1910–11), New York (NL 1904–07), Boston (NL 1908–09); MGR—Brooklyn (NL 1910–13)   SS, 3B, MGR   BR/TR

2,443 games	.272 ba
2,457 hits	84 hr
1,223 rbi	547 sb

One of the finest shortstops of the dead ball era, Dahlen's career total of 7,500 assists ranks second all-time. As the star shortstop of Chicago's White Stock-ings, he batted safely in 42 consecutive games in 1894. An aficionado of the racetrack, Dahlen acquired his nickname for his cantankerous behavior toward umpires. In one memorable episode, he slugged it out with umpire Cy Rigler. On another occasion, he reportedly hurled anti-Semitic insults at a Brooklyn fan while managing the Dodgers.

Dandridge, Ray
1913–
Detroit Stars (1933), Nashville Elite Giants (1933), Newark Dodgers (1934–35), Newark Eagles (1936–38, 1942, 1944)   **3B   BR/TR**

229 games	.335 ba
276 hits	4 hr

Quick as a cat while patrolling third base, Dandridge also had the skill to hit the ball where it was pitched, bunt, and execute the hit-and-run. Dandridge signed with the New York Giants in 1949 at the age of 35, but the parent team never saw fit to promote him to the majors even after he won the MVP award in the American Association in 1950. Dandridge was inducted into the Hall of Fame in 1987.

Dark, Alvin (Blackie)
1922–
Boston (NL 1946–49), New York (NL 1950–56), St. Louis (NL 1956–58), Chicago (NL 1958–59), Philadelphia (NL 1960), Milwaukee (NL 1960); MGR—San Francisco (NL 1961–64), Kansas City (AL 1966–67), Cleveland (AL 1968–71), Oakland (AL 1974–75), San Diego (NL 1977)   **SS, 3B, MGR   BR/TR**

1,828 games	.289 ba
2,089 hits	126 hr
757 rbi	59 sb

A two-sport star in both basketball and baseball, Dark was a spunky, aggressive infielder with good extra-base power and a knack for the hit-and-run. He hit as high as .322 for Boston's last NL pennant winners in 1948 and surpassed .300 three times for the Giants. In 1951, during the Miracle of Coogan's Bluff, he batted .303 with 196 hits, a league-leading 41 doubles, 14 home runs, 114 runs scored, and 69 RBI while missing only one game all season. He later managed the Athletics to the World Series title in 1974.

Darling, Ron
1960–
New York (NL 1983–91), Montreal (NL 1991), Oakland (AL 1991–93 Active)   P   BR/RHP

336 games	2,096 innings
122-98 W–L	3.71 ERA
1,413 k's	

Darling drove managers and fans crazy by nibbling at the strike zone on each batter. No at-bat was complete unless the hitter reached a three-ball count. Even though he threw a fine fastball, Darling became entranced with his forkball. His best years came with the Mets; between 1985 and 1988, his lowest winning percentage was .600, and he won a career-high 17 games in 1988. Like other ex-Mets, Bob Ojeda and David Cone, Darling now wears uniform number 17 in honor of former Mets teammate Keith Hernandez.

Darwin, Danny
1955–
Texas (AL 1978–84), Milwaukee (AL 1985–86), Houston (NL 1986–90), Boston (1991–93 Active)
P   BR/RHP

585 games	2,372 innings
138-135 W–L	3.47 ERA
1,561 k's	32 saves

In 16 years in the major leagues, Darwin has pitched at least 200 innings in only three seasons. Alternating between the starting staff and the bullpen, he has pitched effectively, leading the NL with an ERA of 2.21 in 1990, when he went 11–4.

Daubert, Jacob (Jake)
1884–1924
Brooklyn (NL 1910–18), Cincinnati (NL 1919–24)
1B BL/TL

2,014 games	.303 ba
2,326 hits	56 hr
722 rbi	251 sb

Ten times a .300 hitter and an outstanding fielder, Daubert won the NL batting title twice, in 1913 (.350) and in 1914 (.329). Next to Gil Hodges, Daubert was the greatest first sacker in Brooklyn history. He played on pennant winners in Brooklyn (1916) and Cincinnati (1919) but died tragically at the close of the 1924 season due to complications following postseason surgery. Earlier that season, he had been severely injured by a beaning that was believed to have played a role in his death.

Daulton, Darren (Dutch)
1962–
Philadelphia (NL 1983, 1985–93 Active) C
BL/TR

853 games	.237 ba
623 hits	99 hr
414 rbi	37 sb

Hindered by serious knee injuries early in his Phillies career, the powerfully built Daulton emerged in 1992 as the best-hitting catcher in the NL. That year, he hit .270 with 27 home runs and a league-best 109 RBI. In 1993 he belted 24 homers and knocked in 105 runs.

Dauss, George (Hooks)
1889–1963
Detroit (AL 1912–26) P BR/RHP

538 games	3,390 innings
222-182 W-L	3.30 ERA
1,201 k's	40 saves

Three times a 20-game winner, Dauss remains the winningest pitcher in Tigers history. However, due to his longevity, he also is the losingest pitcher in the franchise's 93 years. Ironically, he won 21 games in 1919, only to lose 21 the following year.

Davis, Charles (Chili)

1960–
San Francisco (NL 1981–87), California (AL 1988–90, 1993 Active), Minnesota (AL 1991–92)
OF   BB/TR

1,743 games	.267 ba
1,677 hits	224 hr
930 rbi	121 sb

One of the few Jamaican-born players to make it to the major leagues, Davis has knocked in at least 90 runs four times in his career. A good off-speed hitter, he batted .277 with 29 homers and 93 RBI in the Twins' 1991 world championship season. A poor outfielder, Davis became a designated hitter after moving to the AL.

Davis, Curt (Coonskin)

1903–1965
Philadelphia (NL 1934–36), Chicago (NL 1936–37), St. Louis (NL 1938–40), Brooklyn (NL 1940–46)
P   BR/RHP

429 games	2,325 innings
158-131 W–L	3.42 ERA
684 k's	33 saves

Davis didn't reach the majors until he was 30, and his performance left fans wondering why. He won 19 games as a rookie and reached 22 victories in 1939. Davis threw his great fastball and snappy curve with a smooth sidearm motion. In addition, he had great control, issuing only 1.85 walks per nine innings. His delivery made him particularly tough on right-handed batters.

Davis, Eric

1962–

Cincinnati (NL 1984–91), Los Angeles (NL
1992–93), Detroit (AL 1993 Active) **OF**
BR/TR

1,063 games	.266 ba
935 hits	202 hr
632 rbi	301 sb

If a vote had been held in 1989 for the best player in
the NL, Davis would have polled the most votes. A rare
combination of speed and power, he had just con-
cluded his fourth straight outstanding season, hitting
34 home runs with 101 RBI. However, a series of injuries to his legs and kidneys since 1990 have seriously
eroded his skills and limited his playing time.

Davis, George

1870–1940

Cleveland (NL 1890–92), New York (NL
1893–1901, 1903), Chicago (AL 1902, 1904–09);
MGR—New York (NL 1895, 1900–01) **SS, 3B,**
OF, MGR **BB/TR**

2,368 games	.295 ba
2,660 hits	73 hr
1,437 rbi	616 sb

A Giants star in the 1890s, Davis batted over .300
every year from 1893 to 1901, and in 1893 he hit
safely in 33 consecutive games. In 1895, he was the
first manager hired by Tammany Hall boss and new
team owner Andrew Freedman, but he lasted only 33
games. Davis became a major figure in the war between
the NL and the fledgling AL after jumping to Chicago
in 1902. He was supposed to remain there as part of
the peace treaty between the two leagues, but due to
the animosity of then-Giants owner John T. Brush for
the junior circuit, he played for the Giants in 1903. He
was quietly returned to the Chisox for the 1904 season;
he finished out his career there in 1909. A member of

the 1906 Chisox Hitless Wonders, he batted .308 in the World Series.

Davis, Harry (Jasper)
1873–1947

New York (NL 1895–96), Pittsburgh (NL 1896–98), Louisville (NL 1898), Washington (NL 1898–99), Philadelphia (AL 1901–11, 1913–17), Cleveland (AL 1912); MGR—Cleveland (AL 1912) **1B, MGR**
BR/TR

1,755 games	.277 ba
1,841 hits	75 hr
951 rbi	285 sb

A slugging first baseman of the dead ball era, Davis led the AL in home runs each year from 1904 to 1907 and in RBI in 1905 and 1906. He played on three Athletics pennant winners and later utilized his expert pitch-stealing skills as a third-base coach.

Davis, Tommy
1939–

Los Angeles (NL 1959–66), New York (NL 1967), Chicago (AL 1968), Seattle (AL 1969), Houston (NL 1969–70), Oakland (AL 1970, 1971), Chicago (NL 1970, 1972), Baltimore (AL 1972–75), California (AL 1976), Kansas City (AL 1976) **OF, DH**
BR/TR

1,999 games	.294 ba
2,121 hits	153 hr
1,052 rbi	136 sb

At the plate, Davis swung as if he had been born wielding a bat. Strong and confident, he hit the ball to all fields. In 1962, he had one of the greatest seasons in NL history, batting a league-high .346 with 230 hits, 27 homers, and 153 RBI. When he led the NL again the following season with a .326 average, his future stardom appeared secure. Unfortunately, he broke his ankle while sliding into a base in 1965 and never ran swiftly again. He then began a long sojourn through the majors as a hired bat.

Davis, Willie

1940–

Los Angeles (NL 1960–73), Montreal (NL 1974), Texas (AL 1975), St. Louis (NL 1975), San Diego (NL 1976), California (AL 1979) OF BL/TL

2,429 games	.279 ba
2,561 hits	182 hr
1,053 rbi	398 sb

Fans would pay money just to see Willie Davis run the bases. His long, fluid gait made him the most exciting man in baseball going from first to third or stretching a double into a triple. He reached double digits in triples five times. Davis might have stolen more bases but for his reluctance to draw more walks, which limited his on-base percentage. In the field, he could outrun the ball, but he will always be remembered for his difficulty with the sun during the 1966 World Series.

Dawson, Andre (The Hawk)

1954–

Montreal (NL 1976–86), Chicago (NL 1987–92), Boston (NL 1993 Active) OF BR/TR

2,431 games	.281 ba
2,630 hits	412 hr
1,492 rbi	312 sb

The National League's Rookie of the Year in 1977 and MVP in 1987, Dawson appears a cinch for future induction into the Hall of Fame. An aggressive hitter who stands on top of the plate and does not like to walk, his achievements are all the more remarkable considering the series of eight operations on both of his knees. In the field, he has one of baseball's strongest arms, but he cannot cover much ground due to his bad wheels. Chicago's Bleacher Bums began bowing in tribute to Dawson's performance during his first year in Wrigley in 1987, when he slammed 49 home runs and knocked in 137 runs.

Day, Leon

1916–

Bacharach Giants (1934), Brooklyn Eagles (1935), Newark Eagles (1936–43, 1946, 1949) **P, OF**
BR/RHP

114 games	667 innings
63-26 W–L	256 k's

In the late thirties and forties, few men pitched more effectively than Leon Day. Using a sidearm motion, he threw a full repertoire of pitches. Day did his best work for the Newark Eagles, going 13–0 in 1937. Also a fine hitter, he played the outfield when he wasn't pitching, and he batted .320 that year.

Dean, Jay (Dizzy)

1911–1974

St. Louis (NL 1930, 1932–37), Chicago (NL 1938–41), St. Louis (AL 1947) **P**   **BR/RHP**

317 games	1,967 innings
150-83 W–L	3.02 ERA
1,163 k's	30 saves

Dean was the colorful leader of the Cardinals' Gas House Gang, a talkative bundle of enthusiasm who drew extra energy from the fans in the stands. The NL's dominant pitcher in 1934 (30–7), he carried St. Louis to victory in the World Series. Unfortunately, he changed his delivery to compensate for a toe broken in the 1937 All-Star Game and hurt his arm as a result. Dean never recaptured his scintillating fastball, and his career slid downhill. He was inducted into the Hall of Fame in 1953 in honor of his abbreviated fling at greatness.

DeCinces, Doug

1950–

Baltimore (AL 1973–81), California (AL 1982–87),
St. Louis (NL 1987)   **3B**   **BR/TR**

1,649 games	.259 ba
1,505 hits	237 hr
879 rbi	58 sb

As the man who replaced Brooks Robinson at third
base for the Orioles, DeCinces had to overcome the
pressure of hearing his talents compared with the Hall
of Famer. His best year in Baltimore was 1978, when
he hit .286 with 28 homers, but after signing as a free
agent with California in 1982, he had his most productive season, hitting .301 with 30 home runs and 97
RBI.

Delehanty, Ed (Big Ed)

1867–1903

Philadelphia (NL 1888–89, 1891–1901), Cleveland
(PL 1890), Washington (AL 1902–03)   **OF, 1B**
BR/TR

1,835 games	.346 ba
2,597 hits	101 hr
1,464 rbi	455 sb

One of five baseball-playing brothers, Ed Delehanty
was the best of the lot. He batted over .400 three times
and his lifetime average ranks fifth all-time. He died
mysteriously in a train accident near Niagara Falls
while still an active player. Big Ed was elected to the
Hall of Fame in 1945.

DeMoss, Elwood (Bingo)

1889–1965

Indianapolis ABC's (1915, 1926), Chicago American
Giants (1917–25), Detroit Stars (1927–29)   **2B**
BR/TR

458 games	.242 ba
398 hits	4 hr
81 sb	

DeMoss was the best second baseman in the Negro Leagues in the twenties, ranging far to either side to snare ground balls. At the plate, he usually batted second due to his proficiency at bunting and executing the hit-and-run.

Denny, John

1952–
St. Louis (NL 1974–79), Cleveland (AL 1980–82), Philadelphia (NL 1982–85), Cincinnati (NL 1986)
P   BR/RHP

325 games	2,148 innings
123-108 W–L	3.59 ERA
1,146 k's	

A hard-throwing pitcher who never hesitated to pitch inside, Denny showed enough flashes of brilliance to always warrant another look from a new team. In 1976, he won only 11 games for St. Louis but his 2.52 ranked as the best ERA in the NL. Arm ailments and inconsistency hindered his career until 1983, when he won 19 games and pitched to an ERA of 2.37 for the pennant-winning Phillies.

Dent, Russell (Bucky)

1951–
Chicago (AL 1973–76), New York (AL 1977–82), Texas (AL 1982–83), Kansas City (AL 1984); MGR—New York (AL 1989)   **SS, MGR**
BR/TR

1,392 games	.247 ba
1,114 hits	40 hr
423 rbi	17 sb

One plate appearance catapulted Dent into a baseball legend. Facing Mike Torrez at Fenway Park in the 1978 one-game postseason playoff to decide the winner of the AL East, he popped a home run into the screen atop the Green Monster to propel the Yankees to victory. In the ensuing World Series against the Dodgers, he continued his stellar play, batting .417 with seven RBI. For the rest of his career, Dent was a steady if unspectacular shortstop and an average hitter.

Derringer, Paul (Duke)

1906–1987

St. Louis (NL 1931–33), Cincinnati (NL 1933–42), Chicago (NL 1943–45)   **P**   **BR/RHP**

579 games	3,645 innings
223-212 W–L	3.46 ERA
1,507 k's	29 saves

Derringer pitched the Reds to back-to-back NL pennants in 1939–40. Physically imposing at 6-feet, 4-inches, he utilized a high leg kick before delivering the ball. Derringer challenged hitters and threw strikes. A workhorse, he pitched at least 200 innings in all but two years of his career and won at least 20 games four times for the Reds, racking up 25 victories in 1939. In 1940, Derringer won the decisive seventh game of the World Series.

DeShields, Delino

1969–

Montreal (NL 1990–93), Los Angeles (NL 1994 Active)   **2B**   **BL/TR**

538 games	.277 ba
575 hits	23 hr
181 rbi	187 sb

DeShields is an emerging star in the NL. A brilliant hitter and fielder with exceptional speed, he has unlimited potential. He hit .289 as a rookie in 1990 and .292 in 1992. The one drawback to his batting is his tendency to strike out; he fanned 151 times in 1991, a poor season for DeShields. In honor of the men who played in the Negro Leagues, DeShields wears his baseball pants very high, evoking the style of that age.

Dickey, Bill
1907–1993
New York (AL 1928–43, 1946); MGR—New York (AL 1946)   C, MGR   BL/TR

1,789 games	.313 ba
1,969 hits	202 hr
1,209 rbi	36 sb

Dickey handled the Yankees pitching staff smartly on eight pennant winners. A clutch hitter who hit over .300 10 times, he knocked in more than 100 runs in four consecutive seasons (1936–39). Dickey was the best catcher in Yankee history. He was inducted into the Hall of Fame in 1954.

Dickson, Murry
1916–1989
St. Louis (NL 1939–40, 1942–43, 1946–48, 1956–57), Pittsburgh (NL 1949–53), Philadelphia (NL 1954–56), Kansas City (AL 1958, 1959), New York (AL 1958)   P   BR/RHP

625 games	3,052 innings
172-181 W–L	3.66 ERA
23 saves	

Dickson started his career with a strong Cardinals outfit but toiled for losing teams thereafter. Blessed with a resilient arm, he started 25–35 games and appeared in relief another 10–20 times a season for most of his career. Dickson went 15–6 for the 1946 world champion Cardinals. In 1951, he miraculously won 20 games for a horrible Pittsburgh team that won a total of only 64 games. He also lost 21 times for the 1952 Pirates and suffered 20 losses for the 1954 Phillies.

Dierker, Larry

1946–

Houston (NL 1964–76), St. Louis (NL 1977)   P
BR/RHP

356 games	2,333 innings
139-123 W–L	3.31 ERA
1,493 k's	1 save

The best of a bright crop of hard-throwing young arms developed by Houston in the sixties, Dierker reached the 20-victory plateau in 1969, when he also pitched 305 innings, struck out 232 batters, and compiled an ERA of 2.33. He won in double digits nine times for the Astros.

Dihigo, Martin

1905–1971

Cuban Stars (1923–27, 1930), Homestead Grays (1928), Philadelphia Hilldales (1929, 1931), Baltimore Black Sox (1931), New York Cubans (1935, 1945)   2B, P, OF   BR/RHP

415 games	.316 ba
453 hits	64 hr
32 sb	309 innings
27-21 W–L	126 k's

Inducted into the Hall of Fame in 1977, Dihigo was one of the greatest Cuban-born players of all time. Like Babe Ruth, he starred as both a pitcher and a hitter. On the mound, he relied on a tremendous fastball. Dihigo was versatile enough to perform brilliantly at any position and in some games he actually played them all.

DiMaggio, Dom (The Little Professor)

1917–

Boston (AL 1940–42, 1946–53)   OF   BR/TR

1,399 games	.298 ba
1,680 hits	87 hr
618 rbi	100 sb

Perpetually caught in the shadow of his older brother, Joe DiMaggio, Dom was an outstanding center fielder in his own right and a fine hitter as well. Primarily a singles and doubles hitter, he scored more than 100 runs six times and averaged a tremendous 105 runs scored for his 10 full seasons. In 1950, DiMaggio hit .328 with a league-leading 11 triples, 131 runs scored, and 15 stolen bases.

DiMaggio, Joe (The Yankee Clipper, Joltin' Joe)

1914–
New York (AL 1936–42, 1946–51)   OF
BR/TR

1,736 games	.325 ba
2,214 hits	361 hr
1,537 rbi	30 sb

Many experts regard DiMaggio as the greatest player to grace the diamond. He did everything on the field and made it look easy. At the plate, his signature stance, with his feet spread wide apart, produced more than 100 RBI nine times. In centerfield, there were few balls he couldn't reach. In 1941, DiMaggio hit safely in 56 games to establish baseball's most fascinating record. A three-time MVP, DiMaggio entered the Hall of Fame in 1955.

Dineen, Bill (Big Bill)

1876–1955
Washington (NL 1898–99), Boston (NL 1900–01), Boston (AL 1902–07), St. Louis (AL 1907–09)   P
BR/RHP

391 games	3,074 innings
170-177 W–L	3.01 ERA
1,127 k's	7 saves

Few fans remember that Dineen won three games pitching for Boston in the first World Series played in the 20th century. After jumping to the American

League, he won more than 20 games in three consecutive years, 1902–1904. Although he slumped to 12 wins in 1905, he pitched a no-hitter that year against the White Sox. Dineen later umpired in the AL from 1909 to 1937.

Dixon, Herbert (Rap)
1902–1945

Harrisburg Giants (1924–28), Baltimore Black Sox (1928–31, 1934), Philadelphia Hilldales (1931), Washington Pilots (1932), Pittsburgh Crawfords (1932, 1934), Philadelphia Stars (1934), Brooklyn Eagles (1935), New York Cubans (1935)   **OF**
BR/TR

395 games	.305 ba
473 hits	36 hr
50 sb	

Dixon combined power and speed to star for the mighty Pittsburgh Crawfords and other teams in the thirties. Defensively, he had good range and a strong arm. Dixon batted .344 in 1935.

Doak, Bill (Spittin' Bill)
1891–1954

Cincinnati (NL 1912), St. Louis (NL 1913–24, 1929), Brooklyn (NL 1924, 1927–28)   **P**
BR/RHP

453 games	2,782 innings
169-157 W–L	2.98 ERA
1,014 k's	16 saves

A famed spitballer of the early 20th century, Doak was permitted to throw his pitch until he retired in 1929. He spent his most productive years in St. Louis, where he won 20 games in 1920. Doak was also instrumental in introducing the Bill Doak Fielder's Glove, which featured a built-in pocket and which helped improve fielding averages throughout baseball.

Dobson, Joe (Burrhead)

1917–

Cleveland (AL 1939–40), Boston (AL 1941–43, 1946–50, 1954), Chicago (AL 1951–53)   P

BR/RHP

414 games	2,170 innings
137–103 W–L	3.62 ERA
992 k's	18 saves

One of Boston's leading hurlers for their pennant contenders in the forties, Dobson won in double digits eight times in his career, scoring 18 triumphs in 1947.

Doby, Larry

1924–

Newark Eagles (1942–43, 1946–47), Cleveland (AL 1947–55, 1958), Chicago (AL 1956–57, 1959), Detroit (AL 1959); MGR—Chicago (AL 1978)

OF, MGR   BL/TR

1,533 games	.283 ba
1,515 hits	253 hr
970 rbi	47 sb

The first black man to play in the AL, Doby signed with Bill Veeck's Cleveland Indians and made his initial appearance in 1947. The following year, he established himself as a star outfielder, hitting .301 in the first of 10 productive seasons. In 1954, he led the AL in both home runs (32) and RBI (126).

Doerr, Bobby

1918–

Boston (AL 1937–44, 1946–51)   2B   BR/TR

1,865 games	.288 ba
2,042 hits	223 hr
1,247 rbi	54 sb

Quiet on the field, Doerr was a fine second baseman with good range and an ability to turn the double play; but he made his mark at the plate, driving in at least 100 runs six times. Few second basemen can make that claim. The Red Sox retired his uniform number 1, and he was inducted into the Hall of Fame in 1986.

Donlin, Mike (Turkey Mike)
1878–1933

St. Louis (NL 1899–1900), Baltimore (AL 1901), Cincinnati (1902–04), New York (NL 1904–11, 1914), Boston (NL 1911), Pittsburgh (NL 1912)
OF   BL/TL

1,049 games	.334 ba
1,286 hits	51 hr
543 rbi	213 sb

One of the most popular players for the turn-of-the-century Giants, Donlin married vaudeville star Mabel Hite and appeared with her on the stage. He was a great hitter who served as captain of the 1908 Giants. His best season came in 1905, when he hit .356 with 216 hits, a league-best 124 runs scored, and 80 RBI.

Donovan, Dick
1927–

Boston (NL 1950–52), Detroit (AL 1954), Chicago (AL 1955–60), Washington (AL 1961), Cleveland (AL 1962–65)   P   BL/RHP

345 games	2,017 innings
122-99 W–L	3.67 ERA
880 k's	5 saves

In July 1955, the Chisox were the surprise of the AL, and Donovan was the ace of the staff, with a 13–4 record. Misfortune befell Chicago when Donovan suffered an attack of appendicitis, and the Sox fell out of the race. He went on to lead the AL in winning percentage in 1957 (.727), when he went 16–6, and in ERA in 1961 for the expansion Senators (2.40). A control artist, Donovan's best pitch was his slider.

Donovan, Patrick (Patsy)
1865–1953

Boston (NL 1890), Brooklyn (NL 1890, 1906–07), Louisville (AA 1891), Washington (AA 1891–92), Pittsburgh (NL 1892–99), St. Louis (NL 1900–03), Washington (AL 1904); MGR—Pittsburgh (NL 1897, 1899), St. Louis (NL 1901–03), Washington (AL 1904), Brooklyn (NL 1906–08), Boston (AL 1910–11)   **OF, MGR**   **BL/TL**

1,821 games	.301 ba
2,253 hits	16 hr
736 rbi	518 sb

In 1894–96, Donovan teamed with Elmer Smith and Jake Stenzel for an all-.300-hitting Pittsburgh outfield. He hit at least .300 11 times overall. A speedy base runner, Donovan led the NL in stolen bases in 1900 (45). In 11 years of managing, he never won a pennant.

Donovan, William (Wild Bill)
1876–1923

Washington (NL 1898), Brooklyn (NL 1899–1902), Detroit (AL 1903–12, 1918), New York (AL 1915–16); MGR—New York (AL 1915–17), Philadelphia (NL 1921)   **P, MGR**   **BR/RHP**

378 games	2,964 innings
186-139 W–L	2.69 ERA
1,552 k's	8 saves

Brooklyn's pitching fortunes tumbled after Donovan defected to the AL Tigers following the 1902 season. Nicknamed for his poor control, he walked over 100 men in 1901, 1902, and 1905. Donovan's best year came in 1907, the first of Detroit's three successive pennant-winning seasons. That year, he compiled a 25–4 record with a 2.19 ERA.

Douglas, Phil (Shufflin' Phil)

1890–1952

Chicago (AL 1912), Cincinnati (NL 1914–15),
Brooklyn (NL 1915), Chicago (NL 1915–19), New
York (NL 1919–22)   P   BR/RHP

299 games	1,708 innings
94-93 W–L	2.80 ERA
683 k's	8 saves

One of the 17 approved post-1920 spitballers, Douglas
enjoyed his greatest success wearing the colors of
McGraw's men in New York. He won 14 games in
1920 and 15 the following year. Douglas pitched 26
innings in the 1921 World Series while winning two
games. He was a heavy drinker and occasionally disap-
peared on a binge. In 1922, after one such absence and
a subsequent fine, he offered to throw a game and was
banished from baseball by Commissioner Landis.

Downing, Al

1941–

New York (AL 1961–69), Oakland (AL 1970),
Milwaukee (AL 1970), Los Angeles (NL 1971–77)
P   BR/LHP

405 games	2,268 innings
123-107 W–L	3.22 ERA
1,639 k's	3 saves

Downing is best remembered today as the man who
served up Hank Aaron's 715th career home run. When
he appeared as a Yankees rookie in 1963, he was touted
as the next Whitey Ford, but although he won in double digits five times and led the AL in strikeouts in
1963 (217), he never fulfilled those expectations.
Downing's best pitch was a blazing fastball; he also
threw a sharp-breaking curve. Moving to the NL, he
won 20 games for the Dodgers in 1971.

Downing, Brian

1950–

Chicago (AL 1973–77), California (AL 1978–90), Texas (AL 1991–92)　**DH, OF, C**　**BR/TR**

2,344 games	.267 ba
2,099 hits	275 hr
1,073 rbi	50 sb

After hitting 56 home runs in his first nine seasons, Downing started lifting weights and appeared at spring training in 1982 with muscles bulging. He became a power hitter overnight, belting 28 homers in 1982 and proceeded to hit 20 or more roundtrippers in six of the next seven seasons. A patient hitter, Downing drew a league-best 106 walks in 1987.

Doyle, Larry (Laughing Larry)

1886–1974

New York (NL 1907–16, 1918–20), Chicago (NL 1916–17)　**2B**　**BL/TR**

1,776 games	.290 ba
1,887 hits	74 hr
793 rbi	298 sb

The Giants' regular second sacker for 13 of his 14 years in the majors, in 1915 Doyle led the NL in hits (189), doubles (40), and batting average (.320). Glad to be a major leaguer in New York, he spoke the immortal words, "It's great to be young and a Giant."

Drabek, Doug

1962–

New York (AL 1986), Pittsburgh (NL 1987–92), Houston (NL 1993 Active)　**P**　**BR/RHP**

260 games	1,732 innings
180-88 W–L	3.21 ERA
1,053 k's	

Another in a long line of refugees from the Yankees organization, Drabek went on to win the NL Cy Young Award in 1999, compiling a 22–6 record. He throws a slider and split-fingered fastball with impeccable control.

Dressen, Charles (Chuck)

1898–1966

Cincinnati (NL 1925–31), New York (NL 1933);
MGR—Cincinnati (NL 1934–37), Brooklyn (NL
1951–53), Washington (AL 1955–57), Milwaukee
(NL 1960–61), Detroit (AL 1963–66)   **3B, MGR**
BR/TR

646 games	.272 ba
603 hits	11 hr
221 rbi	30 sb

An undistinguished player in both baseball and pro
football, Dressen was a combative skipper for a variety
of teams. Boastful of his own ability to lead a team, he
would tell his players, "Hold them until I think of
something." Dressen was a renowned sign stealer.
When he finally got a good team to manage in Brooklyn, he ruined his chances for a long run by demanding
a two-year contract.

Dreyfuss, Barney

1865–1932

Pittsburgh (NL 1900–32)   **Owner**

Part owner of the Louisville team of the NL from 1890
to 1899, Dreyfus acquired the Pirates in 1900 and
served as the team's owner and sole talent evaluator
until his death in 1932. When he moved from Louisville to Pittsburgh, he brought with him Honus Wagner, Fred Clarke, and Rube Waddell, all future Hall of
Famers. After his Pirates won the 1903 NL pennant,
he challenged the AL champions, Boston, to the first
modern World Series. Dreyfuss had a reputation for
being tight-fisted, but he did build the extravagant
Forbes Field in 1909.

Drysdale, Don (Big D)

1936–1993

Brooklyn (NL 1956–57), Los Angeles (NL 1958–69)
P BR/RHP

518 games	3,432 innings
209-166 W–L	2.95 ERA
2,486 k's	6 saves

A 6-foot, 5-inch sidearming right-hander, Drysdale was a great competitor who fiercely protected the inside corner of the plate. He led the NL three times in strikeouts, and in 1962 he won 25 games and the Cy Young Award. A workhorse, Drysdale pitched every fourth day and started more than 40 games in five consecutive years (1962–66). In 1968, he hurled 58 consecutive scoreless innings, a major league record since broken by Orel Hershiser. In the sixties, Drysdale teamed with Sandy Koufax to form one of the greatest one-two pitching duos in major league history. He was inducted into the Hall of Fame in 1984, and his uniform number 53 was retired by the Dodgers.

Duffy, Hugh

1866–1954

Chicago (NL 1888–89), Chicago (PL 1890), Boston (AA 1891), Boston (NL 1892–1900), Milwaukee (AL 1901), Philadelphia (NL 1904–06); MGR— Milwaukee (AL 1901), Philadelphia (NL 1904–06), Chicago (AL 1910–11), Boston (AL 1921–22) **OF, MGR** BR/TR

1,737 games	.324 ba
2,282 hits	106 hr
1,302 rbi	574 sb

Duffy was one of the 19th century's leading batsmen, but he gave little advance warning of his 1894 season. That year, he won the NL triple crown, batting a record .440 with 18 home runs and 145 RBI. Lifting his foot in the air before swinging the bat, in the style of Mel Ott, he batted .300 or better for 10 straight seasons. Fast afoot, Duffy was a terrific ball hawk as well. He was inducted into the Hall of Fame in 1945.

Dunlap, Fred (Sure Shot)
1859–1902
Cleveland (NL 1880–83), St. Louis (UA 1884), St. Louis (NL 1885–86), Detroit (NL 1886–87), Pittsburgh (NL 1888–90), New York (PL 1890), Washington (AA 1891); MGR—Cleveland (NL 1882), St. Louis (UA 1884), St. Louis (NL 1885), Pittsburgh (NL 1889)   **2B, MGR   BR/TR**

965 games	.292 ba
1,159 hits	41 hr
366 rbi	85 sb

In an age when fielders disdained gloves, Dunlap ranked as the best second baseman in baseball. In St. Louis, he teamed with shortstop Jack Glasscock to form the finest double-play duo in the NL. Dunlap had great range and a strong throwing arm. At bat, he showed spunk although he was not an exceptional hitter. Dunlap did produce one remarkable season while playing for St. Louis in the Union Association, cranking out a .412 average.

Duren, Rinold (Ryne)
1929–
Baltimore (AL 1954), Kansas City (AL 1957), New York (AL 1958–61), Los Angeles (AL 1961–62), Philadelphia (NL 1963–64, 1965), Cincinnati (NL 1964), Washington (AL 1965)   **P   BR/RHP**

311 games	589 innings
27-44 W–L	3.83 ERA
630 k's	57 saves

When Duren entered a game in relief for the Yankees, he threw his first warmup pitch, a blazing fastball, 10 feet over the catcher's head and against the backstop. He then wiped off his bottle-shaped eyeglasses and prepared to face the first batter. In 1958 and 1959, Duren was the most intimidating and effective relief pitcher in the AL, saving 34 games for New York with ERAs of 2.02 and 1.88. Arm injuries and a losing battle with the bottle led to Duren's downfall after those glory years. Today he counsels alcohol abusers.

Durocher, Leo (The Lip)
1905–1991
New York (AL 1925, 1928–29), Cincinnati (NL 1930–33), St. Louis (NL 1933–37), Brooklyn (NL 1938–41, 1943, 1945); MGR—Brooklyn (NL 1939–46, 1948), New York (NL 1948–55), Chicago (NL 1966–72), Houston (NL 1972–73)   **SS, MGR BR/TR**

1,637 games	.247 ba
1,320 hits	24 hr
567 rbi	31 sb

There were few things that Durocher did not accomplish during his illustrious baseball career. As a brash youngster on the 1929 Yankees, he antagonized Babe Ruth. Traded to Cincinnati and St. Louis, he took his slick glove and weak bat to the Gas House Gang and became one of its leading members. Durocher made his mark as an abrasive, brilliant manager who would stop at nothing to attain victory. He turned the theretofore hapless Dodgers into pennant winners, took the Giants to the World Series, and nearly pulled off the unthinkable, a Cubs title. A flashy dresser off the field, Durocher was suspended from baseball for the 1947 season for associating with gamblers, but this banishment had no long-term effect on his behavior.

Dwyer, Frank
1868–1943
Chicago (NL 1888–89), Chicago (PL 1890), Cincinnati (AA 1891), Milwaukee (AA 1891), St. Louis (NL 1892), Cincinnati (NL 1892–99); MGR—Detroit (AL 1902)   **P, MGR   BR/RHP**

365 games	2,810 innings
176-152 W–L	3.85 ERA
563 k's	6 saves

Dwyer is one of a select few hurlers who pitched a shut-out in their first major league start, but not many of the players on that list enjoyed a career that matched Dwyer's. Dwyer won 13 consecutive games in 1896 on his way to 24 victories.

Dykes, Jimmy

1896–1976

Philadelphia (AL 1918–32), Chicago (AL 1933–39); MGR—Chicago (AL 1934–46), Philadelphia (AL 1951–53), Baltimore (AL 1954), Cincinnati (NL 1958), Detroit (AL 1959–60), Cleveland (AL 1960–61)   **3B, 2B, MGR   BR/TR**

2,282 games	.280 ba
2,256 hits	108 hr
1,071 rbi	70 sb

Known to generations of Chicago fans as the hot-headed manager of many losing squads, Dykes also enjoyed a long career as a star infielder on the Athletics. In 1929, he batted a career-high .327 with 13 home runs and 79 RBI on the first of three consecutive pennant-winning Philadelphia outfits.

Dykstra, Len (Nails)

1963–

New York (NL 1985–89), Philadelphia (NL 1989–93 Active)   **OF   BL/TL**

1,092 games	.288 ba
1,110 hits	71 hr
349 rbi	257 sb

The Mets said that Dykstra couldn't hit left-handed pitching and eventually traded him due to his vocal objections to being platooned. Known for his scrappy play, he never finishes a game with a clean uniform. Once Dykstra stopped swinging for the fences, he became a much better hitter, reaching .325 in 1990. Few have ever questioned his defensive skills. In the Phillies 1993 pennant-winning season, he batted .305 and scored 143 runs.

E

Earnshaw, George (Moose)

1900–1976

Philadelphia (AL 1928–33), Chicago (AL 1934–35), Brooklyn (NL 1935–36), St. Louis (NL 1936)   P
BR/RHP

319 games	1,915 innings
127-93 W–L	4.38 ERA
1,002 k's	12 saves

Earnshaw teamed with Lefty Grove for Philadelphia to form the leading mound tandem in the AL. He won 24, 22, and 21 games in 1929–31, when the Athletics won three consecutive pennants. Earnshaw threw a hard curve ball at nearly the same velocity as his fastball.

Easterling, Howard

1911–

Cincinnati Tigers (1937), Homestead Grays (1940–43), Washington Homestead Grays (1946), New York Cubans (1949)   3B   BB/TR

179 games	.334 ba
307 hits	8 hr
10 sb	

On the powerful Homestead Grays squads of the early forties, Easterling manned third base and batted behind the legendary Josh Gibson.

Ebbets, Charles

1859–1925

Brooklyn (NL 1883–1925)   MGR, Owner

Ebbets devoted his life to baseball in Brooklyn. He joined the Trolley Dodgers franchise in the American Association in 1883 as a bookkeeper and, after the team joined the National League in 1890, became team president in 1898. Ebbets saved the franchise from being transferred to Baltimore by buying out minority owner and team manager Ned Hanlon in 1905. The Dodgers played in antiquated wooden structures in Gowanus and Broadway Junction until Ebbets purchased land in a sparsely inhabited section of Flatbush to construct a new brick stadium. Ebbets Field, featuring a beautiful marble rotunda, opened in 1913.

Eckersley, Dennis (Eck)
1954–
Cleveland (AL 1975–77), Boston (AL 1978–84), Chicago (NL 1984–86), Oakland (AL 1987–93 Active)   P   BR/RHP

804 games	3,038 innings
183-149 W–L	3.45 ERA
2,198 k's	275 saves

Eckersley's career appeared to be over after he was shuffled from the Red Sox to the Cubs and on to the Athletics as an ineffective spot starter with a proclivity for surrendering home runs. Instead, the Athletics put him in the bullpen, where his spectacular control and aggressive attitude made him baseball's best reliever. Eckersley led the AL in saves in 1988 (45) and 1992 (51) and compiled a minuscule 0.96 ERA in 1989. In 1990, he walked only seven men and struck out 73 in 73 innings.

Ehmke, Howard (Bob)
1894–1959
Buffalo (FL 1915), Detroit (AL 1916–22), Boston (AL 1923–26), Philadelphia (AL 1926–30)   P BR/RHP

427 games	2,820 innings
166-166 W-L	3.75 ERA
1,030 k's	14 saves

Athletics manager Connie Mack shocked the baseball world when he picked Ehmke as his opening-day starter in the 1929 World Series. Although he had pitched only 55 innings the entire season, he stopped the Cubs 3–1 and struck out a record 13 batters.

Elliott, Bob

1916–1966
Pittsburgh (NL 1939–46), Boston (NL 1947–51), New York (NL 1952), St. Louis (AL 1953), Chicago (AL 1953); MGR—Kansas City (AL 1960)   **3B, OF, MGR**   **BR/TR**

1,978 games	.289 ba
2,061 hits	170 hr
1,195 rbi	60 sb

A fierce competitor and great team player, in 1947 Elliott became the first third sacker to win the MVP award. That year, he batted .317 with 22 home runs and 113 RBI for the third-place Boston Braves. Gritty if not graceful at third, Elliott got the job done in the field.

Ellis, Dock

1945–
Pittsburgh (NL 1968–75, 1979), New York (AL 1976–77), Oakland (AL 1977), Texas (AL 1977–79), New York (NL 1979)   **P**   **BB/RHP**

345 games	2,127 innings
138-119 W-L	3.46 ERA
1,136 k's	1 save

Ellis was a freethinker, on and off the mound. After his retirement, he confirmed that he had experimented with drugs and that he was high when he pitched a no-hitter for Pittsburgh in 1970. The following year, he won a career-high 19 games for the Pirates. Traded to the Yankees prior to the 1976 season, he proceeded to notch 17 victories and help New York to its first pennant in 13 years.

Ennis, Del

1925–
Philadelphia (NL 1946–56), St. Louis (NL 1957–58), Cincinnati (NL 1959), Chicago (AL 1959)   **OF   BR/TR**

1,903 games	.284 ba
2,063 hits	288 hr
1,284 rbi	45 sb

Ennis was one of the greatest sluggers in Phillies history. He batted over .300 three times, including a .311 season with the 1950 NL pennant winners, and knocked home at least 100 runs on seven occasions. In 1950, he led the NL with 126 RBI.

Erskine, Carl (Oisk)

1926–
Brooklyn (NL 1948–57), Los Angeles (NL 1958–59)
P   BR/RHP

335 games	1,718 innings
122-78 W–L	4.00 ERA
981 k's	13 saves

One of Brooklyn's top pitchers of the fifties, Erskine had an outstanding curve ball. A spot starter his first four years in the league, he assumed a regular spot in the rotation in 1952 and won 14 games. The following year, his 20–6 record led the NL in winning percentage (.769). In all, he won in double digits in six consecutive seasons (1951–56).

Evans, Darrell

1947–
Atlanta (NL 1969–76, 1989), San Francisco (NL 1976–83), Detroit (AL 1984–88)   **3B, 1B, DH
BL/TR**

2,687 games	.248 ba
2,223 hits	414 hr
1,354 rbi	98 sb

Evans is the only player ever to hit 40 homers in both the National and American Leagues. He became the oldest single-season home run champion when he hit 40 homers in 1985 at the age of 38. A patient hitter, Evans led the NL twice in drawing walks (1973–74) and walked 1,605 times in his career.

Evans, Dwight (Dewey)

1951–

Boston (AL 1972–90), Baltimore (AL 1991)   **OF**
BR/TR

2,606 games	.272 ba
2,446 hits	385 hr
1,384 rbi	78 sb

Opposing runners rarely took an extra base on balls hit to right field because Evans possessed one of the strongest and most accurate arms in the game. A consistent power hitter, he slammed at least 20 homers in 11 seasons and drove home more than 100 runs on four occasions. His best year came in 1987, when he hit .305 with 34 homers and 123 RBI.

Evers, John (Crab)

1881–1947

Chicago (NL 1902–13), Boston (NL 1914–17, 1929), Philadelphia (NL 1917), Chicago (AL 1922); MGR—Chicago (NL 1913, 1921), Chicago (AL 1924)   **2B, MGR**   **BL/TR**

1,783 games	.270 ba
1,658 hits	12 hr
538 rbi	324 sb

A scrappy, testy player, "Crab" turned the double play for the famous Tinkers-to-Evers-to-Chance combination of Cubs infielders in the early twentieth century. Immortalized in Franklin P. Adams's poem, Evers was a mediocre hitter but had few peers in the field. A player who did whatever it took to win, Evers entered the Hall of Fame in 1946.

Ewing, William (Buck)
1859–1906
Troy (NL 1880–82), New York (1883–89, 1891–92), New York (PL 1890), Cleveland (NL 1893–94), Cincinnati (NL 1895–97); MGR—New York (PL 1890), Cincinnati (NL 1895–99), New York (NL 1900)   **C, 1B, OF, MGR**   **BR/TR**

1,315 games	.303 ba
1,625 hits	71 hr
883 rbi	354 sb

Generally regarded as the best catcher of the 19th century, Ewing also played in the infield and outfield. He hit over .300 in 10 seasons. Defensively, he could throw out base runners from a squatting position. Named the Giants' captain in the 1880s, he later jumped to the Players League New York franchise in 1890. Ewing was inducted into the Hall of Fame in 1939.

F

Faber, Urban (Red)
1888–1976
Chicago (AL 1914–33)   **P**   **BB/RHP**

669 games	4,086 innings
254-213 W–L	3.15 ERA
1,471 k's	28 saves

Despite pitching for a second-division White Sox team for 15 of his 20 years with the club, Faber won 254 games, including a career-high 25 in 1921. One of the last of the legal spitballers, he won three World Series games in 1917 to bring the Chisox their last World Series title. He entered the Hall of Fame in 1964.

Face, Roy

1928–

Pittsburgh (NL 1953, 1955–68), Detroit (AL 1968),
Montreal (NL 1969)   P   BB/RHP

848 games	1,375 innings
104-95 W–L	3.48 ERA
877 k's	193 saves

In 1959, Face racked up 17 consecutive wins in relief
before losing his first game. Relying almost exclusively
on a forkball, the diminutive reliever went 18–1 that
year, thus recording the highest winning percentage in
big league history (.947). He also led the NL in saves
three times, including a career-best 28 in 1962.

Fain, Ferris (Burrhead)

1921–

Philadelphia (AL 1947–52), Chicago (AL 1953–54),
Detroit (AL 1955), Cleveland (AL 1955)   1B
BL/TL

1,151 games	.290 ba
1,139 hits	48 hr
570 rbi	46 sb

A two-time AL batting champion (1951 and 1952),
Fain had a knack for getting on base, whether with a
base hit or a walk. He collected more than 100 walks in
five seasons and had an on-base percentage surpassing
.400 every season of his career. Although he was not a
slugger, he could sock doubles. Defensively, Fain had
great range and a strong throwing arm and was regarded as the AL's top fielding first sacker.

Fairly, Ron

1938–

Los Angeles (NL 1958–69), Montreal (NL
1969–74), St. Louis (NL 1975–76), Oakland (AL
1976), Toronto (AL 1977), California (AL 1978)
1B, OF   BL/TL

2,442 games	.266 ba
1,913 hits	215 hr
1,044 rbi	35 sb

Fairly had a smooth left-handed stroke and was a consistent .270 hitter throughout his career. He reached his career high in 1961, when he batted .322 in part-time play.

Falk, Bibb (Jockey)

1899–1989
Chicago (AL 1920–28), Cleveland (AL 1929–31)
OF   BL/TL

1,353 games	.314 ba
1,463 hits	69 hr
784 rbi	46 sb

Outstanding defensively and a strong hitter as well, Falk is frequently overlooked in discussions of the leading AL outfielders of the twenties. He joined the Chisox straight out of college, and his batting average improved once he learned the strike zone. Falk batted .352 with 99 RBI in 1924, .301 with 99 RBI in 1925, and .345 with 108 RBI in 1926. In all, he batted over .300 in eight seasons.

Feller, Bob (Rapid Robert)

1918–
Cleveland (AL 1936–41, 1945–56)   P
BR/RHP

570 games	3,827 innings
266-162 W–L	3.25 ERA
2,581 k's	21 saves

A teenage wonder, Feller blazed fastballs past American Leaguers while still in high school. He utilized an exaggerated leg kick, and his less than perfect control kept batters on edge. When Feller mixed his high hard one, clocked at over 100 miles an hour, with a sharp-breaking curve, he was nearly unhittable. Indeed, he pitched three no-hitters and 12 one-hitters. In his last three

years before joining the Navy in World War II, Feller
won 76 games. Upon returning in 1946, he won 26
games, hurled 10 shutouts, and struck out a then-record 348 batters. Feller was inducted into the Hall of
Fame in 1962.

Fernandez, Sid (El Sid)

1962–
Los Angeles (NL 1983), New York (NL 1984–93),
Baltimore (AL 1994 Active)   P   BL/LHP

257 games	1,590 innings
98-79 W-L	3.15 ERA
1,458 k's	1 save

Mix a nasty, rising fastball, a slow, big-breaking curve
ball, and an awkward delivery and you have Fernandez,
one of the most difficult pitchers to hit in the NL. Batters have hit a combined .205 against him in his career.
However, Fernandez has always had problems with his
stamina, his excessive weight, and his poor control.

Fernandez, Tony

1962–
Toronto (AL 1983–90, 1993), San Diego (NL
1991–92), New York (1993)   SS   BB/TR

1,470 games	.285 ba
1,612 hits	53 hr
543 rbi	202 sb

One of the top fielding shortstops in AL history, Fernandez has been a consistent batter throughout his career, averaging between .257 and .322 each season. He
led the AL twice in fielding percentage (1986 and
1989). Playing mostly on fast artificial surfaces, Fernandez has slapped 274 doubles in his career.

Ferrell, Rick

1905–

St. Louis (AL 1929–33, 1941–43), Boston (AL 1933–37), Washington (AL 1937–41, 1944–45, 1947)   **C**   **BR/TR**

1,884 games	.281 ba
1,692 hits	28 hr
734 rbi	29 sb

Ferrell's induction into the Hall of Fame in 1984 raised some eyebrows among those who doubted his credentials, but he was a strong defensive catcher with a sure throwing arm who handled the knuckle-ball-dominated pitching staff on the Senators. Although he had little punch at the plate, he did hit over .300 four times in a six-year span early in his career. Ironically, his brother, pitcher Wes Ferrell, hit more career homers than he did.

Fielder, Cecil

1963–

Toronto (AL 1985–88), Detroit (AL 1990–93 Active)   **1B**   **BR/TR**

850 games	.259 ba
743 hits	191 hr
590 rbi	

After mixed success as a part-time player with Toronto, Fielder spent one season in Japan before returning to Detroit for the 1990 season as an unheralded and overweight prospect. What happened was phenomenal—he became the first AL'er to belt more than 50 home runs since Maris and Mantle in 1961. He smacked 51 homers and knocked in 132 runs. Despite his large size, Fielder is an agile gloveman at first base. He led the AL in RBI in 1990 (132), in 1991 (133), and in 1992 (124).

Fingers, Rollie

1946–
Oakland (AL 1968–76), San Diego (NL 1977–80),
Milwaukee (AL 1981–82, 1984–85)   P
BR/RHP

944 games	1,701 innings
114-118 W–L	2.90 ERA
1,299 k's	341 saves

Owner of the most perfectly waxed mustache in major
league history, Fingers took an equal amount of care in
disposing of opposing batters. The most effective and
durable relief pitcher without a trick pitch, he relied on
a fastball and slider to stifle rallies. Fingers ranked
number one in career saves at his retirement, and he
won the AL Cy Young Award in 1981. Although he is
best remembered for his work in Oakland, Milwaukee
also retired his uniform number 34. Fingers was inducted into the Hall of Fame in 1992.

Finley, Charles (Chuck)

1962–
California (AL 1986–93 Active)   P   LHP

252 games	1,450 innings
89-76 W–L	3.40 ERA
1,025 k's	

A crackling fastball and sharp-breaking curve ball have
made Finley one of the AL's best lefties. In 1989–91,
he won 16, 18, and 18 games.

Fisk, Carlton (Pudge)

1947–
Boston (AL 1969–80), Chicago (AL 1981–93)   C
BR/TR

2,499 games	.269 ba
2,356 hits	376 hr
1,330 rbi	128 sb

In 1993, Fisk set a new record for games caught by a
major league catcher and was unceremoniously

dumped by the White Sox one week later. He caught hurlers from Bill Lee to Jack McDowell. Fisk played the game all-out and admonished those who did not. He overcame a series of injuries that limited his playing time in the late seventies and actually played better as he aged. At his retirement, Fisk was the leading home run hitter in White Sox history (213). His best season came in 1977, when he batted .315 with 26 home runs and 102 RBI. Fisk's induction into the Hall of Fame is a certainty.

Fitzsimmons, Freddie (Fat Freddie)
1901–1979
New York (NL 1925–37), Brooklyn (NL 1937–43); MGR—Philadelphia (NL 1943–45)   P, MGR
BR/RHP

513 games	3,223 innings
217-146 W–L	3.51 ERA
870 k's	13 saves

Fitzsimmons split his career between both sides of the most heated rivalry in the major leagues—the Dodgers and the Giants. He threw the usual assortment of pitches, plus a knuckle ball, using a delivery that some compared with a windmill. He spun, turned his back to the batter, and then threw the ball with a sidearm release. A fierce competitor, he was literally knocked out of the 1941 World Series, suffering a broken leg when hit by a line drive. A good hitter and fielder, Fitzsimmons led the NL twice in winning percentage, going 19–7 in 1930 (.731) and 16–2 in 1940 (.889).

Flanagan, Mike
1951–
Baltimore (AL 1975–87, 1991–92), Toronto (AL 1987–90)   P   LHP

526 games	2,770 innings
167-143 W–L	3.90 ERA
1,491 k's	4 saves

Flanagan knew how to pitch. Mixing his fastball, curve, and slider, and changing speeds on all his pitches, he kept batters off-stride and fit right in with the other Baltimore aces. In 1979, he won the AL Cy Young Award for a 23–9 season that included a league-high five shutouts.

Fletcher, Art

1885–1950

New York (NL 1909–20), Philadelphia (NL 1920, 1922); MGR—Philadelphia (NL 1923–26), New York (AL 1929)   **SS, MGR   BR/TR**

1,533 games	.277 ba
1,534 hits	32 hr
675 rbi	159 sb

The Giants' aggressive shortstop for nine seasons, Fletcher fit the mold of a McGraw player—a spunky, speedy, intelligent man with good hands and a quick bat. He led NL shortstops in fielding percentage twice. Quick with a vituperative one-liner and always a willing combatant, he was one of the best bench jockeys of his era.

Flick, Elmer

1876–1971

Philadelphia (NL 1898–1901), Philadelphia (AL 1902), Cleveland (AL 1902–10)   **OF   BL/TR**

1,483 games	.313 ba
1,752 hits	48 hr
756 rbi	330 sb

One of the first players to combine speed and power, Flick led the AL in triples for three consecutive years (1905–07) and in stolen bases twice. A superior outfielder with a strong arm, he was nearly traded for Ty Cobb in 1907. Flick's career ended prematurely due to stomach ailments. He was inducted into the Hall of Fame in 1963.

Flood, Curt

1938–

Cincinnati (NL 1956–57), St. Louis (NL 1958–69),
Washington (AL 1971)   **OF   BR/TR**

1,759 games	.293 ba
1,861 hits	85 hr
636 rbi	88 sb

By refusing to report to Philadelphia following his
trade by the Cardinals after the 1969 season, Flood
took a stand that ultimately led to players being
granted their free agency after a given number of years
in the game. On the field, Flood was a superlative center fielder whose reputation was unfairly besmirched by
a line drive in the seventh game of the 1968 World Series that sailed over his head for the series-winning hit.
He batted over .300 six times, including a career-best
.335 in 1967.

Ford, Edwin (Whitey, The Chairman of the Board)

1928–

New York (AL 1950–67)   **P   BL/LHP**

498 games	3,170 innings
236-106 W–L	2.75 ERA
1,956 k's	10 saves

The Yankees' money pitcher, Ford was used primarily
to pitch against the top teams in the league. He combined a good fastball and curve with pinpoint control
and all the tricks of the trade to produce the highest
winning percentage of all 20th-century hurlers. Ford
won the Cy Young Award in 1961; that year, new
manager Ralph Houk pitched him on three days rest
and he responded with 25 victories. He holds many
World Series records, including most career wins (10)
and most consecutive scoreless innings (33⅔). The
Yankees retired his uniform number 16, and he was inducted into the Hall of Fame in 1974.

Ford, Russ
1883–1960
New York (AL 1909–13), Buffalo (FL 1914–15)   P
BR/RHP

199 games	1,487 innings
99-71 W-L	2.59 ERA
710 k's	9 saves

A technician on the mound, Ford originated the use of emery to make the ball sink or sail. The Canadian-born hurler went 26–6 with a tiny 1.65 ERA as a rookie and won 22 games the following year. When the Federal League beckoned in 1914, Ford jumped and won 20 games.

Forsch, Bob
1950–
St. Louis (NL 1974–88), Houston (NL 1988–89)
P   BR/RHP

498 games	2,794 innings
168-136 W-L	3.76 ERA
1,133 k's	3 saves

Forsch was the third-winningest pitcher in Cardinals history (163), trailing only Bob Gibson (251) and Jesse Haines (210). A sinking fastball and a sharp slider were his best pitches. He pitched no-hitters against Philadelphia in 1978 and Montreal in 1983, and in 1977 he won 20 games.

Forsch, Ken
1946–
Houston (NL 1970–80), California (AL 1981–84, 1986)   P   BR/RHP

521 games	2,127 innings
114-113 W-L	3.37 ERA
1,047 k's	51 saves

The brother of Cardinals starter Bob Forsch, Ken Forsch both started and relieved throughout his career. In 1979, he pitched a no-hitter against Atlanta. The

Forsches are the only pair of brothers ever to throw no-hitters. In 1976, Forsch saved 19 games for Houston. He won also 13 times for California as a starter in 1982, when the team won its division title.

Forster, Terry

1952–

Chicago (AL 1971–76), Pittsburgh (NL 1977), Los Angeles (NL 1978–82), Atlanta (NL 1983–85), California (AL 1986)   **P**   **BL/LHP**

614 games	1,105 innings
54-65 W–L	3.23 ERA
791 k's	127 saves

Forster had a great arm, throwing sliders and fastballs past batters throughout his career. The White Sox rushed him to the majors and then couldn't decide if he was a starter or reliever. He saved 29 games in 1972 at the age of 20 and led the AL two years later with 24 saves. Forster's last big year came in 1978, when he saved 22 games for the pennant-winning Dodgers. At the end of his career, the overweight Forster became the subject of fat jokes by comedian David Letterman.

Foster, Andrew (Rube)

1878–1930

Chicago Union Giants, Cuban Giants, Cuban X-Giants, Philadelphia Giants, Chicago Leland Giants, Chicago American Giants   **P, MGR**
BR/RHP

Regarded by many as the father of black baseball, Foster organized the Negro National League in 1920. As a player, he starred on the mound. He created the formidable Chicago American Giants in 1911 and ran the team until 1926. Foster acquired his nickname after he defeated Philadelphia's star hurler Rube Waddell in a game. He was inducted into the Hall of Fame in 1981.

Foster, Bill (Willie)

1904–1978

Memphis Red Sox, Chicago American Giants, Birmingham Black Barons, Homestead Grays, Kansas City Monarchs, Cole's American Giants **P**

BL/LHP

1,659 innings	137-62 W–L
734 k's	12 saves

The younger half-brother of the legendary Rube Foster, Foster was a star in his own right. Excellent control of his dynamic fastball, excellent curve, and tantalizing change-up made him one of the top hurlers of his era. Foster did his best work for the Chicago American Giants.

Foster, George

1948–

San Francisco (NL 1969–71), Cincinnati (NL 1971–81), New York (NL 1982–86), Chicago (AL 1986) **OF**   **BR/TR**

1,977 games	.274 ba
1,925 hits	348 hr
1,239 rbi	51 sb

In the late seventies, Foster starred as the big bopper of the Big Red Machine. Quiet on and off the field, he never attracted the attention of Pete Rose, Johnny Bench, or Joe Morgan. He had a phenomenal season in 1977, with statistics resembling those more common 40 years earlier. He hit .320, while leading the NL in runs scored (124), home runs (52), and RBI (149). Indeed, Foster led the NL in RBI for three consecutive seasons (1976–78). Defensively, he could be a liability because he would not go to the wall to make a catch.

Fournier, Jacques (Jack)

1892–1973

Chicago (AL 1912–17), New York (AL 1918), St. Louis (NL 1920–22), Brooklyn (NL 1923–26), Boston (NL 1927)   **1B**   **BL/TR**

1,530 games	.313 ba
1,631 hits	136 hr
859 rbi	145 sb

An outstanding hitter but a poor fielder, Fournier hit over .300 seven times in his career. When the style of hitting changed after 1920, Fournier kept in stride, increasing his home run and RBI production. He swatted at least 20 homers and drove in more than 100 runs for Brooklyn in three consecutive seasons (1923–25). Brooklyn's boo-birds rode him without mercy, however, due to his defensive ineptitude, and he threatened to retire.

Foutz, Dave (Scissors)

1856–1897

St. Louis (AA 1884–87), Brooklyn (AA 1888–89), Brooklyn (NL 1890–96); MGR—Brooklyn (NL 1893–96)   **1B, OF, P, MGR**   **BR/TR**

1,135 games	.276 ba
1,253 hits	31 hr
548 rbi	280 sb
1,997 innings	147-66 W–L
2.84 ERA	790 k's
4 saves	

As a sidearming right-hander, Foutz teamed with "Parisian Bob" Caruthers to pitch the St. Louis Browns to the top of the AA in the 1880s. A strong hitter, he moved to the outfield after breaking his thumb in 1887. Playing for Brooklyn in 1889, he sparked the Dodgers to the pennant by knocking in 113 runs.

Fowler, John (Bud)

1858–1913

Fowler was the first black to play professional baseball. Appearing in 495 games over 10 years for many teams in various minor leagues, Fowler played a variety of positions. When Jim Crow laws spread across America in the 1890s, he found it increasingly difficult to play alongside whites. In 1895, Fowler organized a black team, called the Page Fence Giants, that was based in Adrian, Michigan.

Fox, Nellie

1927–1975

Philadelphia (AL 1947–49), Chicago (AL 1950–63), Houston (NL 1964–65)   **2B   BL/TR**

2,367 games	.288 ba
2,663 hits	35 hr
790 rbi	76 sb

Nearly 30 years after Fox's retirement, Chicago baseball fans still ask, "Why isn't Nellie Fox in the Hall of Fame?" A hero to the South Side of Chicago, the diminutive, tobacco-chewing second baseman swung a bottle bat and sliced short line drives into left field. A smart contact hitter who batted second in the lineup, Fox never fanned more than 18 times in one season. In the field, Nellie had few equals, and he excelled at turning the double play. In 1959, Fox led the Sox to the pennant and won the AL MVP award. In his honor, the White Sox retired uniform number 2.

Foxx, Jimmie (Double X, Beast)

1907–1967

Philadelphia (AL 1925–35), Boston (AL 1936–42), Chicago (NL 1942, 1944), Philadelphia (NL 1945)
1B   BR/TR

2,317 games	.325 ba
2,646 hits	534 hr
1,922 rbi	87 sb

At the plate, Foxx was an imposing presence. In an age before weightlifting became the norm for ballplayers, his muscles appeared to burst out of his uniform. Foxx relied on his wrist strength to belt line drives that rocketed over the fence. In 1932, he batted .364 with a league-leading slugging percentage of .749, 58 home runs, 151 runs scored, and 169 RBI. Foxx belted 30 homers in each of a record 12 consecutive years, and his total of 17 grand slams ranks third on the all-time list. For his career, he ranks in the top 10 in slugging percentage, homers, and RBI. Foxx was inducted into the Hall of Fame in 1951.

Franco, John

1960–
Cincinnati (NL 1984–89), New York (NL 1990–93
Active)   **P   BL/LHP**

566 games	720 innings
62-47 W–L	2.62 ERA
517 k's	236 saves

One of the NL's top relievers in the eighties, Franco relies heavily on a tailing fastball and a change-up to erase opposing batters. He led the league twice in saves, recording 39 in 1988 and 33 in 1990. In recent years, elbow problems have limited his effectiveness.

Franco, Julio

1958–
Philadelphia (NL 1982), Cleveland (AL 1983–88), Texas (AL 1989–93), Chicago (AL 1994 Active)   **2B BR/TR**

1,546 games	.300 ba
1,784 hits	100 hr
763 rbi	229 sb

At the plate, Franco holds his bat high over his head, horizontal to the ground, before unleashing his swing. He has good power to the opposite field, although he is not a major home run threat. In 1991, one of his five

.300 plus seasons, he led AL batters with a .341 average.

Freehan, Bill

1941–

Detroit (AL 1961, 1963–76)   C   BR/TR

1,774 games	.262 ba
1,591 hits	200 hr
758 rbi	24 sb

A football star at the University of Michigan, Freehan went on to become one of the greatest catchers in Tigers history. Sound defensively, he also batted .300 in 1964 with 18 home runs and 80 RBI. Freehan won five Gold Gloves, and his lifetime fielding percentage of .993 is tied for the best in major league history.

Fregosi, Jim

1942–

Los Angeles (AL 1961–64), California (AL 1965–71), New York (NL 1972–73), Texas (AL 1973–77), Pittsburgh (NL 1977–78); MGR— California (AL 1978–81), Chicago (AL 1986–88), Philadelphia (NL 1991–93 Active)   SS, MGR BR/TR

1,902 games	.265 ba
1,726 hits	151 hr
706 rbi	76 sb

The brightest star on the Angels during their first decade, Fregosi had some robust seasons at the plate and was steady in the field. Traded to the Mets for Nolan Ryan following the 1971 season in New York's perennial quest for a third baseman—a position that Fregosi had never played—he played horribly and was soon back in the AL. After retiring as a player, Fregosi became an effective manager, winning the NL pennant in 1993 with Philadelphia.

French, Larry
1907–1987
Pittsburgh (NL 1929–34), Chicago (NL 1935–41),
Brooklyn (NL 1941–42)   P   BB/LHP

570 games	3,152 innings
197-171 W–L	3.44 ERA
1,187 k's	17 saves

A tough cookie on the mound, French featured a
screwball among his repertoire of pitches. A consistent
winner in the NL, he averaged 14 victories during his
career and won at least 10 games every year but one.
More than 20 percent of his career victories were shutouts, and he led the NL in 1935 and 1936. Ironically,
his last year in the bigs was his best—a 15–4 record
with a scintillating 1.83 ERA for Brooklyn in 1942.

Frey, Linus (Lonny, Junior)
1910–
Brooklyn (NL 1933–36), Chicago (NL 1937, 1947),
Cincinnati (NL 1938–43, 1946), New York (AL
1947–48), New York (NL 1948)   2B, SS
BL/TR

1,535 games	.269 ba
1,482 hits	61 hr
549 rbi	105 sb

A fine defensive second baseman, Frey broke in under
Casey Stengel in Brooklyn and had four fine seasons,
batting .319 as a rookie, before moving on to the Cubs.
Frey played on Cincinnati's pennant winners in 1939
and 1940 and teamed with Eddie Miller at short to create an excellent double play combination.

Friend, Bob (Warrior)
1930–
Pittsburgh (NL 1951–66), New York (NL 1966),
New York (AL 1966)   P   BR/RHP

602 games	3,611 innings
197-230 W-L	3.58 ERA
1,734 k's	11 saves

Friend enjoyed the success and endured the failures that came with pitching more innings than any hurler in Pirates history. He was one of only three pitchers in major league history to lose more than 200 games without winning 200, due in good part to some awful Pittsburgh teams in the early fifties. Indeed, he was shut out 45 times—a record surpassed by only five pitchers. Friend was also active in the formation of the baseball Players Association.

Frisch, Frank (The Fordham Flash)
1898–1973
New York (NL 1919–26), St. Louis (NL 1927–37); MGR—St. Louis (NL 1933–38), Pittsburgh (NL 1940–46), Chicago (NL 1949–51) **2B, 3B, MGR BB/TR**

2,311 games	.316 ba
2,880 hits	105 hr
1,244 rbi	419 sb

A disciple of Giants manager John McGraw, Frisch moved directly from the campus of Fordham University into New York's lineup. After starring in four World Series (1921–24), Frisch's combative personality clashed with McGraw's, and he was traded to St. Louis for Rogers Hornsby in the biggest deal in major league history. A clutch player with a thirst for victory, Frisch played in a record eight World Series as a National Leaguer and batted over .300 in 11 consecutive years. In 1927, he set a fielding record for second basemen of 641 assists, a record that still stands. Frisch managed the Cardinals' Gas House Gang to the World Series title in 1934. After his retirement, he joined the broadcast booth and became baseball's leading raconteur. He was inducted into the Hall of Fame in 1947.

Fryman, Travis

1969–

Detroit (AL 1990–93 Active)   SS   BR/TR

527 games	.277 ba
580 hits	72 hr
311 rbi	32 sb

It took several seasons, but Fryman finally supplanted Alan Trammell, a Detroit institution, at shortstop. Relying on his strong hands and quick wrists, Fryman generates the power of an outfielder. He connected for at least 20 homers and 90 RBI in 1991, 1992, and 1993. In 1993, he became the first Tigers player to hit for the cycle in 43 years.

Furillo, Carl (Skoonj)

1922–1989

Brooklyn (NL 1946–57), Los Angeles (NL 1958–60)
OF   BR/TR

1,806 games	.299 ba
1,910 hits	192 hr
1,058 rbi	48 sb

Furillo was a tough competitor who gave his all to the game and would accept nothing less from his teammates. Although he was an excellent batter who won the NL title in 1953 (.344), he is best remembered for his skill in playing balls that caromed off the beveled right-field wall at Ebbets Field and a rifle arm that intimidated base runners.

G

Gaetti, Gary

1958–

Minnesota (AL 1981–90), California (AL 1991–93), Kansas City (AL 1993 Active)   3B   BR/TR

1,745 games	.252 ba
1,604 hits	245 hr
922 rbi	83 sb

Gaetti's reputation with the Twins was that of a super-charged competitor who would do whatever it took to win. Consecutive seasons in 1986–87 of 30-plus homers and 100 RBI stamped him as the league's best third baseman. Since then, his stock has dropped and his fire has diminished, some believe, due to a conversion to evangelical Christianity.

Gagne, Greg
1961–
Minnesota (AL 1983–92), Kansas City (AL 1993 Active)   SS   BR/TR

1,299 games	.253 ba
995 hits	79 hr
392 rbi	89 sb

Another one of the many farmhands traded away by the Yankees in their fruitless quest for a pennant in the 1980s, Gagne has developed into an excellent defensive shortstop with surprising pop in his bat. Considered the glue of the Twins infield in their World Series title years (1987 and 1991), Gagne also batted .272 in 1989.

Galarraga, Andres (Big Cat)
1961–
Montreal (NL 1985–91), St. Louis (NL 1992), Colorado (NL 1993 Active)   1B   BR/TR

1,062 games	.279 ba
1,083 hits	138 hr
570 rbi	61 sb

America's attention was captured in 1993 by Galarraga's improbable quest to hit the .400 mark. What made this season so remarkable was the contrast with his apparent inability to hit major league pitching during the previous two seasons. As a young player in

Montreal, the slick-fielding Big Cat batted over .300 in 1987 and 1988, but his propensity to strike out soon found him riding the bench. Galarraga likes to extend his arms over the plate and has to be pitched inside.

Galvin, James (Pud)
1856–1902
Buffalo (NL 1879–85), Pittsburgh (AA 1885–86), Pittsburgh (NL 1887–89, 1891–92), Pittsburgh (PL 1890), St. Louis (NL 1892); MGR—Buffalo (NL 1885)   **P, MGR   BR/RHP**

697 games	5,941 innings
360-308 W–L	2.87 ERA
1,799 k's	1 save

Short and stocky, Galvin threw more innings than any pitcher in history except for Cy Young. He starred in Buffalo in the 1880s, where he befriended Mayor Grover Cleveland, the future president. On the mound, Galvin relied on his fastball and pinpoint control. He was also an excellent fielder. Galvin won the first two games in Pittsburgh's NL history and hurled two no-hitters in his career. He was inducted into the Hall of Fame in 1965.

Gant, Ron
1965–
Atlanta (NL 1987–93 Active)   **OF   BR/TR**

858 games	.262 ba
836 hits	147 hr
480 rbi	157 sb

His combination of power and speed makes Gant a valuable commodity for the Braves. He burst upon the major leagues as a home-run-hitting infielder, but defensive problems necessitated a shift to the outfield. In 1990, his first of two consecutive 30–30 seasons, he hit .303 with 32 homers and 33 stolen bases.

Garber, Gene
1947–

Pittsburgh (NL 1969–70, 1972), Kansas City (AL 1973–74, 1987–88), Philadelphia (NL 1974–78), Atlanta (NL 1978–87)   P   BR/RHP

931 games	1,510 innings
96-113 W-L	3.34 ERA
940 k's	218 saves

Aided by an unusual sidearm delivery, Garber became one of the game's top relievers in the seventies and eighties. Few men could match his consistent ability to get key outs in a game. In 1978, Garber stopped Pete Rose's 44-game hitting streak by throwing him an assortment of change-ups. He saved 30 games for the Braves in 1982.

Garcia, Mike (The Big Bear)
1923–1986

Cleveland (AL 1948–59), Chicago (AL 1960), Washington (AL 1961)   P   BR/RHP

428 games	2,174 innings
142-97 W-L	3.27 ERA
1,117 k's	23 saves

A member of the Indians' vaunted pitching staff of the early fifties, which also included Hall of Famers Early Wynn, Bob Lemon, and Bob Feller, Garcia won 79 games in 1951–54 and pitched at least 250 innings each year. His best years came in 1952, when he went 22–11 with a league-high six shutouts and an ERA of 2.37, and 1954, the Indians' pennant-winning year, when he won 19 games and led the AL in ERA (2.64) and shutouts (5).

Gardner, Floyd (Jelly)
1895–1976

Chicago American Giants (1920–30), Homestead Grays (1928), Detroit Wolves (1931)   OF
BL/TR

592 games	.286 ba
595 hits	1 hr
72 sb	

Extremely fast on the base paths, Gardner batted lead-off for the outstanding Chicago American Giants squads of the twenties. His speed and ability to judge fly balls made him one of the best defensive outfielders of his era.

Gardner, Larry

1886–1976

Boston (AL 1908–17), Philadelphia (AL 1918), Cleveland (AL 1919–24) **3B**   **BL/TR**

1,923 games	.289 ba
1,931 hits	27 hr
934 rbi	165 sb

Few fans can still recall the last Red Sox team to capture the World Series title, but Gardner starred at third base for three Boston champions—in 1912, 1915, and 1916. His sacrifice fly drove in the winning run in the 10th inning of the seventh game of the 1912 classic against the Giants. A college boy from the University of Vermont, Gardner also hit .310 with 118 RBI for the Indians' 1920 World Series victors.

Garner, Phil (Scrap Iron)

1948–

Oakland (AL 1973–76), Pittsburgh (NL 1977–81), Houston (NL 1981–87), Los Angeles (NL 1987), San Francisco (NL 1988); MGR—Milwaukee (AL 1992–93 Active) **2B, 3B, MGR**   **BR/TR**

1,860 games	.260 ba
1,594 hits	109 hr
738 rbi	225 sb

Few men played a grittier game than Garner. A throwback to a bygone era, he fought for every advantage on the field. Associated with winners in Oakland, Pittsburgh, and Houston, he batted .500 for the Pirates in the 1979 World Series.

Garr, Ralph (Roadrunner)

1945–

Atlanta (NL 1968–75), Chicago (AL 1976–79), California (AL 1979–80)   OF   BL/TR

1,317 games	.306 ba
1,562 hits	75 hr
408 rbi	172 sb

Garr could flat-out hit. He collected more than 200 hits in three different seasons; and in 1974, he led the NL in batting average (.353), hits (214), and triples (17). A clubhouse comedian, Garr hit over .300 five times but could best be described as an indifferent fielder.

Garver, Ned

1925–

St. Louis (AL 1948–52), Detroit (AL 1952–56), Kansas City (AL 1957–60), Los Angeles (AL 1961)
P   BR/RHP

402 games	2,477 innings
129-157 W–L	3.73 ERA
881 k's	12 saves

The pride of the Browns, Garver won 20 games in 1951, when the last-place St. Louis team lost 100 games. Traded away, Garver wound up with the second-division Tigers and later played for the hapless Athletics. With better teams, his record would surely have improved.

Garvey, Steve

1948–

Los Angeles (NL 1969–82), San Diego (NL 1983–87)   1B   BR/TR

2,322 games	.294 ba
2,599 hits	272 hr
1,308 rbi	83 sb

A former football star at Michigan State, Garvey possessed the most muscular forearms in baseball in the seventies. He worked hard at presenting a squeaky-clean image on and off the field, an image that was exploded by revelations of marital infidelity after his career had ended. On the field, Garvey was indestructible, playing in an NL-record 1,207 consecutive games. He hit over .300 seven times for the Dodgers, knocked in at least 100 runs five times, and led the NL in hits in 1978 (202) and 1980 (200).

Gehrig, Lou (The Iron Horse)
1903–1941
New York (AL 1923–39)   **1B**   **BL/TL**

2,164 games	.340 ba
2,721 hits	493 hr
1,995 rbi	102 sb

Immortalized by the eponymous disease that took his life at an early age, Gehrig is a baseball legend. Quiet and good-natured, he played in the shadow of the flamboyant Babe Ruth. Gehrig compiled baseball's most enduring record—he played in 2,130 consecutive games over the course of 15 seasons. He hit a major league record 23 grand slams and also holds the AL record for RBI in a single season (184 in 1931). Gehrig drove in 100 runs in 13 consecutive seasons; his lifetime total (1,995) places him third on the all-time list. The Yankees retired Gehrig's uniform number 4, and he was inducted into the Hall of Fame in 1939.

Gehringer, Charley (The Mechanical Man)
1903–1993
Detroit (AL 1924–42)   **2B**   **BL/TR**

2,323 games	.320 ba
2,839 hits	184 hr
1,427 rbi	182 sb

Gehringer made the game look easy. Smooth on the field, patient at the plate, his nickname, "The Mechanical Man," belied his baseball smarts. Gehringer excelled at turning the double play, and at the plate he sprayed the ball to all fields. The AL MVP in 1937 when he batted .371, Gehringer was quiet on and off the field. The Tigers retired his uniform number 2, and he was inducted into the Hall of Fame in 1949.

Getzien, Charlie (Pretzels)
1864–1932

Detroit (NL 1884–88), Indianapolis (NL 1889), Boston (PL 1890), Boston (NL 1891), Cleveland (NL 1891), St. Louis (NL 1892)   P   BR/RHP

296 games	2,539 innings
145–139 W–L	3.46 ERA
1,070 k's	1 save

Getzien pitched 8⅔ innings of hitless ball against the St. Louis Browns in the 1887 World Series after going 29–13 during the regular season for the powerful Detroit squad. An artful hurler, he acquired his nickname for his variety of curves. In 1886, Getzien's best year, he won 30 games.

Gibson, Bob (Hoot)
1935–

St. Louis (NL 1959–75)   P   BR/RHP

528 games	3,884 innings
251–174 W–L	2.91 ERA
3,117 k's	6 saves

The 1960s was a golden age for NL pitchers, with stars like Koufax, Drysdale, Marichal, Seaver, and Gibson. Gibson propelled his body toward the batter on every pitch and completed his delivery by standing on one leg to the left of the mound. He intimidated batters with a moving fastball and slider and relished pushing batters off the plate to secure the outside corner. In 1968, Gibson enjoyed the greatest season for any

pitcher since the early years of the 20th century; he
went 22–9 with a miniscule 1.12 ERA, 13 shutouts,
and 268 strikeouts. He won 15 consecutive games that
year. In the World Series, Gibson stifled the Yankees,
Red Sox, and Tigers while completing all but one of his
nine series starts. He fanned 17 Tigers in game one of
the 1968 World Series. Gibson ranks second to
Whitey Ford in World Series victories (seven) and
strikeouts (92), despite making only nine starts to
Ford's 22. Gibson was inducted into the Hall of Fame
in 1981, and the Cardinals retired his uniform number
45.

Gibson, Josh

1911–1947
Homestead Grays (1930–33, 1937–40, 1942–46),
Pittsburgh Crawford (1934–36)   C   BR/TR

439 games	.354 ba
644 hits	141 hr
17 sb	

Inducted into the Hall of Fame in 1972, Gibson
starred for the Pittsburgh Crawfords and Homestead
Grays until his death of a brain tumor at the age of 35.
Hard work made him a fine defensive catcher, and at
the plate he had few equals. Gibson belted some of the
longest balls ever seen in any stadium. Eyewitnesses
claim he once smashed a home run entirely out of Yankee Stadium, the only man ever to do so. He led the
Negro National League in homers nine times.

Gibson, Kirk

1957–
Detroit (AL 1979–87, 1993 Active), Los Angeles (NL
1988–90), Kansas City (AL 1991), Pittsburgh (NL
1992)   OF   BL/TL

1,467 games	.268 ba
1,403 hits	223 hr
763 rbi	271 sb

Gibson plays the game hard all the way and knows no substitute for winning. A former speedy football star at Michigan State, he brought a gridiron mentality to the diamond and suffered many injuries that limited his effectiveness. In 1984, he led the Tigers to the World Series with 27 homers and 91 RBI, but he will always be remembered for his pinch-hit home run in the first game of the 1988 World Series against Dennis Eckersley of the Athletics. Though Gibson was barely able to hobble to the plate, his homer won the game and, in effect, the series, for the Dodgers.

Giles, George
1909–1992

Kansas City Monarchs (NL 1927–28, 1932), St. Louis Stars (NL 1930–31), Detroit Wolves (NL 1932), Homestead Grays (NL 1932), Baltimore Black Sox (NL 1933), Brooklyn Eagles (NL 1936), New York Black Yankees (NL 1936–37), Pittsburgh Crawfords (NL 1938), Philadelphia Stars (NL 1938)
1B   BL/TR

339 games	.309 ba
401 hits	8 hr
24 sb	

Possibly the greatest first baseman in the Negro Leagues, Giles starred for a variety of teams in the thirties. He did his best work for the St. Louis Stars. Giles grandson, Brian Giles, later played second base for the New York Mets in the eighties.

Gilliam, Jim (Junior)
1928–1978

Baltimore Elite Giants (1946–47, 1950), Brooklyn (NL 1953–57), Los Angeles (NL 1958–66)   **2B, 3B, OF   BB/TR**

1,956 games	.265 ba
1,889 hits	65 hr
558 rbi	203 sb

When Gilliam first appeared in a Dodgers uniform in 1953, he was already a polished professional after several seasons in the Negro Leagues and two years in the minors. His impact on Brooklyn was immediate. He batted .278, drawing 100 walks, scoring 125 runs, and smacking an NL-best 17 triples. Gilliam scored at least 100 runs in each of his first four seasons in Brooklyn and continued to star for the team after its move to Los Angeles. The Dodgers retired his uniform number 19.

Giusti, Dave

1939–

Houston (NL 1962, 1964–68), St. Louis (NL 1969), Pittsburgh (NL 1970–76), Chicago (NL 1977), Oakland (AL 1977)   P   BR/RHP

668 games	1,716 innings
100-93 W–L	3.60 ERA
1,103 k's	145 saves

One of a crop of fine young arms developed by Houston in the 1960s, Giusti teamed with Larry Dierker and Don Wilson in the starting rotation for three seasons before moving on to St. Louis and Pittsburgh, where he excelled as a reliever. His rubber arm enabled him to pitch on successive days. In 1971, he led the NL with 30 saves for the World Series champion Pirates. He also had four straight seasons with at least 20 saves (1970–73). His best pitch was a palm ball that made his fastball and slider even more effective.

Glasscock, Jack (Old Battle Axe, Judas)

1859–1947

Cleveland (NL 1879–84), Cincinnati (UA 1884), St. Louis (NL 1885–86), Indianapolis (NL 1887–89), New York (NL 1890–91), St. Louis (NL 1892–93), Pittsburgh (NL 1893–94), Louisville (NL 1895), Washington (NL 1895); MGR—Indianapolis (NL 1889), St. Louis (NL 1892)   SS, MGR   BR/TR

1,736 games	.290 ba
2,040 hits	27 hr
825 rbi	372 sb

The finest-fielding shortstop of his era, Glasscock earned the enmity of many of his fellow ballplayers by his actions in the formation of the Players League in 1890. Accused of spying for the established NL and reneging on his agreement to join the PL, he acquired the nickname "Judas." Ironically, while playing in the weakened NL in 1890, Glasscock hit a league-high .336.

Glavine, Tom

1966–

Atlanta (NL 1987–93 Active)   **P**   **BL/LHP**

208 games	1,357 innings
95-66 W–L	3.53 ERA
769 k's	

Glavine spearheaded the Braves' resurgence in the nineties, winning the NL Cy Young Award in 1991. Rushed to the majors by Atlanta to compensate for years of losing, Glavine lost 17 games in 1988 before going 14–8 the following year. Excellent control of his fastball, curve, and slider combined with an ability to change speeds has made Glavine a big winner. He rarely throws a hittable pitch in the strike zone and has copped 20 wins each year from 1991 to 1993.

Gleason, William (Kid)

1866–1933

Philadelphia (NL 1888–91), St. Louis (NL 1892–94), Baltimore (NL 1894–95), New York (NL 1896–1900), Detroit (AL 1901–02), Philadelphia (NL 1903–08), Chicago (AL 1912); MGR—Chicago (1919–23)   **2B, P, MGR**   **BB/TR**

1,966 games	.261 ba
1,944 hits	15 hr
823 rbi	328 sb
2,389 innings	138-131 W–L
3.79 ERA	744 k's
6 saves	

Gleason enjoyed three careers rolled into one, as a pitcher, hitter, and manager. He won 38 games for the Phillies in 1890 and at least 20 games in each of the next three seasons. After moving to second base, he hit .319 in 1897 with 106 RBI. Gleason is perhaps remembered today as the manager of the Chicago White Sox squad that fixed the 1919 World Series.

Goldsmith, Fred

1852–1939

Troy (NL 1879), Chicago (NL 1880–84), Baltimore (AA 1884)   P   BR/RHP

189 games	1,609 innings
112-68 W–L	2.73 ERA
433 k's	1 save

Goldsmith teamed with Larry Corcoran to form an unbeatable mound duo for the White Stockings in the early 1880s. He won 98 games in his four full seasons for Chicago, and his .875 winning percentage in 1880 (21–3) was the highest for a 20-game winner in the 19th century.

Gomez, Vernon (Lefty, Goofy)

1908–1989

New York (AL 1930–42), Washington (AL 1943)
P   BL/LHP

368 games	2,503 innings
189-102 W–L	3.34 ERA
1,468 k's	9 saves

A comedian off the field, "Goofy" Gomez was all business on the diamond. He played on seven pennant-winning Yankees teams and won 20 games four times.

In World Series play, he won six games without ever suffering a defeat. Gomez also led the AL in ERA and winning percentage twice. In 1934, he snared the pitching triple crown by winning 26 games with an ERA of 2.33 and 158 strikeouts. Despite his slender physique, he threw the ball very hard and changed speeds flawlessly. Some thought his slow curve was his best pitch. Gomez was inducted into the Hall of Fame in 1972.

Gonzalez, Juan

1969–

Texas (AL 1989–93 Active)   **OF**   BR/TR

486 games	.274 ba
497 hits	121 hr
348 rbi	8 sb

Gonzalez has an unlimited future. No young slugger in the past three decades has made as dramatic an entrance into the major leagues. In 1992, he led the AL by smoking 43 home runs and the following year he tied Barry Bonds for the major league lead with 46 homers.

Gooden, Dwight (Doc)

1964–

New York (NL 1984–93 Active)   P   BR/RHP

298 games	2,128 innings
154-81 W–L	3.04 ERA
1,835 k's	1 save

When Hall of Fame pitcher Bob Gibson said that Gooden would never have another season like his 24–4 mark as a 20-year-old in 1985, New York fans said he was crazy, if not jealous. As a precocious rookie, Gooden made pitching look easy, blazing his fastball past batters with pinpoint control. Unfortunately, Gibson has been proven correct. Although Gooden has enjoyed many good seasons since his dramatic start, none have been as spectacular. Indeed, he is now struggling to regain his form following serious rotator cuff surgery. Still, his lifetime winning percentage ranks in the top five all-time, and he remains the most popular athlete in New York. Gooden led the NL in strikeouts in his first two years and has fanned more than 200 men in a season four times in his career.

Goodman, Billy
1926–1984

Boston (AL 1947–57), Baltimore (AL 1957), Chicago (AL 1958–61), Houston (NL 1962) **2B, 1B, 3B** **BL/TR**

1,623 games	.300 ba
1,691 hits	19 hr
591 rbi	37 sb

A slightly built utility man, Goodman brought new respect to the art of playing multiple positions. Expert at hitting to all fields, he led the AL in 1950 (.354) and batted over .300 five times. Filling in for Ted Williams in 1950 after the slugger fractured his elbow in the All-Star Game, Goodman kept the Sox in contention for the pennant, although they ultimately fell short of the Yankees.

Gordon, Joe (Flash)
1915–1978

New York (AL 1938–43, 1946), Cleveland (AL 1947–50); MGR—Cleveland (1958–60), Detroit (AL 1960), Kansas City (AL 1961, 1969) **2B, MGR** **BR/TR**

1,566 games	.268 ba
1,530 hits	253 hr
975 rbi	89 sb

A superior fielder and fine batsman, Gordon was named the AL MVP in 1942 for batting .322 with 18 home runs and 103 RBI. Earlier in his career, in 1939–40, he belted more than 28 homers and knocked in at least 103 runs each season. Following WW II, Gordon was traded to Cleveland for Allie Reynolds in a deal that worked out well for both the Yanks and the Indians. He formed a smart double-play combo with Cleveland player-manager Lou Boudreau, and the two were instrumental in the team's 1948 World Series triumph. While Gordon was managing Cleveland in 1960, his general manager, Frank "Trader" Lane, actually traded him to Detroit, for the Tigers' skipper, Jimmy Dykes.

Gordon, Sid
1917–1975

New York (NL 1941–43, 1946–49, 1955), Boston (NL 1950–52), Milwaukee (NL 1953), Pittsburgh (NL 1954–55)   OF, 3B   BR/TR

1,475 games	.283 ba
1,415 hits	202 hr
805 rbi	19 sb

The Brooklyn-born slugger went on to star for Manhattan's team; in 1948 he contributed 30 homers to the Giants' NL season record of 221. That year was the first of five in which Gordon slammed at least 25 homers. An NL All-Star in 1948–49, Gordon had more than 100 RBI three times in his career.

Gore, George (Piano Legs)
1857–1933

Chicago (NL 1879–86), New York (NL 1887–89, 1891–92), New York (PL 1890), St. Louis (NL 1892); MGR—St. Louis (NL 1892)   OF, MGR
BL/TR

1,310 games	.301 ba
1,612 hits	46 hr
618 rbi	170 sb

One of the unsung stars of the 19th century, Gore was an excellent leadoff batter who displayed the patience to draw walks when it took seven balls to get a free pass. He rapped a league-best .360 in 1880. In 1885, he slammed three doubles and two triples in one game, becoming one of only five National Leaguers to collect five extra-base hits in a single match. Gore's lifestyle so annoyed his pious manager on the White Stockings, Cap Anson, that he was traded to New York, where he continued to star.

Goslin, Leon (Goose)

1900–1971
Washington (AL 1921–30, 1933, 1938), St. Louis (AL 1930–32), Detroit (AL 1934–37)   OF
BL/TR

2,287 games	.316 ba
2,735 hits	248 hr
1,609 rbi	175 sb

Goslin was the only man to take part in all 19 World Series games played by the Washington Senators. Goose was a natural hitter who batted over .300 and drove home more than 100 runs 11 times; he also led AL batters in 1928 (.379). In the 1935 World Series, he knocked in the winning run in the decisive sixth game, bringing Detroit its first title. Goslin was inducted into the Hall of Fame in 1968.

Gossage, Rich (Goose)

1951–
Chicago (AL 1972–76), Pittsburgh (NL 1977), New York (AL 1978–83, 1989), San Diego (NL 1984–87), Chicago (NL 1988), San Francisco (NL 1989), Texas (AL 1991), Oakland (AL 1992–93 Active)   P   BR/RHP

966 games	1,762 innings
121-107 W–L	2.98 ERA
1,473 k's	308 saves

At his best, between 1975 and 1985, opposing batters could barely see Gossage's fastball, let alone hit it. Using a full windup, Gossage hid the ball extremely well before throwing it. He wore a perpetual scowl on the mound, and few batters felt comfortable standing in the box against him. Gossage led the AL in saves in 1975 (26), 1978 (27), and 1980 (33). In 1981, his ERA was 0.77 and he recorded ERAs below 2.00 three other times.

Grace, Mark

1964–
Chicago (NL 1988–93 Active) **1B** **BL/TL**

906 games	.304 ba
1,033 hits	60 hr
453 rbi	49 sb

Grace is a smooth-fielding first baseman in the mold of Keith Hernandez as well as a fine hitter with a gift for hitting doubles. In 1989, he hit .314 with 13 homers, but he did not reached double digits again until 1993. During the 1989 NLCS, he hit a lusty .647, but the Cubs lost to the Giants.

Grant, Charles

?–1932
Page Fence Giants, Columbia Giants, Cuban X-Giants, Philadelphia Giants, New York Black Sox
2B **BR/TR**

After Baltimore Orioles manager John McGraw spotted Charles Grant cavorting on the diamond while his team was in training in Hot Springs, Arkansas, in 1901, he tried to sign him for his major league nine by passing him off as a Cherokee Indian called "Chief Tokohama." Grant practiced with the Orioles, but the ruse backfired when White Sox owner Charles Comiskey recognized Grant.

Grant, Frank

1868–1937
Buffalo (IL), Cuban X-Giants, Harrisburg, Lansing, Colored Capital All-Americans, New York Gorhams, Philadelphia Giants **2B** **BR/TR**

Possibly the greatest black player of the 19th century, Grant was dubbed "the black Dunlap," after St. Louis star second sacker Fred Dunlap. Grant had good power, tremendous range in the field, and a strong throwing arm. In the late 1880s, Grant played three seasons in the International League for Buffalo until Jim Crow attitudes forced him out.

Grant, Jim (Mudcat)

1935–

Cleveland (AL 1958–64), Minnesota (AL 1964–67), Los Angeles (NL 1968), Montreal (NL 1969), St. Louis (NL 1969), Oakland (AL 1970, 1971), Pittsburgh (NL 1970–71)   P   BR/RHP

571 games	2,441 innings
145-119 W–L	3.63 ERA
1,267 k's	53 saves

An entertainer on and off the diamond, Grant went 21–7 in 1965 with the pennant-winning Twins. He led the AL that year in wins, winning percentage, and shutouts (6). In the World Series, he won twice, although the Twins ultimately lost to the Dodgers. After the series, Grant hit the road with his singing group. He won in double digits seven times.

Greenberg, Henry (Hank, Hammerin' Hank)

1911–1986

Detroit (AL 1930, 1933–41, 1945–46), Pittsburgh (NL 1947)   1B, OF   BR/TR

1,394 games	.313 ba
1,628 hits	331 hr
1,276 rbi	58 sb

No Hall of Famer worked harder at his trade than Hank Greenberg. Although he was big and strong, he practiced incessantly to become a better hitter and fielder. Strictly a pull hitter, Greenberg slugged 98 homers and 329 RBI in 1937–38. Greenberg led the

Tigers into four World Series, hitting the pennant-clinching homer in 1945 after returning from four years of military service. He later became the general manager at Cleveland and part-owner of the White Sox. Undoubtedly the greatest Jewish batter in major league history, he was inducted into the Hall of Fame in 1956.

Greenwell, Mike

1963–

Boston (AL 1985–93 Active)   OF   BL/TR

977 games	.307 ba
1,082 hits	97 hr
561 rbi	65 sb

Greenwell burst upon the American League, hitting .328 with 19 homers in his rookie year. Proving it was not a fluke, he batted .325 with 22 home runs and 119 RBI the next year. Alas, he has not produced numbers approaching those since then. After an injury-riddled 1992 season, Greenwell rebounded to hit .315 in 1993.

Grich, Bobby

1949–

Baltimore (AL 1970–76), California (AL 1977–86)
2B   BR/TR

2,008 games	.266 ba
1,833 hits	224 hr
864 rbi	104 sb

Grich was the model for a new breed of middle infielders—slick fielders with power in their bats. He excelled defensively both in turning the double play and in ranging wide for ground balls. At the plate, Grich had his best season in 1979, when he hit .294 with 30 home runs and 101 RBI.

Griffey, Sr., Ken

1950–

Cincinnati (NL 1973–81, 1988–90), New York (AL 1982–86), Atlanta (NL 1986–88), Seattle (AL 1990–91)   **OF**   **BL/TL**

2,097 games	.296 ba
2,143 hits	152 hr
859 rbi	200 sb

Griffey had one of the sweetest swings in the NL during his era. He had great speed and recorded more than his share of infield hits, but most of his blows were line drives. Defensively, he was superb. He made one of the greatest catches in Yankee Stadium history while wearing pinstripes. Griffey's career high was .336 in 1976, but he hit over .300 seven times.

Griffey, Jr., Ken

1969–

Seattle (AL 1989–93 Active)   **OF**   **BL/TL**

734 games	.303 ba
832 hits	132 hr
453 rbi	77 sb

If any player could be considered a natural, it would be Ken Griffey, Jr. Blessed with power, speed, and a flair for the dramatic, he was labeled a star even before he ever stepped on a major league diamond for the first time. He hit over .300 in four consecutive years (1990–93) and slammed more than 20 homers with at least 100 RBI in 1991, 1992, and 1993. In 1993, he tied a major league record by homering in eight consecutive games. Defensively, Griffey evokes memories of Willie Mays.

Griffin, Mike

1865–1908

Baltimore (AA 1887–89), Philadelphia (PL 1890), Brooklyn (NL 1891–98); MGR—Brooklyn (NL 1898)   **OF, MGR**   **BL/TR**

1,511 games	.296 ba
1,753 hits	42 hr
625 rbi	473 sb

The outstanding center fielder of his generation, Griffin also wielded a good bat for Brooklyn in the 1890s, hitting .365 in 1894 and .335 in 1895. A contract dispute with owner Charles Ebbets led to Griffin's early departure from baseball.

Griffith, Clark (The Old Fox)

1869–1955

St. Louis (AA 1891), Boston (AA 1891), Chicago (NL 1893–1900), Chicago (AL 1901–02), New York (AL 1903–07), Cincinnati (AL 1909), Washington (AL 1912–14); MGR—Chicago (AL 1901–02), New York (AL 1903–08), Cincinnati (NL 1909–11), Washington (AL 1912–20) P, MGR BR/RHP

453 games	3,385 innings
237-146 W–L	3.31 ERA
955 k's	6 saves

One of the icons of the game, "the Old Fox" won 20 games in six consecutive seasons for Chicago in the NL before jumping to the upstart American League in 1901 as player-manager of the Chicago franchise. In 1903, he brought AL baseball to New York as player-manager of the team that became known as the Yankees. He purchased part of the Washington Senators in 1914, and his family remained owners of the franchise (later moved to Minnesota) until 1984. Griffith was inducted into the Hall of Fame in 1946.

Grimes, Burleigh (Ol' Stubblebeard)

1893–1985

Pittsburgh (NL 1916–17, 1928–29, 1934), Brooklyn (NL 1918–26), New York (NL 1927), Boston (NL 1930), St. Louis (NL 1930–31, 1933–34), Chicago (NL 1932–33), New York (AL 1934); MGR—Brooklyn (NL 1937–38)   P, MGR   BR/RHP

616 games	4,179 innings
270-212 W–L	3.53 ERA
1,512 k's	18 saves

Snarling at batters from behind a two-day growth of beard, Grimes had few friends on opposing NL teams. He didn't have the best fastball or the best control in the league and didn't field his position particularly well, but he won by utilizing his spitball and by virtue of his gritty determination. He pitched Brooklyn to the 1920 pennant and won the decisive seventh game of the 1931 World Series for St. Louis. Four times a 20-game winner with Brooklyn, Grimes was inducted into the Hall of Fame in 1964.

Grimm, Charley (Jolly Cholly)

1896–1983

Philadelphia (AL 1916), St. Louis (NL 1918), Pittsburgh (NL 1919–24), Chicago (NL 1925–36); MGR—Chicago (NL 1932–38, 1944–49, 1960), Boston (NL 1952), Milwaukee (NL 1953–56)   1B, MGR   BL/TL

2,166 games	.290 ba
2,299 hits	79 hr
1,078 rbi	57 sb

One of the most popular players of any era, Grimm acquired his nickname, "Jolly Cholly," from his banjo-playing and heavily accented storytelling. An outstanding defensive first baseman, he also slugged .345 in 1923 with 99 RBI and batted over .300 in five seasons. As a manager, he led the Cubs during their last period of glory in the thirties and forties, winning pennants in 1932, 1935, and 1945.

Grissom, Marquis

1967–

Montreal (NL 1989–93 Active)   OF   BR/TR

588 games	.277 ba
610 hits	43 hr
231 rbi	230 sb

Regarded as a can't-miss star, Grissom hasn't disappointed. He led the NL in steals in 1991 (76) and 1992 (78) and has showed increasing power at the plate. Defensively, he is a ball hawk who plays very shallow in centerfield and utilizes good speed to track down fly balls.

Groat, Dick

1930–

Pittsburgh (NL 1952, 1955–62), St. Louis (NL 1963–65), Philadelphia (NL 1966–67), San Francisco (NL 1967)   SS   BR/TR

1,929 games	.286 ba
2,138 hits	39 hr
707 rbi	14 sb

The glue of the 1960 World Series champion Pirates team, Groat won the NL MVP award that year, batting a league-high .325. A master of the hit-and-run and a strong opposite-field hitter, Groat was a consistent performer throughout his 14-year career. On defense, he teamed with Bill Mazeroski to form the top double-play duo of his era.

Groh, Henry (Heinie)

1889–1968

New York (NL 1912–13, 1922–26), Cincinnati (NL 1913–21), Pittsburgh (NL 1927);

MGR—Cincinnati (NL 1918)   3B, SS, MGR

BR/TR

1,676 games	.292 ba
1,774 hits	26 hr
566 rbi	180 sb

Groh swung the weirdest-looking bat in the major leagues—the so-called bottle bat, a 46-ounce piece of lumber with a thin handle and a thick barrel. A small man at 5-feet, 7-inches and 160 pounds, he choked up on the handle and slapped the ball out of the infield. He led the NL in doubles in 1917 (39) and 1918 (28). Groh went on to play in five different World Series for the Reds, Giants, and Pirates, batting .474 for the 1922 series-winning Giants.

Grote, Jerry

1942–

Houston (NL 1963–64), New York (NL 1966–77), Los Angeles (NL 1977–78, 1981), Kansas City (AL 1981)   C   BR/TR

1,421 games	.252 ba
1,092 hits	39 hr
404 rbi	15 sb

Grote was an ornery guy with a burning desire to win and a truculence that often offended sportswriters. His performance on the field won the respect of his teammates and opponents alike throughout the NL. Defensively, he was superb at blocking pitches in the dirt, and he possessed a strong, accurate arm. Grote called a smart game and knew when to get tough with his talented pitching staff. At the plate, he used a closed stance and was at his best when he tried to poke the ball to the opposite field. He batted a career-high .295 in 1975, but defense was his main game.

Grove, Robert (Lefty)

1900–1975

Philadelphia (AL 1925–33), Boston (AL 1934–41)

P   BL/LHP

616 games	3,940 innings
300-141 W-L	3.06 ERA
2,266 k's	55 saves

Hot-tempered early in his career, Grove overcame control problems to become one of the greatest left-handers in major league history. Possessor of a great rising fastball, he only began throwing curves after joining the Red Sox in 1934. Grove won 20 games eight times, led the AL in strikeouts for seven consecutive seasons, and in 1931 went 31–4 for the Athletics. With the fourth best lifetime winning percentage (.680), Grove was inducted into the Hall of Fame in 1947.

Guerrero, Pedro (Pete)

1956–

Los Angeles (NL 1978–88), St. Louis (NL 1988–92)

OF, 3B, 1B   BR/TR

1,536 games	.300 ba
1,618 hits	215 hr
898 rbi	97 sb

Stolen by the Dodgers from Cleveland in a minor league trade, Guerrero became one of the leading sluggers in the NL in the 1980s. He belted 32 homers in 1982 and 1983, driving home 100 and 103 runs. His best year was probably in 1985, when he led the NL in slugging percentage (.577) while hitting .320 with 33 homers. At the plate, Guerrero liked to extend his arms and had a strong dislike to being pitched inside. In 1988, he showed his objection to being hit by David Cone's slow curve by flinging his bat at the hurler and precipitating a brawl. Both in the field and on the bases, his skills were below average.

Guidry, Ron (Louisiana Lightning, Gator)

1950–

New York (AL 1975–88)   P   LHP

368 games	2,392 innings
170-91 W–L	3.29 ERA
1,778 k's	4 saves

Guidry generated tremendous power from his compact frame. With his great fastball and superlative slider, he could blow the ball past hitters. Found wanting by the Yankees in brief call-ups in 1975 and 1976, he emerged during the 1977 season to win 16 games, plus one in the World Series. In 1978, Guidry had a year pitchers dream about, going 25–3 with a 1.74 ERA, 248 strikeouts, and nine shutouts. He also won 20 games in 1983 and 1985. A great fielder, Guidry hurt his arm in 1987 and retired the following year.

Guillen, Ozzie

1964–

Chicago (AL 1985–93 Active)   SS   BL/TR

1,229 games	.267 ba
1,149 hits	14 hr
388 rbi	141 sb

When San Diego obtained former Cy Young winner LaMarr Hoyt from the White Sox in 1984, they surrendered a minor league prospect named Ozzie Guillen. Hoyt was soon out of baseball, but Guillen has developed into the best White Sox shortstop since fellow Venezuelan Luis Aparicio fielded the position in the 1950s. Named the AL Rookie of the Year in 1985 and awarded a Gold Glove in 1990, he is a smooth fielder with good range and a quick release. At the plate, he is a pesky hitter who shows little patience; he drew only 11 walks in 1991—a major league record for players with more than 150 games.

Gullett, Don

1951–

Cincinnati (NL 1970–76), New York (AL 1977–78)

P   BR/LHP

266 games	1,390 innings
109-50 W–L	3.11 ERA
921 k's	11 saves

Pitching pundits who looked at Gullett pitch agreed on two things: his fastball moved like a laser, but future arm trouble was inevitable. Unfortunately, the prediction proved correct. When Gullett's arm was sound, he was nearly unbeatable. Except for 1972, when he went 9–10, his lowest winning percentage was .607; and in only two years did he lose as many as 10 games. The Yankees signed Gullett to one of the first big free-agent contracts, but after two seasons of recurring arm miseries he retired.

Gura, Larry

1947–

Chicago (NL 1970–73, 1985), New York (AL 1974–75), Kansas City (AL 1976–85)   P
BB/LHP

403 games	2,047 innings
126-97 W–L	3.76 ERA
801 k's	14 saves

Larry Gura rubbed Billy Martin the wrong way, and the Yanks traded the lefty to Kansas City prior to the 1976 season. He averaged 15 wins per year from 1978 to 1982 for the Royals and took special delight in beating the Yankees. Gura was particularly effective against left-handed hitters.

Guzman, Juan

1966–

Toronto (AL 1991–93 Active)   P   RHP

84 games	540 innings
40-11 W–L	3.28 ERA
482 k's	

Few pitchers have made a more auspicious debut in the majors. Joining the Blue Jays midway through the 1991 season, Guzman won 10 games. He went 16–5 in his sophomore year, as Toronto became the first non-U.S. team to win the World Series. He relies on a fastball, slider, and splitter for his success.

Gwynn, Tony
1960–
San Diego (NL 1982–93 Active)   **OF**   **BL/TR**

1,585 games	.329 ba
2,039 hits	66 hr
650 rbi	263 sb

Gwynn has been the NL's best hitter for the past decade, winning four batting titles. He batted over .300 every year since 1983 and led the league in hits four times. An intelligent hitter who studies his swing on videotape regularly, Gwynn hits the ball to all fields. At the plate, Gwynn uses the smallest and lightest bat in the majors. The only criticisms that can be leveled against him are that he lacks power and is not a big run producer. Defensively, he has made himself into one of the best right fielders in the league through hard work.

H

Hack, Stan (Smiling Stan)
1909–1979
Chicago (NL 1932–47); MGR—Chicago (NL 1954–56), St. Louis (NL 1958)   **3B, MGR**
BL/TR

1,938 games	.301 ba
2,193 hits	57 hr
642 rbi	165 sb

Playing his entire career on the North Side of Chicago, Hack earned accolades as one of the most popular players in Cubs history. Although he was not a power hitter, he did bat over .300 six times. His career highs came in 1938 (.320) and 1945 (.323), both pennant-winning seasons for the Cubs. He scored at least 100 runs in six consecutive seasons (1936–41). In the field, he did not have great range.

Haddix, Harvey (The Kitten)

1925–

St. Louis (NL 1952–56), Philadelphia (NL 1956–57), Cincinnati (NL 1958), Pittsburgh (NL 1959–63), Baltimore (AL 1964–65)   P

BL/LHP

453 games	2,235 innings
136-113 W–L	3.63 ERA
1,575 k's	21 saves

A 20-game winner as a Cardinal rookie in 1953, Haddix was a crafty hurler. In one of the legendary games of major league history, he pitched a perfect game for 12 innings against the Milwaukee Braves in 1959, only to lose the game in the 13th inning.

Hadley, Irving (Bump)

1904–1963

Washington (AL 1926–31, 1935), Chicago (AL 1932), St. Louis (AL 1932–34), New York (AL 1936–40), New York (NL 1941), Philadelphia (AL 1941)   P   BR/RHP

528 games	2,945 innings
161-165 W–L	4.24 ERA
1,318 k's	25 saves

After toiling for a decade on losing teams in Washington and St. Louis, Hadley learned what it was like to live on the sunny side of the street following a trade to the Yanks prior to the 1936 season. He went from a sub-.500 pitcher to a record of 14–4 in his first year in pinstripes and appeared in four consecutive world series. In 1937, Hadley beaned the Tigers' star catcher, Mickey Cochrane, forcing his premature retirement.

Hafey, Charles (Chick)

1903–1973

St. Louis (NL 1924–31), Cincinnati (NL 1932–35, 1937)   **OF   BR/TR**

1,283 games	.317 ba
1,466 hits	164 hr
833 rbi	70 sb

Hafey overcame poor eyesight and sinus troubles to develop into one of the leading batsmen of his generation. A consistent .300 hitter, he led the NL in 1931 (.349). In 1929, he tied an NL record by getting a hit in 10 consecutive plate appearances. Defensively, Hafey possessed the strongest arm in the NL. Unfortunately, Hafey's sinus problems forced his early retirement. He was inducted into the Hall of Fame in 1971.

Hahn, Frank (Noodles)

1879–1960

Cincinnati (NL 1899–1905), New York (AL 1906)
P   BL/LHP

243 games	2,029 innings
130-94 W–L	2.55 ERA
917 k's	

Dwight Gooden's phenomenal success as a teenage strikeout artist sent researchers scurrying to the history books looking for other precocious hurlers. Invariably, they found the name of Noodles Hahn, who fanned 239 men in 1901 as a 22-year-old pitcher and led the NL in strikeouts at the ages of 20 and 21 as well. Four times a 20-game winner in his first five seasons, Hahn also pitched a no-hitter in 1900, but his career ended abruptly due to arm problems.

Haines, Jesse (Pop)

1893–1978

Cincinnati (NL 1918), St. Louis (NL 1920–37)   **P
BR/RHP**

555 games	3,208 innings
210-158 W–L	3.64 ERA
981 k's	10 saves

Haines threw a sharp-breaking curve ball that batters beat into the ground. Never a strikeout pitcher, he also gave up more hits than innings pitched in his career. Yet he won because he was tough to hit with men on base. Haines pitched a no-hitter in 1924 and won three games in the World Series in 1926 and 1930. In later years, he developed a highly effective knuckle ball. Haines was inducted into the Hall of Fame in 1970.

Hall, Dick

1930–

Pittsburgh (NL 1952–57, 1959), Kansas City (AL 1960), Baltimore (AL 1960–66, 1969–71), Philadelphia (NL 1967–68)   **P**   BR/RHP

495 games	1,259 innings
93-75 W–L	3.32 ERA
741 k's	68 saves

Signed as a bonus baby outfielder by the Pirates in 1952 straight out of Swarthmore College, Hall was one of the rare intellectuals of major league ball. Tall (6 feet, 6 inches) and slender, he became a pitcher who demonstrated excellent control using an unorthodox sidearm and submarine delivery. Hall loved to engage in hijinks in the bullpen, but on the mound he was all business. In 1964, he went 9–1 with a tiny 1.85 ERA.

Hallahan, Bill (Wild Bill)

1902–1981

St. Louis (NL 1925–36), Cincinnati (NL 1936–37), Philadelphia (NL 1938)   **P**   BR/LHP

324 games	1,740 innings
102-94 W–L	4.03 ERA
856 k's	8 saves

When Hallahan released his blazing fastball, he could never be sure where it was headed. His notable lack of control led to his nickname, "Wild Bill." He led the NL three times in bases on balls and twice in strike-outs. In the 1931 World Series, he was the Cardinals' most valuable pitcher, winning twice.

Hamilton, Bill (Sliding Billy)

1866–1940

Kansas City (AA 1888–89), Philadelphia (NL 1890–95), Boston (NL 1896–1901) **OF**

BR/TL

1,591 games	.344 ba
2,158 hits	40 hr
736 rbi	912 sb

An excellent batter, Hamilton formed part of one of the best-hitting outfields in history with Ed Delehanty and Sam Thompson for the Phillies teams of the late 1890s. He batted over .300 in 12 consecutive seasons, and his lifetime average ranks as the sixth best in the history of the game. Hamilton is best remembered for his base-running exploits. His record of 912 career steals stood for many years after his retirement until it was broken by Lou Brock; he scored more than one run per game throughout his career. Hamilton was inducted into the Hall of Fame in 1961.

Hands, Bill

1940–

San Francisco (NL 1965), Chicago (NL 1966–72), Minnesota (AL 1973–74), Texas (AL 1974–75) **P**

BR/RHP

374 games	1,951 innings
111-110 W–L	3.35 ERA
1,128 k's	14 saves

Hands's best pitch, a sharp-breaking slider that painted the outside corner at the knees, made him extremely tough on right-handed batters. When the Cubs threatened to win the NL East in 1969, he won 20 games with a tidy 2.49 ERA. In 1968–70, he won a total of

54 games; he teamed with Ferguson Jenkins to form an outstanding pitching tandem for the first Cubs team in over two decades to taste success.

Hanlon, Ned
1857–1937

Cleveland (NL 1880), Detroit (NL 1881–88), Pittsburgh (NL 1889, 1891), Pittsburgh (PL 1890), Baltimore (NL 1892); MGR—Pittsburgh (NL 1889, 1891), Pittsburgh (PL 1890), Baltimore (NL 1892–98), Brooklyn (NL 1899–1905), Cincinnati (NL 1906–07)   OF, MGR   BL/TR

1,267 games	.260 ba
1,317 hits	30 hr
517 rbi	329 sb

A fine center fielder during his playing days, Hanlon's reputation rests on his managing the brilliant Baltimore Orioles of the 1890s. He stressed bunting, the hit-and-run, and stealing bases. In 1899, he moved to Brooklyn when the Orioles and the Bridegrooms merged rosters and took most of his stars north. His team became known as the Brooklyn Superbas, after a popular entertainment troupe called Hanlon's Superbas. Hanlon won five NL pennants between 1894 and 1900.

Harder, Mel (Chief)
1909–

Cleveland (AL 1928–47)   P, MGR   BR/RHP

582 games	3,426 innings
223-186 W–L	3.80 ERA
1,160 k's	23 saves

Famed as the man DiMaggio couldn't hit, Harder pitched more games in a Cleveland uniform than any other man. He ranks second only to Bob Feller for most franchise victories. Harder won in double digits for 11 consecutive seasons, copping 20 victories in 1934 and 22 in 1935. In retirement, he became the

Indians' longtime pitching coach and nurtured the great pitching staffs of the fifties. The Indians retired his uniform number 18.

Hargrove, Mike
1949–

Texas (AL 1974–78), San Diego (NL 1979), Cleveland (AL 1979–85); MGR—Cleveland (AL 1991 Active) **1B, MGR** **BL/TL**

1,666 games	.290 ba
1,614 hits	80 hr
686 rbi	24 sb

When Hargrove stepped into the batter's box, stadium concessionaires let out a cheer. His series of nervous adjustments at the plate—tugging his cap, hitching his pants, twisting his thumb, practicing his swing—all amounted to a human rain delay. What made these habits pardonable was his innate ability to hit the baseball. Hargrove hit over .300 six times in his career, including .323 as a rookie.

Harrah, Toby
1948–

Washington (AL 1969, 1971), Texas (AL 1972–78, 1985–86), Cleveland (AL 1979–83), New York (AL 1984); MGR—Texas (AL 1992) **3B, SS, 2B**
BR/TR

2,155 games	.264 ba
1,954 hits	195 hr
918 rbi	238 sb

Harrah was a throwback to the era before guaranteed multiyear contracts when gritty play predominated. A power-hitting middle infielder, he also had good speed and a strong throwing arm. Patient at the plate, he was regularly among the AL's best in drawing walks, twice reaching the century mark. In 1982, he batted .304 with 25 homers and 78 RBI.

Harris, Stanley (Bucky)
1896–1977

Washington (AL 1919–1928), Detroit (AL 1929, 1931); MGR—Washington (AL 1924–28, 1935–42, 1950–54), Detroit (AL 1929–33, 1955–56), Boston (AL 1934), Philadelphia (NL 1943), New York (AL 1947–48)   2B, MGR   BR/TR

1,263 games	.274 ba
1,297 hits	9 hr
506 rbi	166 sb

An outstanding second baseman, good hitter, and smart base runner, Harris was the "boy manager" of the 1924 World Series champion Washington Senators at the age of 27. A players' manager, Harris piloted teams for 29 years; he ranks fourth in career victories (2,157), behind Mack, McCarthy, and Lasorda. In 1947, he led the Yankees to the World Series title.

Harris, Vic
1905–1978

Toledo Tigers (1923), Cleveland Tate Stars (1924), Cleveland Browns (1924), Chicago American Giants (1924), Homestead Grays (1925–33, 1935–36), Detroit Wolves (1932), Pittsburgh Crawfords (1934), Washington Homestead Grays (1937–43, 1945)
OF, MGR   BL/TR

477 games	.299 ba
541 hits	24 hr
15 sb	

Harris spent 23 years with the Homestead Grays, both in Pittsburgh and in Washington. A powerful hitter and a devastating base runner, Harris batted .370 for the 1935 Grays.

Hartnett, Charles (Gabby)
1900–1972
Chicago (NL 1922–40), New York (NL 1941);
MGR—Chicago (NL 1938–40)   C, MGR
BR/TR

1,990 games	.297 ba
1,912 hits	236 hr
1,179 rbi	28 sb

Hartnett's famous "homer in the gloamin'" at Wrigley Field won the 1938 pennant for the Cubs. Talkative behind the plate, "Gabby" possessed an outstanding throwing arm and excelled at handling a pitching staff. He set NL career records for chances and putouts. An aggressive leader, Hartnett was inducted into the Hall of Fame in 1955.

Harvey, Bryan
1963–
California (AL 1987–92), Florida (NL 1993 Active)
P   BR/RHP

309 games	376 innings
17-25 W–L	2.34 ERA
438 k's	171 saves

When the California Angels left Harvey unprotected during the 1992 expansion draft, experts figured that no one would take a flier on his injured arm and multimillion-dollar contract. Florida spent big bucks, however, and he responded with an outstanding year. Harvey's best pitch is a nasty splitter; he also throws a slider and fastball. In 1991, he led the AL in saves (46).

Hearn, Jim
1921–
St. Louis (NL 1947–50), New York (NL 1950–56),
Philadelphia (NL 1957–59)   P   BR/RHP

396 games	1,703 innings
109-89 W–L	3.81 ERA
669 k's	8 saves

Hearn won 12 games as a Cardinals rookie in 1947 but hit the skids in 1948 and 1949 as his ERA rose to 5.14. Traded to the Giants in 1950, he became a key contributor to the Miracle of Coogan's Bluff the following year when he went 17–9. Hearn's best pitch was a sinker ball.

Heath, Jeff
1915–1975

Cleveland (AL 1936–45), Washington (AL 1946), St. Louis (AL 1946–47), Boston (NL 1948–49)   **OF**
BL/TR

1,383 games	.293 ba
1,447 hits	194 hr
887 rbi	56 sb

Heath was a consistent contributor to the Cleveland offense for a decade. After hitting .343 with 21 homers and 112 RBI as a rookie in 1938, he enjoyed another great year in 1941 when he batted .340 with 24 home runs and 123 RBI. Both years, he led the AL in triples, with 18 in 1938 and 20 in 1941.

Hebner, Richie
1947–

Pittsburgh (NL 1968–76, 1982–83), Philadelphia (NL 1977–78), New York (NL 1979), Detroit (AL 1980–82), Chicago (NL 1984–85)   **3B, 1B**
BL/TR

1,908 games	.276 ba
1,694 hits	203 hr
890 rbi	38 sb

Possibly the only gravedigger to star in the major leagues, Hebner was a strong low-ball hitter who swatted over .290 five times. His best year came in 1972, when he hit .300 with 19 homers and 72 RBI. In the field, Hebner was no better than average.

Hecker, Guy (Blond Guy)
1856–1938
Louisville (AA 1882–89), Pittsburgh (NL 1890);
MGR—Pittsburgh (NL 1890)   P, 1B, MGR
BR/TR

703 games	.283 ba
810 hits	19 hr
103 rbi	123 sb
2,906 innings	173-146 W–L
2.92 ERA	1,099 k's
1 save	

An outstanding pitcher who could also hit with authority, Hecker turned in a phenomenal 1884 campaign for Louisville, winning 52 games, completing 72 of his 73 game starts, pitching 670 innings, and striking out 385 batters—all league-leading figures. In 1886, his .341 batting average led the AA, and he still managed to win 26 games on the mound.

Hegan, Jim
1920–1984
Cleveland (AL 1941–42, 1946–57), Detroit (AL 1958), Philadelphia (NL 1958–59), San Francisco (NL 1959), Chicago (NL 1960)   C   BR/TR

1,666 games	.228 ba
1,087 hits	92 hr
525 rbi	15 sb

Widely acclaimed as the finest defensive catcher of his generation, Hegan made a specialty of catching the Indians' 20-game winners—Feller, Wynn, Garcia, and Score. Though he was never a strong hitter, he did smack 14 homers in both 1948 and 1950.

Heilmann, Harry (Slug)
1894–1951
Detroit (AL 1914, 1916–29), Cincinnati (NL 1930, 1932)   OF, 1B   BR/TR

2,148 games	.342 ba
2,660 hits	183 hr
1,539 rbi	112 sb

If it was an odd-numbered year in the 1920s, you could count on Heilmann winning the AL batting title. After all, he led the league in 1921, 1923, 1925, and 1927. Among his contemporaries, only Rogers Hornsby was a better right-handed batter. Heilmann is tied for ninth place in lifetime batting average. One of the best players never to play in the World Series, he was inducted into the Hall of Fame in 1952.

Henderson, Dave (Hendu)

1958–

Seattle (AL 1981–86), Boston (AL 1986–87), San Francisco (NL 1987), Oakland (AL 1988–93 Active)
OF   **BR/TR**

1,482 games	.259 ba
1,275 hits	192 hr
677 rbi	48 sb

A stylish fielder and clutch hitter, Henderson wrote his name into Red Sox lore with his 1986 postseason heroics. The team was down 3–1 in games against the Angels when he smacked a dramatic ninth-inning, two-out homer that enabled the Sox to prolong the ALCS. In the World Series against the Mets, he homered again in the 10th inning of the sixth game to position Boston for its first title since 1918, only to see the team's expectations dashed by the Mets' remarkable rebound.

Henderson, Rickey

1957–

Oakland (AL 1979–84, 1989–93), New York (AL 1985–89), Toronto (AL 1993)   **OF**   **BR/TL**

1,993 games	.291 ba
2,139 hits	220 hr
784 rbi	1,095 sb

Unquestionably the greatest leadoff batter in the history of the game, Henderson has a combination of speed and power like few players before him. He currently holds major league records for career stolen bases and for leading off the game with a home run. Henderson has led the AL in stolen bases 11 times, including a major league record of 130 thefts in 1982. His best year might have been his first in the Bronx, when he hit .314 with a phenomenal 146 runs scored, 24 homers, and 72 RBI. Defensively, he has a reputation for inconsistent play and a poor arm, but at his best he covers a great deal of ground while making his unique "snatch catch."

Hendrick, George

1949–
Oakland (AL 1971–72), Cleveland (AL 1973–76), San Diego (NL 1977–78), St. Louis (NL 1978–84), Pittsburgh (NL 1985), California (AL 1985–88)
OF   BR/TR

2,048 games	.278 ba
1,980 hits	267 hr
1,111 rbi	59 sb

A quiet man who refused to talk to the press, Hendrick starred for a variety of teams throughout his long career. His best success came in St. Louis, where he hit .300 three times and knocked in more than 100 RBI twice. Defensively, Hendrick had good range and a strong arm.

Hendrix, Claude

1889–1944
Pittsburgh (NL 1911–13), Chicago (FL 1914–15), Chicago (NL 1916–20)   **P   BR/RHP**

360 games	2,371 innings
144-116 W–L	2.65 ERA
1,092 k's	17 saves

An outstanding pitcher who won 29 games in the Federal League in 1914 and 20 games twice in the NL, Hendrix left the majors under a cloud of suspicion in 1920. Believed to have fixed a game he had started earlier in the season, he was removed from his regular start before a game in September and never appeared in another major league game.

Henke, Tom (The Terminator)

1957–

Texas (AL 1982–84, 1993 Active), Toronto (AL 1985–92)   **P**   **RHP**

553 games	697 innings
37-35 W-L	2.67 ERA
774 k's	260 saves

When Henke enters the game, opposing teams know the end is near. He combines a blazing fastball and an elusive forkball to stifle AL hitters. In every year since 1986, Henke has recorded at least 20 saves and averaged more than one strikeout per inning.

Henneman, Mike

1961–

Detroit (AL 1987–93 Active)   **P**   **RHP**

432 games	605 innings
56-30 W-L	3.00 ERA
429 k's	128 saves

A sinker, slider pitcher, Henneman has survived as the ace of the Tigers bullpen since 1987 without a trick pitch or delivery. He has won in double digits three times and saved at least 20 games in five seasons.

Henrich, Tommy (Old Reliable)

1913–

New York (AL 1937–42, 1946–50)   **OF**
BL/TL

1,284 games	.282 ba
1,297 hits	183 hr
795 rbi	37 sb

Ruled a free agent by Commissioner Landis, Henrich signed with the Yankees, where he teamed with Joe DiMaggio and Charlie Keller in one of the most potent outfields in New York's illustrious history. Henrich was a serious man who worked hard for his success. Nicknamed "Old Reliable" for his ability to deliver in the clutch, Henrich drove home at least 85 runs in five seasons. His ninth-inning home run won game one of the 1949 World Series 1–0.

Herman, Floyd (Babe)
1903–1987
Brooklyn (NL 1926–31, 1945), Cincinnati (NL 1932, 1935–36), Chicago (NL 1933–34), Pittsburgh (NL 1935), Detroit (AL 1937)   **OF, 1B   BL/TL**

1,552 games	.324 ba
1,818 hits	181 hr
997 rbi	94 sb

Unusual events just kept happening to Herman on the ballfield, whether sliding into third base when two of his Brooklyn teammates already occupied the base, or circling under fly balls that eventually missed his glove and plunked him on the head or shoulder. The pride of Brooklyn's Daffiness Boys, Herman was an outstanding slugger who batted .393 (second in the NL) with 35 home runs and 130 RBI, in 1930.

Herman, William (Billy)
1909–1992
Chicago (NL 1931–41), Brooklyn (NL 1941–43, 1946), Boston (NL 1946), Pittsburgh (NL 1947); MGR—Pittsburgh (NL 1947), Boston (AL 1964–66)   **2B, MGR   BR/TR**

1,922 games	.304 ba
2,345 hits	47 hr
839 rbi	67 sb

A masterful defensive second baseman who excelled at turning the double play, Herman was also perhaps the best hit-and-run artist of all time. He was a team player who led the Cubs to pennants in 1932, 1935, and 1938 and helped bring Brooklyn its first flag in 21 years in 1941. Named to 10 All-Star games, Herman was inducted into the Hall of Fame in 1975.

Hernandez, Guillermo (Willie)

1954–

Chicago (NL 1977–83), Philadelphia (NL 1983), Detroit (AL 1984–89)   P   BL/LHP

744 games	1,044 innings
70-63 W–L	3.38 ERA
788 k's	147 saves

On the heels of his Cy Young Award season in 1984, when he went 9–3 with 32 saves, Hernandez foreswore the nickname "Willie" for his given name, Guillermo. He had seven years of only mixed success in the NL, but his screwball helped him to become an outstanding reliever for Detroit.

Hernandez, Keith (Mex)

1953–

St. Louis (NL 1974–83), New York (NL 1983–89), Cleveland (AL 1990)   1B   BL/TL

2,088 games	.296 ba
2,182 hits	162 hr
1,071 rbi	98 sb

The finest-fielding first baseman of his generation, Hernandez was equally adept at ranging to his right for grounders, and fielding bunts and throwing rapidly to second. Hernandez had a strong arm and never hesitated to use it. At bat, he was great in clutch situations and knocked in at least 90 runs six times. A scientific hitter, Hernandez sprayed the ball to all fields but showed his most power to right- and left-center. In spite of his many accomplishments, he was an insecure player prone to inexplicable batting slumps, and he needed regular encouragement to succeed. In 1979, he led the NL in batting (.344) and was named co-winner of the MVP award.

Hershiser, Orel (Bulldog)

1958–
Los Angeles (NL 1983–93 Active)   P   BR/RHP

322 games	2,020 innings
128-96 W–L	2.95 ERA
1,371 k's	5 saves

Hershiser's boyish looks belie his fierce determination on the mound. An outstanding repertoire of curves, sliders, and fastballs thrown with pinpoint control made him the top pitcher of the game in 1988, when he set a major league record by hurling 59 consecutive scoreless innings. That year, he went 23–8 and single-handedly pitched the Dodgers to the pennant and the World Series. The following year, he led the NL in innings pitched for the third successive year, but he suffered a serious rotator cuff injury. Following surgery in 1990, Hershiser had difficulty recapturing his earlier form.

Herzog, Charles (Buck)

1885–1953
New York (NL 1908–09, 1911–13, 1916–17), Boston (NL 1910–11, 1918–19), Cincinnati (NL 1914–16), Chicago (NL 1919–20); MGR— Cincinnati (NL 1914–16)   2B, 3B, SS, MGR
BR/TR

1,493 games	.259 ba
1,370 hits	20 hr
445 rbi	312 sb

Herzog went directly from the University of Maryland into the starting lineup of the New York Giants in 1908 and enjoyed a long and sometimes controversial career. He engaged in a series of brawls with Ty Cobb during one spring training, withstood a near-mutiny by his charges while managing Cincinnati, was stabbed by an irate fan who thought he was involved in the fix of the 1919 World Series, and testified against Rube Benton, who not only knew of the fix but bet on the outcome. A snappy second baseman on three consecutive Giants pennant winners (1911–13), Herzog batted .290 in 1911.

Herzog, Dorrel (Whitey, The White Rat)

1931–

Washington (AL 1956–58), Kansas City (AL 1958–60), Baltimore (AL 1961–62), Detroit (AL 1963); MGR—Texas (AL 1973), California (AL 1974), Kansas City (AL 1975–79), St. Louis (NL 1980–90)   OF, MGR   BL/TL

634 games	.257 ba
414 hits	25 hr
172 rbi	13 sb

The winningest manager ever for the Royals and second only to Red Schoendienst in Cardinals history, Herzog was a master motivator and manipulator of talent. He won three division titles in Kansas City but lost out to the Yanks each time. He was criticized for lifting his relief pitchers too frequently. In St. Louis, he won the World Series in 1982; he took pennants in 1985 and 1987, only to lose both times in seven games. Herzog's teams were known for their aggressive style, strong pitching, and sound defense.

Higbe, Kirby

1915–1985

Chicago (NL 1937–39), Philadelphia (NL 1939–40), Brooklyn (NL 1941–43, 1946–47), Pittsburgh (NL 1947–49), New York (NL 1949–50)   P
BR/RHP

418 games	1,952 innings
118-101 W–L	3.69 ERA
971 k's	24 saves

A hard-throwing right-hander who led the NL in walks four times and in strikeouts once, Higby won 22 games for the Dodgers in 1941, when the Brooks won their first pennant in 21 years. In 1947, he revealed that a petition was circulating among Dodgers players protesting the inclusion of Jackie Robinson on the roster. He was not one of the signees, but he was soon traded to Pittsburgh.

Higgins, Michael (Pinky)

1909–1969

Philadelphia (AL 1930, 1933–36), Boston (AL 1937–38, 1946), Detroit (AL 1939–44, 1946); MGR—Boston (AL 1955–62)   **3B, MGR**
BR/TR

1,802 games	.292 ba
1,941 hits	140 hr
1,075 rbi	61 sb

A quiet man off the field, Higgins was anything but reserved with a bat in his hands. He hit over .300 four times and knocked in 106 runs in consecutive seasons (1937–38). His major league record for consecutive hits—12 in a row in 1938—still stands.

Higuera, Ted

1958–

Milwaukee (AL 1985–91, 1993 Active)   **P**   **LHP**

196 games	1,321 innings
93–59 W–L	3.46 ERA
1,046 k's	

Sidelined in 1991 by a rotator cuff injury, Higuera had been the top left-hander in the AL prior to being hurt. Frequently compared with his Mexican countryman, Fernando Valenzuela, Higuera throws a tantalizing screwball as well as a good fastball and curve. He won 20 games in 1986 and 18 in 1987, but he was plagued by injuries starting in 1989.

Hill, Preston (Pete)

1880–1951

Chicago American Giants (1914–17), Detroit Stars (1920–21), Milwaukee Bears (1923), Baltimore Black Sox (1924–25)   **OF**   **BL/TR**

117 games	.312 ba
127 hits	6 hr
9 sb	

Possibly the finest black player of the early 20th century, Hill starred at the plate and in the field. He smacked the ball to all fields, and defensively he showed great range and a strong arm.

Hiller, John

1943–

Detroit (AL 1965–70, 1972–80)   **P**   **BR/LHP**

545 games	1,242 innings
87–76 W–L	2.83 ERA
1,036 k's	125 saves

Hiller recovered from a heart attack to become the greatest relief pitcher in Tigers history. In 1973, he went 10–5 with an AL-best 38 saves and a minuscule 1.44 ERA; the following year, he won 17 games in relief while pitching 150 innings.

Hines, Paul

1852–1935

Chicago (NL 1876–77), Providence (NL 1878–85),
Washington (NL 1886–87), Indianapolis (NL
1888–89), Pittsburgh (NL 1890), Boston (NL 1890),
Washington (AA 1891) OF BR/TR

1,481 games	.301 ba
1,881 hits	56 hr
751 rbi	153 sb

The only man to play for Providence in each year of its
NL tenure, Hines won the NL triple crown in 1878
with a .358 batting average, four home runs, and 50
RBI. He was probably the first deaf man to play in the
major leagues.

Hisle, Larry

1947–

Philadelphia (NL 1968–71), Minnesota (AL
1973–77), Milwaukee (AL 1978–82) OF
BR/TR

1,197 games	.273 ba
1,146 hits	166 hr
674 rbi	128 sb

Highly touted as a Phillies rookie, Hisle struggled in
Philadelphia but hit his stride in Minnesota, developing into a strong power hitter and a fine outfielder. His
best year came in 1977, when he hit .302 with 28
home runs and an AL-high 119 RBI. In 1978, he
signed a free-agent contract with Milwaukee and became an instant success, belting 34 homers with 115
RBI. Unfortunately, the extremely popular Hisle suffered a severe shoulder injury that limited his effectiveness thereafter.

Hodges, Gil

1924–1972

Brooklyn (NL 1943, 1947–57), Los Angeles (NL 1958–61), New York (NL 1962–63);
MGR—Washington (AL 1963–67), New York (NL 1968–71)   1B, MGR   BR/TR

2,071 games	.273 ba
1,921 hits	370 hr
1,274 rbi	63 sb

No player commanded more respect, both on his own team and around the league, than Gil Hodges. He had an inner strength that inspired confidence in his teammates as a player and in his troops as a manager. Signed by Brooklyn as a catcher, Hodges moved to first base in 1948, a position where he excelled, due in part to his enormous hands and quick feet. At bat, he was a powerful pull hitter who tended to step in the bucket and have trouble with curve balls. Nevertheless, he slammed at least 20 homers in 11 consecutive seasons (1949–59) and knocked in at least 100 runs in seven consecutive years (1949–55). As a manager, he led the previously inept Mets to the World Series title in 1969. It remains one of baseball's great injustices that Hodges is not in the Hall of Fame.

Hoerner, Joe

1936–

Houston (NL 1963–64), St. Louis (NL 1966–69), Philadelphia (NL 1970–72, 1975), Atlanta (NL 1972–73), Kansas City (AL 1973–74), Texas (AL 1976), Cincinnati (NL 1977)   P   BR/LHP

493 games	562 innings
39-34 W–L	2.99 ERA
412 k's	99 saves

Hoerner was a sidearm sinker-baller who made life difficult for left-handed batters. Brought in almost exclusively to face lefties he often proved to be unhittable. Hoerner spent his best years in St. Louis, where he saved at least 13 games a season in 1966–69.

Hoffer, Bill (Wizard)
1870–1959

Baltimore (NL 1895–98), Pittsburgh (NL 1898–99), Cleveland (AL 1901)　P　**BR/RHP**

161 games	1,254 innings
92-46 W–L	3.75 ERA
314 k's	3 saves

In his first three seasons in the big leagues, Hoffer compiled a record of 77–25 and appeared headed for stardom. Unfortunately, he won only 14 games thereafter due to a sore arm. He retired after an abortive comeback in 1901 with Cleveland.

Hogan, James (Shanty)
1906–1967

Boston (NL 1925–27, 1933–35), New York (NL 1928–32), Washington (AL 1936–37)　C
BR/TR

989 games	.295 ba
939 hits	61 hr
474 rbi	6 sb

Hogan proved that you could be fat and still play major league baseball. Ridiculed by fans and press alike, he shrugged off criticism of his 250-pound frame to hit over .300 in four consecutive seasons for the Giants (1928–31). In the offensive-crazy season of 1930, he hit .339 with 13 homers and 75 RBI.

Holland, Bill
1901–

Detroit Stars, Chicago American Giants, New York Lincoln Giants, Brooklyn Royal Giants, New York Black Yankees, Philadelphia Stars　P　**BR/RHP**

1,336 innings	99-81 W–L
575 k's	5 saves

Holland did his best pitching for the New York Black Yankees in the thirties. He had an overpowering fastball and an effective curve.

Holmes, Tommy (Kelly)

1917–

Boston (NL 1942–51), Brooklyn (NL 1952);
MGR—Boston (NL 1951–52)   **OF, MGR**
BL/TL

1,320 games	.302 ba
1,507 hits	88 hr
581 rbi	40 sb

A quiet, undemonstrative player, Holmes was a great hitter with extra-base power and an uncanny ability to put his bat on the ball. In 1945, he batted .352 with 47 doubles, 28 home runs, 125 runs scored, and 117 RBI. That year, he became the only player ever to lead his league both in homers and fewest strikeouts, whiffing only nine times.

Holtzman, Ken

1945–

Chicago (NL 1965–71, 1978–79), Oakland (AL 1972–75), Baltimore (AL 1976), New York (AL 1976–78)   **P   BR/LHP**

451 games	2,867 innings
174-150 W–L	3.49 ERA
1,601 k's	3 saves

An independent thinker on the mound, Holtzman rarely threw to first base to hold the runner on. He won 20 games in 1973 and was an important starting pitcher for the three-time champion Athletics of 1972–74. Holtzman pitched two no-hitters for the Cubs and hit a home run in the 1974 World Series after not batting for the entire regular season. During his tenure with the Yankees, he was ostracized by manager Billy Martin and rarely pitched in 1977.

Hooper, Harry

1887–1974

Boston (AL 1909–20), Chicago (AL 1921–25)   **OF**
BL/TR

2,309 games	.281 ba
2,466 hits	75 hr
817 rbi	375 sb

Batting leadoff for the four-time champion Red Sox squads of the 1910s, Harry Hooper set the table for a dynamic offense. Although he played in the shadow of Tris Speaker for much of his career, he was a brilliant outfielder who perfected the sliding catch, and he possessed a powerful arm. Hooper was inducted into the Hall of Fame in 1971.

Hooton, Burt (Happy)

1950–

Chicago (NL 1971–75), Los Angeles (NL 1975–84), Texas (AL 1985)   **P**   **BR/RHP**

480 games	2,652 innings
151-136 W–L	3.38 ERA
1,491 k's	7 saves

How many pitchers can claim to have introduced a pitch? The dour Hooton baffled National League batters for more than a dozen years with the knuckle-curve. He made a big splash in the majors by fanning 15 Mets in a late-season start in 1971. As a Cubs rookie in 1972, he hurled a no-hitter against the weak-hitting Phillies. After being traded to the Dodgers in 1975, Hooton ran off 12 victories in a row. In his best season, 1978, he won 19 games with a 2.71 ERA. Hooton's career was limited by persistent arm trouble thereafter.

Horlen, Joe

1937–

Chicago (AL 1961–71), Oakland (AL 1972)   **P**
BR/RHP

361 games	2,002 innings
116–117 W–L	3.11 ERA
1,065 k's	4 saves

No matter how well Horlen pitched, he was never assured of victory when he played for the anemic-hitting White Sox of the sixties. In 1964, his ERA was a meager 1.88, yet he was only able to amass a record of 13–8. Only when he won the AL ERA crown in 1967 (2.06) did he earn as many as 19 victories. Between 1964 and 1968, the highest ERA he had was 2.88, but his won-lost record was a disappointing 67–56. Horlen credited his pitching success to a cut fastball that moved away from right-hand batters.

Horner, Bob

1957–
Atlanta (NL 1978–86), St. Louis (NL 1988)   **3B, 1B   BR/TR**

1,020 games	.277 ba
1,047 hits	218 hr
685 rbi	14 sb

Horner never got to ride the buses in the minor leagues; he stepped directly from the campus of Arizona State University into the Atlanta Braves' starting lineup. His short, quick swing generated tremendous power, producing at least 20 homers in seven seasons. In 1986, he slammed four home runs in one game. Defensively, Horner was a man without a position.

Hornsby, Rogers (Rajah)

1896–1963
St. Louis (NL 1915–26, 1933), New York (NL 1927), Boston (NL 1928), Chicago (NL 1929–32), St. Louis (AL 1933–37); MGR—St. Louis (NL 1925–26), New York (NL 1927), Boston (NL 1928), Chicago (NL 1930–32), St. Louis (AL 1933–37, 1952), Cincinnati (NL 1952–53)   **2B, SS, MGR BR/TR**

2,259 games	.358 ba
2,930 hits	301 hr
1,584 rbi	135 sb

The major leagues' greatest right-handed batter, Hornsby averaged .402 in 1921–25, including .424 in 1924 (a 20th-century high). At bat, he stood well off the plate. Rajah won six consecutive batting titles (1920–25) and managed St. Louis to its first NL pennant and World Series crown in 1926. Traded in 1927 to the Giants, he began a hegira around the majors, due in part to his irascible nature. As a manager, he had little patience for those without his skills, which usually meant his entire roster. Off the diamond, Hornsby had a mania for gambling on the horses. He was inducted into the Hall of Fame in 1942.

Horton, Willie

1942–

Detroit (AL 1963–77), Texas (AL 1977), Cleveland (AL 1978), Oakland (AL 1978), Toronto (AL 1978), Seattle (AL 1979–80)   **OF, DH**   **BR/TR**

2,028 games	.273 ba
1,993 hits	325 hr
1,163 rbi	20 sb

The heavily muscled Horton struck a menacing stance in the batter's box, and every pitcher was well aware of his awesome power. He started his career with a bang, slamming 29 homers in 1965 and 27 the following year. When the Tigers won the World Series in 1968, Horton belted 36 roundtrippers. A series of leg injuries limited his playing time throughout his career, but his total of 262 homers ranks fourth in Tigers history.

Hough, Charlie

1948–

Los Angeles (NL 1970–80), Texas (AL 1980–90), Chicago (AL 1991–92), Florida (NL 1993 Active)
P   BR/RHP

837 games	3,686 innings
211-207 W–L	3.70 ERA
2,297 k's	61 saves

It appears that Hough might pitch forever. Since he began throwing the knuckle ball full time, he has just rolled on year after year, impervious to advancing age. Hough started his career in the Dodgers bullpen but became a starter after moving over to Texas in the AL. The ace of the Rangers staff, he won 17 games in 1986 and 18 the following year. A native of South Florida, Hough was a canny draft choice of the expansion Florida Marlins.

Houk, Ralph (Major)

1919–
New York (AL 1947–54); MGR—New York (AL 1961–63, 1966–73), Detroit (AL 1974–77), Boston (AL 1981–84)   **C, MGR   BR/TR**

| 91 games | .272 ba |
| 43 hits | 20 rbi |

As third-string catcher during the run of five consecutive championship seasons for the Yanks (1949–53), Houk saw minimum active duty. He acquired fame as the manager who replaced Casey Stengel on the Yankees, leading them to the pennant in his first three seasons at the helm. Houk moved to the general manager's office at New York but could not stem the Yankees' slide from the top. He returned to manage the team in the late sixties, but he could not serve under new Yankees' owner George Steinbrenner. Thereafter, he enjoyed long tenures at both Detroit and Boston. Always regarded as a players' manager, Houk was not a master tactician in the dugout. Instead, he relied on creating an atmosphere of goodwill to motivate his players.

Howard, Elston (Ellie)

1929–1980

Kansas City Monarchs (1948–50), New York (AL 1955–67), Boston (AL 1967–68)   C, OF

BR/TR

1,605 games	.274 ba
1,471 hits	167 hr
762 rbi	9 sb

The first black player to wear Yankees pinstripes, Howard was an outstanding defensive catcher and smart hitter. Blocked by Yogi Berra from becoming the regular catcher until 1961, he played left field and first base. In 1961, he batted .348 with 21 homers, and in 1964 he was voted the AL MVP for his .313 average and defensive brilliance. Howard had a strong, accurate arm and excelled at blocking pitches in the dirt. At bat, he used a closed batting stance to slam balls to the opposite field. The Yankees retired his uniform number 32.

Howard, Frank (Hondo)

1936–

Los Angeles (NL 1958–64), Washington (AL 1965–71), Texas (AL 1972), Detroit (AL 1972–73); MGR—San Diego (NL 1981), New York (NL 1983)

OF, 1B, MGR   BR/TR

1,902 games	.273 ba
1,774 hits	382 hr
1,119 rbi	8 sb

Howard was the gentle giant of the ballfield, a Paul Bunyanesque figure whose 6-foot, 7-inch frame housed a bundle of enthusiasm and energy. Touted by the Dodgers as a great power prospect, he did belt 31 homers in 1962, but he truly tormented AL pitchers while swinging for the Senators. From 1968 to 1970, he slugged 44, 48, and 44 home runs.

Hoy, William (Dummy)
1862–1961

Washington (NL 1888–89, 1892–93), Buffalo (PL 1890), St. Louis (AA 1891), Cincinnati (NL 1894–97, 1902), Louisville (NL 1898–99), Chicago (AL 1901) **OF** **BL/TR**

1,796 games	.287 ba
2,044 hits	40 hr
726 rbi	594 sb

Hoy was one of the swiftest center fielders of his generation, and he accomplished great things at bat without being able to hear or speak. Twice a .300 hitter, Hoy lived to throw out the first ball in the third game of the 1961 World Series at Cincinnati.

Hoyt, Lamarr
1955–

Chicago (AL 1979–84), San Diego (NL 1985–86)
P **BR/RHP**

244 games	1,311 innings
98-68 W–L	3.99 ERA
681 k's	10 saves

Recipient of the AL Cy Young Award in 1983, when he won 24 games despite a 3.66 ERA that ranked 17th in the league, Hoyt epitomized the contemporary White Sox slogan, "Winning Ugly." A workhorse on the mound, he slumped in 1984 and was traded to San Diego, where his career was ended by an injury.

Hoyt, Waite (Schoolboy)
1899–1984

New York (NL 1918, 1932), Boston (AL 1919–20), New York (AL 1921–30), Detroit (AL 1930–31), Philadelphia (AL 1931), Brooklyn (NL 1932, 1937–38), Pittsburgh (NL 1933–37) **P**
BR/RHP

674 games	3,762 innings
237-182 W–L	3.59 ERA
1,206 k's	52 saves

A schoolboy hero in Brooklyn, Hoyt kept his boyish good looks throughout his 20-year career. He starred on the Yankees' powerhouse teams of the 1920s, winning 22 games in 1927 and 23 the following year, plus six World Series games in six seasons. An intelligent, articulate player, Hoyt broadcast Cincinnati games for over 20 years after his retirement from the field. He was inducted into the Hall of Fame in 1969.

Hrabosky, Al (The Mad Hungarian)

1949–

St. Louis (NL 1970–77), Kansas City (AL 1978–79), Atlanta (NL 1980–82)   **P   BR/LHP**

545 games	722 innings
64-35 W–L	3.10 ERA
548 k's	97 saves

A theatrical reliever, Hrabosky went into a trancelike state before delivering each pitch. He stalked the mound and stared menacingly at opposing batters, but in actuality his good fastball and slider, not his dramatics, struck batters out. In 1975, he went 13–3, with an NL-best 22 saves and a stingy 1.66 ERA.

Hrbek, Kent (Herbie)

1960–

Minnesota (AL 1981–93 Active)   **1B   BL/TR**

1,666 games	.283 ba
1,675 hits	283 hr
1,033 rbi	37 sb

Hrbek ranks second to Harmon Killebrew in career home runs and RBI among Twins players. He hit at least 20 homers every year from 1984 to 1991 and has knocked in more than 90 RBI five times. Despite a bulky build, Hrbek is a fine-fielding first baseman.

Hubbell, Carl (King Carl, The Meal Ticket)

1903–1988

New York (NL 1928–43)   P   BB/LHP

535 games	3,590 innings
253-154 W–L	2.97 ERA
1,677 k's	33 saves

Hubbell was the greatest left-hander in Giants history. His favorite pitch was the screwball, which he threw at different speeds. A master at mixing pitches, Hubbell had great control and could spot his less-than-overpowering fastball. A great clutch performer, he won two MVP awards and pitched the Giants into the World Series three times. In the 1934 All-Star Game, he made baseball history by striking out Ruth, Gehrig, Foxx, Simmons, and Cronin in succession. Hubbell's uniform number 11 was retired by the Giants, and he was inducted into the Hall of Fame in 1947.

Hudlin, Willis (Ace)

1906–

Cleveland (AL 1926–40), Washington (AL 1940), St. Louis (AL 1940, 1944), New York (NL 1940)   P
BR/RHP

491 games	2,613 innings
158-156 W–L	4.41 ERA
677 k's	31 saves

A consistent big winner for the Indians, Hudlin reached double digits in victories in all but two seasons between 1927 and 1937. As a rookie in 1927, he won 18 games. Hudlin's best pitch was a sinker ball.

Huggins, Miller (Mighty Mite)

1879–1929

Cincinnati (NL 1904–09), St. Louis (NL 1910–16); MGR—St. Louis (NL 1913–17), New York (AL 1918–29)   2B, MGR   BB/TR

1,586 games	.265 ba
1,474 hits	9 hr
318 rbi	324 sb

A combative second baseman who was a graduate of Cincinnati Law School, Huggins is remembered today as the manager of the teams that began the Yankees dynasty; he won six pennants and three World Series. He was elected to the Hall of Fame in 1964.

Hughes, Sammy
1910–1973
Louisville Black Caps (1930–31), Pittsburgh Crawfords (1931), Washington Pilots (1932), Washington Elite Giants (1933, 1936–37), Nashville Elite Giants (1934), Columbus Elite Giants (1935), Baltimore Elite Giants (1938–40, 1942, 1946)   **2B**
BR/TR

287 games	.296 ba
320 hits	15 hr
10 sb	

Widely acclaimed as the best defensive second baseman ever to play in the Negro Leagues, Hughes had excellent skills at the plate and in the field. He sent rockets to all fields and had the ability to drop a bunt or play hit-and-run. Defensively, he ranged far to his left and right, and he had a great throwing arm.

Hughson, Cecil (Tex)
1916–1993
Boston (AL 1941–44, 1946–49)   **P**   **BR/RHP**

225 games	1,375 innings
96-54 W–L	2.94 ERA
693 k's	17 saves

The Red Sox uncovered a gem in Hughson, who won 22 games in 1942 and 20 in 1946. In between, he went 18–5 in 1944. Unfortunately, Hughson's career was cut short by arm miseries.

Hunt, Ron

1941–

New York (NL 1963–66), Los Angeles (NL 1967),
San Francisco (NL 1968–70), Montreal (NL
1971–74), St. Louis (NL 1974)   **2B**   **BR/TR**

1,483 games	.273 ba
1,429 hits	39 hr
370 rbi	65 sb

The darling of the New Breed of fan that followed the
Mets in their infancy, Hunt became the first Met to
start in the All-Star Game in 1963. A scrappy hitter
with little power, Hunt specialized in getting hit by
pitches. Wearing a loose-fitting uniform, he stood
right on top of the plate and dared pitchers to plunk
him. In 1971, moundsmen obliged Hunt a record 50
times.

Hunter, Jim (Catfish)

1946–

Kansas City (AL 1965–67), Oakland (AL 1968–74),
New York (AL 1975–79)   **P**   **BR/RHP**

500 games	3,449 innings
224-166 W–L	3.26 ERA
2,012 k's	1 save

Hunter first emerged as a star late in the 1968 season
when he pitched a perfect game against the Twins. He
had a smooth, easy delivery and pinpoint control of his
fastball, curve, and slider. Hunter challenged hitters; as
a result, he surrendered more than his share of homers,
but most came with no runners on base. Batters hit an
amazing number of deep flies against him that outfielders caught on the warning track. A tremendous
clutch pitcher, he won at least 21 games in five successive seasons (1971–75). Hunter won the Cy Young
Award in 1974 for his 25 victories. He hurled a remarkable 30 complete games and won 23 times in his
first season for the Yankees the following year. Arm injuries ended his career prematurely, but his stellar re-

cord resulted in his induction into the Hall of Fame in 1987.

Hurst, Bruce

1958–

Boston (AL 1980–88), San Diego (NL 1989–92),
Colorado (NL 1993 Active)　P　　**BL/LHP**

371 games	2,379 innings
143-112 W–L	3.87 ERA
1,665 k's	

Hurst knows how to pitch. Utilizing a great curve and change-up while spotting his fastball, he has continued to stifle opposing batters for over a decade. He won in double digits every year from 1983 to 1992, although arm trouble limited his play in 1993. Hurst enjoyed his breakthrough season in 1986, when he went 13–8 for the Red Sox's last pennant-winning team. In the World Series that fall, he defeated the Mets twice but could not stop them a third time in game seven.

Hutchinson, Fred (Hutch)

1919–1964

Detroit (AL 1939–40, 1946–53); MGR—Detroit
(AL 1952–54), St. Louis (NL 1956–58), Cincinnati
(NL 1959–64)　P, **MGR**　　**BL/RHP**

242 games	1,464 innings
95-71 W–L	3.73 ERA
591 k's	7 saves

A top-flight pitcher for the Tigers, Hutchinson enjoyed five consecutive winning seasons (1946–50) as a starter. He turned to managing after his playing days and won the 1961 NL pennant in Cincinnati—the Reds' first flag in 21 years. A big bear of a man with an explosive temper but a heart of gold, Hutchinson was a very popular skipper; the Reds retired his uniform number 1. He fought a gallant battle with cancer but succumbed following the 1964 season.

Hutchison, Bill (Wild Bill)

1859–1926

Kansas City (UA 1884), Chicago (NL 1889–95), St. Louis (NL 1897)   P   BR/RHP

375 games	3,083 innings
184-163 W–L	3.58 ERA
1,236 k's	3 saves

A graduate of Yale University, Hutchison won a phenomenal 123 games in 1890–92 for Chicago after his delayed arrival in the majors. He had poor control of his one pitch, a strong fastball, and when the mound was moved to 60 feet, 6 inches from home plate, his performance deteriorated.

I

Irvin, Monte

1919–

Newark Eagles (1937–42, 1945–48), New York (NL 1949–55), Chicago (NL 1956)   OF   BR/TR

764 games	.293 ba
731 hits	99 hr
443 rbi	28 sb

Irvin spent most of his most productive years in the Negro Leagues and didn't join the Giants until he was 30 years old. He and Hank Thompson were the first blacks to play for the Giants. In 1951, he sparked New York's miraculous comeback to overtake the Dodgers in the pennant race when he batted .312 with 24 home runs and a league-best 121 RBI. At the plate, he swung from a wide stance and took a short stride. Irvin was inducted into the Hall of Fame in 1973.

J

Jackson, Joe (Shoeless Joe)

1889–1951

Philadelphia (AL 1908–09), Cleveland (AL
1910–15), Chicago (AL 1915–20)   OF   BL/TR

1,332 games	.356 ba
1,772 hits	54 hr
785 rbi	202 sb

Jackson's exclusion from the Hall of Fame remains one
of baseball's worst injustices. One of the truly great hitters in baseball history, his lifetime average ranks third
all-time. Swinging a bat nicknamed "Black Betsy,"
Jackson drove line shots to all fields with the sweetest
swing in the big show. Implicated in the Black Sox
scandal of 1919 along with seven Chicago teammates,
he was barred from baseball by Commissioner Landis.
Despite his alleged involvement in the fix, he hit .375
with six RBI in the 1919 World Series.

Jackson, Larry (Cocky)

1931–1990

St. Louis (NL 1955–62), Chicago (NL 1963–66),
Philadelphia (NL 1966–68)   P   BR/RHP

558 games	3,262 innings
194–183 W–L	3.40 ERA
1,709 k's	20 saves

Jackson utilized the complete repertoire of fastball,
curve, and slider to baffle NL batters for the better part
of two decades. A workhorse, he led the NL in starts
(38) and innings pitched (282) in 1960 and in wins in
1964 (24). Unfortunately, for most of his career he
played on second-division teams.

Jackson, Reggie (Mr. October, Buck)

1946–

Kansas City (AL 1967), Oakland (AL 1968–75, 1987), Baltimore (AL 1976), New York (AL 1977–81), California (AL 1982–86)   **OF, DH**
BL/TL

2,820 games	.262 ba
2,584 hits	563 hr
1,702 rbi	228 sb

Jackson was a flamboyant performer who thrived on pressure situations. In five World Series, he batted .357 with 10 home runs and 24 RBI. In the 1977 series, he slammed three home runs on three successive at-bats in the decisive sixth game to cement the Yankees' victory. Jackson is the only man to hit more than 100 home runs for three different franchises. Ironically, his best individual season performance—41 home runs and 111 RBI with a .300 average in 1980—did not produce a pennant winner, as the Yanks fell to the Royals in the ALCS. At the plate, Jackson took a hearty cut with each swing, and his strikeouts could be as dramatic as his long homers—witness his strikeout against Bob Welch in the 1977 World Series. In the field, he grew less proficient with advancing age, and duty as the designated hitter became the only way to get his bat into the lineup. He was inducted into the Hall of Fame in 1993.

Jackson, Travis (Stonewall)

1903–1987

New York (NL 1922–36)   SS, 3B   **BR/TR**

1,656 games	.291 ba
1,768 hits	135 hr
929 rbi	71 sb

Baseball contemporaries of Jackson felt that his induction into the Hall of Fame in 1982 was long overdue. A great team player who fielded brilliantly, he had outstanding range and a superior throwing arm. At bat,

Jackson was dangerous in the clutch, and he hit over .300 six times. In 1930, he batted a career-high .339.

Jackson, Vincent (Bo)

1962–
Kansas City (AL 1986–90), Chicago (AL 1991, 1993 Active)   OF, DH   BR/TR

619 games	.247 ba
542 hits	128 hr
372 rbi	81 sb

Jackson was an advertising agency's dream whose face became one of the most recognizable in America. Considered by many to be one of the greatest athletes in sports history, he excelled at football and made his mark in baseball with his prodigious home runs. Prior to his hip injury and resulting replacement surgery, Jackson was the fastest man in sports; his recovery alone stamps him as the hardest-working and most courageous man in sports. In his most complete season on the diamond, he smashed 32 homers with 105 RBI in 1989. Frequently, it is feast or famine for Jackson; he also struck out 172 times that season and regularly fanned more than 125 times per year.

Jamieson, Charlie (Cuckoo)

1893–1969
Washington (AL 1915–17), Philadelphia (AL 1917–18), Cleveland (AL 1919–32)   OF
BL/TL

1,779 games	.303 ba
1,990 hits	18 hr
552 rbi	132 sb

A consistent .300 hitter throughout his 18-year career, Jamieson batted .345 in 1923 and .359 in 1924 for Cleveland. In 1923, he led the AL with 222 hits, and he scored 130 runs. Jamieson was a fine left fielder with one of the most accurate throwing arms of his generation.

Jansen, Larry

1920–

New York (NL 1947–54), Cincinnati (NL 1956)   P
BR/RHP

291 games	1,765 innings
122-89 W–L	3.58 ERA
842 k's	10 saves

Between 1947 and 1951, Jansen was one of the top right-handers in the NL, winning a total of 96 games. His nifty 21–5 debut in 1947 would have ordinarily attracted a great deal of attention in New York, but that was also the season that Jackie Robinson broke the color barrier in Brooklyn. In 1951, he led the NL with 23 wins and proved unbeatable down the stretch in the Giants' miraculous comeback.

Jefferies, Gregg

1967–

New York (NL 1987–91), Kansas City (AL 1992), St. Louis (NL 1993 Active)   2B, 3B   BB/TR

759 games	.290 ba
830 hits	68 hr
363 rbi	128 sb

Rushed by the Mets to the major leagues and then pampered once he arrived, Jefferies never fulfilled the high expectations of the Mets management. Scouts raved about his short, quick stroke from either side of the plate and his fine speed, but they must have been looking the other way when he played the field. Inept at any position for the Mets, Jefferies appears to have finally found a home at first base for the Cardinals. He led the NL in doubles in 1990 (40), but many of his hardest-hit balls always seemed to go directly into a fielder's glove. Jefferies enjoyed a breakthrough season under the relaxed leadership of Joe Torre in St. Louis in 1993, batting .342.

Jenkins, Clarence (Fats)

1898–1968

New York Lincoln Giants (1920, 1928, 1930–31, 1934), Atlantic City Bacharach Giants (1922, 1928–29), Harrisburgh Giants (1923–27), Pittsburgh Crawfords (1932, 1938), New York Black Yankees (1932, 1936–38), Brooklyn Eagles (1935)

OF, MGR   BL/TL

468 games	.324 ba
610 hits	13 hr
47 sb	

The swift-footed Jenkins also played professional basketball in the twenties. He did his best work for the New York Black Yankees in the thirties.

Jenkins, Ferguson (Fergie)

1943–

Philadelphia (NL 1965–66), Chicago (NL 1966–73, 1982–83), Texas (AL 1974–75, 1978–81), Boston (AL 1976–77)   **P   BR/RHP**

664 games	4,500 innings
284-226 W–L	3.34 ERA
3,192 k's	7 saves

A Cubs hero who won 20 or more games for six consecutive seasons between 1967 and 1972, Jenkins was renowned for his remarkable durability as well as his great slider and precise control. He won the Cy Young Award in 1971 in recognition of his league-leading 24 victories and 30 complete games. Cubdom was shocked by his trade to Texas in 1974, but Fergie showed his stuff by winning 25 games. He was inducted into the Hall of Fame in 1991.

Jennings, Hugh (Hughie Ee-yah)
1869–1928

Louisville (AA 1891), Louisville (NL 1892–93),
Baltimore (NL 1893–99), Brooklyn (NL
1899–1900, 1903), Philadelphia (NL 1901–02),
Detroit (AL 1907, 1909, 1912, 1918);
MGR—Detroit (AL 1907–20), New York (NL
1924)　SS, 1B, MGR　BR/TR

1,285 games	.312 ba
1,532 hits	18 hr
840 rbi	359 sb

The outstanding shortstop on the great Orioles squads
of the 1890s, Jennings made a speciality of getting hit
by pitched balls. In 1896, he batted .401 and was
plunked 49 times. As manager of the dominant Tigers
teams of Ty Cobb's era, he popularized yelling
"Eeyah" to encourage his players.

Jensen, Jackie
1927–1982

New York (AL 1950–52), Washington (AL
1952–53), Boston (AL 1954–59, 1961)　OF
BR/TR

1,438 games	.279 ba
1,463 hits	199 hr
929 rbi	143 sb

Jensen arrived at the Yankees' spring training camp in
1950 as a much-heralded college football player who
had stardom written all over him. Unfortunately, there
was no room in the Yankees outfield for any rookie. He
was eventually shipped to Washington and on to Boston, where his career flowered. A powerful slugger with
great speed, Jensen led the AL in RBI in 1955 (116),
1958 (122), and 1959 (112), and in stolen bases in
1954 (22). A fear of flying cut Jensen's career short.

John, Tommy

1943–

Cleveland (AL 1963–64), Chicago (AL 1965–71),
Los Angeles (NL 1972–74, 1976–78), New York (AL
1979–82, 1986–89), California (AL 1982–85),
Oakland (AL 1985)   P   BR/LHP

760 games	4,710 innings
288-231 W–L	3.34 ERA
2,245 k's	4 saves

John wanted to pitch forever. After a tendon transfer operation in 1975, "the man with the bionic arm" continued to baffle batters until the age of 45. At his best, John threw a sinking fastball (some claimed it was a spitter or a scuffed ball) and a sharp-breaking curve, utilizing a motion that resembled a man relaxing in a rocking chair. His pitches forced batters to beat the ball into the ground. John enjoyed his best years in Yankee pinstripes in 1979–80, when he won 43 games and pitched a total of 541 innings.

Johnson, Bob (Indian Bob)

1906–1982

Philadelphia (AL 1933–42), Washington (AL 1943),
Boston (AL 1944–45)   OF   BR/TR

1,863 games	.296 ba
2,051 hits	288 hr
1,283 rbi	96 sb

Johnson spent the majority of his career toiling for second-division clubs, but he kept slamming the ball wherever he played. He hit over .300 five times and pushed across more than 100 runs eight times. If he were active today, Johnson might be hailed as a future Hall of Famer. Johnson played in seven All-Star Games.

Johnson, Byron Bancroft (Ban)

1864–1931

American League (1901–27)   EXECUTIVE

A former sports editor for a Cincinnati newspaper, Ban Johnson founded the American League, which emerged in 1901 as a serious rival to the established National League. He was a hands-on executive and the American League was a well-run organization. Johnson sought to create respect for umpires; he also improved the public's perception of baseball as an honest enterprise.

Johnson, Davey

1943–
Baltimore (AL 1965–72), Atlanta (NL 1973–75), Philadelphia (NL 1977–78), Chicago (NL 1978); MGR—New York (NL 1984–90), Cincinnati (NL 1993 Active)   **2B, MGR   BR/TR**

1,435 games	.261 ba
1,252 hits	136 hr
609 rbi	33 sb

A thinking man's second baseman, Johnson was part of the great Orioles teams that won the World Series in 1966 and 1970. He excelled in the field and swung a dangerous bat, hitting 18 homers for the Birds in 1971. Traded to "the launching pad" in Atlanta, Johnson shocked baseball by crushing 43 home runs, 25 more than he collected in any other season. As manager, he produced the greatest record in Mets history by utilizing a laid-back style that let his talented players play.

Johnson, Deron

1938–1992
New York (AL 1960–61), Kansas City (AL 1961–62), Cincinnati (NL 1964–67), Atlanta (NL 1968), Philadelphia (NL 1969–73), Oakland (AL 1973–74), Milwaukee (AL 1974), Boston (AL 1974, 1975, 1976), Chicago (AL 1975)   **1B, 3B, DH, OF BR/TR**

1,765 games	.244 ba
1,447 hits	245 hr
923 rbl	11 sb

After being buried in the Yankees' minor league system, Johnson emerged in 1964 as a slugging first baseman for the Reds, belting 21 roundtrippers that season. The next year, he put up his best numbers—32 homers, a league-best 130 RBI, and a .287 batting average. Traded along to Philadelphia, he produced back-to-back power seasons in 1970–71, crushing a total of 61 homers.

Johnson, Howard (HoJo)

1960–

Detroit (AL 1982–84), New York (NL 1985–93), Colorado (NL 1994 Active)   **3B**   **BB/TR**

1,351 games	.253 ba
1,148 hits	211 hr
698 rbi	219 sb

No matter what Johnson has accomplished in the major leagues, there have always been skeptics who doubt his ability. As a young third baseman for the pennant-winning Tigers in 1984, he was benched by manager Sparky Anderson for the World Series. When he emerged for the Mets as a power hitter with stolen-base tools, Cardinals manager Whitey Herzog claimed he used a corked bat. Nevertheless, Johnson remains a great fastball hitter who can turn on any pitch, although curve balls continue to give him problems. Hojo got into the habit of having great seasons only every other year, belting 36 homers in 1987, 36 in 1989, and a league-best 38 in 1991, when he also led the NL with 117 RBI. Defensively, Johnson is erratic and prone to making errors in bunches.

Johnson, Randy

1963–

Montreal (NL 1988–89), Seattle (AL 1989–93
Active)   **P**   **BR/LHP**

165 games	1,073 innings
68-56 W–L	3.78 ERA
1,126 k's	1 save

A gangly left-hander, the 6-foot, 10-inch Johnson became a pitcher rather than a thrower midway through the 1992 season. Comparable in some ways to Nolan Ryan, he threw the ball extremely hard and had a great curve, but he could not control his pitches. Johnson led the AL in strikeouts in 1992 (241) and 1993 (308). He threw a no-hitter in 1990 against Detroit.

Johnson, Walter (The Big Train)

1887–1946

Washington (AL 1907–27); MGR—Washington
(AL 1929–32), Cleveland (AL 1933–35)   **P, MGR**
BR/RHP

802 games	5,921 innings
417-279 W–L	2.16 ERA
3,509 k's	34 saves

No pitcher has ever thrown a ball faster than Walter Johnson. Using a smooth, sweeping delivery, he pitched 110 shutouts—a major league record that will probably never be broken. Johnson's 416 career victories rank second only to Cy Young, and his 3,509 lifetime strikeouts remained the major league record for over 60 years. Beloved by teammates and opponents alike, he was inducted as an inaugural member of the Hall of Fame in 1936.

Johnson, William (Judy)

1900–1989

Philadelphia Hilldales (1921–29, 1931–32),
Homestead Grays (1930), Pittsburgh Crawfords
(1932–36)   **3B**   **BR/TR**

728 games	.303 ba
816 hits	19 hr
51 sb	

Inducted into the Hall of Fame in 1975, Johnson was generally regarded as the Negro Leagues' best third baseman of the twenties and thirties. Smart both at the plate and in the field, he led the Philadelphia Hilldales to three pennants. In 1929, he batted .406. Johnson went on to work as a scout for the Philadelphia Phillies from 1959 to 1973.

Johnston, Jimmy
1889–1967
Chicago (AL 1911), Chicago (NL 1914), Brooklyn (NL 1916–25), Boston (NL 1926), New York (NL 1926)   **3B, OF, 2B   BR/TR**

1,377 games	.294 ba
1,493 hits	22 hr
410 rbl	169 sb

When the Federal League crumbled following the 1915 season, Johnston learned firsthand the law of supply and demand as it applied to baseball. If he wanted to play ball, he was compelled to accept the salary offer of owner Charles Ebbets rather than fulfill the contract he had signed with a Federal League team. A versatile fielder, Johnston played most regularly at third base. At the bat, he hit for a good average, although he was not a big run producer. He played in the 1916 and 1920 World Series for Brooklyn. Johnston's best seasons came in 1921–23, when he hit .325 twice and .319 once.

Jones, Cleon
1942–
New York (NL 1963–75), Chicago (AL 1976)   **OF
BR/TL**

1,213 games	.281 ba
1,196 hits	93 hr
524 rbi	91 sb

Jones was the first solid hitter developed by the Mets franchise. He sprayed the ball to all fields while swinging from a slightly closed stance. A rarity in baseball, Jones batted right and threw left. In 1969, the year of the Miracle Mets, he led the NL in batting for much of the season before settling for a .340 average. He hit .319 two years later. Jones excelled defensively by utilizing his good speed and strong throwing arm.

Jones, Doug

1957–

Milwaukee (AL 1982), Cleveland (AL 1986–91), Houston (NL 1992–93), Philadelphia (NL 1994 Active)   P   **BR/RHP**

427 games	620 innings
41-50 W–L	3.06 ERA
499 k's	190 saves

Jones pitches to the credo of "slow, slower, and slowest." Although hitters know what is coming, they are regularly caught off-stride and are way out in front with their swings. He has saved at least 32 games in four different seasons, with a career-high 43 saves in 1990.

Jones, Fielder

1871–1934

Brooklyn (NL 1896–1900), Chicago (AL 1901–08), St. Louis (FL 1914–15); MGR—Chicago (AL 1904–08), St. Louis (FL 1914–15), St. Louis (AL 1916–18)   OF, MGR   **BL/TR**

1,793 games	.284 ba
1,924 hits	20 hr
632 rbi	359 sb

A consistent .300 hitter for Brooklyn early in his career, Jones saw his average fall after he jumped to the

White Sox in the rival AL in 1901. He was also a first-rate center fielder. He later managed the White Sox "Hitless Wonders," who shocked the baseball world by defeating an outstanding Cubs squad in the 1906 World Series. An innovative manager who positioned his fielders according to the skills of the opposing batter, Jones was also renowned as an umpire-baiter.

Jones, Randy

1950–

San Diego (NL 1973–80), New York (NL 1981–82)

P   BR/LHP

305 games	1,933 innings
100-123 W–L	3.42 ERA
735 k's	2 saves

Jones threw an assortment of soft stuff to home plate but always kept batters off-stride with a deceptive motion and pinpoint control. He was a fast worker who threw an inordinate number of ground balls. As a result, Jones needed a strong infield to complement his skills. In 1976, Jones put it all together to win the NL Cy Young Award with a record of 22–14 and 25 complete games.

Jones, Sam (Sad Sam)

1892–1966

Cleveland (AL 1914–15), Boston (AL 1916–21),
New York (AL 1922–26), St. Louis (AL 1927),
Washington (AL 1928–31), Chicago (AL 1932–35)

P   BR/RHP

647 games	3,883 innings
229-217 W–L	3.84 ERA
1,223 k's	31 saves

Only a handful of pitchers have lasted for 22 years in the major leagues, among them "Sad Sam" Jones, whose downcast demeanor earned him his moniker. Traded to the Red Sox in 1916 for the immortal Tris Speaker, he led the AL in winning percentage in 1918

(.762), but by 1922 he had joined the shuttle of players to the Yankees. In 1923, he enjoyed his greatest thrill when he hurled a no-hitter against the Athletics.

Joss, Addie

1880–1911

Cleveland (AL 1902–10)   **P**   **BR/RHP**

286 games	2,327 innings
160-97 W–L	1.89 ERA
920 k's	5 saves

Joss had it all—a crackling fastball, a sharp curve, and excellent control. One of the tallest hurlers of his era, he used a pinwheel motion and threw sidearm. Joss also helped his cause by fielding his position smoothly. In a major league debut that augured things to come, he tossed a one-hitter. Joss pitched a perfect game in 1908 and a no-hitter in 1910, both against the White Sox. Of his 160 career victories, 45 were shutouts. His 1.89 lifetime ERA ranks second to Ed Walsh. Tragically, he died from meningitis at the start of the 1911 season. In a display of player loyalty, a group of AL All-Stars played a charity benefit game against Cleveland, with all of the proceeds going to the Joss family. He was inducted into the Hall of Fame in 1978.

Joyner, Wally (Wally World)

1962–

California (AL 1986–91), Kansas City (AL 1992–93 Active)   **1B**   **BL/TL**

1,136 games	.286 ba
1,224 hits	138 hr
649 rbi	44 sb

Joyner entered the AL in 1986 with a flourish, hitting .290 with 22 homers and 100 RBI and fielding his position brilliantly. When he knocked out 34 home runs and 117 RBI the following year, it appeared he was on his way to a superlative career. Unfortunately, Joyner has approached those numbers only once since.

Judge, Joe

1894–1963
Washington (AL 1915–32), Brooklyn (NL 1933),
Boston (AL 1933–34)   1B   BL/TL

2,171 games	.298 ba
2,352 hits	71 hr
1,034 rbi	213 sb

A smart base runner and an outstanding defensive first
baseman, Judge was one of many Brooklyn-born sand-
lotters to star in the majors. He spent all but two years
of his career in Washington and starred on pennant
winners in 1924 and 1925, batting .324 and .314.

Jurges, Bill

1908–
Chicago (NL 1931–38, 1946–47), New York (NL
1939–45); MGR—Boston (AL 1959–60)   SS,
MGR   BR/TR

1,816 games	.258 ba
1,613 hits	43 hr
656 rbi	36 sb

A scrappy infielder and a joker off the field, Jurges
played short on three Cubs pennant winners in the
thirties. Though never a great batter, he fielded his position brilliantly and led NL shortstops in fielding percentage four times. In the 1932 season, Jurges was shot
by a mentally disturbed female fan who then tried to
commit suicide.

Justice, David

1966–
Atlanta (NL 1989–93 Active)   OF   BL/TL

553 games	.270 ba
527 hits	111 hr
360 rbi	26 sb

Justice has one of the sweetest swings in the game
today. He swatted 28 homers as a rookie in 1990 and

followed that with successive seasons of 21 roundtrippers; before exploding for 40 more in 1993.

K

Kaat, Jim (Kitty)
1938–

Washington (AL 1959–60), Minnesota (AL 1961–73), Chicago (AL 1973–75), Philadelphia (NL 1976–79), New York (AL 1979–80), St. Louis (NL 1980–83)　P　BL/LHP

898 games	4,530 innings
283-237 W–L	3.45 ERA
2461 k's	18 saves

Kaat is the winningest pitcher in Twins history; he accumulated 189 victories during his 1961–73 tenure in Minnesota. He was a tremendous athlete, perhaps the greatest fielding pitcher of all-time, and an outstanding hitter. Kaat's best season came in 1966, when he won 25 games and pitched 304 innings.

Kaline, Al
1934–

Detroit (AL 1953–74)　OF　BR/TR

2,834 games	.297 ba
3,007 hits	399 hr
1,583 rbi	137 sb

Kaline became the youngest batting champion in major league history when he topped the AL in 1955 at the age of 20. He compiled outstanding career totals due to consistent, if not outstanding, performance. Kaline hit over .300 nine times, although he never hit more than 29 homers in a season and knocked in over 100 runs only three times. He was an excellent outfielder with an accurate and powerful throwing arm. Kaline was inducted into the Hall of Fame in 1980.

Kamm, Willie

1900–1988

Chicago (AL 1923–31), Cleveland (AL 1931–35)

3B   BR/TR

1,693 games	.281 ba
1,643 hits	29 hr
826 rbi	125 sb

In 1922, the White Sox paid the minor league San Francisco Seals $100,000—then a record price—for the contract of Willie Kamm. It was a wise purchase, because Kamm became the all-time Chisox third baseman. A superlative player who led the AL in fielding six times, he was the master of the hidden-ball trick.

Kauff, Benny

1890–1961

New York (AL 1912), Indianapolis (FL 1914), Brooklyn (FL 1915), New York (NL 1916–20)   **OF**

BL/TL

859 games	.311 ba
961 hits	49 hr
454 rbi	234 sb

Known as the Ty Cobb of the Federal League, Kauff won the batting crown and stolen-base race in both years of the league's existence, batting .370 and .342. McGraw's Giants sought Kauff for his batting prowess and his presumed attraction for New York's Jewish fans. Unfortunately, the little (5-foot, 7-inch) outfielder never duplicated those figures at the Polo Grounds, although he did bat .308 for the Giants' pennant-winning team in 1917. Commissioner Landis barred Kauff from baseball because of his reputed involvement with a gang that stole automobiles.

Keefe, Tim (Sir Timothy)

1857–1933

Troy (NL 1880–82), New York (AA 1883–84), New York (NL 1885–89, 1891), New York (PL 1890), Philadelphia (NL 1891–93)   **P**   **BR/RHP**

599 games	5,047 innings
342-225 W–L	2.62 ERA
2,545 k's	2 saves

One of the first pitchers to employ a change of pace, Keefe won a record 19 consecutive games in 1888. Nicknamed "Sir Timothy" for his aristocratic airs, he won 40 games twice and played on three pennant winners. Between 1880 and 1888, Keefe completed all but ten of his 444 starting assignments. In recognition of his 342 career victories, which place him eighth on the all-time list, the Hall of Fame inducted him in 1964.

Keeler, Willie (Wee Willie)

1872–1923

New York (NL 1892–93, 1910), Brooklyn (NL 1893, 1899–1902), Baltimore (NL 1894–98), New York (AL 1903–09)   **OF**   **BL/TL**

2,123 games	.341 ba
2,932 hits	33 hr
810 rbi	495 sb

Famed for "hitting 'em where they ain't," Keeler perfected the bunt and the Baltimore chop to collect at least 200 hits eight years in a row. A slight man at 5 feet, 4 inches and 140 pounds, he slapped a record 202 singles in 1898. Batting second in the Orioles lineup, he excelled at the hit-and-run. A fast runner and a fine fielder, he entered the Hall of Fame in 1939.

Kell, George

1922–

Philadelphia (AL 1943–46), Detroit (AL 1946–52), Boston (AL 1952–54), Chicago (AL 1954–56), Baltimore (AL 1956–57)   **3B**   **BR/TR**

1,795 games	.306 ba
2,054 hits	78 hr
870 rbi	51 sb

An excellent fielder with an outstanding throwing arm, Kell led the AL third basemen in fielding percentage seven times. At the plate, he batted over .300 nine times. In 1949, he hit a career high of .343—a mark that led the AL. Kell was extremely tough to strike out, fanning only 287 times in his entire career. Although he was not a big run producer, Kell was inducted into the Hall of Fame in 1983.

Keller, Charlie (King Kong)

1916–1990
New York (AL 1939–43, 1945–49, 1952), Detroit (AL 1950–51)   OF   BL/TR

1,170 games	.286 ba
1,085 hits	189 hr
760 rbi	45 sb

A member of the outstanding Yankees outfield that also featured Joe DiMaggio and Tommy Henrich, the muscular Keller was a power-hitting lefty who frequently dented the seats at Yankee Stadium. He hit at least 21 homers in each of his full seasons between 1940 and 1946 and reached 30 three times. Patient at the plate, Keller led the AL in walks twice and drew more than 100 free passes five times. His best year came in 1941, when he hit .298 with 33 homers, 122 RBI, and 102 runs scored. After 1946, Keller's career as a full-time player was curtailed due to chronic back problems.

Kelley, Joe
1871–1943

Boston (NL 1891), Pittsburgh (NL 1892), Baltimore
(NL 1892–98), Brooklyn (NL 1899–1901),
Baltimore (AL 1902), Cincinnati (NL 1902–06),
Boston (NL 1908); MGR—Cincinnati (NL
1902–05), Boston (NL 1908)   OF, 1B, MGR
BR/TR

1,853 games	.317 ba
2,220 hits	65 hr
1,194 rbi	443 sb

One of the vitriolic Orioles of the 1890s, Kelley was a
superb left fielder with a strong arm and great speed. A
player with star appeal, he batted over .300 for 11 consecutive seasons, including .393 in 1894. Kelley was inducted into the Hall of Fame in 1971.

Kelly, George (Highpockets)
1895–1984

New York (NL 1915–17, 1919–26), Pittsburgh (NL
1917), Cincinnati (NL 1927–30), Chicago (NL
1930), Brooklyn (NL 1932)   1B   BR/TR

1,622 games	.297 ba
1,778 hits	148 hr
1,020 rbi	65 sb

The long-legged Kelly was a slick fielder and a strong
clutch hitter for McGraw's Giants. He batted over
.300 in six consecutive seasons (1921–26) and led the
NL in RBI in 1920 (94) and in 1924 (136). Kelly's
arm was one of the best ever for a first baseman; he was
regularly used as the cut-off man for outfield throws.
He was inducted into the Hall of Fame in 1973.

Kelly, Michael (King)

1857–1894

Cincinnati (NL 1878–79), Chicago (NL 1880–86), Boston (NL 1887–89, 1891–92), Boston (PL 1890), Cincinnati (AA 1891), Boston (AA 1891), New York (NL 1893); MGR—Boston (NL 1887), Boston (PL 1890), Cincinnati (AA 1891)   **OF, C, MGR**
BR/TR

1,455 games	.308 ba
1,813 hits	69 hr
950 rbi	315 sb

One of baseball's biggest celebrities of the 19th century, Kelly's daring base running elicited the chant "Slide, Kelly, slide." He played on five pennant winners with Chicago in the 1880s. After he won the batting title in 1886, the White Stockings sold him to Boston for the grand sum of $10,000. Kelly entered the Hall of Fame in 1945.

Keltner, Ken

1916–1991

Cleveland (AL 1937–44, 1946–49), Boston (AL 1950)   **3B   BR/TR**

1,526 games	.276 ba
1,570 hits	163 hr
852 rbi	39 sb

Keltner was the AL's leading third baseman in the forties, earning All-Star accolades seven times. His best season was 1948, when he batted .297 with 31 homers and 119 RBI. But his most memorable game came on July 17, 1941, when he made several outstanding defensive plays that helped to halt Joe DiMaggio's 56-game hitting streak.

Kennedy, William (Brickyard)

1867–1915

Brooklyn (NL 1892–1901), New York (NL 1902), Pittsburgh (NL 1903)   **P   BR/RHP**

405 games	3,021 innings
187-159 W–L	3.96 ERA
797 k's	9 saves

Brickyard Kennedy had fun on and off the field. His booming voice announced his arrival to everyone in a room, and his drinking bouts and occasional lame-brained play resulted in several fines. On the mound, he led Brooklyn in starts and innings pitched every year from 1893 to 1898. He won more than 20 games four times in his career, including 20 for the pennant-winning 1900 squad.

Key, Jimmy

1961–

Toronto (AL 1984–92), New York (AL 1993 Active)

P   LHP

351 games	1,932 innings
134-87 W–L	3.37 ERA
1,117 k's	10 saves

Key's style on the mound evokes memories of Whitey Ford. He is a crafty left-hander with a good, though not great, fastball, an excellent curve ball, and precise control. Key changes speeds to keep opposing batters off-stride, and his curve induces many ground-ball outs. Key won 17 games in 1987 and has reached double digits every year in his career. After winning two games for Toronto in the 1992 World Series, he signed a free-agent contract with the Yankees, where he went 18–6.

Killebrew, Harmon (Killer)

1936–

Washington (AL 1954–60), Minnesota (AL 1961–74), Kansas City (AL 1975)   **1B, 3B, OF**

BR/TR

2,435 games	.256 ba
2,086 hits	573 hr
1,584 rbi	19 sb

Killebrew often sent baby boomers across America to bed unhappy after his booming home runs defeated their favorite team. Soft-spoken and a gentle strongman, he had enormous forearms that powered more than 40 home runs in eight seasons; he led the AL in 1959 (42), 1962 (48), 1963 (45), 1964 (49), 1967 (44), and 1969 (49). At his retirement, his 573 career homers ranked fifth in major league history. The Twins retired his uniform number 3, and he was inducted into the Hall of Fame in 1984.

Killen, Frank (Lefty)

1870–1939

Milwaukee (AA 1891), Washington (NL 1892, 1898–99), Pittsburgh (NL 1893–98), Boston (NL 1899), Chicago (NL 1900)   P   BL/LHP

321 games	2,511 innings
164-131 W–L	3.78 ERA
725 k's	

A Pittsburgh native, Killen enjoyed his best years in the Steeltown, leading the NL in wins in 1893 (36) and 1896 (30). He suffered a broken arm and a serious spike wound in 1894–95 and suffered through two mediocre seasons.

Kimbro, Henry (Jumbo)

1912–

Washington Elite Giants (1937–38), Baltimore Elite Giants (1939–50)   OF   BL/TL

490 games	.315 ba
725 hits	23 hr
31 sb	

Kimbro was a defensive standout and base-running genius who played in five East-West Negro Leagues All-Star Games in the forties. He batted a robust .363 in 1947.

Kinder, Ellis (Old Folks, Old Rubber Arm)

1914–1968

St. Louis (AL 1946–47), Boston (AL 1948–55), St. Louis (NL 1956), Chicago (AL 1956–57)   P
BR/RHP

484 games	1,479 innings
102-71 W–L	3.43 ERA
749 k's	102 saves

Kinder was a late bloomer who didn't reach the majors until he was past the age of 30. He enjoyed great success as a Red Sox starter, winning 23 games in 1949 with six shutouts. Shifted to the bullpen, he became the AL's top reliever, saving 14 games in 1951 and 27 in 1953.

Kiner, Ralph

1922–

Pittsburgh (NL 1946–53), Chicago (NL 1953–54), Cleveland (AL 1955)   OF   BR/TR

1,472 games	.279 ba
1,451 hits	369 hr
1,015 rbi	22 sb

Kiner was the NL's premier slugger in the late forties and early fifties—an era when he basically was the Pirates' entire offense on some very weak teams. He was a scientific hitter who either won or shared the NL home run crown in each of his first seven years in the majors. A dead-pull hitter, Kiner improved his production after learning the strike zone. He engaged in some memorable contract battles with the Pirates' owner, noted skinflint Branch Rickey. When asked to explain his emphasis on the long ball, Kiner coined the phrase "Home run hitters drive Cadillacs." Some critics have disparaged his all-around play, but he earned induction into the Hall of Fame in 1975.

King, Charles (Silver)

1868–1938

Kansas City (NL 1886), St. Louis (AA 1887–89), Chicago (PL 1890), Pittsburgh (NL 1891), New York (NL 1892–93), Cincinnati (NL 1893), Washington (NL 1896–97)   P   BR/RHP

398 games	3,190 innings
204-153 W–L	3.18 ERA
1,229 k's	6 saves

King pitched effectively from 45 and 50 feet, winning an AA-high 45 games in 1888, but he didn't adapt well to the lengthened distance of 60 feet, 6 inches and the introduction of the pitching rubber in 1893. He threw a mighty fastball with a deceptive delivery, and having to retain contact with the rubber hindered his style and limited his success.

Kingman, Dave (Kong)

1948–

San Francisco (NL 1971–74), New York (NL 1975–77, 1981–83), San Diego (NL 1977), California (AL 1977), New York (AL 1977), Chicago (NL 1978–80), Oakland (AL 1984–86)   OF, 1B, DH   BR/TR

1,941 games	.236 ba
1,575 hits	442 hr
1,210 rbi	85 sb

Kingman did one thing on the ballfield—hit home runs—and he did it very well; but as an all-around player, he was less than proficient. He hit below .250 11 times; only in the friendly confines of Wrigley Field did he reach the .280 level. Swinging from his heels on every pitch, he struck out at least 100 times in 13 seasons. Defensively, he was a man without a position, shuffling from third to first to the outfield. Off the field, Kingman protected his privacy and rarely got along with the working press.

Klein, Charles (Chuck)

1904–1958

Philadelphia (NL 1928–33, 1936–39, 1940–44), Chicago (NL 1934–36), Pittsburgh (NL 1939)   **OF**
BL/TR

1,753 games	.320 ba
2,076 hits	300 hr
1,201 rbi	79 sb

The Phillies' home park, Baker Bowl, was a hitters' paradise, and no batter enjoyed it more than Klein. He put up great numbers between 1928 and 1933. In 1930, he set an NL mark with 107 extra-base hits and scored a 20th-century record 158 runs. He won the MVP award in 1932 and copped the triple crown the following year, batting .368 with 28 home runs and 120 RBI. Klein belted four home runs in a single game in 1936, only the fourth man to do so. The strong-armed Klein also made 44 assists in the outfield in 1930. He was inducted into the Hall of Fame in 1980.

Kling, Johnny (Noisy)

1875–1947

Chicago (NL 1900–08, 1910–11), Boston (NL 1911–12), Cincinnati (NL 1913); MGR—Boston (NL 1912)   **C, MGR**   **BR/TR**

1,260 games	.272 ba
1,151 hits	20 hr
513 rbi	123 sb

Kling was the finest defensive catcher of his generation. He helped the Cubs to a record 116 victories in 1906, although they lost the World Series to the White Sox's "Hitless Wonders." A talented pool player, Kling won the world title in 1908. While he sat out the entire 1909 season in a contract dispute, he spent his time running his billiards hall. Considered one of the finest Jewish players of all time, Kling later owned the minor league Kansas City Blues. He acquired his nickname, "Noisy," because he was so quiet.

Kluszewski, Ted (Klu)

1924–1988

Cincinnati (NL 1947–57), Pittsburgh (NL 1958–59), Chicago (AL 1959–60), Los Angeles (AL 1961)   1B   BL/TL

1,718 games	.298 ba
1,766 hits	279 hr
1,028 rbi	20 sb

Kluszewski was an awesome sight at home plate in the sleeveless uniform of the Reds in the mid-fifties. Klu had the biggest biceps in the NL, and he used his strength to slam 40, 49, and 47 home runs for Cincinnati in 1953–55. He knocked in more than 100 RBI four times. In 1954, he hit .326 with a league-leading 49 homers and 141 RBI. Only a slipped disc and continuing back problems prevented Kluszewski from rewriting the record books.

Knepper, Bob

1954–

San Francisco (NL 1976–80, 1989–90), Houston (NL 1981–89)   P   BL/LHP

445 games	2,708 innings
146-155 W–L	3.68 ERA
1,473 k's	1 save

A feminist's nightmare, Knepper gained considerable notoriety late in his career due to his outspoken objection to coverage of the game by women sportswriters. He endured on the mound despite some severe reversals, winning 17 games in 1978, losing 15 in 1982, winning 17 in 1986, and losing 17 in 1987. Knepper failed to hold the lead in the ninth inning of the fateful sixth game of the 1986 NLCS, and the Mets rebounded to win the pennant in the 16th inning.

Knowles, Darold

1941–

Baltimore(AL 1965), Philadelphia (NL 1966),
Washington (AL 1966–71), Oakland (AL 1971–74),
Chicago (NL 1975–76), Texas (AL 1977), Montreal
(NL 1978), St. Louis (NL 1979–80)   P

BL/LHP

765 games	1,092 innings
66-74 W-L	3.12 ERA
681 k's	143 saves

The one certainty in the 1973 World Series between
the Athletics and the Mets was that this lefty reliever
would appear on the mound. In seven appearances, he
surrendered only one unearned run and saved two victories. Knowles bounced around the major leagues and
in 1970 saved 27 games for the Senators despite losing
14 times.

Konetchy, Ed (Big Ed)

1885–1947

St. Louis (NL 1907–13), Pittsburgh (NL 1914),
Pittsburgh (FL 1915), Boston (NL 1916–18),
Brooklyn (NL 1919–21), Philadelphia (NL 1921)

1B   BR/TR

2,085 games	.281 ba
2,150 hits	75 hr
992 rbi	255 sb

Often overlooked in discussions of dead ball stars, Ko-
netchy ranks with the best Cardinals first basemen of
all time and later led Brooklyn to the pennant in 1920.
He batted over .300 four times and was a sharp fielder.

Konstanty, Jim

1917–1976

Cincinnati (NL 1944), Boston (NL 1946),
Philadelphia (NL 1948–54), New York (AL
1954–56), St. Louis (NL 1956)   P   BR/RHP

433 games	945 innings
66-48 W–L	3.46 ERA
268 k's	74 saves

Konstanty will always be remembered for his one great season in the big leagues in 1950. That year, he received the NL MVP award after winning 16 games and saving 22 in the Phillies' pennant-winning season. His best pitch was a palm ball.

Koosman, Jerry (Kooz)

1942–

New York (NL 1967–78), Minnesota (AL 1979–81), Chicago (AL 1981–83), Philadelphia (NL 1984–85)

P   BR/LHP

612 games	3,839 innings
222-209 W–L	3.36 ERA
2556 k's	17 saves

Koosman helped eradicate the Mets' image as losers. During his rookie season, fans watched with joy as he blew his fastball past batters and froze them with his sharp-breaking curve. What's more, he pitched with a boyish enthusiasm and was not averse to brushing hitters off the plate and occasionally plunking a batter when the situation called for it. He won 19 games with a 2.08 ERA and seven shutouts as a rookie in 1968; only the outstanding debut of Johnny Bench prevented him from winning the frosh award. He won 20 games for both the Mets and the Twins and went undefeated in three World Series decisions, including the decisive fifth game of the 1969 classic. Koosman remains one of the most popular Mets in the team's history.

Koufax, Sandy

1935–

Brooklyn (NL 1955–57), Los Angeles (NL 1958–66)

P   BR/LHP

397 games	2,324 innings
165-87 W–L	2.76 ERA
2,396 k's	9 saves

Many experts proclaim Koufax as the greatest left-hander in the history of the National League. Throwing directly overhand, he had a fastball that rose through the strike zone and a curve that dropped off the table. Once he acquired control of his pitches, he was nearly unhittable. Between 1962 and 1966, when he retired due to an arthritic elbow, he dominated hitters, gaining the ERA title each year, winning 25 or more games three times, striking out more than 300 batters three times, and leading the league in shutouts three times. Koufax earned three Cy Young Awards and pitched four no-hitters, including a perfect game against Chicago in 1965. The Dodgers retired his uniform number 32, and he was inducted into the Hall of Fame in 1972.

Kremer, Ray (Wiz)
1893–1965
Pittsburgh (NL 1924–33)   P   BR/RHP

308 games	1,954 innings
143-85 W–L	3.76 ERA
516 k's	10 saves

A fun-loving prankster who enjoyed the occasional cocktail, Kremer excelled on the mound. Although he didn't reach the majors until the age of 31, he twice led the NL in wins (20 in both 1926 and 1930) and ERA (2.61 in 1926 and 2.47 in 1927), and he suffered only one losing season in the big leagues at the age of 38. In the hit-crazy year of 1930, Kremer managed to win 20 games despite an ERA of 5.02. His success was due in part to his good move to first base.

Kruk, John (Jake)

1961–

San Diego (NL 1986–89), Philadelphia (NL
1989–93 Active)   **1B, OF   BL/TL**

1,080 games	.300 ba
1,044 hits	93 hr
531 rbi	54 sb

Kruk rarely completes a game with a clean uniform. An
outstanding hitter with an open stance, he hits most of
his balls to center and left field. Despite his pear-
shaped body and excess weight, Kruk is a fine defensive
first baseman and a smart base runner.

Kuenn, Harvey

1930–1988

Detroit (AL 1952–59), Cleveland (AL 1960), San
Francisco (NL 1961–65), Chicago (NL 1965–66),
Philadelphia (NL 1966); MGR—Milwaukee (AL
1975, 1982–83)   **OF, SS, MGR   BR/TR**

1,833 games	.303 ba
2,092 hits	87 hr
671 rbi	68 sb

The AL's Rookie of the Year in 1953, Kuenn led the
league in hits (209) while batting .308. An outstanding
hitter, although not a great run producer, he led the AL
in base hits four times but received his greatest publicity when he was traded for Rocky Colavito prior to the
1960 season. As manager of the Brewers, he led Harvey's Wallbangers into the 1982 World Series.

Kuhel, Joe

1906–1984

Washington (AL 1930–37, 1944–46, 1948–49),
Chicago (AL 1938–43, 1946–47); MGR—
Washington (AL 1948–49)   **1B, MGR   BL/TL**

2,104 games	.277 ba
2,212 hits	131 hr
1,049 rbi	176 sb

An outstanding fielder at first base, Kuhel also wielded a potent bat, hitting .300 three times and collecting 100 RBI twice. In 1933, he hit .322 with 107 RBI for the pennant-winning Senators, the last Washington team to win the flag.

L

Labine, Clem
1926–
Brooklyn (NL 1950–57), Los Angeles (NL 1958–60), Detroit (AL 1960), Pittsburgh (NL 1960–61), New York (NL 1962)   **P**   **BR/RHP**

513 games	1,079 innings
77-56 W–L	3.63 ERA
551 k's	96 saves

The ace of the Brooklyn bullpen and one of the top relievers of the fifties, Labine relied on a natural sinker to record outs. He went 13–5 in 1955 and led the NL in saves in 1956 (19) and 1957 (17). In one of his rare starts, Labine pitched a 1–0, 10-inning shutout against the Yankees in the sixth game of the 1956 World Series.

Lajoie, Napoleon (Nap, Larry)
1874–1959
Philadelphia (NL 1896–1900), Philadelphia (AL 1901–02, 1915–16), Cleveland (AL 1902–14); MGR—Cleveland (AL 1905–09)   **2B, 1B, MGR**
BR/TR

2,480 games	.338 ba
3,242 hits	83 hr
1,599 rbi	380 sb

How many players could state that their team was named in their honor? Lajoie, baseball's best second baseman, could after Cleveland became known as the "Naps." Scintillating in the field, he also retired with the second-most career RBI. After jumping to the up-start American League in 1901, Nap batted .426, winning the title by the greatest margin (.086) in major league history. Lajoie was elected to the Hall of Fame in 1937.

Landis, Kenesaw Mountain
1866–1944
EXECUTIVE

Baseball's first commissioner, Landis ruled the game with an iron hand from 1920 to 1944. His first involvement with baseball came when he heard the Federal League's antitrust suit from his seat on the federal bench in Illinois. By delaying any decision until the league folded, he won the admiration of baseball's leaders, who later turned to him to clean up the game after the Chicago White Sox scandal in the 1919 World Series. Judge Landis banned eight members of the team, although they were never convicted by a court. Despite barring more than a dozen players for gambling or illegal behavior, he turned the other cheek when Ty Cobb and Tris Speaker, two of the game's icons, were implicated in a conspiracy to fix games. Landis also disliked the growing farm systems of various teams; he freed players like Tommy Henrich who he felt had been illegally blocked from advancing to the majors. He entered the Hall of Fame in 1944.

Lange, Bill (Little Eva)
1871–1950

Chicago (NL 1893–99)	OF	BR/TR
811 games	.330 ba	
1,055 hits	39 hr	
578 rbi	399 sb	

Love ended the baseball career of Lange, perhaps the best all-around player of the 19th century. Extremely popular with Chicago's fans, he excelled both at the plate and in the field. He batted over .324 in every season but his rookie year. In 1895, Lange batted .389; no Cub has hit for a higher average since. Great speed and a powerful arm made him one of the best ball hawks of his generation. Yet Lange brought his career to a premature close in order to marry his sweetheart, whose father objected to her marrying a ballplayer.

Langston, Mark

1960–

Seattle (AL 1984–89), Montreal (NL 1989), California (AL 1990–93 Active)   P   BR/LHP

334 games	2,329 innings
144-126 W–L	3.60 ERA
2,001 k's	

Langston has great stuff—a high, rising fastball, a sharp-breaking curve, and a snappy slider. Strikeouts are his game, and he led the AL in three of his first four seasons in the league. Langston's best year came in 1991, when he went 19–8.

Lanier, Max

1915–

St. Louis (NL 1938–46, 1949–51), New York (NL 1952–53), St. Louis (AL 1953)   P   BR/LHP

327 games	1,619 innings
108-82 W–L	3.01 ERA
821 k's	17 saves

Underpaid as a member of the Cardinals pitching staff, Lanier jumped to the Mexican League early in the 1946 season after having won all six of his starts that season. He was allowed to return to St. Louis in 1949 but was never as effective as he had been prior to his departure.

Lansford, Carney

1957–

California (AL 1978–80), Boston (AL 1981–82), Oakland (AL 1983–92)   3B   BR/TR

1,862 games	.290 ba
2,074 hits	151 hr
874 rbi	204 sb

An aggressive team leader on the great Athletics squads of the eighties, Lansford played in three World Series for Oakland. Earlier in his career, he led the AL in batting (.336 in 1981). Lansford suffered a serious knee injury in an off-season snowmobile accident in 1990. He retired after the 1992 season.

Larkin, Barry

1964—
Cincinnati (NL 1986--93 Active)   SS   **BR/TR**

935 games	.298 ba
1,045 hits	78 hr
419 rbi	162 sb

One of the game's biggest stars, Larkin is an outstanding hitter and superlative fielder. In addition, he projects an image of sportsmanship that baseball wishes its other stars would emulate. Larkin batted .342 in 1989 and has hit over .300 in every season since. In 1991, he cracked 20 home runs, and in 1992, he drove home 78 runs.

Larsen, Don

1929—
St. Louis (AL 1953), Baltimore (AL 1954, 1965), New York (AL 1955–59), Kansas City (AL 1960–61), Chicago (AL 1961), San Francisco (NL 1962–64), Houston (NL 1964–65), Chicago (NL 1967)   P   **BR/RHP**

412 games	1,548 innings
81-91 W–L	3.78 ERA
849 k's	23 saves

Considered a throw-in in the 17-player swap between New York and Baltimore, Larsen turned his career around in the Bronx. After a combined record of 10–33 for his first two years in the majors, he went

39–17 in his first four seasons in New York. Larsen pitched the most memorable game in baseball history—a perfect game against Brooklyn in game five of the 1956 World Series.

LaRussa, Tony

1944–

Kansas City (AL 1963), Oakland (AL 1968–71), Atlanta (NL 1971), Chicago (NL 1973); MGR—Chicago (AL 1979–86), Oakland (AL 1986–93 Active)   2B, MGR   BR/TR

132 games	.199 ba
35 hits	7 rbi

LaRussa is generally regarded as the current genius among major league managers. Armed with a law degree and a computer, he analyzes player performances in a myriad of situations so that he will always have an edge when he needs to make a move. LaRussa always calls in his relief ace, Dennis Eckersley, at the start of an inning and never warms him up without bringing him into a game. The results have been fantastic. As a strategist, he always seems to get the best of his opponents by making the right play at the right time. LaRussa won the 1989 World Series with the Athletics, although he fell short in the 1988 and 1990 fall classics.

Lary, Frank (The Yankee-Killer)

1930–

Detroit (AL 1954–64), New York (NL 1964, 1965), Milwaukee (NL 1964), Chicago (AL 1965)   P
BR/RHP

350 games	2,162 innings
128-116 W–L	3.49 ERA
1,099 k's	11 saves

Yankee fans moaned when Lary took the mound against the Bombers, for they sensed a frustrating afternoon ahead. Indeed, his 28–13 lifetime record against

New York proved the only medicine effective against baseball's leading dynasty. Lary could never explain his unique success against the Yanks; his special record even overshadowed his two 20-victory seasons.

Lasorda, Tommy

1927–

Brooklyn (NL 1954–55), Kansas City (AL 1956); MGR—Los Angeles (NL 1976–93 Active)   P, MGR   BL/LHP

26 games	58 innings
0-4 W–L	6.52 ERA
37 k's	

A public relations genius, Lasorda completed his 17th season as the Dodgers' skipper in 1993 and surpassed Wilbert Robinson as the second-winningest manager in team history. Despite all his schmaltz about "bleeding Dodger blue," he projects a sensitivity about team unity and the feeling of family that is unique to the Dodgers organization. His lifetime record is 1,420–1,280.

Latham, Walter (Arlie, The Freshest Man on Earth)

1860–1952

Buffalo (NL 1880), St. Louis (AA 1883–89), Chicago (PL 1890), Cincinnati (NL 1890–95), St. Louis (NL 1896), Washington (NL 1899), New York (NL 1909); MGR—St. Louis (NL 1896)   3B, MGR
BR/TR

1,627 games	.269 ba
1,833 hits	27 hr
398 rbi	739 sb

Latham was one of the most colorful personalities ever to put on a baseball uniform. As funny as a clown, he also was the fastest man in baseball during his era. He scored more than 100 runs in nine seasons, including an AA-high 152 in 1888 for the powerful Browns outfit. At third base, Latham possessed the strongest throwing arm in the game, although he permanently injured his wing in a publicity stunt. In retirement, he took on the role of baseball's goodwill ambassador; in 1909, he became the game's first full-time coach, hiring on with the New York Giants.

Lavagetto, Harry (Cookie)
1912–1990
Pittsburgh (NL 1934–36), Brooklyn (NL 1937–41, 1946–47); MGR—Washington (AL 1957–60), Minnesota (AL 1961)   **3B, 2B, MGR   BR/TR**

1,043 games	.269 ba
945 hits	40 hr
486 rbi	63 sb

One of the most popular players in Brooklyn, Lavagetto was serenaded each game by a local restaurateur carrying balloons inscribed with his name. A fine hitter, Lavagetto was an NL All-Star from 1938 to 1941 before enlisting in the armed forces. After his return, he became a reserve but made baseball history in the fourth game of the 1947 World Series, breaking up a no-hit bid by Yankees pitcher Bill Bevens when he doubled against the right-field wall at Ebbets Field with two outs in the bottom of the ninth. His hit won the game that many experts consider the most dramatic in major league history.

Law, Vern (Deacon)
1930–
Pittsburgh (NL 1950–51, 1954–67)   **P**
BR/RHP

483 games	2,672 innings
162-147 W–L	3.77 ERA
1,092 k's	13 saves

Law was the ace of the Pirates staff that won the 1960 World Series. He won 20 games in the regular season and two more in the series. Law threw a full complement of pitches and effectively hit his spots and changed speeds to baffle batters.

Lazzeri, Tony (Poosh 'Em Up)
1903–1946
New York (AL 1926–37), Chicago (NL 1938), Brooklyn (NL 1939), New York (NL 1939)   2B
BR/TR

1,740 games	.292 ba
1,840 hits	178 hr
1,191 rbi	148 sb

A powerful hitter for a middle infielder, Lazzeri was the first big Italian-American baseball star. He was a smart, heady player who had the courage to battle epilepsy throughout his career. As a member of the great Yankees teams that featured Babe Ruth, Lou Gehrig, and, later, Joe DiMaggio, Lazzeri held his own in the lineup, batting over .300 five times, including a career-high .354 in 1929, and driving in more than 100 runs on seven occasions. Lazzeri was inducted into the Hall of Fame in 1991.

Leach, Tommy
1877–1969
Louisville (NL 1898–99), Pittsburgh (NL 1900–12, 1918), Chicago (NL 1912–14), Cincinnati (NL 1915)   OF, 3B   BR/TR

2,156 games	.269 ba
2,143 hits	63 hr
810 rbi	361 sb

Leach alternated between the outfield and third base throughout his career. Very small and fast, he led the NL in homers in 1902 with six; all were inside-the-park feats. Leach led the NL in runs scored in 1909 (126) and 1913 (99).

Lee, Bill (Big Bill)
1909–1977

Chicago (NL 1934–43, 1947), Philadelphia (NL 1943–45), Boston (NL 1945–46)   P   BR/RHP

462 games	2,864 innings
169-157 W–L	3.54 ERA
998 k's	13 saves

A big, hard-throwing righty, Lee starred for two Cubs pennant winners in 1935 and 1938. Both years, he led the NL in winning percentage, going 20–6 in 1935 and 22–9 three years later. He also had the lowest ERA in 1938 (2.66). Lee's high leg kick intimidated batters.

Lee, Bill (Spaceman)
1946–

Boston (AL 1969–78), Montreal (NL 1979–82)   P   BL/LHP

416 games	1,944 innings
119-90 W–L	3.62 ERA
713 k's	19 saves

A rebel in a baseball uniform, Lee brought a sixties-generation attitude to the game. He tweaked the noses of baseball's establishment, from manager Don Zimmer to commissioner Bowie Kuhn. On the mound, he threw a terrific curve and change-up and spotted his fastball with precise control. In the seventh game of the 1975 World Series, Lee threw one change-up too many to Tony Perez, who smacked a homer that led the Red Sox to another heartbreaking loss in series play. Lee's career took a downward turn after he suffered a severe shoulder injury during a brawl at Yankee Stadium in 1976. Lee won 17 games in three consecutive seasons (1973–75).

Lee, Thornton (Lefty)
1906–

Cleveland (AL 1933–36), Chicago (AL 1937–47), New York (NL 1948)   P   BL/LHP

375 games	2,331 innings
117–124 W–L	3.56 ERA
937 k's	10 saves

Lee became one of the top lefties in the AL in the pre-war years, winning in double digits for five consecutive years, topped by 22 victories, a league-leading 30 complete games, and a 2.37 ERA in 1941. Injuries limited his usefulness in 1942–44, but he won 15 times in 1945.

Leever, Sam (The Goshen Schoolmaster)

1871–1953
Pittsburgh (NL 1898–1910)   P   BR/RHP

388 games	2,660 innings
194–100 W–L	2.47 ERA
847 k's	13 saves

In 1899, Leever set a host of rookie pitching records for the Pirates that stand to this day, going 21–23, pitching 379 innings, and hurling four shutouts among his 35 complete games. He went on to win the second-most games in team history and currently ranks second in Pirates annals in career winning percentage, shutouts, and complete games as well. A control artist, Leever walked fewer than two men per nine innings. In his best year, 1903, he went 25–7 and led the NL in winning percentage (.781), ERA (2.06), and shutouts (7).

LeFlore, Ron

1948–
Detroit (AL 1974–79), Montreal (NL 1980),
Chicago (AL 1981–82)   OF   BR/TR

1,099 games	.288 ba
1,283 hits	59 hr
353 rbi	455 sb

Billy Martin gave LeFlore a chance to earn a livelihood in baseball following a stint in prison; he responded by playing exciting ball both at bat and on the base paths. LeFlore batted .316 in 1976 and .325 in 1977. In 1978, he led the AL in runs scored (126) and stolen bases (68). Following a move to Montreal, he stole 97 bases to lead the NL.

Leibrandt, Charlie

1956–
Cincinnati (NL 1979–82), Kansas City (AL 1984–89), Atlanta (NL 1990–92), Texas (AL 1993 Active)   **P**   **BR/LHP**

394 games	2,308 innings
140-119 W–L	3.71 ERA
1,121 k's	2 saves

Leibrandt's best pitch is a change-up, and he throws it about 70 percent of the time. He has been a big winner in both leagues, earning 60 victories in four successive seasons for Kansas City (1985–88) and reaching 15 triumphs in both 1991 and 1992 for Atlanta; yet his World Series failures for the Braves sealed his departure from Atlanta.

Lemon, Bob

1920–
Cleveland (AL 1941–42, 1946–58); MGR—Kansas City (AL 1970–72), Chicago (AL 1977–78), New York (AL 1978–79, 1981–82)   **P, MGR** **BL/RHP**

460 games	.232 ba
274 hits	37 hr
147 rbi	2,850 innings
207-128 W–L	3.23 ERA
1,277 k's	22 saves

Lemon started his career as an outfielder and didn't become a pitcher until the age of 26. Relying mostly on his tremendous sinker, he won 20 games seven times in the nine-year span between 1948 and 1956. Lemon hurled a no-hitter in 1948 against Detroit. Inducted into the Hall of Fame in 1976, he later managed the Yankees to the World Series title in 1978.

Lemon, Chet

1955–
Chicago (AL 1975–81), Detroit (AL 1982–90)   **OF**
BR/TR

1,988 games	.273 ba
1,875 hits	215 hr
884 rbi	58 sb

Lemon was a fine defensive center fielder who also wielded a powerful bat. He batted .300 three times, swatting a career-best .318 in 1979 when he led the AL in doubles (44). In 1977, he set an AL record by making 512 put-outs.

Leonard, Dennis

1951–
Kansas City (AL 1974–86)   **P**   **RHP**

312 games	2,187 innings
144-106 W–L	3.70 ERA
1,323 k's	1 save

A fastball, slider pitcher, Leonard was one of the AL's top righty starters of the seventies and the ace of the Royals staff. He won 20 games three times for Kansas City.

Leonard, Emil (Dutch)

1909–1983
Brooklyn (NL 1933–36), Washington (AL 1938–46), Philadelphia (NL 1947–48), Chicago (NL 1949–53)   **P**   **BR/RHP**

640 games	3,218 innings
191-181 W–L	3.25 ERA
1,170 k's	44 saves

By the good graces of the knuckle ball, Leonard pitched effectively for 20 years as a starter and reliever. He spent his most productive years as a member of the

Senators' staff of knuckleballers, winning 20 games in 1939 and at least 17 on three other occasions.

Leonard, Hubert (Dutch)

1892–1952
Boston (AL 1913–18), Detroit (AL 1919–21, 1924–25)   P   BL/LHP

331 games	2,192 innings
139-112 W–L	2.76 ERA
1,160 k's	13 saves

Leonard threw a "legal" spitball five years after the pitch was outlawed in 1920. As a starter for the 1914 Red Sox, he enjoyed one of the most remarkable seasons in major league history, going 19–5 with a league-best, minuscule 0.96 ERA in 224 innings.

Leonard, Jeffrey (Hac-Man, Penitentiary Face)

1955–
Los Angeles (NL 1977), Houston (NL 1978–81), San Francisco (NL 1981–88), Milwaukee (AL 1988), Seattle (AL 1988–90)   OF   BR/TR

1,415 games	.266 ba
1,342 hits	144 hr
723 rbi	163 sb

An aggressive player, Leonard made few friends among his opponents. He played the game with a snarl on his face, earning him the nickname "Penitentiary Face." A free-swinger, his best seasons came with the Giants. He batted .302 with 86 RBI in 1984 and .280 with 19 homers for the division-winning 1987 team.

Leonard, Walter (Buck)

1907–
Washington Homestead Grays (1934–48)   1B
BL/TL

382 games	.324 ba
514 hits	71 hr
10 sb	

Named to the Hall of Fame in 1972 for his excellent play in the Negro Leagues, Leonard teamed with Josh Gibson to form a duo that resembled the Ruth-Gehrig combo in terms of power. Leonard won the Negro NL batting title in 1948 (.391). He was a great team player with an outstanding personality.

Lindstrom, Freddie (Lindy)

1905–1981

New York (NL 1924–32), Pittsburgh (NL 1933–34), Chicago (NL 1935), Brooklyn (NL 1936)   **3B, OF**
BR/TR

1,438 games	.311 ba
1,747 hits	103 hr
779 rbi	84 sb

Were it not for bad hops on two ground balls hit toward Lindstrom, a young rookie reserve, in the eighth and twelfth innings of the seventh game of the 1924 World Series, the Giants would have secured the title. He overcame the pain of that bad luck and went on to a sterling career. Lindstrom hit at least .300 seven times and twice accumulated 231 hits in a season. He was inducted into the Hall of Fame in 1976.

Lloyd, John (Pop, El Cuchara)

1884–1964

Chicago American Giants (1914, 1917), New York Lincoln Giants (1914, 1916, 1926–30), Brooklyn Royal Giants (1918–20), Columbus Buckeyes (1921), Atlantic City Bacharach Giants (1922, 1924–25, 1931–32), Philadelphia Hilldales (1923), New York Harlem Stars (1931); MGR—(1921–31)
SS   BL/TR

477 games	.368 ba
651 hits	26 hr
56 sb	

Contemporaries compared Lloyd to Pittsburgh's star shortstop Honus Wagner for his outstanding play on the field and his demeanor off the diamond. Babe Ruth called him the best player he had ever seen. After playing 12 years in Cuba, he acquired the nickname of "El Cuchara" ("the Shovel") for his defensive abilities at shortstop. He moved to first base in 1928 and batted an astronomical .564 for the New York Lincoln Giants. Lloyd was inducted into the Hall of Fame in 1977.

Loes, Billy

1929–

Brooklyn (NL 1950, 1952–56), Baltimore (AL 1956–59), San Francisco (NL 1960–61)   **P**
BR/RHP

316 games	1,190 innings
80-63 W–L	3.55 ERA
645 k's	32 saves

The only pitcher ever to claim that he lost a ground ball in the sun, Loes also reportedly predicted that the Yanks would beat his own team, the Dodgers, prior to one World Series. As for the grounder, hit by Raschi, that Loes couldn't handle, a World Series highlights film clearly shows the sun shining between the two decks behind home plate. Loes won 50 games in 1952–55, but he said that he never wanted to win 20 games, because then he would be expected to do it again.

Lofton, Kenny

1967–

Houston Astros (NL 1991), Cleveland Indians (AL 1992–93 Active)   **OF**   **BL/TL**

316 games	.299 ba
364 hits	6 hr
84 rbi	138 sb

A tremendous fly chaser, Lofton ranks with the best centerfielders in the American League. After two full years in the majors, he has two AL stolen base crowns, swiping 66 bags in 1992 and 70 in 1993. Lofton batted a robust .325 in 1993 and scored 116 runs.

Logan, Johnny
1927–

Boston (NL 1951–52), Milwaukee (NL 1953–61), Pittsburgh (NL 1961–63)   SS   **BR/TR**

1,503 games	.268 ba
1,407 hits	93 hr
547 rbi	19 sb

An aggressive player who was the sparkplug of the Braves infield, Logan engaged Don Drysdale in one of the most memorable brawls in Ebbets Field history in 1957. His best season came in 1955, when he batted .297 with 13 homers, 83 RBI, and a league-high 37 doubles.

Lolich, Michael (Mickey)
1940–

Detroit (AL 1963–75), New York (NL 1976), San Diego (NL 1978–79)   P   **BB/LHP**

586 games	3,638 innings
217-191 W–L	3.44 ERA
2,832 k's	11 saves

No other great pitcher ever looked less like an athlete than the portly Lolich. Owner of a wicked slider and a moving fastball, he was extremely tough on left-handed batters, particularly when he dropped to a side-arm delivery. A workhorse whose appetite for pitching matched the heroics of the early 20th-century stars,

Lolich's total of 367 innings in 1971 was the highest in the AL since 1912. Lolich starred in the 1968 World Series, winning three starts against the Cardinals.

Lollar, Sherm (Dad)

1924–1977

Cleveland (AL 1946), New York (AL 1947–48), St. Louis (AL 1949–51), Chicago (AL 1952–63)   C
BR/TR

1,752 games	.264 ba
1,415 hits	155 hr
808 rbi	20 sb

Lollar's intelligence behind the plate made him the equivalent of an assistant manager on the field. Hurlers trusted his pitch selection and appreciated his defensive skills in throwing out potential base stealers. A dry wit, Lollar was well liked by his teammates. At the plate, he slugged 20 homers in 1958 and 22 in 1959, when the White Sox won their first pennant in four years. He knocked in 84 runs in each of those years.

Lombardi, Ernie (Schnozz)

1908–1977

Brooklyn (NL 1931), Cincinnati (NL 1932–41), Boston (NL 1942), New York (NL 1943–47)   C
BR/TR

1,853 games	.306 ba
1,792 hits	190 hr
990 rbi	8 sb

The slowest runner in the majors, Lombardi had to earn all of his hits, because infielders played him very deep. He seldom struck out and he hit the ball hard to all fields. Indeed, Lombardi never fanned more than 25 times in a single season. He led NL batters in 1938 (.342). Defensively, he had few equals, throwing the ball rapidly with a sidearm delivery without rising from

his crouch. Lombardi was inducted into the Hall of
Fame in 1986.

Lonborg, Jim
1942–
Boston (AL 1965–71), Milwaukee (AL 1972),
Philadelphia (NL 1973–79)   **P   BR/RHP**

425 games	2,464 innings
157-137 W–L	3.86 ERA
1,475 k's	4 saves

An avid skier, Lonborg suffered an off-season mishap
on the slopes that rerouted what might have been a
great career. Injured following his 22–9 season in
1967, he did not reach double digit wins again until
1971. Although he became an effective starter for the
Phillies in the mid-seventies, winning 17 games in
1974 and 18 in 1976, he never threw with the same
velocity after his knee injury.

Long, Herman (Germany)
1866–1909
Kansas City (AA 1889), Boston (NL 1890–1902),
New York (AL 1903), Detroit (AL 1903),
Philadelphia (NL 1904)   SS   **BL/TR**

1,874 games	.277 ba
2,127 hits	91 hr
1,054 rbi	534 sb

A fine fielder and outstanding hitter, Long joined the
Boston Beaneaters in 1890 and played regularly on five
pennant winners ever that decade. In 1896, he hit a
career-high .343 with 100 RBI.

Lopat, Ed (Steady Eddie)
1918–1992
Chicago (AL 1944–47), New York (AL 1948–55),
Baltimore (AL 1955); MGR—Kansas City (AL
1963–64)   **P, MGR   BL/LHP**

340 games	2,439 innings
166-112 W–L	3.21 ERA
859 k's	3 saves

Lopat had three speeds on his fastball—slow, slower, and slowest. Batters were convinced they could cream his assortment of soft curves and change-ups, but they regularly retreated to the dugout shaking their heads. At his best in big games, Lopat went 4–1 in World Series play. After a 21–9 season in 1951, he hurt his arm in the World Series that fall and thereafter was limited to pitching once a week.

Lopes, Davey

1945–

Los Angeles (NL 1972–81), Oakland (AL 1982–84), Chicago (NL 1984–86), Houston (NL 1986–87)

2B, OF   BR/TR

1,812 games	.263 ba
1,671 hits	155 hr
614 rbi	557 sb

An outstanding base runner who was rarely thrown out attempting to steal a base, Lopes was an integral member of four Dodgers pennant winners. He led the NL in steals in 1975 (77) and 1976 (63). At the plate, he was a notorious first-ball hitter who had surprising power for a middle infielder. In 1979, he launched 28 homers and drove home 73 runs while batting .265.

Lopez, Al

1908–

Brooklyn (NL 1928–35), Boston (NL 1936–40), Pittsburgh (NL 1940–46), Cleveland (AL 1947); MGR—Cleveland (AL 1951–56), Chicago (AL 1957–65, 1968–69)   **C, MGR   BR/TR**

1,950 games	.261 ba
1,547 hits	52 hr
652 rbi	46 sb

Most star players who turn to managing find limited success. Not so Al Lopez, who finished second 10 times in 14 full seasons and was the only AL manager to finish ahead of the Yankees between 1949 and 1964. As a player in Brooklyn, he hit over .300 in 1930 and in 1933. His defensive skills were also first rate. At his retirement, Lopez held the major league record for most games caught (1,918)—a record later broken by Carlton Fisk. He was inducted into the Hall of Fame in 1977.

Lowe, Bobby (Link)
1868–1951
Boston (NL 1890–1901), Chicago (NL 1902–03), Pittsburgh (NL 1904), Detroit (AL 1904–07); MGR—Detroit (AL 1904)   **2B, OF, MGR**
BR/TR

1,818 games	.273 ba
1,929 hits	71 hr
984 rbi	302 sb

The first player in major league history to hit four home runs in a single game (1894), Lowe performed his feat against "Icebox" Chamberlain on a Boston field used temporarily after a fire destroyed the Beaneaters' regular park. Lowe crowded some lusty hitting into that season, batting .346 with 17 homers and 115 RBI. A versatile player, he spent most of his time at second base.

Lucas, Charles (Red)
1902–1986
New York (NL 1923), Boston (NL 1924), Cincinnati (NL 1926–33), Pittsburgh (NL 1934–38)   **P**
BL/RHP

396 games	.281 ba
404 hits	3 hr
190 rbi	2 sb
2,542 innings	157-135 W–L
3.72 ERA	602 k's
7 saves	

An outstanding batsman as well as a pitcher, Lucas was frequently deployed as a pinch hitter. He was a control artist on the mound, walking only 18 men in 220 innings in 1933. Lucas spent his most productive years pitching for awful clubs in Cincinnati but managed to record 19 wins in 1929 and reach double digits each year from 1927 to 1933.

Luderus, Fred

1885–1961
Chicago (NL 1909–10), Philadelphia (NL 1910–20)
1B   BL/TR

1,346 games	.277 ba
1,344 hits	84 hr
642 rbi	55 sb

In the four-year span between 1911 and 1914, Luderus was one of the leading sluggers in the National League, belting 56 home runs. In 1915, playing on one of five Phillies pennant-winning squads in the 20th century, he batted a career-high .315 and slugged an impressive .438 in the World Series.

Lundgren, Carl

1880–1934
Chicago (NL 1902–09)   P   BR/RHP

179 games	1,322 innings
91-55 W–L	2.42 ERA
535 k's	6 saves

Lundgren compiled outstanding records for the Cubs dynasty of the early 20th century, going 65–27 in

1904–07. In 1907, he manufactured a tiny ERA of 1.17.

Lundy, Dick (King Richard)
1898–1965

Atlantic City Bacharach Giants (1918–28), Philadelphia Hilldales (1919), Baltimore Black Sox (1929–32), Philadelphia Stars (1933), Brooklyn Eagles (1934), New York Cubans (1935), Newark Dodgers (1935), Newark Eagles (1937)   SS
BB/TR

584 games	.317 ba
685 hits	51 hr
43 sb	

Few shortstops ranged as far afield or had as strong a throwing arm as Lundy. At the plate, he batted a robust .484 in 1921. As manager of the Bacharach Giants, he led his team to pennants in 1926 and 1927.

Luque, Dolf (The Pride of Havana)
1890–1957

Boston (NL 1914–15), Cincinnati (NL 1918–29), Brooklyn (NL 1930–31), New York (NL 1932–35)
P   BR/RHP

550 games	3,220 innings
194-179 W–L	3.24 ERA
1,130 k's	28 saves

A tough competitor who did not hesitate to throw inside to defend his share of home plate, Luque was Cincinnati's top hurler during the team's lean years in the twenties. He twice won the NL ERA crown, and he enjoyed a phenomenal season in 1923, going 27–8 with a 1.93 ERA and six shutouts. He was the first Latin-born pitcher to win 20 games. Later in his career, Luque became a top-flight reliever at the Polo Grounds, where he sparkled in the 1933 World Series.

Luzinski, Greg (The Bull)

1950–

Philadelphia (NL 1970–80), Chicago (AL 1981–84)

OF, DH   BR/TR

1,821 games	.276 ba
1,795 hits	307 hr
1,128 rbi	37 sb

Built like a football player, Luzinski crushed line drives to the deepest part of ballparks. A power hitter who maintained a near-.300 average in his prime, he socked at least 30 homers four times and drove home more than 100 runs on four occasions. His best year was probably in 1977, when he hit .309 with 39 home runs and 130 RBI. Defensively, he had limited range and could be a liability.

Lyle, Albert (Sparky)

1944–

Boston (AL 1967–71), New York (AL 1972–78), Texas (AL 1979–80), Philadelphia (NL 1980–82), Chicago (AL 1982)   **P   BL/LHP**

899 games	1,390 innings
99-76 W–L	2.88 ERA
873 k's	238 saves

Following the Yankees' acquisition of Goose Gossage prior to the 1978 season, Lyle went from Cy Young to Sayonara. Irreverent in the locker room but all business on the mound, he threw the sharpest-breaking slider in the AL and was very effective against right-handed batters. Lyle was originally sent to the Yanks by Boston in exchange for Danny Cater; the trade was undoubtedly one of the worst in Red Sox history. Lyle led the AL in saves in 1972 (35) and 1976 (23); he also earned the Cy Young Award in 1977 for his 13 wins, 26 saves, and tiny 2.17 ERA.

Lynn, Fred

1952–

Boston (AL 1974–80), California (AL 1981–84),
Baltimore (AL 1985–88), Detroit (AL 1988–89), San
Diego (NL 1990)   **OF**   **BL/TL**

1,969 games	.283 ba
1,960 hits	306 hr
1,111 rbi	72 sb

Lynn's sweet swing produced fantastic offensive numbers in his rookie season—a .331 batting average, 21
homers, 105 RBI, and a league-leading 103 runs
scored and 47 doubles. In one memorable game at
Tiger Stadium, Lynn collected 10 RBI. The Hall of
Fame beckoned. However, something went wrong, because he enjoyed only one other year with comparable
figures. In 1979, he led the AL in batting (.333) and hit
39 roundtrippers with 122 RBI. Defensively, Lynn was
one of the best; he had good range and sure hands.

Lyons, Jimmy

?

Brooklyn Royal Giants (1914), Chicago American
Giants (1920–24)   **OF**   **BL/TR**

217 games	.292 ba
222 hits	15 hr
76 sb	

Contemporaries said that Lyons ran faster than Cool
Papa Bell. He starred in the Chicago American Giants
outfield. At the plate, the diminutive, five-foot, 6-inch
Lyons was a superb bunter. Defensively, he was a tremendous fly chaser.

Lyons, Ted

1900–1986

Chicago (AL 1923–42, 1946); MGR—Chicago (AL 1946–48) **P, MGR** **BB/RHP**

594 games	4,161 innings
260-230 W–L	3.67 ERA
1,073 k's	23 saves

In Lyons's 21 years on the South Side, the Sox finished in the first division only five times. A workhorse who completed nearly 75 percent of his starts, he threw with a herky-jerky delivery and won 20 games three times before hurting his arm in 1931. Then he developed a knuckle ball and continued as a successful hurler. Among pitchers who lasted more than 20 years, Lyons is the only one never to record 100 strikeouts in a single season, topping out at 74 in 1933. Ironically, he went 10–21 that year. The Sox retired his uniform number 16, and he was inducted into the Hall of Fame in 1955.

M

Mack, Cornelius (Connie)

1862–1956

Washington (NL 1886–89), Buffalo (PL 1890), Pittsburgh (NL 1891–96); MGR—Pittsburgh (NL 1894–96), Philadelphia (AL 1901–50) **C, MGR** **BR/TR**

723 games	.245 ba
659 hits	5 hr
265 rbi	127 sb

No man personified a franchise as strongly as Connie Mack did the Philadelphia Athletics. Assuming control of the team in its inaugural season in the American League in 1901, he managed it for 50 years. Mack always wore a business suit in the dugout and used a rolled-up scorecard to rally his team. He had two outstanding squads in 1910–14 and 1929–31, but he sold the team's stars rather than meet their salary demands. As a result, his A's were perennial losers. Mack was inducted into the Hall of Fame in 1937.

Mack, Shane

1963–

San Diego (NL 1987–88), Minnesota (AL 1990–93 Active) OF   BR/TR

713 games	.295 ba
653 hits	56 hr
291 rbi	76 sb

Mack's trade to Minnesota transformed him from a prospect to an everyday .300 hitter. He cracked the .300 barrier in his first three years in the Twin Cities and helped Minnesota to the World Series in 1991 by batting .310 with 18 homers.

Mackey, Biz

1897–1959

Indianapolis ABC's (1920–22), Philadelphia Hilldales (1923–31), Philadelphia Stars (1933–35), Baltimore Elite Giants (1936–39), Newark Eagles (1939–41, 1945–47) C, MGR   BB/TR

833 games	.322 ba
971 hits	66 hr
51 sb	

A five-time All-Star, Mackey was one of the most admired men in the Negro Leagues. Behind the plate, he had few equals defensively; he was a past master at blocking balls in the dirt and throwing out attempted base stealers. As a member of the Elite Giants, he taught the young Roy Campanella the tricks of the trade. Mackey batted a lusty .364 to lead the Hilldales to the pennant in 1923. As manager of the Newark Eagles, he tutored Monte Irvin, Don Newcombe, and Larry Doby.

MacPhail, Larry

1890–1975
Cincinnati (NL 1934–36), Brooklyn (NL 1939–42),
New York (AL 1945–47)   **EXECUTIVE**

One of baseball's great innovators, the combative Mac-
Phail introduced night baseball to the major leagues in
Cincinnati and began commercial air transportation
for teams. He built winners in Cincinnati and Brooklyn and helped sustain the Yankees' success. Possibly
his most important decision took place off the diamond. In 1939, MacPhail hired Red Barber to broadcast Brooklyn's games, breaking the unwritten agreement among the three New York teams not to air their
games. Barber's announcing style created legions of
new fans for the team. MacPhail's son Lee later worked
as an executive for the Orioles and Yankees and served
a term as president of the American League; his grandson Andy is currently the Minnesota general manager.

Maddox, Garry

1949–
San Francisco (NL 1972–75), Philadelphia (NL
1975–86)   **OF**   **BR/TR**

1,749 games	.285 ba
1,802 hits	117 hr
754 rbi	248 sb

Hall of Famer and Mets announcer Ralph Kiner once
observed that two-thirds of the earth is covered by
water and Maddox covers the other third. Clearly the
best defensive center fielder of his generation, he used
his great speed and sense of anticipation to track down
fly balls. At the plate, he was a good line-drive hitter
who batted .330 with 68 RBI in 1976.

Maddux, Greg

1966–
Chicago (NL 1986–92), Atlanta (NL 1993 Active)
P   **BR/RHP**

248 games	1,709 innings
115-85 W–L	3.19 ERA
1,134 k's	

Don't let his slender frame deceive you—Maddux throws hard and is not averse to pitching inside. Within the cozy confines of Wrigley Field, he developed into the NL's top right-hander, winning the Cy Young Award in 1992. That year, he won 20 games for the first time and compiled a tidy 2.18 ERA. In Atlanta, in 1993, he went 20–10 with a league best 2.36 ERA.

Madlock, Bill (Mad Dog)
1951–
Texas (AL 1973), Chicago (NL 1974–76), San Francisco (NL 1977–79), Pittsburgh (NL 1979–85), Los Angeles (NL 1985–87), Detroit (AL 1987)   **3B BR/TR**

1,806 games	.305 ba
2,008 hits	163 hr
860 rbi	174 sb

A four-time batting champion in the NL, Madlock was one of the best pure hitters of his era. Few remember that the Cubs obtained him from Texas in exchange for future Hall of Famer Ferguson Jenkins, but Madlock batted .313 his first year in Chicago and led the NL in the following two seasons. His two other batting titles came with Pittsburgh in 1981 and 1983.

Magee, Sherwood (Sherry)
1884–1929
Philadelphia (NL 1904–14), Boston (NL 1915–17), Cincinnati (NL 1917–19)   **OF   BR/TR**

2,085 games	.291 ba
2,169 hits	83 hr
1,176 rbi	441 sb

Magee spent the first 11 years of his career with the Phillies but had the misfortune of being traded the year before Philadelphia won its first pennant in 1915. A powerful batter in the dead ball era, he consistently hit 30 doubles a year and led the NL in RBI on four occasions. Magee played his entire career with epilepsy.

Maglie, Sal (The Barber)
1917–1992
New York (NL 1945, 1950–55), Cleveland (AL 1955–56), Brooklyn (NL 1956–57), New York (AL 1957–58), St. Louis (NL 1958)   **P**   **BR/RHP**

303 games	1,723 innings
119-62 W–L	3.15 ERA
862 k's	14 saves

Maglie was the type of competitor that you loved if he was on your team but hated if he was your opponent. Nicknamed "the Barber" because he had no compunction about "shaving" batters with inside pitches, Maglie enjoyed his best days with the Giants. Readmitted to the National League following his defection to the Mexican League in 1946, he threw the ball hard and had an exceptional curve. In 1950, he went 18–4; the following year he propelled the Giants to the Miracle of Coogan's Bluff with a 23–6 record. Maglie pitched for all three New York teams in the fifties and was the Dodgers' hurler when Don Larsen pitched a perfect game in the 1956 World Series.

Malarcher, Dave (Gentleman Dave)
1894–1982
Chicago American Giants (1920–34)   **3B**
BB/TR

513 games	.270 ba
507 hits	5 hr
81 sb	

Malarcher earned his nickname, "Gentleman Dave," because of his genteel manners both on and off the field. He graduated from the University of New Orleans before beginning his career in baseball. Most fans regarded Malarcher as the best third baseman in the Negro Leagues. It came as no surprise when he replaced Rube Foster as manager of the Chicago American Giants in 1926.

Malone, Perce (Pat)

1902–1943
Chicago (NL 1928–34), New York (AL 1935–37)
P BB/RHP

357 games	1,915 innings
134-92 W–L	3.74 ERA
1,024 k's	26 saves

Malone was one mean pitcher on the mound. He commanded the inside part of the plate by knocking down any batter who crowded it. In 1929–30, he led the NL in victories, racking up 42. He also pitched the most shutouts (5) and fanned the most batters (166) in 1929. When not pitching, Malone was a fierce bench jockey.

Maloney, Jim

1940–
Cincinnati (NL 1960–70), California (AL 1971) P
BL/RHP

302 games	1,849 innings
134-84 W–L	3.19 ERA
1,605 k's	4 saves

A Cincinnati bonus baby, Maloney threw one of the best fastballs in the NL during the sixties. After he learned to control his temper, he won 23 games in 1963 and 20 in 1965. Maloney pitched no-hitters against the Cubs and Astros, yet he lost a 1–0, 11-inning game to the Mets in 1965 after holding them hitless for the first 10 frames and fanning 18 batters.

Malzone, Frank

1930–

Boston (AL 1955–65), California (AL 1966) 3B

BR/TR

1,441 games	.274 ba
1,486 hits	133 hr
728 rbi	14 sb

A dependable third baseman for the Red Sox over the course of a decade, Malzone won three Gold Glove awards and consistently batted between .260 and .295. He drove in a career-high 103 RBI as a rookie in 1957. A six-time All-Star, Malzone rarely walked or struck out.

Mantle, Mickey

1931–

New York (AL 1951–68) OF, 1B BB/TR

2,401 games	.298 ba
2,415 hits	536 hr
1,509 rbi	153 sb

One of the most gifted athletes ever to play the game, Mantle's career was nevertheless hampered by a series of leg injuries. Blessed with brilliant speed and power from both sides of the plate, he won the AL triple crown in 1956, batting .353 with 52 homers and 130 RBI. More dangerous when batting right-handed, Mantle led the AL in home runs four times and runs scored six times, surpassing the century mark in nine consecutive years (1953–61). Undemonstrative as a young man, Mantle was booed regularly until 1960, when the arrival of Roger Maris seemed to shift the burden of high fan expectations off his shoulders. In retirement, Mantle's legend has grown and he is loved as never before. The Yankees retired his uniform number 7, and he was inducted into the Hall of Fame in 1974.

Manush, Henry (Heinie)

1901–1971

Detroit (AL 1923–27), St. Louis (AL 1928–30),
Washington (AL 1930–35), Boston (AL 1936),
Brooklyn (NL 1937–38), Pittsburgh (NL 1938–39)
OF   BL/TL

2,008 games	.330 ba
2,524 hits	110 hr
1,183 rbi	114 sb

Manush starred with Ty Cobb and Harry Heilmann in
the greatest-hitting Tigers outfield in the team's history. Although he choked up on the bat and didn't
swing for the fences, he led the AL in doubles in 1928
and in 1929, and his line drives earned him a batting
title in 1926 (.378). In 1933, his bat sparked the Senators to the pennant. Manush was inducted into the
Hall of Fame in 1964.

Maranville, Walter (Rabbit)

1891–1954

Boston (NL 1912–20, 1929–33, 1935), Pittsburgh
(NL 1921–24), Chicago (NL 1925), Brooklyn (NL
1926), St. Louis (NL 1927–28); MGR—Chicago
(NL 1925)   SS, 2B, MGR   BR/TR

2,605 games	.258 ba
1,605 hits	28 hr
884 rbi	291 sb

Some experts questioned Maranville's induction into
the Hall of Fame in 1954, but his meager lifetime average (.258) belied his overall contributions to the game.
A great fielder who made the basket catch famous and a
fine clutch hitter, Maranville led the 1914 Miracle
Braves to the World Series crown. A funny, fun-loving
man, Maranville was one of the most popular players
of his era.

Marberry, Fred (Firpo)
1898–1976

Washington (AL 1923–32, 1936), Detroit (AL 1933–3), New York (NL 1936) P BR/RHP

551 games	2,067 innings
148-88 W–L	3.63 ERA
822 k's	101 saves

A fastballing reliever in the mold of modern firemen, Marberry threw with an exaggerated windup and was extremely difficult to hit in the late-afternoon shadows. He led the AL in games pitched six times and in games saved on five occasions. His best season came in 1929 when he both started and relieved, going 19–12 with 11 saves.

Marcelle, Oliver (Ghost)
1897–1949

Brooklyn Royal Giants (1918–19), Atlantic City Bacharach Giants (1920–23, 1925–28), New York Lincoln Giants (1924–25), Baltimore Black Sox (1929), Brooklyn Royal Giants (1930) 3B BR/TR

349 games	.305 ba
442 hits	12 hr
41 sb	

The Negro Leagues best-fielding third baseman in the twenties, Marcelle did his best work for the Bacharach Giants, where he teamed with shortstop Dick Lundy to make the left side of the infield impregnable. He excelled at charging bunts and throwing out the batter while on the dead run. A Creole from New Orleans, Marcelle was a tempestuous player who would fight his own teammates as well as opponents. Offensively, he sprayed the ball to all fields.

Marichal, Juan (The Dominican Dandy)

1937–

San Francisco (NL 1960–73), Boston (AL 1974), Los Angeles (NL 1975)   P   BR/RHP

471 games	3,507 innings
243-142 W–L	2.89 ERA
2,303 k's	2 saves

When Marichal pitched a one-hitter against Philadelphia in his major league debut, it was a harbinger of things to come. He used an exaggerated windup that included a very high leg kick, and he released the ball from every conceivable angle and at a multitude of speeds. Marichal had 12 consecutive winning seasons (1960–71), won 20 games six times, and pitched a no-hitter in 1963 against Houston. He won 26 games in 1968 and 25 in both 1963 and 1966. The Giants retired his uniform number 27, and he was inducted into the Hall of Fame in 1983.

Marion, Marty (Slats)

1917–

St. Louis (NL 1940–50), St. Louis (AL 1952–53); MGR—St. Louis (NL 1951), St. Louis (AL 1952–53), Chicago (AL 1954–56)   SS, MGR BR/TR

1,572 games	.263 ba
1,448 hits	36 hr
624 rbi	35 sb

If the Hall of Fame rated defensive skills as highly as it does batting prowess, Marion would have entered baseball's shrine long ago. Tall for a shortstop at 6 feet, 2 inches, Marion seemed to cover the entire left side of the Cardinals infield. At the plate, he was productive too, knocking in 70 or more runs twice.

Maris, Roger
1934–1985
Cleveland (AL 1957–58), Kansas City (AL
1958–59), New York (AL 1960–66), St. Louis (NL
1967–68) **OF**   **BL/TR**

1,463 games	.260 ba
1,325 hits	275 hr
851 rbi	21 sb

A dead-pull hitter, Maris exhibited streaks of great play
and home run punch with Cleveland and Kansas City
before the Yankees acquired him prior to the 1960 season. He proceeded to win the MVP award in recognition of his 39 homers and league-high 112 RBI. The
following year, Maris became a household name when
he belted 61 home runs to break Babe Ruth's single-
season record of 60. His strong outfield play, particularly his rifle arm, and his aggressive base running made
Maris a complete player. The Yankees retired his uniform number 9.

Marquard, Richard (Rube)
1889–1980
New York (NL 1908–15), Brooklyn (NL 1915–20),
Cincinnati (NL 1921), Boston (NL 1922–25) **P**
BB/LHP

536 games	3,306 innings
201-177 W–L	3.08 ERA
1,593 k's	19 saves

A sophisticated urbanite from Cleveland, Marquard
was no rube on or off the diamond. He was nicknamed
"Rube" because he threw left-handed like Rube Waddell, a dominant pitcher of his day. Purchased by the
Giants from Indianapolis for the record sum of
$11,000 in 1908, Marquard led the Giants to pen-
nants in 1911–13 as he won 73 games. In 1912, he
won a record 19 straight games; and in 1915, he
pitched a no-hitter against Brooklyn. The following

year, Marquard led Brooklyn to their first pennant in 16 years. He was inducted into the Hall of Fame in 1971.

Marshall, Mike

1943–

Detroit (AL 1967), Seattle (AL 1969), Houston (NL 1970), Montreal (NL 1970–73), Los Angeles (NL 1974–76), Atlanta (NL 1976–77), Texas (AL 1977), Minnesota (AL 1978–80), New York (NL 1981) P
BR/RHP

723 games	1,386 innings
97-112 W-L	3.14 ERA
880 k's	188 saves

Marshall marched to his own drummer. He earned a doctorate in kinesiology and applied his own theories to pitching. He believed that he could pitch as frequently as was needed; he put this theory to the test in 1974, when he made 106 game appearances for the Dodgers. That year, he won the NL Cy Young Award in recognition of his 15 relief victories, 208 innings pitched, 2.42 ERA, and league-best 21 saves. Marshall's best pitch was a screwball.

Martin, Billy (The Kid)

1928–1989

New York (AL 1950–53, 1955–57), Kansas City (AL 1957), Detroit (AL 1958), Cleveland (AL 1959), Cincinnati (NL 1960), Milwaukee (NL 1961), Minnesota (AL 1961); MGR—Minnesota (AL 1969), Detroit (AL 1971–73), Texas (AL 1973–75), New York (AL 1975–79, 1983, 1985, 1988), Oakland (AL 1980–82) 2B, MGR   BR/TR

1,021 games	.257 ba
877 hits	64 hr
333 rbi	34 sb

An abrasive personality, Billy Martin was loved by his teammates and hated by his opponents. Labeled as

Casey Stengel's boy when he arrived in New York, he rarely hit for a high average but always seemed to make his hits count. In the seventh game of the 1952 World Series, Martin made a game-saving catch of an infield pop-up. The following year, he drove home the decisive run in the sixth and final game of the World Series and batted .500 with 12 hits. As a manager, Martin resurrected several franchises from the depths of their division and led the Yankees to victory in the 1977 World Series. Martin enjoyed a combustible relationship with Yankees team owner George Steinbrenner, who fired him four times. The Yankees retired his uniform number 1.

Martin, John (Pepper, the Wild Horse of the Osage)

1904–1965
St. Louis (NL 1928, 1930–40, 1944)   OF, 3B
BR/TR

1,189 games	.298 ba
1,227 hits	59 hr
501 rbi	146 sb

Martin epitomized the Cardinals' Gas House Gang—rough, hell-bent, and profane. He became a national star in the 1931 World Series when he hit .500 and stole five bases to lead St. Louis to victory over Philadelphia. Martin led the NL in stolen bases three times.

Martinez, Dennis (El Presidente)

1955–
Baltimore (AL 1976–86), Montreal (NL 1986–93), Cleveland (AL 1994 Active) P   BR/RHP

558 games	3,384 innings
208-165 W–L	3.64 ERA
1,831 k's	6 saves

No one questioned the quality of Martinez's stuff when he pitched for Baltimore in the seventies and eighties, but he never became a big winner. His career eventually ground to a halt due to a drinking problem, and it took a trade to Montreal for Martinez to regain his effectiveness. The highlight of his career came when he pitched a perfect game against the Dodgers in 1991. In his native Nicaragua, Martinez is a national hero.

Martinez, Felix (Tippy)

1950–
New York (AL 1974–76), Baltimore (AL 1976–86), Minnesota (AL 1988)   P   LHP

546 games	834 innings
55-42 W–L	3.45 ERA
632 k's	115 saves

The Yankees couldn't wait for Martinez to develop, so they included him in a mammoth trade with the Orioles in 1976. It was a trade that haunted them for a decade as he became one of the top lefty stoppers in the game. Armed with good control of a variety of pitches and an excellent move to first base, Martinez won 10 games in 1979 and went 9–3 with 21 saves in the Orioles 1983 championship season.

Mathews, Bobby

1851–1898
New York (NL 1876), Cincinnati (NL 1877), Providence (NL 1879, 1881), Boston (NL 1881–82), Philadelphia (AA 1883–87)   P   BR/RHP

323 games	2,734 innings
166-136 W–L	3.00 ERA
1,199 k's	3 saves

A five-year veteran of the old National Association, Mathews spent an additional 10 seasons in the AA and NL, winning a combined total of 297 games—more than any other pitcher not in the Hall of Fame. A small man at 5 feet, 5 inches and 140 pounds, he was among the first pitchers to throw the curve ball and the spitter. Despite playing for a weak-hitting Mutuals of New York team in the NA, he won a combined total of 100 games in three seasons (1873–75). After spending many years with unstable franchises, Mathews joined the Philadelphia Athletics of the AA. There he enjoyed his greatest success, winning 30 games in three consecutive years (1883–85).

Mathews, Eddie
1931–
Boston (NL 1952), Milwaukee (NL 1953–65), Atlanta (NL 1966), Houston (NL 1967), Detroit (AL 1967–68); MGR—Atlanta (NL 1972–74)   **3B, MGR**   **BL/TR**

2,391 games	.271 ba
2,315 hits	512 hr
1,453 rbi	68 sb

The NL's best third baseman in the 1950s, Mathews became the first slugger in major league history at that position. He smacked more than 30 homers in nine consecutive seasons (1953–61) and became the seventh player to hit 500 career home runs. Mathews led the NL in homers in 1953 (47) and 1959 (46). Defensively, he made himself into a good fielder through practice. The Braves retired his uniform number 41, and he was inducted into the Hall of Fame in 1978.

Mathewson, Christy (Big Six, Matty)
1880–1925
New York (NL 1900–16), Cincinnati (NL 1916); MGR—Cincinnati (NL 1916–18)   **P, MGR BR/RHP**

635 games	4,780 innings
373-188 W–L	2.13 ERA
2,502 k's	28 saves

A graduate of Bucknell, Mathewson brought baseball a degree of respectability that had been lacking. He was the epitome of the all-American boy. On the mound, his best pitch was the "fadeaway," or screwball. He won 30 or more games four times, including a modern

National League record of 37 in 1908. In the 1905 World Series, "Big Six," whose nickname was borrowed from New York's biggest fire engine, secured his immortality when he shut out the Athletics three times.

Matlack, Jon

1950–

New York (NL 1971–77), Texas (AL 1978–83)   P

BL/LHP

361 games	2,363 innings
125-126 W–L	3.18 ERA
1,516 k's	3 saves

Matlack's career was an example of the whole not equaling the sum of its parts. He had great stuff—a moving fastball, a sharp breaking ball, and excellent control—yet he never matched the outstanding achievements of his cohorts, Seaver and Koosman. He blamed his mediocre performance on his being pushed around in the Mets rotation and poor run support, but he often did not pitch well when the game was on the line. Matlack won at least 13 games in each of his first five years in the bigs and later won 15 games for Texas.

Matthews, Gary (Sarge)

1950–

San Francisco (NL 1972–76), Atlanta (NL 1977–80), Philadelphia (NL 1981–83), Chicago (NL 1984–87), Seattle (AL 1987)   OF   BR/TR

2,033 games	.281 ba
2,011 hits	234 hr
978 rbi	183 sb

Matthews was an outspoken team leader wherever he played. A consistent .280 hitter with good power, he belted at least 20 homers three times and cracked over 20 doubles in 10 seasons. His best season came in 1979, when he hit .304 with 27 homers and 90 RBI.

Mattingly, Don (The Hit Man, Donny Baseball)

1961–

New York (AL 1982–93 Active) **1B**   **BL/TL**

1,560 games	.309 ba
1,908 hits	214 hr
999 rbi	14 sb

Before he was slowed by a back injury in 1990, Mattingly was generally regarded as the best player in baseball, hitting for high average, belting home runs, and fielding his position brilliantly. Between 1984 and 1989, Mattingly set a host of records. In 1984, he led the AL in batting (.343), base hits (207), and doubles (44). The next year, he led the league in doubles (48) and RBI (145). In 1986, he finished second in batting to Wade Boggs (.352) and led the AL in hits (238, a new Yankee record) and doubles (53). Finally, in 1987, Mattingly tied the major league record when he cracked home runs in eight consecutive games.

Mauch, Gene

1925–

Brooklyn (NL 1944, 1948), Pittsburgh (NL 1947), Chicago (NL 1948–49), Boston (NL 1950–51), St. Louis (NL 1952), Boston (AL 1956–57);
MGR—Philadelphia (NL 1960–68), Montreal (NL 1969–75), Minnesota (AL 1976–80), California (AL 1981–82, 1985–87) **2B, MGR**   **BR/TR**

304 games	.239 ba
176 hits	5 hr
62 rbi	6 sb

Though considered by his peers to be a managerial genius, Mauch was never able to win a pennant, let alone a World Series. He came close in 1964, 1982, and 1986, but the Phillies and the Angels both suffered classic collapses. Mauch's reputation derived from his strategic maneuvers and game preparation. His lifetime record was 1,902–2,037.

Maxwell, Charlie (Smokey)

1927–

Boston (AL 1950–52, 1954), Baltimore (AL 1955),
Detroit (AL 1955–62), Chicago (AL 1962–64)   OF
BL/TL

1,133 games	.264 ba
856 hits	148 hr
532 rbi	18 sb

If it was a summer weekend in the late fifties, you could count on Maxwell hitting a home run. He specialized in belting roundtrippers on Sunday, connecting 40 times in his career. Maxwell posted his best numbers in 1956, batting .326 with 28 home runs and 87 RBI.

May, Lee (The Big Bopper)

1943–

Cincinnati (NL 1965–71), Houston (NL 1972–74),
Baltimore (AL 1975–80), Kansas City (AL 1981–82)
1B, DH   BR/TR

2,071 games	.267 ba
2,031 hits	354 hr
1,244 rbi	39 sb

May fit in nicely in the early days of the Big Red Machine, smashing 38 homers in 1969 and 39 in 1971, but he was sent packing to Houston in exchange for future Hall of Famer Joe Morgan prior to the 1972 season. May continued his lusty hitting in the spacious Astrodome, driving home 105 runs in 1973 and a league-best 109 runs in 1976.

Mayberry, John

1949–

Houston (NL 1968–71), Kansas City (AL 1972–77),
Toronto (AL 1978–82), New York (AL 1982)   1B
BL/TL

1,620 games	.253 ba
1,379 hits	255 hr
879 rbi	20 sb

The free-swinging Mayberry was one of the most dangerous sluggers in the AL during the seventies. After failing to produce in Houston, he found a home in Kansas City, averaging 26 homers and 94 RBI in 1972–75. Patient at the plate, he also led the AL in walks in 1973 (122) and 1975 (119).

Mays, Carl (Sub)

1891–1971
Boston (AL 1915–19), New York (AL 1919–23),
Cincinnati (NL 1924–28), New York (NL 1929)   P
BL/RHP

490 games	3,021 innings
207-126 W–L	2.92 ERA
862 k's	31 saves

A sullen, intense competitor, Mays was already one of the least-liked men in the major leagues when one of his submarine pitches struck Cleveland shortstop Ray Chapman in the head, killing him. There was a short-lived campaign to ban him from the game, but Mays survived. He pitched his best ball in 1921, leading the AL in wins (27), winning percentage (.750), innings pitched (336), and saves (7). Mays won at least 20 games five times. There is little doubt that if it were not for that fatal pitch, Mays would be in the Hall of Fame today.

Mays, Willie (The "Say Hey" Kid)

1931–
Birmingham Black Barons (1948–50), New York
(NL 1951–52, 1954–57), San Francisco (NL
1958–72), New York (NL 1972–73)   OF
BR/TR

2,992 games	.302 ba
3,283 hits	660 hr
1,903 rbi	338 sb

Unquestionably the greatest player in the second half of the 20th century, Mays was a unique powerhouse who excelled at all aspects of the game—he could hit, hit with power, run, field, and throw. He sparked the Giants to the 1954 World Series crown by hitting .345 with 41 home runs and 110 RBI. His catch of Vic Wertz's 475-foot fly ball in game one of the series has been called baseball's finest. Typically, after a game at the Polo Grounds, he would play stickball on the streets of Harlem. After the Giants moved to the West Coast, Mays adjusted his batting style to take advantage of the prevailing winds at Candlestick Park. On the base paths, Mays led the NL in steals for four consecutive years (1956–59). His flair for the dramatic exhilarated fans. Ironically, he never led the NL in RBI but ranks third all-time. The Giants retired his uniform number 24, and he was inducted into the Hall of Fame in 1979.

Mazeroski, Bill (Maz)
1936–
Pittsburgh (NL 1956–72)   **2B**   **BR/TR**

2,163 games	.260 ba
2,016 hits	138 hr
853 rbi	27 sb

Were it not for one fateful October afternoon at Forbes Field in Pittsburgh, Mazeroski would be remembered primarily as a smart-fielding second sacker who excelled at turning the double play. At bat, he was a steady .260 hitter with little power. But on October 13, 1960, leading off in the bottom of the ninth, Mazeroski slammed a home run over the left-field wall to win the World Series for the Pirates. It brought a shocking end to the most unpredictable World Series ever played.

McAuliffe, Dick
1939–
Detroit (AL 1960–73), Boston (AL 1974–75)   **2B,**
SS   **BL/TR**

1,763 games	.247 ba
1,530 hits	197 hr
974 rbi	63 sb

Most middle infielders are content to get on base for the power hitters in the lineup, but McAuliffe combined both abilities. He pounded the ball around spacious Tiger Stadium and also drew a fair number of walks, twice surpassing 100 in a season. Never a high-average hitter, he posted a career-best .274 in both 1966 and 1973 and crunched at least 11 homers in 10 consecutive seasons.

McCarthy, Joe
1887–1978
MGR—Chicago (NL 1926–30), New York (AL 1931–46), Boston (AL 1948–50)   **MGR**

The winningest manager of all time, with a .615 percentage, McCarthy had one pennant winner with Chicago and eight with the Yankees, including seven World Series champs. In 16 years with New York, he finished below second place only twice. Although denigrated as a "push-button" manager when he skippered the great Yankees teams of the 1930s, he earned the respect of all his players. McCarthy was a stickler for fundamentals, and he developed a style of conduct on and off the field that became known as "Yankee class." He was inducted into the Hall of Fame in 1957.

McCarthy, Tommy
1863–1922
Boston (UA 1884), Boston (NL 1885, 1892–95), Philadelphia (NL 1886–87), St. Louis (AA 1888–91), Brooklyn (NL 1896); MGR—St. Louis (AA 1890)   **OF, MGR**   **BR/TR**

1,275 games	.292 ba
1,496 hits	44 hr
666 rbi	468 sb

An innovative player, McCarthy was adept at the hit-and-run and at stealing opponents signs. In 1888, he stole 93 bases to lead the St. Louis Browns to the American Association pennant. In Boston, McCarthy teamed with Hugh Duffy in the "Heavenly Twins" outfield. He entered the Hall of Fame in 1946.

McCarver, Tim

1941–
St. Louis (NL 1959–61, 1963–69, 1973–74), Philadelphia (NL 1970–72, 1975–80), Montreal (NL 1972), Boston (AL 1974–75)   C   BL/TR

1,909 games	.271 ba
1,501 hits	97 hr
645 rbi	61 sb

Most fans today think of McCarver as the erudite announcer for the Mets and CBS network sports, forgetting that during the sixties he was the NL's best catcher. Fast afoot, he lined the ball sharply to all fields and in 1966 led the league in triples (13). In 1964, he batted .288 in regular-season play and swatted a lusty .478 in the World Series, including a game-winning three-run homer in the 10th inning of game five. While playing for Philadelphia later in his career, McCarver gained fame as Steve Carlton's personal catcher.

McCormick, Frank (Buck)

1911–1982
Cincinnati (NL 1934, 1937–45), Philadelphia (NL 1946–47), Boston (NL 1947–48)   1B   BR/TR

1,534 games	.299 ba
1,711 hits	128 hr
951 rbi	27 sb

Cincinnati's leading run producer on the 1939–40 pennant-winning teams, McCormick batted a robust .332 in 1939 while driving home a league-high 128 runs. The following year, he knocked in 127 runs and was voted the league MVP. For three consecutive years in 1938–40, McCormick led the NL in hits. Defensively, he starred as well, surpassing all NL first-basemen in fielding percentage four times.

McCormick, Jim

1856–1918

Indianapolis (NL 1878), Cleveland (NL 1879–84), Cincinnati (UA 1884), Providence (NL 1885), Chicago (NL 1885–86), Pittsburgh (NL 1887); MGR—Cleveland (NL 1879–80, 1882)   **P, MGR**
BR/RHP

492 games	4,275 innings
265-214 W–L	2.43 ERA
1,704 k's	1 save

At 225 pounds, McCormick was one of the heaviest hurlers of the 19th century. He used his heft to hurl the baseball past his opponents in the 1880s. He left Cleveland midway through the 1884 season to join the outlaw Union Association and won a total of 40 games that year. McCormick consistently pitched to a low ERA; he led the NL in 1883 (1.84) and the UA in 1884 (1.54). After returning to the NL, he had one more banner year, going 31–11 for Chicago in 1886.

McCovey, Willie (Stretch)

1938–
San Francisco (NL 1959–73, 1977–80), San Diego (NL 1974–76), Oakland (AL 1976)   **1B, OF**
BL/TL

2,588 games	.270 ba
2,211 hits	521 hr
1,555 rbi	26 sb

McCovey's practice swings sent tremors of anticipation throughout the ballpark as fans and players alike waited for him to slam one over the outfield fence. A truly fearsome slugger, he ranks number one among NL lefty hitters in career home runs. His 18 career grand slams rank second to Gehrig's record of 23 slams. McCovey led the NL in homers and RBI twice and won the league MVP award in 1969. Probably the most popular player in San Francisco Giant history, McCovey was inducted into the Hall of Fame in 1986.

McDaniel, Lindy

1935–

St. Louis (NL 1955–62), Chicago (NL 1963–65), San Francisco (NL 1966–68), New York (AL 1968–73), Kansas City (AL 1974–75)   P
BR/RHP

987 games	2,139 innings
141-119 W–L	3.45 ERA
1,361 k's	172 saves

It didn't take long for McDaniel to reach the majors, and once he arrived, he stayed long enough to pitch in the third-most games in big league history. After a few seasons as a Cardinals starter, he found his niche in the bullpen and emerged as one of the top relievers of the fifties. Relying heavily on a forkball, he led the NL in saves three times. After his career hit the skids, McDaniel was traded to the Yankees; there he recaptured his former glory, saving 29 games in 1970 and winning 12 times in 1973.

McDougald, Gil

1928–

New York (AL 1951–60)   2B, 3B, SS   BR/TR

1,336 games	.276 ba
1,291 hits	112 hr
576 rbi	45 sb

Versatility personified, McDougald alternated between three infield positions for Casey Stengel's Yanks. A brash, cocky youngster, he was named AL Rookie of the Year in 1951, when he batted .306 with 14 home runs and also sparkled in the field. At bat, McDougald stood far from the plate, adopting an extreme open stance while holding his bat high over his head.

McDowell, Jack (Black Jack)

1966–

Chicago (AL 1987–93 Active)   P   RHP

166 games	1,162 innings
81-49 W–L	3.46 ERA
791 k's	

Generally regarded as the contemporary pitcher who most resembles the hurlers of yesterday, McDowell is a workhorse who takes command of home plate and is tough to beat once he gains the lead. He won 20 games in 1992 and 22 more in 1993. Off the field, he plays the guitar in a rock band.

McDowell, Sam (Sudden Sam)

1942–

Cleveland (AL 1961–71), San Francisco (NL 1972–73), New York (AL 1973–74), Pittsburgh (NL 1975)   P   BL/LHP

425 games	2,492 innings
141-134 W–L	3.17 ERA
2,453 k's	14 saves

When McDowell was scheduled to pitch, batters often felt the need to take the day off. Not only was he the hardest thrower in the AL, his control was so poor that most hitters were reluctant to get a deep toehold in the batter's box. Some thought he would one day equal Koufax in stature, but poor control on and off the mound led to his demise. McDowell led the AL in strikeouts in five of the six years between 1965 and 1970, with totals ranging from 225 to 325. Yet he won 20 games only once, in 1970. In his best year, 1976, he surrendered just 178 hits in 273 innings, fanned 325, and led the AL in ERA (2.18).

McGee, Willie

1958–

St. Louis (NL 1982–90), Oakland (AL 1990), San
Francisco (NL 1991–93 Active)   OF   BB/TR

1,592 games	.298 ba
1,832 hits	61 hr
685 rbi	317 sb

The Yankees came to rue the day they traded McGee
to the Cardinals for lefty reliever Bob Sykes. The
speedy outfielder batted .296 as a rookie, sparking the
Cardinals to the World Series title. McGee led the NL
in hitting in both 1985 (.353) and 1990 (.335), although he was traded to Oakland late in 1990 and won
the title by default. At the plate, he has the unusual
ability to look awful on one or two swings, only to slap
the next offering for a base hit. Although he has batted
leadoff, McGee does not draw very many walks.

McGinnity, Joe (Iron Man)

1871–1929

Baltimore (NL 1899), Brooklyn (NL 1900),
Baltimore (AL 1901–02), New York (NL 1902–08)
P   BR/RHP

465 games	3,441 innings
264-142 W–L	2.66 ERA
1,068 k's	24 saves

Nicknamed for his work in a foundry, McGinnity was
truly an iron man on the mound, pitching both ends of
doubleheaders five times in his career. He won three
twin bills in August 1903. McGinnity relied on guile,
control, and a special pitch—an underhanded curve
ball that he dubbed "Old Sal"—to baffle batters. He
won more than 20 games in eight consecutive seasons
and set a modern NL record by pitching 434 innings in
1903. McGinnity was inducted into the Hall of Fame
in 1946.

McGraw, Frank (Tug)

1944–
New York (NL 1965–67, 1969–74), Philadelphia
(NL 1975–84)   P   BR/LHP

824 games	1,514 innings
96-92 W–L	3.14 ERA
1,109 k's	180 saves

A screwball on and off the field, McGraw relied on the
scroogie as his out pitch. As a young player, he created
a stir when he became the first Mets hurler to beat
Sandy Koufax. He developed into the best lefty reliever
in the NL. The Mets rallied behind his battle cry, "You
Gotta Believe," to win the 1973 pennant after being
stuck in last place well into August. Traded to the Phillies, he pitched them to their first and only World Series title in 1980.

McGraw, John (Little Napoleon, Muggsy)

1873–1934
Baltimore (AA 1891), Baltimore (NL 1892–99), St.
Louis (NL 1900), Baltimore (AL 1901–02), New
York (NL 1902–06); MGR—Baltimore (NL 1899),
Baltimore (AL 1901–02), New York (NL 1902–32)
3B, MGR   BL/TR

1,099 games	.334 ba
1,309 hits	13 hr
462 rbi	436 sb

As the vitriolic leadoff batter for the scrappy Baltimore
Orioles teams of the 1890s and later the combative
manager of the New York Giants from 1902 to 1932,
John McGraw came to personify baseball. After his
playing career ended due to a serious spike wound suffered at third base, he became a full-time field boss. His
autocratic style inspired both intense admiration and
deep-seated hatred among both players and fans. Yet
McGraw's disciples continue to follow his credo of the
game to the present day. His Giants teams won 10

pennants and three World Series. McGraw was inducted into the Hall of Fame in 1937.

McGregor, Scott
1954–
Baltimore (AL 1976–88)   P   LHP

356 games	2,140 innings
138-108 W–L	3.99 ERA
904 k's	5 saves

McGregor knew how to pitch. Blessed with excellent control and the ability to change speeds on all his pitches, he kept batters off-stride. Once considered the crown jewel of the Yankees' farm system, he wound up in Baltimore as a result of a 1976 trade that sent Ken Holtzman and Doyle Alexander to New York. By 1980, he was a 20-game winner, and he later scored 18 triumphs in the Orioles' 1983 championship season.

McGriff, Fred (Crimedog)
1963–
Toronto (AL 1986–90), San Diego (NL 1991–93), Atlanta (NL 1993 Active)   1B   BL/TL

1,034 games	.281 ba
1,001 hits	228 hr
616 rbi	38 sb

Don Mattingly blocked McGriff's ascent to the Yankees' first-base job, so New York traded him to Toronto for the forgettable reliever Dale Murray. The team made many other bad trades in the eighties, but this one takes the prize for the worst. McGriff developed into one of the most feared sluggers in the game, leading both the AL and the NL in homers. He has cracked at least 30 long flies every year since 1988.

McGuire, James (Deacon)
1863–1936

Toledo (AA 1884), Detroit (NL 1885, 1888),
Philadelphia (NL 1886–88), Cleveland (AA 1888),
Rochester (AA 1890), Washington (AA 1891),
Washington (NL 1892–99), Brooklyn (NL
1899–1901), Detroit (AL 1902–03, 1912), New
York (AL 1904–07), Boston (AL 1907–08),
Cleveland (AL 1908, 1910); MGR—Washington
(NL 1898), Boston (AL 1907–08), Cleveland (AL
1909–11)   **C, MGR**   **BR/TR**

1,781 games	.278 ba
1,749 hits	45 hr
787 rbi	117 sb

In a 26-year career that ranked as baseball's longest
until the record was broken by Nolan Ryan in 1993,
McGuire played for 13 franchises. A gentlemanly
player, "Deacon" played his best seasons for the awful
Washington Senators of 1894–98, batting a career-
high .343 in 1897. After he had clocked more than two
decades of catching with only rudimentary protective
equipment, McGuire's gnarled and twisted fingers became the subject of a famous sports photograph.

McGwire, Mark
1963–

Oakland (AL 1986–93 Active)   **1B**   **BR/TR**

943 games	.249 ba
800 hits	229 hr
632 rbi	6 sb

No batter has ever hit more home runs in his first six
full seasons than Mark McGwire. His 49 homers as a
rookie surpassed the old mark by 11. Make a mistake
to McGwire and the ball will go out of the yard. Yet his
batting averages indicate that he can be pitched to. In
1989–91, he batted .231, .235, and .201. Defensively,
McGwire is a smooth fielder who has good range.

McInnis, John (Stuffy)

1890–1960

Philadelphia (AL 1909–17), Boston (AL 1918–21),
Cleveland (AL 1922), Boston (NL 1923–24),
Pittsburgh (NL 1925–26), Philadelphia (NL 1927);
MGR—Philadelphia (NL 1927)   **1B, MGR**
BR/TR

2,128 games	.307 ba
2,405 hits	20 hr
1,062 rbi	172 sb

A member of the Athletics' $100,000 infield, McInnis
played on three Philadelphia pennant winners. In
1912, he hit .327 with 101 RBI. McInnis was a
smooth fielder who led AL first basemen six times in
fielding percentage.

McKechnie, Bill (Deacon)

1886–1965

Pittsburgh (NL 1907, 1910–12, 1918, 1920), Boston
(NL 1913), New York (AL 1913), Indianapolis (FL
1914), Newark (FL 1915), New York (NL 1916),
Cincinnati (NL 1916–17); MGR—Newark (FL
1915), Pittsburgh (NL 1922–26), St. Louis (NL
1928–29), Boston (NL 1930–37), Cincinnati (NL
1938–46)   **3B, MGR**   **BB/TR**

845 games	.251 ba
713 hits	8 hr
240 rbi	127 sb

The only manager to take three different franchises
(Pittsburgh, St. Louis, and Cincinnati) to the World
Series, "Deacon" McKechnie was a quiet man and a
lay preacher. As a strategist, he played for one run at a
time and favored strong defensive players. He preferred
big, strong pitchers and loved the curve ball. He was
inducted into the Hall of Fame in 1962.

McLain, Denny

1944–

Detroit (AL 1963–70), Washington (AL 1971),
Oakland (AL 1972), Atlanta (NL 1972)   P
BR/RHP

280 games	1,886 innings
131-91 W–L	3.39 ERA
1,282 k's	2 saves

The last pitcher to win 30 games in one season, McLain went 31–6 for the world champion Tigers in 1968. He won 20 games on two other occasions, but unfortunately his legacy will be tarnished by his subsequent fall from grace. Following his suspension from baseball by commissioner Bowie Kuhn, McLain's career deteriorated rapidly. While he was active, his off-field regimen included the consumption of mass quantities of Coca-Cola.

McMahon, Don

1930–1987

Milwaukee (NL 1957–62), Houston (NL 1962–63), Cleveland (AL 1964–66), Boston (AL 1966–67), Chicago (AL 1967–68), Detroit (AL 1968–69), San Francisco (NL 1969–74)   P   BR/RHP

874 games	1,310 innings
90-68 W–L	2.96 ERA
1,003 k's	153 saves

Popular with his teammates wherever he played, the Brooklyn-born McMahon made bullpen work his forte in the fifties. In common with other relievers of the period, he suffered through off-seasons, but when his fastball was humming, he compiled big numbers. In 1959, he recorded an NL-best 15 saves; he also produced five seasons with an ERA below 2.00.

McMahon, John (Sadie)

1867–1954

Philadelphia (AA 1889–90), Baltimore (AA 1890–91), Baltimore (NL 1892–96), Brooklyn (NL 1897)   P   BR/RHP

321 games	2,634 innings
173-127 W–L	3.51 ERA
967 k's	4 saves

An unlikely candidate for workhorse given his rotund figure, McMahon teamed with Hall of Fame catcher Wilbert Robinson to form the "Dumpling Battery" for Baltimore in the 1890s. He featured a fine fastball and curve and helped his own cause by fielding his position well. McMahon was a carouser, but it was a shoulder injury that ended his career prematurely.

McManus, Marty

1900–1966

St. Louis (AL 1920–26), Detroit (AL 1927–31), Boston (AL 1931–33), Boston (NL 1934); MGR—Boston (AL 1932–33)   2B, 3B, MGR BR/TR

1,831 games	.289 ba
1,926 hits	120 hr
996 rbi	126 sb

McManus was a consistent performer in the infield who did his best work for the Browns in the twenties. He knocked in at least 90 runs four times and in 1922 batted .312 with 11 homers and 109 RBI—gaudy stats for a middle infielder.

McMillan, Roy

1930–

Cincinnati (NL 1951–60), Milwaukee (NL 1961–64), New York (NL 1964–66); MGR—Milwaukee (AL 1972), New York (NL 1975) SS, MGR   BR/TR

2,093 games	.243 ba
1,639 hits	68 hr
594 rbi	41 sb

McMillan's defensive brilliance made him valuable at any batting average. He anchored Cincinnati's infield in the fifties and led NL shortstops in fielding percentage four times. McMillan ranged smoothly to either side, and his soft hands rarely misplayed a bounce.

McNally, Dave

1942–
Baltimore (AL 1962–74), Montreal (NL 1975) P
BR/LHP

424 games	2,730 innings
184-119 W–L	3.24 ERA
1,512 k's	2 saves

A member of the Orioles' vaunted pitching staff in the sixties and seventies, McNally won at least 20 games in four consecutive seasons. Like his fellow hurlers, he changed speeds and threw strikes. Along with Andy Messersmith, McNally refused to sign a contract for the 1975 season; however, he knew he was at the end of his career and took his action just to test the reserve clause. He retired rather than sign with a new club for 1976.

McPhee, John (Bid)

1859–1943
Cincinnati (AA 1882–89), Cincinnati (NL 1890–99); MGR—Cincinnati (NL 1901–02) 2B, MGR BR/TR

2,135 games	.271 ba
2,250 hits	53 hr
727 rbi	568 sb

The finest-fielding second sacker of the 19th century, McPhee played all but four years of his career without a glove. Nevertheless, he led the AA and the NL in fielding percentage nine times and in double plays 11 times. Only Frankie Frisch handled more chances (in 1927) than McPhee did in 1886. Off the field, he was a gentleman who was well liked by teammates and opposing players alike.

McRae, Hal

1945–

Cincinnati (NL 1968, 1970–72), Kansas City (AL 1973–87); MGR—Kansas City (1992–93 Active)

DH, OF, MGR   BR/TR

2,084 games	.290 ba
2,091 hits	191 hr
1,097 rbi	109 sb

McRae's aggressive style rubbed off on his Kansas City teammates and helped transform them into perennial pennant contenders. Strong at the plate although weak in the field, he became the league's best designated hitter. In 1976, McRae hit .332 and finished a controversial second to teammate George Brett in the batting race amid charges of racism. As skipper of the Royals, he manages his son, center fielder Brian McRae.

McReynolds, Kevin (Big Mac)

1959–

San Diego (NL 1983–86), New York (NL 1987–91), Kansas City (AL 1992–93 Active)   **OF   BR/TR**

1,451 games	.266 ba
1,393 hits	207 hr
786 rbi	91 sb

In the field or at bat, McReynolds often gave the impression that he would rather be somewhere else. His nonchalant attitude bordered on indifference, and fans found it hard to accept his efforts. A consistent batter and outstanding outfielder, McReynolds never appeared comfortable in the spotlight. His best season came in New York in 1988, when he hit .288 with 27 home runs and 99 RBI.

Meadows, Lee (Specs)

1894–1963

St. Louis (NL 1915–19), Philadelphia (NL 1919–23), Pittsburgh (NL 1923–29)   P
BB/RHP

490 games	3,160 innings
188-180 W–L	3.37 ERA
1,063 k's	7 saves

"Specs" Meadows was the first modern major league pitcher to wear glasses. He struggled on some poor Cardinals teams but hit his stride when he arrived in Pittsburgh in 1923. He won 19 games for the Pirates' pennant winners in 1925 and 1927 and led the NL with 20 wins in 1926.

Medwick, Joe (Ducky Wucky, Muscles)

1911–1975

St. Louis (NL 1932–40, 1947–48), Brooklyn (NL 1940–43, 1946), New York (NL 1943–45), Boston (NL 1945)   OF   BR/TR

1,984 games	.324 ba
2,471 hits	205 hr
1,383 rbi	42 sb

Medwick was a notorious first-ball, fastball hitter. He was a free swinger who hacked at any pitch within his reach. Moody and temperamental in nature, Medwick was a combative player who nearly caused a riot during the seventh game of the 1934 World Series with his fierce slide into Detroit third baseman Marv Owen. Indifferent in the field, he lived to swing the bat. Medwick batted over .300 12 times and earned the NL MVP award in 1937 when he hit for the triple crown. He was inducted into the Hall of Fame in 1968.

Melton, Bill

1945–

Chicago (AL 1968–75), California (AL 1976),
Cleveland (AL 1977)   3B   BR/TR

1,144 games	.253 ba
1,004 hits	160 hr
591 rbi	23 sb

Sure Comiskey Park had distant outfield fences, but it
took 60 years, until 1970, for Melton to become the
first White Sox player to hit 30 home runs in a single
season. The following year, he became the first Chisox
slugger to lead the AL in homers (33). On another
team, he would have been just another power-hitting
third baseman, but on the White Sox his feats made
history.

Mendez, Jose

1887–1928

Cuban Stars, Stars of Cuba, All-Nations, Los Angeles
White Sox, Chicago American Giants, Detroit Stars,
Kansas City Monarchs   P   RHP

Many experts rate Mendez, a great hurler from Cuba,
as one of the best pitchers of any era. Giants manager
John McGraw considered him the equal of Christy
Mathewson. A small, slender man, Mendez threw a
blazing fastball and a big, breaking curve. Mendez put
in his best years as player-manager with the Kansas
City Monarchs in the mid-twenties.

Mercer, George (Win)

1874–1903

Washington (NL 1894–99), New York (NL 1900),
Washington (AL 1901), Detroit (AL 1902)   P
BR/RHP

333 games	2,470 innings
131-164 W–L	3.99 ERA
528 k's	10 saves

Washington's best pitcher in the 1890s, Mercer won 25 games in 1896 and 20 more in 1897. After going 15–18 for Detroit in 1902, he was named as manager for the following season, but he committed suicide in San Francisco while on a barnstorming tour that winter.

Merkle, Fred

1888–1956
New York (NL 1907–16), Brooklyn (NL 1916–17), Chicago (NL 1917–20), New York (AL 1925–26)
1B   BR/TR

1,638 games	.273 ba
1,580 hits	60 hr
733 rbi	272 sb

Unjustly remembered as the perpetrator of the biggest blunder in baseball history—failing to touch second base on a Giants single to the outfield in a crucial game against the Cubs in 1908—Merkle was actually one of the smartest men on the team, highly respected by both his teammates and manager John McGraw. He played on five pennant winners and batted a career-high .309 in 1912.

Messersmith, Andy

1945–
California (AL 1968–72), Los Angeles (NL 1973–75, 1979), Atlanta (NL 1976–77), New York (AL 1978)
P   BR/RHP

344 games	2,230 innings
130-99 W–L	2.86 ERA
1625 k's	15 saves

When Messersmith was healthy, he dominated games—or even an entire season, as in 1971 when he won 20 games, or in 1974 when he went 20–6. He compiled five seasons (1971–75) with an ERA under 3.00 and struck out over 200 men in three different seasons. Messersmith refused to sign a contract for the

1975 season, and an arbitrator declared him a free agent for 1976.

Meusel, Bob (Long Bob)

1896–1977
New York (AL 1920–29), Cincinnati (NL 1930)
OF   BR/TR

1,407 games	.309 ba
1,693 hits	156 hr
1,067 rbi	139 sb

Meusel's manager, Miller Huggins, once described his sullen outfielder's attitude as one of "just plain indifference." Meusel also exasperated the New York fans with his lackadaisical style. He had great physical tools—he was a powerful hitter with home run strength, good speed, and the strongest and most accurate arm in the major leagues. Meusel batted over .300 his first five seasons with the Yankees and seven times overall, and he knocked in at least 100 runs five times. In 1925, when the Yanks finished a disappointing seventh, Meusel led the AL in homers (33) and RBI (138).

Meusel, Emil (Irish)

1893–1963
Washington (AL 1914), Philadelphia (NL 1918–21), New York (NL 1921–26), Brooklyn (NL 1927)   **OF**
BR/TR

1,289 games	.310 ba
1,521 hits	106 hr
819 rbi	113 sb

The older brother of the Yankees' star outfielder, Bob Meusel, Emil Meusel put up numbers nearly identical to those of his sibling. The two brothers faced each other in the World Series in 1921–23. In 1922, Meusel batted .331 and chased home 132 runs; in the following year, he led the NL with 125 RBI.

Meyers, John (Chief)

1880–1971

New York (NL 1909–15), Brooklyn (NL 1916–17), Boston (NL 1917)   C   BR/TR

992 games	.291 ba
826 hits	14 hr
363 rbi	44 sb

A Mission Indian from California who attended Dartmouth College, "Chief" Meyers was a highly intelligent man who starred as the Giants' regular catcher on three pennant winners. In 1912, he batted a career-high .358. After being traded to Brooklyn in 1916, he won another pennant with the Robins.

Milan, Clyde (Deerfoot)

1887–1953

Washington (AL 1907–22); MGR—Washington (AL 1922)   OF, MGR   BL/TR

1,982 games	.285 ba
2,100 hits	17 hr
617 rbi	495 sb

The fleet-footed Milan played alongside the great Walter Johnson throughout his career in Washington. He batted over .300 four times, including a .322 mark in 1920. Milan led the AL in stolen bases in 1912 (88) and 1913 (75). Defensively, he played shallow in order to cut off short line drives.

Miller, Edmund (Bing)

1894–1966

Washington (AL 1921), Philadelphia (AL 1922–26, 1928–34), St. Louis (AL 1926–27), Boston (AL 1935–36)   OF   BR/TR

1,820 games	.312 ba
1,936 hits	116 hr
990 rbi	128 sb

Miller was a contact hitter who rarely walked or struck out; after 1923, he never fanned more than 26 times in any season. He starred in the Athletics outfield with Mule Haas and Al Simmons on three pennant winners (1929–31). His double in game five of the 1929 World Series was the series-winning hit.

Miller, Stu

1927–

St. Louis (NL 1952–54, 1956), Philadelphia (NL 1956), New York (NL 1957), San Francisco (NL 1958–62), Baltimore (AL 1963–67), Atlanta (NL 1968)   **P   BR/RHP**

704 games	1,694 innings
105-103 W–L	3.24 ERA
1,164 k's	154 saves

Miller was noted for throwing the ball at three speeds—slow, slower, and slowest. He constantly kept batters off-stride with his assortment of junk. He led the NL in saves in 1961 (17) and the AL in saves in 1963 (27). In one of baseball memorable moments, Miller was literally blown off the mound by a gust of wind during the All-Star Game at Candlestick Park in 1961. To his amazement, the umpire called Miller's move a balk.

Minoso, Saturnio (Minnie)

1922–

New York Cubans (1945–48), Cleveland (AL 1949, 1951, 1958–59), Chicago (AL 1951–57, 1960–61, 1964, 1976, 1980), St. Louis (NL 1962), Washington (AL 1963)   **OF   BR/TR**

1,835 games	.298 ba
1,963 hits	186 hr
1,023 rbi	205 sb

The first black man to wear the White Sox uniform, Minoso homered in his first at-bat. An exciting player who could hit and run with the game's best, Minnie was a favorite with the fans wherever he played. In the batter's box, he crowded the plate and regularly led the

AL in getting hit by pitches. He was a strong batter who knocked in more than 100 runs in four seasons. He was named the *Sporting News* Rookie of the Year in 1951, and his uniform number 9 was later retired by Chicago. In 1976, at the age of 56, Minoso became the oldest active player to get a hit.

Mitchell, Clarence

1891–1963

Detroit (AL 1911), Cincinnati (NL 1916–17), Brooklyn (NL 1918–22), Philadelphia (NL 1923–28), St. Louis (NL 1928–30), New York (NL 1930–32)   P   BL/LHP

390 games	2,217 innings
125-139 W–L	4.12 ERA
544 k's	9 saves

Mitchell was known to be a pitcher who could hit, but no one could have foreseen what transpired on October 10, 1920, in the fifth game of the 1920 World Series, when he was brought into the game in relief by the Dodgers in the fifth inning. Mitchell came to bat with the bases loaded, no men out, and his team trailing 7–0. Mitchell slammed a line drive directly to Cleveland second baseman Bill Wambsganss, who completed an unassisted triple play. Mitchell was a spitballer who ironically recorded his highest victory total in his last full season, winning 13 games in 1931.

Mitchell, Kevin (Mitch, World)

1962–

New York (NL 1984, 1986), San Diego (NL 1987), San Francisco (NL 1987–91), Seattle (AL 1992), Cincinnati (NL 1993 Active)   OF, 3B   BR/TR

993 games	.282 ba
969 hits	190 hr
612 rbi	27 sb

Trouble seems to follow Mitchell around from team to team. Traded by four franchises because of his poor attitude, he is still in demand because of his awesome bat. Mitchell broke in slowly with the Mets, but he hit his stride with the Giants when he won the NL MVP award in 1989 in recognition of his .291 average and league-leading 47 homers, 125 RBI, and .635 slugging percentage. In the field, Mitchell is inconsistent at best.

Mize, Johnny (The Big Cat)
1913–1993
St. Louis (NL 1936–41), New York (NL 1942, 1946–49), New York (AL 1949–53)   1B
BL/TR

1,884 games	.312 ba
2,011 hits	359 hr
1,337 rbi	28 sb

Mize had the rare ability to hit for power and make consistent contact. In 1947, he became the only major leaguer player to hit 50 home runs while striking out fewer than 50 times. A burly, physical man who credited his phenomenal eyesight for his success, Mize led the NL in homers four times and played on five consecutive World Series champion Yankees teams as a part-time first sacker and pinch hitter extraordinaire. His 216 homers during the 1940s led all major leaguers. Mize was inducted into the Hall of Fame in 1981.

Mogridge, George
1889–1962
Chicago (AL 1911–12), New York (AL 1915–20), Washington (AL 1921–25), St. Louis (AL 1925), Boston (NL 1926–27)   P   BL/LHP

398 games	2,265 innings
132-131 W–L	3.23 ERA
679 k's	20 saves

Mogridge spent his best years in New York, toiling for the Yankees before their glory days. He won 16 games in 1918 and consistently pitched to an ERA below

3.00. Traded to Washington, he twice won 18 games for the Nats; he also won 16 times for the 1924 world champion squad.

Molitor, Paul

1956–

Milwaukee (AL 1978–92), Toronto (AL 1993 Active)
3B, 2B, DH, 1B   BR/TR

2,016 games	.306 ba
2,492 hits	182 hr
901 rbi	434 sb

As Molitor keeps producing one outstanding season after another, people are beginning to tout his eventual candidacy for the Hall of Fame. Were it not for a series of injuries earlier in his career, he would now be approaching 3,000 hits. Using a short, quick stroke, Molitor hits line drives to all fields and has outstanding extra-base power. Frequently batting leadoff, he has scored 1,275 runs in his career, leading the AL three times. Defensively, Molitor has played all the infield positions except for shortstop. He has outstanding speed and has stolen more than 40 bases four times. In 1987, Molitor excited the nation by hitting safely in 39 consecutive games and in 1993 he starred in the World Series, batting .500 with 12 hits.

Monbouquette, Bill (Monbo)

1936–

Boston (AL 1958–65), Detroit (AL 1966–67), New York (AL 1967–68), San Francisco (NL 1968)   P
BR/RHP

343 games	1,961 innings
114-112 W–L	3.68 ERA
1,122 k's	3 saves

Monbouquette persevered on some poor Red Sox teams in the early sixties, winning 20 games in 1963 and no-hitting the White Sox in 1962. He won in double digits each year from 1960 to 1965.

Monday, Rick

1945–

Kansas City (AL 1966–67), Oakland (AL 1968–71), Chicago (NL 1972–76), Los Angeles (NL 1977–84)

OF   BL/TL

1,986 games	.264 ba
1,619 hits	241 hr
775 rbi	98 sb

The first player drafted in the initial universal draft, held in 1965, Monday signed with the Kansas City Athletics. Although he never became the superstar the scouts expected, Monday had several good years with the Cubs and Dodgers. In 1976, he batted .272 with 32 homers for the Cubs; and in 1981, he cracked a clutch home run to win the NL pennant for the Dodgers. Ironically, Monday grew up a Dodgers fan and would have signed with them were it not for the introduction of the draft.

Montgomery, Jeff

1962–

Cincinnati (NL 1987), Kansas City (AL 1988–93 Active)   **P   RHP**

396 games	528 innings
34-27 W–L	2.52 ERA
427 k's	160 saves

The unheralded closer of the Royals bullpen, Montgomery tallied 141 saves in 1990–93. In 1993, he saved 45 games and had a 2.27 ERA.

Moore, Joe (Jo-Jo)

1908–

New York (NL 1930–41)   **OF   BL/TR**

1,335 games	.298 ba
1,615 hits	79 hr
513 rbi	46 sb

A notorious first-ball, fastball hitter, Moore batted leadoff for the Giants and was effective at slapping the ball past the infield to get on base. At his best in the mid-thirties, Moore knocked out more than 200 hits twice and scored more than 100 runs in three consecutive seasons (1934–36).

Moore, Mike

1959–
Seattle (AL 1982–88), Oakland (AL 1989–92), Detroit (AL 1993 Active)   **P   RHP**

400 games	2,544 innings
145-151 W-L	4.16 ERA
1,541 k's	2 saves

An extremely slow worker on the mound, Moore won 17 games for the tail-enders in Seattle in 1985. When free agency rolled around, he escaped to a championship Athletics team in 1989, winning 66 games in his four seasons in Oakland.

Moore, Terry

1912–
St. Louis (NL 1935–42, 1946–48);
Mgr—Philadelphia (NL 1954)   **OF, MGR**
BR/TR

1,298 games	.280 ba
1,318 hits	80 hr
513 rbi	82 sb

Moore was the outstanding fly chaser of his generation, and some regard him as one of the greatest center fielders in major league history. Named to the All-Star team each year from 1939 to 1942, he batted a career-high .304 with 17 home runs in 1940.

Morgan, Joe

1943–
Houston (NL 1963–71, 1980), Cincinnati (NL 1972–79), San Francisco (NL 1981–82), Philadelphia (NL 1983), Oakland (AL 1984)   **2B**
BL/TR

2,649 games	.271 ba
2,517 hits	268 hr
1,133 rbi	689 sb

Morgan brought a special dimension to the game. No other second baseman in the past 60 years combined speed and power like he did. After escaping the distant fences of the Astrodome, he connected for more than 20 homers four times and knocked in a career-high 111 runs in 1976. A key member of the Big Red Machine in the seventies, Morgan earned the NL MVP award in 1975 and 1976, when he batted .327 and .320. Patient at the plate, he walked more than 100 times in eight seasons. He had a habit of flapping his left arm prior to each pitch. In the field, Morgan was renowned for using the smallest glove in the majors, but it never hindered his defensive skills.

Morris, Ed (Cannonball)

1862–1937
Columbus (AA 1884), Pittsburgh (AA 1885–86), Pittsburgh (NL 1887–89), Pittsburgh (PL 1890)   P
BR/LHP

311 games	2,678 innings
171-122 W–L	2.82 ERA
1,217 k's	1 save

A fine fastball, curve, and change-up comprised Morris's repertoire on the mound, but his determination was his greatest asset. In 1886, he won 41 games and established a still-standing single-season NL record for shutouts by a lefty with 12. Like many players of that period, Morris fought a long battle with the bottle, and it shortened his career.

Morris, Jack

1955–
Detroit (AL 1977–90), Minnesota (AL 1991), Toronto (AL 1992–93)   P   RHP

526 games	3,683 innings
244-180 W–L	3.83 ERA
2,378 k's	

The chief proponent of the split-fingered fastball today, Morris is a likely candidate for induction into the Hall of Fame. A four-time 20-game winner, he earned more victories in the eighties than any other hurler. Morris pitched on three World Series winners and won the seventh game of the thrilling 1991 World Series by a score of 1-0 in 10 innings.

Morrison, Johnny (Jughandle Johnny)

1895–1966
Pittsburgh (NL 1920–27), Brooklyn (NL 1929–30)
P   BR/RHP

297 games	1,535 innings
103-80 W–L	3.65 ERA
546 k's	23 saves

Morrison became the top NL reliever of the twenties after winning 25 games as a starter in 1923. Owner of the best curve ball in the majors, Morrison was aptly nicknamed "Jughandle Johnny."

Moses, Wally

1910–1990
Philadelphia (AL 1935–41, 1949–51), Chicago (AL 1942–46), Boston (AL 1946–48)   **OF**   BL/TL

2,012 games	.291 ba
2,138 hits	89 hr
679 rbi	174 sb

Moses's career was filled with peculiarities. He batted over .300 in his first seven years in the majors, yet he never reached that figure again. Not a power hitter, he smacked 25 home runs in 1937 but never hit more than eight in any other season. Moses hit .345 in 1936 and .320 the following year, and he was a fine outfielder with a strong throwing arm. When his playing career ended, Moses served as a batting instructor for a variety of teams.

Mossi, Don (The Sphinx, Dumbo)

1929–

Cleveland (AL 1954–58), Detroit (AL 1959–63), Chicago (AL 1964), Kansas City (AL 1965)   P
BL/LHP

460 games	1,548 innings
101-80 W–L	3.43 ERA
932 k's	50 saves

One of the most recognizable men in baseball in the fifties due to his oversized ears, Mossi teamed with Ray Narleski to form an excellent one-two punch in the Indians bullpen. Traded to the Tigers, he became a starter and won 17 games in 1959. Mossi threw hard and developed an excellent curve and change-up.

Mostil, Johnny (Bananas)

1896–1970

Chicago (AL 1918, 1921–29)   OF   BR/TR

972 games	.301 ba
1,054 hits	23 hr
376 rbi	176 sb

Mostil was one of the best defensive outfielders of the twenties. He played a shallow center field and simply outran most balls hit over his head. He also had one of the strongest throwing arms in major league history. At the plate, he batted a career-high .325 in 1924 and led the AL the following year in runs scored (135), walks (90), and stolen bases (43). In spring training in 1927, Mostil attempted suicide; he played only sporadically thereafter.

Mota, Manuel (Manny)

1938–

San Francisco (NL 1962), Pittsburgh (NL 1963–68), Montreal (NL 1969), Los Angeles (NL 1969–80, 1982)   OF   BR/TR

1,536 games	.304 ba
1,149 hits	31 hr
438 rbi	50 sb

Few doubted that Mota could wake up any winter morning, grab a bat, and slap a hit past an infielder. When his career appeared to be over, Mota became a pinch hitter deluxe; he still holds the career major league record of 150 pinch hits.

Mullane, Tony (Count)

1859–1944

Detroit (NL 1881), Louisville (AA 1882), St. Louis (AA 1883), Toledo (AA 1884), Cincinnati (AA 1886–89), Cincinnati (NL 1890–93), Baltimore (NL 1893–94), Cleveland (NL 1894)   P   BB/TB

784 games	.243 ba
661 hits	8 hr
128 rbi	112 sb
4,531 innings	284-220 W–L
3.05 ERA	1,803 k's
15 saves	

Mullane was one of the early showmen of baseball, combining good looks and a flair for the unusual to carve out his success. His combativeness led him into frequent sparring matches with club owners over his financial value, but he was a definite gate attraction, particularly when he switched pitching arms during a game. He won at least 30 games each year from 1882 to 1887, although he was suspended in 1885.

Mullin, George (Wabash George)

1880–1944

Detroit (AL 1902–13), Washington (AL 1913), Indianapolis (FL 1914), Newark (FL 1915)   P

BR/RHP

487 games	3,686 innings
228-196 W–L	2.82 ERA
1,482 k's	8 saves

Mullin was a workhorse whose 42 complete games in 1904 are the second most in AL history. Control was a problem early in his career, and he led the AL in allowing the most walks in four consecutive years (1903–06); however, he was a hard thrower who was also among the league leaders in strikeouts. In 1907, Mullin became the only man to lose 20 games for a pennant winner. Nevertheless, he ranks with the best hurlers in Tigers history. Mullin won 20 games five times and went 29-8 in 1909, as well as capturing two victories in the World Series. A pitcher who could also wield an effective bat in his own cause, he no-hit the Browns in 1912.

Mungo, Van Lingle

1911–1985
Brooklyn (NL 1931–41), New York (NL 1942–43, 1945)   P   BR/RHP

364 games	2,113 innings
120-115 W–L	3.47 ERA
1,242 k's	16 saves

The man with the mellifluous name and raging temper, Mungo had a great fastball and a hot head. Mean-spirited on the mound, he not only berated his opponents but even attacked his own teammates for committing errors behind him. His fastball enabled him to lead the NL in strikeouts in 1936 (238). That year capped the end of a five-year span during which he won 81 games. After injuring his arm in the 1937 All-Star Game, Mungo was never the same as a pitcher.

Munson, Thurman (Thurm)

1947–1979
New York (AL 1969–79)   C   BR/TR

1,423 games	.292 ba
1,558 hits	113 hr
701 rbi	48 sb

Gruff and frequently uncommunicative with the press, Munson let his outstanding performance on the field speak for him. The supreme clutch hitter in the AL in his generation, he played with a tenacity that endeared him to fans. During his career, he was the top catcher in the AL, batting over .300 five times; in 1975–77, he batted .300 with 100 RBI each year. Munson batted .373 in three World Series. Knee injuries slowed him down in 1979, and he had already begun talking of retirement before his death in a plane crash later that season. Only the brevity of his career has kept Munson from induction into the Hall of Fame.

Murcer, Bobby

1946–
New York (AL 1965–74, 1979–83), San Francisco (NL 1975–76), Chicago (NL 1977–79) **OF**
BL/TR

1,908 games	.277 ba
1,862 hits	252 hr
1,043 rbi	127 sb

Acclaimed as the pocket-sized version of Mickey Mantle, Murcer shifted from shortstop to the outfield like his hero and also had home-run pop in Yankee Stadium, but all other comparisons were unjust. At his best in 1971, he batted .331 with 25 home runs and 94 RBI. Murcer finally played on a Yankees pennant winner in his second tour of duty with the team, in 1981. A very popular player with the fans, Murcer currently broadcasts Yankees games on television.

Murphy, Dale

1956–
Atlanta (NL 1976–90), Philadelphia (NL 1990–92), Colorado (NL 1993) **OF, 1B** BR/TR

2,180 games	.265 ba
2,111 hits	398 hr
1,266 rbi	161 sb

Everybody's favorite player in Atlanta, Murphy played brilliantly on the field and led an exemplary life off it. He belted at least 30 homers six times, leading the NL in 1984 (36) and in 1985 (37). He also led the league in RBI in 1982 (109) and 1983 (121) and won the NL MVP award in both years. Defensively, Murphy adapted well to the outfield after shifting from catcher and won five Gold Glove awards.

Murphy, Johnny (Fireman)

1908–1970

New York (AL 1932, 1934–43, 1946), Boston (AL 1947)   P   BR/RHP

415 games	1,045 innings
93-53 W–L	3.50 ERA
378 k's	107 saves

Baseball's best reliever in the thirties, Murphy established records that were not broken until the sixties. His out pitch was a sharp-breaking curve ball. In 1936–39, Murphy played an important role in the Yankees' four consecutive World Series titles. He won 13 times in relief in 1937 and led the AL in saves four times. Murphy later became a general manager and helped build the 1969 World Champion Mets.

Murray, Eddie

1956–

Baltimore (AL 1977–88), Los Angeles (NL 1989–91), New York (NL 1992–93), Cleveland (AL 1994 Active)   1B, DH   BB/TR

2,598 games	.290 ba
2,820 hits	441 hr
1,662 rbi	92 sb

Pitchers quickly learned one thing about Eddie Murray—don't pitch to him with the bases loaded. A tremendous clutch hitter under ordinary circumstances, he became lethal with the bags full, batting well over .400 for his career. Equally adept at smashing the long ball from both sides of the plate, this future Hall of Famer has posted remarkably consistent numbers each year. A hero in Baltimore, where he knocked in over 100 runs five times, Murray had his uniform number 33 retired by the Orioles. Murray's reluctance to grant interviews has not endeared him to the working press.

Murtaugh, Danny

1917–1976
Philadelphia (NL 1941–43, 1946), Boston (NL 1947), Pittsburgh (NL 1948–51); Mgr—Pittsburgh (NL 1957–64, 1967, 1970–71, 1973–76)   **2B, MGR   BR/TR**

767 games	.254 ba
661 hits	8 hr
219 rbi	49 sb

The second-winningest manager in Pittsburgh history, trailing only Fred Clarke, Murtaugh went 1,115-950 during four separate tenures at the Pirates' helm. Loved by players and fans alike, he won the World Series in 1960 and 1971 for the Pirates. An affable man, he was the ultimate players' manager. The Pirates retired his uniform number 40.

Musial, Stan (Stan the Man)

1920–
St. Louis (NL 1941–63)   **OF, 1B   BL/TL**

3,026 games	.331 ba
3,630 hits	475 hr
1,951 rbi	78 sb

Simply the greatest left-handed hitter in National League history, Musial had an unique corkscrew batting stance with his head peaking over his right shoulder at the pitcher. He excelled in Brooklyn, so much so that the Flatbush faithful accorded him the nickname "The Man." Musial batted over .300 in 17 seasons and won seven NL batting titles. He currently ranks fourth in career hits and fifth in RBI. The all-time St. Louis leader in home runs (475), he was inducted into the Hall of Fame in 1969.

Mussina, Mike

1968–
Baltimore (AL 1991–93 Active)   **P**   **RHP**

69 games	496 innings
36-16 W–L	3.25 ERA
299 k's	

It was a short hop from the campus of Stanford University to the major leagues for this well-educated right-hander. Mussina throws two different fastballs that dart in opposite directions. Outstanding control and the ability to change speeds make him one of the top young pitchers in the game today. In his first full season in the majors, 1992, he went 18-5 with a 2.54 ERA, and his .783 winning percentage led AL hurlers.

Mutrie, Jim

1851–1938
Mgr—New York (AA 1883–84), New York (NL 1885–91)   **Mgr**

Mutrie's lifetime winning percentage of .611 is surpassed only by Joe McCarthy's .614. A bit of a dandy, he was very popular among his players and won pennants with New York in the AA in 1884 and with the Giants in the NL in 1888 and 1889. While managing his NL entry, he admiringly described them as "my Giants," and the nickname stuck.

Myer, Charles (Buddy)

1904–1974
Washington (AL 1925–27, 1929–41), Boston (AL 1927–28)   **2B, SS, 3B**   **BL/TR**

1,923 games	.303 ba
2,131 hits	38 hr
850 rbi	156 sb

One of the greatest bunters in the history of the game, Myer utilized his speed to beat out many infield hits. He also led the AL in stolen bases in 1928 (30). In 1935, he led the AL in batting (.349); he hit over .300 eight times. Excellent defensively as well, he led the AL in fielding percentage in both 1931 and 1938. Born in Mississippi, Myer was one of the few Jewish stars in major league ball.

Myers, Randy

1962–
New York (NL 1985–89), Cincinnati (NL 1990–91), San Diego (NL 1992), Chicago (NL 1993 Active)   P   **BL/LHP**

448 games	613 innings
32-42 W–L	3.07 ERA
622 k's	184 saves

Rambo in a baseball uniform, Myers spends nearly all his free time lifting weights. His obsession with improving his strength ultimately led to his departure from the Mets. His fastball, which has been timed at over 95 miles an hour, ranks with the best in baseball. In 1993, Myers saved an NL-record 53 games.

N

Nash, Billy

1865–1929
Richmond (AA 1884), Boston (NL 1885–89, 1891–95), Boston (PL 1890), Philadelphia (NL 1896–98); Mgr—Philadelphia (NL 1896)   **3B, MGR**   **BR/TR**

1,549 games	.275 ba
1,606 hits	60 hr
977 rbi	265 sb

Nash's hometown of Richmond fielded a major league franchise for only six weeks late in the 1884 season, but it was there that he made his debut. Joining Boston the following season, he began a long association with the Beaneaters as an outstanding hit-and-run specialist. Nash also showed occasional power, as his 10 homers and 123 RBI in 1893 attest.

Nehf, Art
1892–1960
Boston (NL 1915–19), New York (NL 1919–26), Cincinnati (NL 1926–27), Chicago (NL 1927–29)
P   BL/LHP

451 games	2,707 innings
184-120 W–L	3.20 ERA
844 k's	13 saves

When the Giants won four consecutive pennants, in 1921–24, Nehf played a major role, winning 66 games. Obtained from Boston, where he pitched brilliantly for a weak club, he starred on a pennant-winning club. In World Series play, Nehf won four games and compiled a stingy ERA of 2.12 in 79 innings.

Nettles, Graig (Puff)
1944–
Minnesota (AL 1967–69), Cleveland (AL 1970–72), New York (AL 1973–83), San Diego (NL 1984–86), Atlanta (NL 1987), Montreal (NL 1988)   3B
BL/TR

2,700 games	.248 ba
2,225 hits	390 hr
1,314 rbi	32 sb

It took the spotlight of the 1978 World Series for the nation to appreciate Nettles's magic at third base. In the third game, he robbed the Dodgers of at least five runs with his outstanding diving stops and started New York on the way to the title. A dead-pull hitter, Nettles was ideal for Yankee Stadium, and he led the AL in home runs in 1976 (32). In his career, he belted at least

20 homers in 11 seasons. Nettles also established an AL record by recording 412 assists at third base in 1971.

Newcombe, Don (Newk)
1926–

Newark Eagles (1944–45), Brooklyn (NL 1949–51, 1954–57), Los Angeles (NL 1958), Cincinnati (NL 1958–60), Cleveland (AL 1960)   P   BL/RHP

344 games	2,154 innings
149-90 W–L	3.56 ERA
1,129 k's	7 saves

Newcombe was the first black pitcher to win 20 games in the major leagues. A big man physically, he used an overhand delivery to unleash his mighty fastball, a pitch that he used to intimidate batters. Newcombe won at least 20 games in three seasons but missed two years to military service at the height of his career. His best years came in 1955 (20-5) and 1956 (27-7); he led NL hurlers in winning percentage both seasons. Any criticism of Newcombe started and ended with his failures during World Series play against the Yankees—he was winless in four decisions with an astronomical 8.59 ERA. After his career ended, Newcombe revealed his addiction to alcohol, and he has worked for the past 20 years counseling players.

Newhouser, Hal (Prince Hal)
1921–

Detroit (AL 1939–53), Cleveland (AL 1954–55)   P   BL/LHP

488 games	2,993 innings
207-150 W–L	3.06 ERA
1,796 k's	26 saves

After starting his career with five subpar seasons, Newhouser turned it around in 1944 by winning an AL-best 29 games against only nine losses. When he followed this up by gaining 25 victories the next season, critics labeled him a wartime pitcher. However, Newhouser also won 97 games in the first five postwar campaigns. Beset by arm troubles thereafter, he lost his effectiveness. In recognition of his outstanding career, the Hall of Fame inducted him in 1992.

Newsom, Louis (Bobo, Buck)
1907–1962
Brooklyn (NL 1929–30, 1942–43), Chicago (NL 1932), St. Louis (AL 1934–35, 1938–39, 1943), Washington (AL 1935–37, 1942, 1943, 1946–47, 1952), Boston (AL 1937), Detroit (AL 1939–41), Philadelphia (AL 1944–46, 1952–53), New York (AL 1947), New York (NL 1948)   P   BR/RHP

600 games	3,759 innings
211-222 W–L	3.98 ERA
2,082 k's	21 saves

Newsom called himself "Buck" and everyone else "Bobo." A good talker who was great fun off the field, he played for nearly every team in both leagues during his peripatetic career. On the mound, he utilized an unusual windup, swinging his arms in opposite directions prior to delivering the ball. He threw hard but had rather poor control. A tough competitor, Newsom once pitched seven innings with a broken leg. He was one of only two pitchers in major league history to win more than 200 games and yet end his career with a losing record. He won 20 games in 1938–40 but lost 20 on three occasions as well.

Nichols, Charles (Kid)
1869–1953
Boston (NL 1890–1901), St. Louis (NL 1904–05), Philadelphia (NL 1905–06); Mgr—St. Louis (NL 1904–05)   P, MGR   BB/RHP

620 games	5,056 innings
361-208 W–L	2.95 ERA
1,868 k's	17 saves

"Kid" Nichols was the greatest pitcher in Boston's National League history. He won more than 30 games in seven of eight seasons between 1891 and 1898 and garnered 300 victories before the age of 31. Nichols used a fastball and change of pace with pinpoint control to baffle batters. He was inducted into the Hall of Fame in 1949.

Nicholson, Bill (Swish)

1914–

Philadelphia (AL 1936), Chicago (NL 1939–48), Philadelphia (NL 1949–53) **OF**   **BL/TR**

1,677 games	.268 ba
1,484 hits	235 hr
948 rbi	27 sb

Prone to strike out, when Nicholson did make contact the ball flew out of the park. He led the NL in homers and RBI in 1943 and 1944—29, 128 and 33, 122. In 1944 Nicholson blasted homers in four consecutive plate appearances over two games. In the second game of the doubleheader on the second day, in which he homered yet again, Nicholson was actually walked intentionally with the bases loaded.

Niekro, Joe

1944–

Chicago (NL 1967–69), San Diego (NL 1969), Detroit (AL 1970–72), Atlanta (NL 1973–74), Houston (NL 1975–85), New York (AL 1985–87), Minnesota (AL 1987–88) **P**   **BR/RHP**

702 games	3,584 innings
221-204 W–L	3.59 ERA
1,747 k's	16 saves

The junior member of the knuckle ball firm of Niekro and Niekro, Joe Niekro never enjoyed the adulation accorded his brother Phil, but he made headlines in 1987 when he reached into his back pocket for a little extra and pulled out a nail file. A mainstay on the Astros staff in the eighties, he became Houston's all-time leader in career wins, compiling 41 wins in 1979–80.

Niekro, Phil (Knucksie)
1939–

Milwaukee (NL 1964–65), Atlanta (NL 1966–83, 1987), New York (AL 1984–85), Cleveland (AL 1986–87), Toronto (AL 1987)   P   BR/RHP

864 games	5,404 innings
318-274 W–L	3.35 ERA
3,342 k's	29 saves

A certain Hall of Famer, Niekro holds all the major Atlanta Braves pitching records. He won at least 20 games three times and led the NL in wins twice, in 1974 (20) and 1979 (21). Niekro often pitched on three days' rest and started 43, 42, and 44 games in 1977–79—unheard-of figures in modern baseball. Perhaps the only prize that eluded him was the opportunity to pitch in a World Series game; he spent 24 seasons without playing on a pennant winner.

Nolan, Gary
1948–

Cincinnati (NL 1967–77), California (AL 1977)   P   BR/RHP

250 games	1,674 innings
110-70 W–L	3.08 ERA
1,039 k's	

Arm injuries cut short what might have been a Hall of Fame career for Nolan. Throwing a sharp-breaking curve and an overpowering fastball, he mowed down NL batters from his rookie season onward. He won 14 games, struck out 206 batters, and compiled a tidy 2.58 ERA as a freshman. In 1970, he went 18-7, and he later won 15 games in 1972, 1975, and 1976 before his arm gave out.

Nuxhall, Joe

1928–

Cincinnati (NL 1944, 1952–60, 1962–66), Kansas City (AL 1961), Los Angeles (AL 1962)   P
BL/LHP

526 games	2,302 innings
135-117 W–L	3.90 ERA
1,372 k's	19 saves

The fun-loving Nuxhall was the youngest pitcher ever to appear in a major league game, hurling at the tender age of 15 for the wartime Reds in 1944. After resurfacing in 1952, he enjoyed a productive career, winning 17 games in 1955 and 15 in 1963. After he retired, Nuxhall began a long career as the radio voice of the Reds.

O

O'Dell, Billy (Digger)

1933–

Baltimore (AL 1954–59), San Francisco (NL 1960–64), Milwaukee (NL 1965), Atlanta (NL 1966), Pittsburgh (NL 1966–67)   P   BB/LHP

479 games	1,817 innings
105-100 W–L	3.29 ERA
1,133 k's	48 saves

O'Dell was a fast worker on the mound who rarely took any time between pitches. Starting and relieving throughout his career, he won 14 games for Baltimore in 1958 and 19 for the pennant-winning 1962 Giants. Transferred full-time to the bullpen in Milwaukee, he won 10 games and saved another 18 in 1965. Off the field, O'Dell was the life of the party.

Odom, John (Blue Moon)

1945–

Kansas City (AL 1964–67), Oakland (AL 1968–75), Cleveland (AL 1975), Atlanta (NL 1975), Chicago (AL 1976)   P   BR/RHP

295 games	1,508 innings
84-85 W–L	3.70 ERA
857 k's	1 save

When Charley Finley ran the Athletics, he invented nicknames for all of his most promising young players. Thus, Odom became "Blue Moon." Rushed to the major leagues by Kansas City, he didn't blossom until the team moved to Oakland in 1968. He went 16-10 in 1968 and later won 15 times in 1969 and 1972. In 1976, Odom combined with his relievers to no-hit the White Sox.

O'Doul, Francis (Lefty)

1897–1969

New York (AL 1919–20, 1922), Boston (AL 1923), New York (NL 1928, 1933–34), Philadelphia (NL 1929–30), Brooklyn (NL 1931–33)   OF
BL/TL

970 games	.349 ba
1,140 hits	113 hr
542 rbi	36 sb

A converted pitcher, O'Doul was a confident hitter who led the NL in batting twice, with averages of .398 in 1929 and .368 in 1932. In 1929, his 254 hits were the most ever by a National League player. A sharp dresser, O'Doul might have made the Hall of Fame if he had become a regular player sooner.

O'Farrell, Bob

1896–1988
Chicago (NL 1915–25, 1934), St. Louis (NL
1925–28, 1933, 1935), New York (NL 1928–32),
Cincinnati (NL 1934); Mgr—St. Louis (NL 1927),
Cincinnati (NL 1934)   **C, MGR**   **BR/TR**

1,492 games	.273 ba
1,120 hits	51 hr
549 rbi	35 sb

An excellent backstop with a powerful throwing arm,
O'Farrell earned the NL MVP award in 1926 when he
batted .293 with seven homers and 68 RBI. That year,
the Cardinals won their first pennant in team history
and went on to capture the World Series.

Oglivie, Ben

1949–
Boston (AL 1971–73), Detroit (AL 1974–77),
Milwaukee (AL 1978–86)   **OF**   **BL/TL**

1,754 games	.273 ba
1,615 hits	235 hr
901 rbi	87 sb

A productive batter who smashed an AL-high 41 homers in 1980 while driving in 118 runs, Oglivie was
called "Ogilvie" for most of his career. Such is the ano-
nymity that comes from playing in Milwaukee. On the
Brewers' pennant-winning team in 1982, he crushed
34 homers and had 102 RBI.

Ojeda, Bob (Bobby O)

1957–
Boston (AL 1980–85), New York (NL 1986–90),
Los Angeles (NL 1991–92), Cleveland (AL 1993
Active)   **P**   **BL/LHP**

349 games	1,881 innings
115-98 W–L	3.62 ERA
1,125 k's	1 save

A master at changing speeds and moving the ball in and out just on the edge of the strike zone, Ojeda pitched brilliantly for the Mets in 1986, going 18-5 with a 2.57 ERA. During spring training of 1993, he was seriously injured in the tragic boating accident that took the lives of teammates Steve Olin and Tim Crews.

Olerud, John

1968–

Toronto (AL 1989–93 Active)   **1B**   **BL/TL**

552 games	.297 ba
544 hits	71 hr
289 rbi	1 sb

Olerud stands a long way off the plate, but at 6 feet, 5 inches, he can still reach the outside corner with the bat. His sweet swing gave promise of great success in the majors, a promise that was finally fulfilled in 1993 when he flirted with the .400 mark before settling for an AL-best .363. Olerud overcame a brain aneurysm suffered in college to become a professional athlete.

Oliva, Pedro (Tony)

1940–

Minnesota (AL 1962–76)   **OF**   **BL/TR**

1,676 games	.304 ba
1,917 hits	220 hr
947 rbi	86 sb

Serious knee injuries prevented Oliva from posting the kind of career statistics necessary for induction into the Hall of Fame. Even so, his candidacy has many boosters. Oliva's sweet swing won AL batting titles in his first two years in the league, and he took a third crown in 1971. Oliva led the circuit in hits five times. He made seven All-Star teams (1964–70) and earned one Gold Glove (1966).

Oliver, Al (Scoop)

1946–

Pittsburgh (NL 1968–77), Texas (AL 1978–81),
Montreal (NL 1982–83), San Francisco (NL 1984),
Philadelphia (NL 1984), Los Angeles (NL 1985),
Toronto (AL 1985)   OF, 1B, DH   BL/TL

2,368 games	.303 ba
2,743 hits	219 hr
1,326 rbi	84 sb

Oliver received his most publicity ever for complaining
that he had not received the acclaim he deserved for his
batting accomplishments. In spite of his 2,743 career
hits, he will probably garner few votes for the Hall of
Fame. Consistency was Oliver's hallmark. He batted
over .300 11 times, including every year from 1976 to
1983. In 1982, Oliver's .331 led the NL.

Olson, Gregg

1966–

Baltimore (AL 1988–93 Active)   P   RHP

320 games	350 innings
17-21 W–L	2.26 ERA
347 k's	160 saves

Named the AL Rookie of the Year in 1989 for his scintillating work in the Baltimore bullpen, Olson won five
games, saved 27 others, and compiled a tidy 1.69 ERA.
Olson's curve ranks with the best in the league.

Olson, Ivan (Ivy)

1885–1965

Cleveland (AL 1911–14), Cincinnati (NL 1915),
Brooklyn (NL 1915–24)   SS, 2B   BL/TR

1,572 games	.258 ba
1,575 hits	13 hr
446 rbi	156 sb

Olson's boyhood friend Casey Stengel used to say that
as a youth, Ivy terrorized the neighborhood. But he
was no match for the ferocity of Brooklyn's fans, who

made the inconsistent shortstop the butt of their frequent catcalls. Olson was a scrappy player who led the NL in hits in 1919 (164), but his defensive shortcomings earned the fans' wrath.

O'Malley, Walter
1903–1979
Brooklyn (NL 1933–57), Los Angeles (NL 1958–69)
OWNER

O'Malley started his association with the Brooklyn Dodgers as the lawyer representing their major creditor, the Brooklyn Trust Company. He began purchasing team shares, and by 1950, he had become principal owner after outsmarting his rival, Branch Rickey. O'Malley enjoyed the fruits of Rickey's astute assemblage of talent, winning pennants in 1952, 1953, 1955, and 1956, and either leading the league in attendance or finishing second behind Milwaukee throughout the decade. Unhappy with the pocketsized Ebbets Field, O'Malley moved Brooklyn's beloved Dodgers after the 1957 season, setting up shop in Los Angeles. He uncovered a gold mine out west; the Dodgers have been baseball's most consistently successful franchise over the last three decades.

O'Neil, John (Buck)
1911–
Memphis Red Sox (1937), Kansas City Monarchs (1938–43, 1946–50); Mgr—Kansas City Monarchs (1948–55)   1B, MGR   BR/TR

335 games	.288 ba
402 hits	11 hr
29 sb	

O'Neill was a fine hitter for the Monarchs, batting .350 in 1946; but he is best known for managing the team from 1948 to 1955. In 1962, he became the first black coach hired by a major league team when he joined the Chicago Cubs.

O'Neill, James (Tip)

1858–1915

New York (NL 1883), St. Louis (AA 1884–89,
1891), Chicago (PL 1890), Cincinnati (NL 1892)
OF   BR/TR

1,054 games	.326 ba
1,386 hits	52 hr
435 rbi	161 sb

The greatest Canadian player of the 19th century,
O'Neill began his career on the mound, but an arm
injury in 1883 led him to switch to the outfield. He
starred for Von der Ahe's colorful Browns teams of the
eighties, leading the AA in batting in 1887 (.435) and
1888 (.335).

O'Neill, Paul

1963–

Cincinnati (NL 1985–92), New York (AL 1993
Active) OF   BL/TL

940 games	.268 ba
834 hits	116 hr
486 rbi	63 sb

Like many other strong left-handed batters, O'Neill is
a deadly low-ball hitter. Not strictly a pull hitter, he
smashes line drives to all fields, and his home runs
barely scrape the top of the fence. Defensively, he ranks
with the best due to his powerful throwing arm. Runners advance at their own risk. In 1991, he cracked 28
homers and drove home 91 RBI; in 1993, he recorded
his highest average, .311, for the Yankees.

O'Neill, Steve

1891–1962

Cleveland (AL 1911–23), Boston (AL 1924), New
York (AL 1925), St. Louis (AL 1927–28);
Mgr—Cleveland (AL 1935–37), Detroit (AL
1943–48), Boston (AL 1950–51), Philadelphia (NL
1952–54) C, MGR   BR/TR

1,590 games	.263 ba
1,259 hits	13 hr
537 rbi	30 sb

The leading defensive catcher of the teens and twenties, O'Neill excelled at blocking the plate. At bat, he hit over .300 in three consecutive years (1920–22). In 1920, the year Cleveland won the pennant, he batted .321.

Orosco, Jesse
1957–
New York (NL 1979, 1981–87), Los Angeles (NL 1988), Cleveland (AL 1989–91), Milwaukee (AL 1992–93 Active)   P   BR/LHP

714 games	932 innings
66-63 W–L	2.85 ERA
826 k's	130 saves

Mets fans will always remember Orosco as the pitcher who secured the last out in both the NLCS and World Series in 1986. Acquired by the Mets in exchange for Jerry Koosman in 1978, he became the top NL lefty reliever by relying on his sharp-breaking slider and moving fastball. In 1983, he won 13 games, saved 17 more, and recorded an ERA of 1.47. The following year, he saved 31 games.

O'Rourke, Jim (Orator Jim)
1850–1919
Boston (NL 1876–78, 1880), Providence (NL 1879), Buffalo (NL 1881–84), New York (NL 1885–89, 1891–92, 1904), New York (PL 1890), Washington (NL 1893); Mgr—Buffalo (NL 1881–84), Washington (NL 1893)   OF, C, MGR   BR/TR

1,774 games	.310 ba
2,304 hits	50 hr
1,010 rbi	191 sb

O'Rourke's storied career stretched from the inaugural season of the National League in 1876 to a cameo appearance in 1904. He collected the first hit in the history of the league and caught nine innings of the pennant-clinching game for the New York Giants at the age of 52. A graduate of Yale Law School, "Orator Jim" had an unusually sophisticated vocabulary for a 19th-century baseball player. He was inducted into the Hall of Fame in 1945.

Orr, Dave
1859–1915
New York (AA 1883, 1884–87), New York (NL 1883), Brooklyn (AA 1888), Columbus (AA 1889), Brooklyn (PL 1890) 1B, MGR BL/TR

791 games	.342 ba
1,126 hits	37 hr
270 rbi	66 sb

Few players in the 19th century were more beloved than Dave Orr, a gentle giant who stood 5 feet, 11 inches and weighed 250 pounds. He led the American Association in batting in 1884 (.354) and remains the only one of four 19th-century players to achieve a lifetime slugging percentage higher than .500 and not be elected to the Hall of Fame. Still in his prime in 1890, he suffered a debilitating stroke that ended his career.

Orth, Al (The Curveless Wonder)
1872–1948
Philadelphia (NL 1895–1901), Washington (AL 1902–04), New York (AL 1904–09) P
BL/RHP

440 games	3,354 innings
204-189 W–L	3.37 ERA
948 k's	6 saves

Orth was one of the top control pitchers in the history of the game, issuing only 1.77 walks per nine innings. His nickname, "the Curveless Wonder," derived from his total lack of a curve ball. Instead he threw fastballs, change-ups, and spitters. Orth's best year came in New

York in 1906, when he led the AL in wins (27), complete games (36), and innings pitched (338). Ironically, the next season he lost 21 games.

Osteen, Claude

1939–

Cincinnati (NL 1957, 1959–61), Washington (AL 1961–64), Los Angeles (NL 1965–73), Houston (NL 1974), St. Louis (NL 1974), Chicago (AL 1975)   P
BL/LHP

541 games	3,460 innings
196-195 W–L	3.30 ERA
1,612 k's	1 save

For many years, Osteen was the best number-three pitcher in the majors when he backed Koufax and Drysdale on the Dodgers. After toiling for the expansion Senators, he earned a promotion to Los Angeles in a trade for slugger Frank Howard. Joining the NL's best pitching staff, Osteen won an average of 16 games each season between 1965 and 1973.

Otis, Amos

1947–

New York (NL 1967, 1969), Kansas City (AL 1970–83), Pittsburgh (NL 1984)   OF   BR/TR

1,998 games	.277 ba
2,020 hits	193 hr
1,007 rbi	341 sb

The Mets originally hoped to groom Otis to fill their perpetual need at third base, but they made the mistake of trading him to Kansas City, where he starred as the AL's top defensive center fielder for more than a decade. A slender man with good power to the gaps, he twice led the AL in doubles and hit 26 home runs in 1973. A smart base runner, Otis also led the AL in stolen bases in 1971 (52).

O'Toole, Jim (Tootie)

1937–

Cincinnati (NL 1958–66), Chicago (NL 1967)   P

BB/LHP

270 games	1,615 innings
98–84 W–L	3.57 ERA
1,039 k's	4 saves

Once the hot-tempered O'Toole gained control of both his emotions and his fastball, he became one of the NL's best left-handers of the early sixties. From 1960 to 1964, he won a total of 81 games, including 19 in 1961, the year the Reds won the NL pennant.

Ott, Mel (Master Melvin)

1909–1958

New York (NL 1926–47); Mgr—New York (NL 1942–48)   OF, 3B, MGR   BL/TR

2,730 games	.304 ba
2,876 hits	511 hr
1,860 rbi	89 sb

Ott perfected a highly unusual batting stance; he stood deep in the box, close to the plate, and raised his front foot high in the air before taking a very short stride into the pitch. Whatever the peculiarities of his style, Ott's .322 average in 1928 is the highest mark ever achieved by a teenager. Although he was not a big man physically, standing only 5 feet, 9 inches and weighing 165 pounds, he generated great power, and his 511 career home runs were an NL record at his retirement. He led the league in taters six times. Though he was a great team player, Ott's easygoing manner did not translate into success as a manager. The Giants retired his uniform number four, and he was inducted into the Hall of Fame in 1951.

Overall, Orval (Jumbo)

1881–1947

Cincinnati (NL 1905–06), Chicago (NL 1906–10, 1913)   **P**   **BB/RHP**

218 games	1,535 innings
108-71 W–L	2.23 ERA
935 k's	12 saves

One of a handful of collegians in major league ball in the rough-and-ready days of the early 20th century, Overall attended the University of California before joining the Reds in 1905. As a rookie, he pitched 318 innings, but the Reds were unimpressed with his 23 losses and traded him to Chicago the following season. It was a trade they would regret, because Overall developed into one of the best pitchers in baseball. Pitching for the powerful Cubs squad, he went 82-38 in five seasons before hurting his arm.

Owen, Mickey

1916–

St. Louis (NL 1937–40), Brooklyn (NL 1941–45), Chicago (NL 1949–51), Boston (AL 1954)   **C**   **BR/TR**

1,209 games	.255 ba
929 hits	14 hr
378 rbi	36 sb

Although he was a fine defensive catcher, Owen will forever be remembered as the goat of the 1941 World Series for failing to catch the third strike that would have ended the fourth game in a Dodgers victory. Instead, the ball—some say it was a Hugh Casey spitter—rolled to the backstop, enabling Tommy Henrich to reach first base. Given this opening, the Yankees rallied to win that game and went on to secure the series title the following day. Owen jumped to the Mexican League in 1946.

P

Pafko, Andy (Pruschka, Handy Andy)
1921–
Chicago (NL 1943–51), Brooklyn (NL 1951–52),
Milwaukee (NL 1953–59)   OF, 3B   BR/TR

1,852 games	.285 ba
1,796 hits	213 hr
976 rbi	38 sb

When the Dodgers obtained Pafko midway through
the 1951 season, their competitors in the NL groaned
because he filled the only available spot in their star-
laden lineup. After all, he had hit .300 three times in
Chicago, knocked in at least 100 runs twice, and was
coming off a 1950 season in which he crushed 36 homers. Yet what looked great on paper never quite materi-
alized on the field. Within two years, Pafko was on his
way to Milwaukee.

Page, Joe (Fireman)
1917–1980
New York (AL 1944–50), Pittsburgh (NL 1954)   P
BL/LHP

285 games	790 innings
57-49 W–L	3.53 ERA
519 k's	76 saves

The hard-drinking, fun-loving Page starred in the Yankees bullpen in the late forties. In 1947 and 1949, he
led the AL in both relief victories and saves, winning a
combined 27 games and saving 44 over the two years.

Paige, Leroy (Satchel)

1906–1982

Birmingham Black Barons (1927–30), Cleveland
Cubs (1931), Pittsburgh Crawfords (1931–34,
1936), Kansas City Monarchs (1935, 1940–47,
1950), St. Louis Stars (1937), Cleveland (AL
1948–49), St. Louis (AL 1951–1953), Kansas City
(AL 1965)　P　　**BR/RHP**

1,584 innings	123-79 W–L
1,177 k's	8 saves

Paige was the biggest celebrity in the Negro Leagues
and he knew it; he demanded 10–15 percent of the
receipts for each game. He knew all the tricks of pitching and had a special flair on the mound. Paige had an
excellent fastball, curve, and change-up, but his pinpoint control set him apart from other hurlers. His specialty was a hesitation pitch in which he broke his delivery and tossed a change of pace. Paige made his
debut in the major leagues at the age of 42, becoming
the majors' oldest rookie player. That year, he attracted
a record crowd for a night game, drawing 78,382 at
Cleveland, and pitched his second consecutive shutout. Paige's age was always in doubt, and he did nothing to clear up the mystery. In 1965, he made his final
appearance in the majors. Some of his expressions have
become a part of the vernacular, such as "Don't look
back—something might be gaining on you." He was
inducted into the Hall of Fame in 1971.

Palmeiro, Rafael

1964–

Chicago (NL 1986–88), Texas (AL 1989–93),
Baltimore (AL 1994)　**1B, OF**　　**BL/TL**

1,046 games	.296 ba
1,144 hits	132 hr
526 rbi	50 sb

The Cubs traded Palmeiro because they thought, not-
withstanding his sweet stroke and his potential to lead

the league in batting, he would never hit for power and drive in enough runs. Once again, they miscalculated. Palmeiro has developed into one of the best hitters in the AL. In 1990, he led the circuit in hits (191); the following year, he hit a league-best 49 doubles, cracked 26 homers, and drove home 88 runs while batting .322. In 1993 he slammed a career-best 37 home runs. Defensively, Palmeiro has few equals.

Palmer, Jim

1945–
Baltimore (AL 1965–67, 1969–84)   P
BR/RHP

558 games	3,948 innings
268-152 W–L	2.86 ERA
2,212 k's	4 saves

A perfectionist, Palmer believed he should pitch a shutout every time he strode out to the mound. The problem is, his stuff was so good that others expected him to as well. Palmer burst upon the scene as a hard-throwing 20-year-old with a curve that dropped off the table and the poise of a veteran. He won 15 games in 1966 and shut out the Dodgers in the World Series. Although his career was in jeopardy the next year due to a sore arm, he rebounded in 1969 to go 16-4, and he never looked back. A three-time Cy Young Award winner, Palmer pitched more than 300 innings in four seasons despite the reputation of complaining like a hypochondriac. He won at least 20 games in eight of nine seasons (1970–78), and his lifetime ERA ranks fifth among those who have pitched at least 3,000 innings. Probably one of the handsomest men ever to play baseball, Palmer has modeled and worked in television since his retirement. He was inducted into the Hall of Fame in 1990, his first year of eligibility.

Pappas, Milt (Gimpy)

1939–

Baltimore (AL 1957–65), Cincinnati (NL 1966–68),
Atlanta (NL 1968–70), Chicago (NL 1970–73)   P
BR/RHP

520 games	3,186 innings
209-164 W–L	3.40 ERA
1,728 k's	4 saves

Pappas's career is peppered with oddities. He was one of only two men to win 200 games in a career without winning 20 games in any one season. His lifetime record of 209-164 is statistically superior to that of Don Drysdale's 209-166, yet he has never received serious consideration for induction into the Hall of Fame. He was one strike away from pitching a perfect game in 1972, yet Pappas will always be remembered for being traded to Cincinnati for an "old" Frank Robinson in one of the most lopsided trades in major league history.

Parker, Dave (The Cobra)

1951–

Pittsburgh (NL 1973–83), Cincinnati (NL 1984–87), Oakland (AL 1988–89), Milwaukee (AL 1990), California (AL 1991), Toronto (AL 1991)
OF, DH   BL/TR

2,466 games	.290 ba
2,712 hits	339 hr
1,493 rbi	154 sb

An awesome physical specimen, Parker could hit with power, steal bases, and throw bullets from his position in right field. He won two batting titles in Pittsburgh (.338 in 1977 and .334 in 1978) but was driven out of town due to fan antagonism fueled by his involvement with drugs. Resurfacing in his hometown of Cincinnati, Parker smashed 42 doubles, 34 homers, and drove in 125 runs in 1985. Were it not for his drug conviction, Parker would be a serious candidate for the Hall of Fame.

Parnell, Mel (Dusty)

1922–
Boston (AL 1947–56)   P   BL/LHP

289 games	1,752 innings
123-75 W–L	3.50 ERA
732 k's	10 saves

Other lefties cringed at the idea of pitching in Fenway Park, but Parnell never let the specter of the Green Monster bother him. In 1949, he went 25-7 and led the AL in games won, complete games (27), and innings pitched (295). Four successful seasons followed, but an injured wing ended his career prematurely.

Parrish, Lance

1956–
Detroit (AL 1977–86), Philadelphia (NL 1987–88), California (AL 1989–92), Seattle (AL 1992), Cleveland (AL 1993)   C   BR/TR

1,878 games	.253 ba
1,712 hits	317 hr
1,032 rbi	27 sb

Parrish arrived in the major leagues after a stint as a bodyguard for rock singer Tina Turner, and he looked every inch the part. His muscles made him a feared power hitter who smashed at least 20 homers in seven of eight seasons (1980–86), but a recurring back injury limited his success thereafter.

Pascual, Camilo (Little Patato)

1934–
Washington (AL 1954–60), Minnesota (AL 1961–66), Washington (AL 1967–69), Cincinnati (NL 1969), Los Angeles (NL 1970), Cleveland (AL 1971)   P   BR/RHP

529 games	2,930 innings
174-170 W–L	3.63 ERA
2,167 k's	10 saves

Pascual threw one of the best curve balls in the American League during the fifties and sixties. Pitching for the perennial tail-enders in Washington, he went a combined 38 games below .500 between 1954 and 1958, but he rebounded to win 17 games in 1959. When the Senators moved to Minnesota in 1961, Pascual's career blossomed. He led the AL in strikeouts in three consecutive years (1961–63), winning 20 games twice and leading the AL in shutouts twice.

Passeau, Claude
1909–

Pittsburgh (NL 1935), Philadelphia (NL 1936–39), Chicago (NL 1939–47) **P   BR/RHP**

444 games	2,719 innings
162-150 W–L	3.32 ERA
1,104 k's	21 saves

A durable and consistent hurler, Passeau pitched at least 217 innings each year between 1936 and 1945. In 1945, he helped the Cubs to their last pennant by winning 17 games and later pitched a one-hit shutout in the third game of that year's World Series. Passeau was always suspected of throwing a spitter and he never denied it.

Peckinpaugh, Roger
1891–1977

Cleveland (AL 1910, 1912–13), New York (AL 1913–21), Washington (AL 1922–26), Chicago (AL 1927); Mgr—New York (AL 1914), Cleveland (AL 1928–33, 1941) **SS, MGR   BR/TR**

2,012 games	.259 ba
1,876 hits	48 hr
739 rbi	207 sb

Peckinpaugh was one of the top AL shortstops of his era. Strong defensively and fast afoot, he was a pesky hitter who batted .305 for the 1919 Yanks. At the age of 23 he managed the final 17 games of the 1914 regular season. Traded to Washington, Peckinpaugh was named the AL MVP in 1925 but suffered through an awful World Series in which he committed eight errors.

Pelty, Barney (The Yiddish Curver)

1880–1939

St. Louis (NL 1903–12), Washington (AL 1912)   P
BR/RHP

266 games	1,908 innings
92-117 W–L	2.63 ERA
693 k's	4 saves

Pitching for the Browns in the first decade of the 20th century could not have been an easy assignment. Between 1903 and 1912, their best finish was a fourth-place showing in 1908. Two of the Brownies' best players were Jewish—batting champ George Stone and pitcher Barney Pelty. Pelty's best season was 1906, when his tiny 1.59 ERA (second in the AL) produced 16 wins. He was stingy in surrendering the long ball, throwing only 22 gopher balls in his career.

Peña, Tony

1957–

Pittsburgh (NL 1980–86), St. Louis (NL 1987–89),
Boston (AL 1990–93 Active)   C   BR/TR

1,750 games	.262 ba
1,536 hits	99 hr
633 rbi	79 sb

An excellent catcher, Peña has the lowest squat of any backstop in memory. He keeps one leg outstretched on the ground, offering his pitchers a target at the batter's knees. Peña's throws are fast and accurate. At the plate, he is a wild swinger who rarely walks. Peña never gets cheated on his swings. His spent his most productive years in Pittsburgh, batting .301 in 1983 and .288 in 1986.

Pendleton, Terry

1960–

St. Louis (NL 1984–90), Atlanta (NL 1991–93
Active)   **3B**   **BB/TR**

1,401 games	.273 ba
1,446 hits	104 hr
717 rbi	119 sb

Pendleton revised his earlier reputation as a great fielder but mediocre hitter after arriving in Atlanta. Signed by the Braves as a free agent in 1991, he won the NL's MVP award in 1991, when he batted a league-high .319 with 22 home runs and 86 RBI. Proving his newly found offense was no fluke, Pendleton batted .311 with 21 home runs and 105 RBI the next season as the Braves won the second of two consecutive pennants.

Pennock, Herb (The Knight of Kennett Square)

1894–1948

Philadelphia (AL 1912–15), Boston (AL 1915–22, 1934), New York (AL 1923–33)   **P**   **BB/LHP**

617 games	3,571 innings
240-162 W–L	3.60 ERA
1,227 k's	33 saves

Pennock pitched for three of the strongest AL franchises between 1910 and 1930. After joining the Boston-to-New York shuttle of the 1920s, he led the AL in winning percentage in his first season in pinstripes. An artist on the hill, he had great control and threw an assortment of curves and change-ups to baffle batters. Pennock is one of only two pitchers to win a game before the age of 20 and past the age of 40. Perfect at 5-0 in World Series competition for the Yanks, Pennock entered the Hall of Fame in 1948.

Pepitone, Joe (Pepi)

1940–

New York (AL 1962–69), Houston (NL 1970), Chicago (NL 1970–73), Atlanta (NL 1973) **1B, OF BL/TL**

1,397 games	.258 ba
1,315 hits	219 hr
721 rbi	41 sb

A free spirit on and off the field, Pepitone could hit with power, run, throw, and field superbly. Yet his career always suggested the question, What if . . . ? His was a story of unfulfilled potential. His highest batting average in New York was .271 in 1963, and he belted 28 home runs with 100 RBI the following year. Pepitone did lead the AL in introducing the hair dryer into the locker room.

Perez, Tony (Doggie)

1942–

Cincinnati (NL 1964–76, 1984–86), Montreal (NL 1977–79), Boston (AL 1980–83), Philadelphia (NL 1983); Mgr—Cincinnati (NL 1993) **1B, 3B, MGR BR/TR**

2,777 games	.279 ba
2,732 hits	379 hr
1,652 rbi	49 sb

One of the best clutch hitters of his generation, Perez knocked in at least 90 runs 12 times, including 11 consecutive years from 1967 to 1977. He used a closed batting stance to spray the ball to all fields, but he showed particular power to left- and right-center.

Perranoski, Ron

1936–

Los Angeles (NL 1961–67, 1972), Minnesota (AL 1968–71), Detroit (AL 1971–72), California (AL 1973) **P BL/LHP**

737 games	1,174 innings
79-74 W–L	2.79 ERA
687 k's	179 saves

The Dodgers' top reliever in the sixties, Perranoski won 16 games and saved an additional 21 while compiling a 1.67 ERA in 1963. He pitched on three pennant winners for Los Angeles. Traded to Minnesota, he led the AL in saves in 1969 (31) and 1970 (34).

Perritt, William (Pol)

1892–1947

St. Louis (NL 1912–14), New York (NL 1915–21), Detroit (AL 1921)   P   BR/RHP

256 games	1,469 innings
92-78 W–L	2.89 ERA
543 k's	8 saves

One of the top starting pitchers in the teens, Perritt won 18 games twice and 17 once for the Giants in 1916–18. On September 9, 1916, he pitched two complete games against Philadelphia, winning one 3-1 and the other 3-0.

Perry, Gaylord

1938–

San Francisco (NL 1962–71), Cleveland (AL 1972–75), Texas (AL 1975–77, 1980), San Diego (NL 1978–79), New York (AL 1980), Atlanta (NL 1981), Seattle (AL 1982–83), Kansas City (AL 1983)   P   BR/RHP

777 games	5,350 innings
314-265 W–L	3.11 ERA
3,534 k's	11 saves

Did he or didn't he? In his 1984 autobiography, Perry answered the curious when he confessed to having thrown the spitter during his career. Actually, it was Perry's slider that transformed him into a winning pitcher—his 21 wins in 1966 topped the senior circuit. A strong, durable hurler, he started no fewer than 37 games in every year between 1967 and 1975 and cur-

…ntly ranks fifth on the all-time list of innings pitched. …raded to Cleveland in 1972, Perry won the Cy Young Award amid allegations that he threw the spitter. In 1978, he became the first hurler to win the Cy Young Award in both leagues following a 21-6 season in San Diego. Perry currently ranks sixth on the all-time strikeout list. In recognition of his many lifetime achievements, the Hall of Fame inducted Perry in 1991.

Perry, Jim

1936–

Cleveland (AL 1959–63, 1974–75), Minnesota (AL 1963–72), Detroit (AL 1973), Oakland (AL 1975)

P   **BR/RHP**

630 games	3,285 innings
215-174 W–L	3.45 ERA
1,576 k's	10 saves

Jim Perry pitched his entire career without generating anywhere near the level of controversy that surrounded his younger brother Gaylord. He led the AL in wins in 1960 (18) and again in 1970 (24). The Perrys hold the record for the most wins by a pair of brothers in major league history (529).

Pesky, Johnny

1919–

Boston (AL 1942, 1946–52), Detroit (AL 1952–54), Washington (AL 1954); Mgr—Boston (AL 1963–64, 1980)   **SS, 3B, MGR**   **BL/TR**

1,270 games	.307 ba
1,455 hits	17 hr
404 rbi	53 sb

Pesky was the only major leaguer to lead his league in hits in his first three seasons. He smacked a total of 620 hits in 1942 and 1946–47 to spark the potent Red Sox attack. Pesky rarely struck out, fanning only 218 times in his career. Defensively, he is best remembered for his indecision on a relay throw in the seventh game of the

1946 World Series, a play on which Country Slaughter scored the winning run.

Peters, Gary

1937–

Chicago (AL 1959–69), Boston (AL 1970–72) P
BL/LHP

359 games	2,081 innings
124-103 W–L	3.25 ERA
1,420 k's	5 saves

The practical joker of the White Sox teams of the 1960s, Peters won the AL Rookie of the Year award in 1963, when he won 19 games and led the league in ERA (2.33). The next year, he won 20 games; and in 1966, he led the AL in ERA again (1.98). Peters became a winner after developing an effective slider. The best-hitting pitcher of his generation, he frequently helped his cause at the plate.

Peterson, Fritz

1942–

New York (AL 1966–74), Cleveland (AL 1974–76),
Texas (AL 1976) P   BB/LHP

355 games	2,218 innings
133-131 W–L	3.30 ERA
1,015 k's	1 save

A control specialist, Peterson never walked more than 49 men in a single season. Unfortunately, he pitched for the Yanks during their 12-year drought without a pennant winner. Peterson won 20 games in 1970, securing his last victory on the final day of the season. Though he was known as a flake on the field, the baseball world was still shocked to learn he had exchanged his wife and family for those of teammate Mike Kekich.

Petrocelli, Rico

1943–

Boston (AL 1963, 1965–76) SS, 3B   BR/TR

1,553 games	.251 ba
1,352 hits	210 hr
773 rbi	10 sb

Petrocelli had a swing perfectly suited for Fenway Park, and his high flies and line drives frequently cleared the Green Monster. In 1969, he cranked 40 homers, and he totaled 57 more in the following two seasons.

Petry, Dan

1958–

Detroit (AL 1979–87, 1990–91), California (AL 1988–89), Atlanta (NL 1991), Boston (AL 1991) P

RHP

370 games	2,080 innings
125-104 W–L	3.94 ERA
1,063 k's	1 save

Petry pitched in Jack Morris's shadow on the Tigers, but he racked up six seasons with double-digit win totals. In 1983, he went 19-11; and in the Tigers' title season in 1984, he snatched 18 triumphs.

Pfeffer, Edward (Jeff)

1888–1972

St. Louis (AL 1911), Brooklyn (NL 1913–21), St. Louis (NL 1921–24), Pittsburgh (NL 1924) P

BR/RHP

347 games	2,407 innings
158-112 W–L	2.77 ERA
836 k's	10 saves

A big, hard-throwing righty, Pfeffer was the ace of Brooklyn's pitching staff in the teens, going 25-11 in 1916 when the Dodgers won their first pennant since 1900. When Brooklyn won again in 1920, Pfeffer chipped in for 16 wins. The Dodgers thought he was through in 1921, but he rebounded to cop 19 victories in 1922.

Pfeffer, Fred (Dandelion, Fritz)

1860–1932

Troy (NL 1882), Chicago (NL 1883–89, 1891, 1896–97), Chicago (PL 1890), Louisville (NL 1892–95), New York (NL 1896); Mgr—Louisville (NL 1892)   **2B, MGR**   **BR/TR**

1,670 games	.255 ba
1,671 hits	94 hr
1,019 rbi	382 sb

A leader among men, Pfeffer inspired trust in his teammates and fans alike. On the field, he was the NL's best second baseman of the 1880s and the defensive anchor of Chicago's famed Stonewall Defense, which also featured Cap Anson, Thomas Burns, and Ned Williamson. Pfeffer was instrumental in procuring talent for the Players League Chicago franchise, drawing his White Stockings teammates to the new league. Popular with the fans in Chicago and Louisville, the German-speaking Pfeffer was suspended by the NL in 1895 for trying to organize a rival league, but fan outrage led to his reinstatement by the Louisville team against the NL's wishes. His admirers raised $500 to pay his fine to the league. A thinking man's player, Pfeffer published a tome entitled *Scientific Baseball* in 1889.

Pfiester, Jack (Jack the Giant Killer)

1878–1953

Pittsburgh (NL 1903–04), Chicago (NL 1906–11)
P   **BR/LHP**

149 games	1,067 innings
71-44 W–L	2.02 ERA
503 k's	

Nicknamed "Jack the Giant Killer" for his uncanny ability to beat the Cubs' arch rivals, Pfiester won 63 games against only 33 losses in 1906–09. In his career, he went 15-5 against McGraw's men. In 1907, Pfiester led the NL in ERA (1.15).

Phillippe, Charles (Deacon)

1872–1952

Louisville (NL 1899), Pittsburgh (NL 1900–11)   P
BR/RHP

372 games	2,607 innings
189-109 W–L	2.59 ERA
929 k's	12 saves

Phillippe became the first 20th-century World Series hero when he won three games in the 1903 World Series against the Red Sox. No slouch in the regular season, he earned 20 victories in each of his first five seasons in the NL.

Pierce, Billy

1927–

Detroit (AL 1945, 1948), Chicago (AL 1949–61),
San Francisco (NL 1962–64)   P   BL/LHP

585 games	3,306 innings
211-169 W–L	3.27 ERA
1,999 k's	32 saves

Pierce won 186 games for Chicago, a record for Chisox lefties. Small in stature, he threw a good fastball; and when he developed a slider in 1953, his career took off. That year, he went 18-12 with a 2.72 ERA and a league-leading 186 strikeouts. In 1958, Pierce came within one out of pitching a perfect game against Washington. He won 20 games twice, and after being traded to the Giants, pitched them to the World Series in 1962. The White Sox retired his uniform number 19.

Piersall, Jimmy

1929–

Boston (AL 1950, 1952–58), Cleveland (AL
1959–61), Washington (AL 1962–63), New York
(NL 1963), Los Angeles (AL 1963–64), California
(AL 1965–67)   OF   BR/TR

1,734 games	.272 ba
1,604 hits	104 hr
591 rbi	115 sb

Piersall was driven to succeed by an overbearing father, and the pressures of major league baseball ultimately drove him to a nervous breakdown. Given to colorful, uninhibited behavior, Piersall was a fan favorite wherever he played. He was a great defensive center fielder who played very shallow, in part to compensate for a weak throwing arm, but he covered a tremendous amount of ground. When he hit his 100th career home run while playing for Casey Stengel's Mets in 1963, Piersall ran backward around the bases.

Piniella, Lou (Sweet Lou)
1943–

Baltimore (AL 1964), Cleveland (AL 1968), Kansas City (AL 1969–73), New York (AL 1974–84); Mgr—New York (AL 1986–88), Cincinnati (NL 1990–92), Seattle (AL 1993 Active)   **OF, DH, MGR   BR/TR**

1,747 games	.291 ba
1,705 hits	102 hr
766 rbi	32 sb

Piniella loved to practice his batting stroke—in the dugout, in front of a mirror, on the field, anywhere. He could probably have stepped to the plate in the middle of winter and gotten a base hit. If they needed a clutch hit during a game, Piniella was the man his managers and teammates wanted at the plate. Extremely popular with the fans during his playing career, Piniella batted .300 six times in his career. Hot-tempered and explosive, his tirades as a player and manager have become legendary. He managed Cincinnati to victory in the 1990 World Series.

Pinson, Vada
1936–

Cincinnati (NL 1958–68), St. Louis (NL 1969), Cleveland (AL 1970–71), California (AL 1972–73), Kansas City (AL 1974–75)   **OF   BL/TL**

2,469 games	.286 ba
2,757 hits	256 hr
1,170 rbi	305 sb

Pinson ran like a deer and belted the ball to all fields, yet his name is rarely mentioned today in discussions of great outfielders of the sixties. He collected more than 200 hits in four seasons and led the NL twice, in 1961 (208) and 1963 (204). In Cincinnati's pennant-winning year, 1961, he batted a career-high .343.

Pipp, Wally

1893–1965
Detroit (AL 1913), New York (AL 1915–25), Cincinnati (NL 1926–28)   **1B**   **BL/TL**

1,872 games	.281 ba
1,941 hits	90 hr
996 rbi	125 sb

Pipp became famous as the man whose stomachache kept him out of the lineup, giving Lou Gehrig his chance at bat. By the time he recovered, he had lost his job. He was traded to Cincinnati the following year. Pipp was a fine-fielding first baseman who hit .329 in 1922 and drove home 113 runs in 1924.

Pizarro, Juan

1937–
Milwaukee (NL 1957–60), Chicago (Al 1961–66), Pittsburgh (NL 1967–68, 1974), Boston (Al 1968–69), Cleveland (AL 1969), Oakland (Al 1969), Chicago (NL 1970–73), Houston (NL 1973)   **P**
BL/LHP

488 games	2,034 innings
131–105 W–L	3.43 ERA
1,522 Wo	28 saves

Pizarro threw a great fastball, but he didn't become a winner until he joined the Chisox and changed his delivery. In 1962–63, he won a combined 35 games against only 17 losses.

Plank, Eddie (Gettysburg Eddie)
1875–1926

Philadelphia (AL 1901–14), St. Louis (FL 1915), St. Louis (AL 1916–17)   P   **BL/LHP**

623 games	4,495 innings
362-194 W–L	2.35 ERA
2,246 k's	23 saves

Plank joined the Athletics straight off the campus of Gettysburg College. He completed more games (410) and pitched more shutouts (69) than any other left-hander in major league history. A finesse pitcher, he won 20 games eight times and was the first lefty to win 300 games in his career. Plank entered the Hall of Fame in 1946.

Podres, Johnny
1932–

Brooklyn (NL 1953–55, 1957), Los Angeles (NL 1958–66), Detroit (AL 1966–67), San Diego (NL 1969)   P   **BL/LHP**

440 games	2,265 innings
148-116 W–L	3.68 ERA
1,435 k's	11 saves

A hero for all time in Brooklyn, Podres pitched a 2-0 shutout in the seventh game of the 1955 World Series to provide the Brooks with their only title. A master of the change-up, he used a deceptive motion that hid the ball from the batter. Podres also led the NL in ERA in 1957 (2.66) and in winning percentage in 1961 (.783), when he went 18-5. In six World Series starts, he won four games with a scintillating 2.11 ERA.

Poles, Spottswood (Spot)
1886–1962

Philadelphia Giants (1909–1910), New York Lincoln Giants (1911–1914, 1916–1917, 1919), Brooklyn Royal Giants (1912), New York Lincoln Stars (1915)   **OF**   **BB/TR**

66 games	.292 ba
79 hits	2 hr
6 sb	

Often called "the black Ty Cobb," Poles ran like a deer and played an aggressive game on the base paths. He usually batted leadoff on account of his phenomenal speed. Defensively, he roamed center field, where he could grab any ball hit in the air.

Pollet, Howie

1921–1974

St. Louis (NL 1941–43, 1946–51), Pittsburgh (NL 1951–53, 1956), Chicago (NL 1953–55), Chicago (AL 1956)   P   BL/LHP

403 games	2,107 innings
131-116 W–L	3.51 ERA
934 k's	20 saves

Pollet had two big seasons for the Cardinals, winning 21 games in 1946 and 20 more in 1949. In 1946, he led the NL in wins, innings pitched (266), and ERA (2.10). St. Louis finished the season tied for first with Brooklyn. Pollett defeated the Dodgers in the first playoff game of a best-of-three series that the Cardinals ultimately swept to win the pennant.

Posey, Cumberland (Cum)

1891–1946

Homestead Grays   OF, MGR

A pioneer in the Negro Leagues, Posey became manager of the Homestead Grays in 1916 and later owned the team. One of the greatest sports franchises of all time, the Grays proved a formidable rival to the Pittsburgh Crawfords and the Kansas City Monarchs. Posey treated his players well, paying them good salaries and providing them with the best possible accommodations. He was a well-educated man who attended Penn State.

Post, Wally

1929–1982

Cincinnati (NL 1949, 1951–57, 1960–63),
Philadelphia (NL 1958–60), Minnesota (AL 1963),
Cleveland (AL 1964) **OF   BR/TR**

1,204 games	.266 ba
1,064 hits	210 hr
699 rbi	19 sb

A right-handed slugger who was murder on left-handers, Post belted 76 homers in 1955–56 and slammed another 20 as a part-timer on the pennant-winning Reds team in 1961.

Potter, Nelson (Nels)

1911–1990

St. Louis (NL 1936), Philadelphia (AL 1938–41,
1948), Boston (AL 1941), St. Louis (AL 1943–48),
Boston (NL 1948–49) **P   BL/RHP**

349 games	1,686 innings
92-97 W–L	3.99 ERA
747 k's	22 saves

The war years brought glory to the Brownies when Potter pitched them to the 1944 AL pennant. He won a career-best 19 games and surrendered only six home runs in 232 innings. His best pitches were a screwball and a slider, although he was suspended in 1946 for throwing a spitball.

Powell, Jack

1874–1944

Cleveland (NL 1897–98), St. Louis (NL
1899–1901), St. Louis (AL 1902–03, 1905–12),
New York (AL 1904–05) **P   BR/RHP**

578 games	4,389 innings
245-254 W–L	2.97 ERA
1,621 k's	15 saves

An old warhorse, Powell was one of only two major league hurlers to win more than 200 games with a sub-

.500 winning percentage, It was his misfortune to pitch for a series of second-division clubs; otherwise, his lifetime mark might have been much improved. Powell won 20 games four times in his career, but his long tenure with the Browns dragged his record below .500.

Powell, John (Boog)

1941–
Baltimore (AL 1961–74), Cleveland (AL 1975–76), Los Angeles (NL 1977) **1B, OF** **BL/TR**

2,042 games	.266 ba
1,776 hits	339 hr
1,187 rbi	20 sb

A giant of a man physically, Powell belted 34 homers in 1966, 37 in 1969, and 35 in 1970. In each season, Baltimore reached the World Series. Although he was not a fast runner, Powell was nimble around the first base bag and clearly presented a big target.

Power, Vic

1931–
Philadelphia (AL 1954), Kansas City (AL 1955–58), Cleveland (AL 1958–61), Minnesota (AL 1962–64), Los Angeles (AL 1964), Philadelphia (NL 1964), California (AL 1965) **1B** **BR/TR**

1,627 games	.284 ba
1,716 hits	126 hr
658 rbi	45 sb

Power was buried in the Yankees' minor league system because he did not fit the team's image of the sort of personality that their first black player should have. He was an outspoken, flashy player who did not suffer racial injustice quietly. After he was traded to the Athletics, Power took special delight in beating the Yankees. A strong hitter, he was also the finest defensive first baseman of his generation. He batted .319 in 1955 and .312 in 1958.

Pratt, Derrill (Del)

1888–1977

St. Louis (AL 1912–17), New York (AL 1918–20), Boston (AL 1921–22), Detroit (AL 1923–24)   **2B**

BR/TR

1,836 games	.292 ba
1,996 hits	43 hr
966 rbi	246 sb

An outstanding batter and fielder, Pratt took great pride in his work. When St. Louis owner Phil Ball accused the entire team of not giving their best effort in a game, Pratt sued him for slander and won an out-of-court settlement. Of course, he was summarily traded as retribution. In 1916, Pratt led the AL in RBI (103)—not a bad feat for a second baseman.

Puckett, Kirby

1961–

Minnesota (AL 1984–93 Active)   **OF**   **BR/TR**

1,538 games	.318 ba
1,996 hits	164 hr
874 rbi	125 sb

The most popular player ever to wear a Twins uniform, Puckett always plays the game with youthful enthusiasm. When he first arrived in Minnesota, he was a singles hitter; but after smacking 31 homers in his third season, he propelled himself into the spotlight as a powerhouse in the lineup. Puckett led the AL in base hits four times and batting average once (.339 in 1989). Ironically, he batted .356 the year before without winning the crown. Defensively, he covers a lot of ground and has a strong and accurate arm.

Purkey, Bob

1929–

Pittsburgh (NL 1954–57, 1966), Cincinnati (NL 1958–64), St. Louis (NL 1965)   **P**   **BR/RHP**

386 games	2,114 innings
129-115 W–L	3.79 ERA
793 k's	9 saves

A smart hurler who studied batters' weaknesses, Purkey threw a full assortment of pitches, including the knuckle ball. A big winner during the five-year span from 1958 to 1962, he went 23-5 for the Reds in 1962, but it wasn't good enough to take the team to a second consecutive pennant.

Q

Quinn, Jack
1883–1946
New York (AL 1909–12, 1919–21), Boston (NL 1913), Baltimore (FL 1914–15), Chicago (AL 1918), Boston (AL 1922–25), Philadelphia (AL 1925–30), Brooklyn (NL 1931–32), Cincinnati (NL 1933)   P   BR/RHP

756 games	3,920 innings
247-218 W–L	3.29 ERA
1,329 k's	57 saves

Born John Quinn Picus in the Pennsylvania mine country, Quinn was the last of the legal spitballers. He faked throwing a wet one on every pitch and actually enjoyed his greatest success past the age of 40. He won 18 games for the Athletics in 1928 and led the NL in saves in both 1931 and 1932.

Quisenberry, Dan (Quiz)
1953–
Kansas City (AL 1979–88), St. Louis (NL 1988–89), San Francisco (NL 1990)   P   BR/RHP

674 games	1,043 innings
56-46 W–L	2.76 ERA
379 k's	244 saves

Always ready with a quip, Quisenberry looked at the lighter side of baseball throughout his career. On the mound, his submarine delivery baffled batters for over a decade. Quisenberry lead the AL in saves five times. His best year was 1983, when he saved 45 games and pitched to an ERA of 1.94.

R

Radatz, Dick (The Monster)
1937–
Boston (AL 1962–66), Cleveland (AL 1966–67), Chicago (NL 1967), Detroit (AL 1969), Montreal (NL 1969)   P   BR/RHP

381 games	693 innings
52-43 W–L	3.13 ERA
745 k's	122 saves

Between 1962 and 1964, Radatz was the most feared pitcher in the AL. He stood 6 feet, 5 inches and threw an explosive fastball with a sidearm motion. His pitches were extremely difficult for right-handed batters. Radatz went 40-24 with 78 saves and recorded well over one strikeout per inning in this span. Unlike the relievers of today, who pitch to one or two batters per outing, Radatz averaged more than two innings an appearance.

Radbourn, Charles (Old Hoss)
1854–1897
Buffalo (NL 1880), Providence (NL 1881–85), Boston (NL 1886–89), Boston (PL 1890), Cincinnati (NL 1891)   P   BB/RHP

528 games	4,535 innings
309-195 W–L	2.67 ERA
1,830 k's	2 saves

"Old Hoss" epitomized the durability of 19th-century hurlers. In 1884, he established a number of one-season pitching records that will never be broken—59 wins, 73 complete games, 678 innings pitched, and 441 strikeouts. That year, Radbourn pitched Providence to victory in the World Series against the New York Metropolitans of the American Association. He was inducted into the Hall of Fame in 1939.

Radcliffe, Ted (Double Duty)

1902–

Detroit Stars (1928–29), St. Louis Stars (1930), Detroit Wolves (1931), Homestead Grays (1931, 1933), Pittsburgh Crawfords (1932), Cleveland Giants (1933), Columbus Blue Birds (1933), Chicago American Giants (1934, 1942–43), Brooklyn Eagles (1935), Memphis Red Sox (1938–39), Cleveland Red Sox (1941), Birmingham Black Barons (1942, 1944)

C, P   BR/RHP

296 games	.282 ba
303 hits	20 hr
13 sb	542 innings
53-33 W–L	138 k's
9 saves	

Nicknamed "Double Duty" by newsman Damon Runyon, Radcliffe alternated between the mound and the backstop during his career. Short and stocky, he had a dynamic throwing arm behind the plate; on the mound, he relied on his fastball and a spitball.

Raines, Tim (Rock)

1959–

Montreal (NL 1979–90), Chicago (AL 1991–93 Active)   OF   BB/TR

1,819 games	.298 ba
2,050 hits	124 hr
710 rbi	751 sb

One of the best leadoff hitters in the history of the game, Raines's combination of speed and power has been matched only by Rickey Henderson. Raines led the NL in steals in 1981–84, with a personal best of 90 swipes in 1983. He also led the NL in batting in 1986 (.334).

Ramos, Pedro (Pete)
1935–
Washington (AL 1955–60), Minnesota (AL 1961), Cleveland (AL 1962–64), New York (AL 1964–66), Philadelphia (NL 1967), Pittsburgh (NL 1969), Cincinnati (NL 1969), Washington (AL 1970)   P
BB/RHP

582 games	2,355 innings
117-160 W–L	4.08 ERA
1,305 k's	55 saves

The Cuban-born right-hander had great stuff, but while playing on last-place teams in Washington, he led the AL in most losses for four consecutive seasons (1958–61). After moving to the bullpen, he enjoyed more success, especially in 1964 when he sparked the Yankees to the pennant. Off the field, Ramos was known for his cowboy boots, Cuban cigars, and partying.

Randolph, Willie
1954–
Pittsburgh (NL 1975), New York (AL 1976–88), Los Angeles (NL 1989–90), Oakland (AL 1990), Milwaukee (AL 1991), New York (NL 1992)   2B
BR/TR

2,202 games	.276 ba
2,210 hits	54 hr
687 rbi	271 sb

Yankees fans took Randolph for granted; only after his departure did they realize what they no longer had. He excelled at turning double plays, had good range to either side, and possessed a strong throwing arm. At bat, Randolph was at his best when he drove the ball to the opposite field. He was an extremely patient hitter who rarely swung at the first strike. In his best year, 1980, he topped the AL with 119 walks, batted .294, had a .429 on-base average, and scored 99 runs. For his career, he drew 1,243 walks.

Raschi, Vic (The Springfield Rifle)
1919–1988
New York (AL 1946–53), St. Louis (NL 1954–55), Kansas City (AL 1955)   P   BR/RHP

269 games	1,819 innings
132-66 W–L	3.72 ERA
944 k's	3 saves

The first great Italian-American pitcher in the majors, Raschi never had an effective curve ball, relying instead on his overhand fastball and slider. In his eight years with the Yanks, he won 120 and lost only 50, for a winning percentage of .706. On the mound, Raschi was all business and he was at his best in pressure situations. He won 21 games each year from 1949 to 1951, but after a knee injury limited his effectiveness in 1953, he was unceremoniously dumped by the Yankees.

Reardon, Jeff
1955–
New York (NL 1979–81), Montreal (NL 1981–86), Minnesota (AL 1987–89), Boston (AL 1990–92), Atlanta (NL 1992), Cincinnati (NL 1993 Active)   P   BR/RHP

869 games	1,122 innings
72-77 W–L	3.11 ERA
873 k's	365 saves

Until he was bested by Lee Smith, Reardon held the major league record for career saves. In his finest outings, he utilized a high-rising fastball and sharp-breaking slider that batters could not touch. Reardon saved at least 40 games each season in 1985, 1988, and 1991. Groomed by the Mets as a bullpen ace, Reardon has never started a game in the major leagues.

Redding, Dick (Cannonball)

1891–1940

New York Lincoln Giants, Lincoln Stars, Indianapolis ABC's, Chicago American Giants, Brooklyn Royal Giants, Bacharach Giants P, MGR **RHP**

598 innings	45-44 W–L
142 k's	2 saves

Arguably the hardest-throwing right-hander in baseball history, "Cannonball" Redding was often compared to Walter Johnson. Like "the Big Train," he threw only one pitch—a blazing fastball—for much of his career, developing a curve only after his number-one pitch lost its steam.

Reese, Harold (Pee Wee, The Little Colonel)

1918–

Brooklyn (NL 1940–42, 1946–57), Los Angeles (NL 1958) SS **BR/TR**

2,166 games	.269 ba
2,170 hits	126 hr
885 rbi	232 sb

A gentleman on and off the field, Reese captained the Dodgers and openly supported Jackie Robinson's entry into the major leagues. Sure-handed in the field and a solid hitter, he boosted his power numbers by playing in cozy Ebbets Field. He scored an NL-high 132 runs in 1949 and drove home at least 60 runs eight times. Reese was the only man to play in every game of the seven World Series match-ups between Brooklyn and the Yankees. In a memorable evening at Ebbets Field on his birthday in 1957, more than 30,000 fans held lighted candles in the darkened ballpark in tribute to him. The Dodgers have retired his uniform number one, and he was inducted into the Hall of Fame in 1984.

Regan, Phil (The Vulture)

1937–

Detroit (AL 1960–65), Los Angeles (NL 1966–68), Chicago (NL 1968–72), Chicago (AL 1972) P

BR

551 games	1,372 innings
96-81 W–L	3.84 ERA
743 k's	92 saves

Regan was an effective spot starter for the Tigers, winning a career-high 15 games in 1963, but he made his mark in the Dodgers bullpen. In 1966, he acquired his nickname, "the Vulture," when he earned 14 relief wins, saved an NL-high 21 more, and compiled a stingy 1.62 ERA. Traded to the Cubs in 1968, he led the NL again with 25 saves. Although it was never proven, most observers believed that Regan threw a spitball or greaseball throughout his career.

Reiser, Pete (Pistol Pete)

1919–1981

Brooklyn (NL 1940–42, 1946–48), Boston (NL 1949–50), Pittsburgh (NL 1951), Cleveland (AL 1952) OF BL/TR

861 games	.295 ba
786 hits	58 hr
368 rbi	87 sb

The legend of Pete Reiser continues to grow more than 50 years after he first appeared in a major league game. An enormously gifted athlete, he had great speed, hit with power, and had a fierce competitive drive to excel. Acquired by the Dodgers from St. Louis in a controversial trade, Reiser batted an NL-high .343 in his first full season in 1941. He also led the league in runs (117), doubles (39), and triples (17) while fielding brilliantly. The next year, he was in the middle of another superlative season when he ran headlong into the brick outfield wall at St. Louis's Sportsman's Park in pursuit of a fly ball. He suffered a fractured skull and never performed at the same level again. After missing the 1943–45 seasons in the military, he returned in 1946, only to break his ankle. The following season, he ran into the wall at Ebbets Field and suffered another fractured skull. This time, he was finished as a productive player.

Reulbach, Ed (Big Ed)
1882–1961
Chicago (NL 1905–13), Brooklyn (NL 1913–14), Newark (FL 1915), Boston (NL 1916–17)   P
BR/RHP

399 games	2,632 innings
182-106 W–L	2.28 ERA
1,138 k's	13 saves

On September 26, 1908, the Cubs were in hot pursuit of the first-place Giants but found themselves short of pitchers for a doubleheader at Brooklyn. Reulbach shut out the Superbas in the opener and then came back to blank them again in the nightcap, making him the only man ever to pitch a doubleheader shutout. Although he never received the publicity accorded the Cubs' star hurler, "Three Finger" Brown, Reulbach led the NL in winning percentage for three consecutive years, from 1906 to 1908.

Reuschel, Rick (Big Daddy)
1949–
Chicago (NL 1972–81, 1983–84), New York (AL 1981), Pittsburgh (NL 1985–87), San Francisco (NL 1987–91)   P   BR/RHP

557 games	3,548 innings
214-191 W–L	3.37 ERA
2,015 k's	5 saves

Like a cat with nine lives, Reuschel came back from serious injuries on at least three occasions when most observers considered him washed up. A mountain of a man, he looked more like the farmer he was in the off-season than a top athlete. On the mound, he threw a natural sinker and a sharp curve, but his biggest asset was his pinpoint control. Reuschel won 20 games and compiled a stingy 2.79 ERA for the 1977 Cubs. Released after a major shoulder injury, Reuschel bounced from the Cubs to the Yankees, back to the Cubs, and on to the Pirates before he regained his success. Then traded to the Giants, he won 36 games in 1988–89, relying on little more than his guile.

Reuss, Jerry

1949–

St. Louis (NL 1969–71), Houston (NL 1972–73), Pittsburgh (NL 1974–78, 1990), Los Angeles (NL 1979–87), Cincinnati (NL 1987), California (AL 1987), Chicago (AL 1988–89), Milwaukee (AL 1989) P   BL/LHP

628 games	3,669 innings
220-191 W–L	3.64 ERA
1,907 k's	11 saves

A flaky left-hander, Reuss won the most games in major league history without ever winning 20 games in any one season. He threw a good fastball and slider on his way to three 18-victory seasons.

Reynolds, Allie (Superchief)

1915–

Cleveland (AL 1942–46), New York (AL 1947–54) P   BR/RHP

434 games	2,492 innings
182-107 W–L	3.30 ERA
1,423 k's	49 saves

Labeled a quitter in Cleveland, Reynolds went on to become one of the game's best clutch pitchers in New York, winning World Series games in each of the Yankees' five consecutive championship years (1949–53). In his first year in New York, he led the AL in winning percentage (.704). A fast worker, Reynolds's best pitch was his explosive fastball. He pitched two no-hitters in 1951. After injuring his back in a team bus crash in Philadelphia in 1953, Reynolds lost much of his effectiveness, and he retired after the next season.

Rhoden, Rick

1953–
Los Angeles (NL 1974–78), Pittsburgh (NL 1979–86), New York (AL 1987–88), Houston (NL 1989)   **P**   **BR/RHP**

413 games	2,593 innings
151-125 W–L	3.59 ERA
1,419 k's	1 save

Rhoden was a dependable starting pitcher who could fill the third slot on any staff. He relied on his fastball and slider to get batters out, and he won in double digits 10 times. At the plate, Rhoden carried a big stick and often helped his own cause with timely base hits.

Rice, Edgar (Sam)

1890–1974
Washington (AL 1915–33), Cleveland (AL 1934)
OF   **BL/TR**

2,404 games	.322 ba
2,987 hits	34 hr
1,078 rbi	351 sb

A speedy outfielder who led the AL in steals in 1920 (63), Rice was a consistently strong hitter for two decades. A lightweight at only 150 pounds, he nevertheless showed good strength at the plate, knocking out over 200 hits six times. He hit over .300 in 13 seasons, with a career-high .350 in 1925, when he led Washington to the pennant. In the World Series that year, he made a miraculous game-saving catch while tumbling into the temporary stands in right-center field. Forty years later, he confirmed that he had made the catch legally. Rice was inducted into the Hall of Fame in 1963.

Rice, Jim

1953–

Boston (AL 1974–89)   OF, DH   BR/TR

2,089 games	.298 ba
2,452 hits	382 hr
1,451 rbi	58 sb

At the plate, Rice stood deep in the box and took a short stride before snapping his strong wrists at the pitch. He powered the ball to all fields and showed particular strength to right-center. In 1978, Rice was honored as the AL MVP after he accumulated 400 total bases; he was the last player to achieve that mark. He knocked in over 100 RBI in eight seasons, with a career-high 139 in 1978.

Richard, James Rodney (J.R.)

1950–

Houston (NL 1971–80)   P   BR/RHP

238 games	1,606 innings
107-71 W–L	3.15 ERA
1,493 k's	

Richard's career was tragically ended by a stroke in 1980, at a time when he was emerging as the dominant pitcher in baseball. Towering over batters on the mound, he intimidated batters by throwing fastballs at over 95 miles an hour. He won 20 games in 1976 and 18 in each of the next three seasons. Richard led the NL in strikeouts in 1978 (303) and again in 1979 (313); but when he felt his right arm go dead in 1980, neither team personnel nor the media believed him.

Richards, Paul

1908–1986

Mgr—Chicago (AL 1951–54, 1976), Baltimore (AL 1955–61)   MGR

Richards revived the moribund franchises in Chicago and Baltimore. In the early fifties, he transformed the Chisox from perennial losers into an exciting, running team cheered on by the fans' chant of "Go, Go!" The acknowledged master of the pitching staff, Richards molded Baltimore's Baby Birds in the early 1960s. Under his tutelage, Steve Barber, Chuck Estrada, and Milt Pappas became outstanding hurlers, and the Orioles began their three-decade contention for the top of the American League.

Richardson, Bobby
1935–
New York (AL 1955–66)   **2B**   BR/TR

1,412 games	.266 ba
1,432 hits	34 hr
390 rbi	73 sb

A deeply religious man, Richardson seemed out of place on the hell raising Yankees squads of the fifties and sixties. He formed a great double-play combo with fellow good citizen Tony Kubek. After knocking in only 26 runs for the entire 1960 season, he drove in 12 runs in the World Series against the Pirates, including six in one game, thus establishing two series records. A fine fielder and a spunky high fastball hitter, Richardson batted .302 with a league-best 209 hits from his accustomed leadoff spot for the 1962 Yanks.

Richardson, Hardy (Old True Blue)
1855–1931
Buffalo (NL 1879–85), Detroit (NL 1886–88), Boston (NL 1889), Boston (PL 1890), Boston (AA 1891), Washington (NL 1892), New York (NL 1892)
2B, OF   BR/TR

1,331 games	.299 ba
1,688 hits	70 hr
822 rbi	205 sb

One of the NL's best sluggers in the 1880s, Richardson was one of the famous Big Four who were sold to Detroit in 1885 for $7,000. The transaction made the Wolverines instant pennant contenders. A versatile performer, Richardson played all nine positions at various times in his career, although he performed most often at second base. In 1886, he led the NL in home runs with 11.

Rickey, Wesley (Branch)

1881–1965
St. Louis (AL 1905–06, 1914), New York (AL 1907); Mgr—St. Louis (AL 1913–15), St. Louis (NL 1919–25)   C, MGR, GM   BL/TR

120 games	.239 ba
82 hits	3 hr
27 rbi	8 sb

Rickey revolutionized baseball. Had he retired in 1945, he would still be remembered as the man who invented the farm system, stockpiling hundreds of players on minor league teams to ensure a steady supply of talent. His success in St. Louis and Brooklyn produced dynasties in both cities. However, his lasting legacy stems from his decision in 1945 to sign Jackie Robinson to a minor league contract with the Dodger's top farm club in Montreal, thereby breaking the color barrier. The Dodgers were quick to sign other top black talents and quickly became the most popular team in the nation. Known throughout his career as a skinflint, he ultimately lost control of the Dodgers in a power struggle with Walter O'Malley and later became the chief executive of the Pittsburgh franchise. Rickey was inducted into the Hall of Fame in 1967.

Righetti, Dave (Rags)

1958–
New York (AL 1979, 1981–90), San Francisco (NL 1991–93)   P   BL/LHP

688 games	1,333 innings
79-76 W–L	3.33 ERA
1,069 k's	252 saves

The Yankees could never decide what to do with Righetti's talented arm. Some talent evaluators within the organization felt that he belonged in the bullpen because he seemed to tire after the sixth inning. Others pointed to his no-hitter on July 4, 1983, as proof that he should start. Righetti never won more than 14 games as a starter. He found more success in the bullpen, where he saved 46 games in 1986, then a major league record. He relied on a fastball and a slider to muzzle the opposing bats.

Rijo, Jose

1965–

New York (AL 1984), Oakland (AL 1985–87), Cincinnati (NL 1988–93 Active)   P   BR/RHP

292 games	1,544 innings
97-77 W–L	3.13 ERA
1,323 k's	3 saves

Rushed to the major leagues by the Yankees in 1984 to counter the Met's superrookie Dwight Gooden, Rijo pitched poorly and was sent to Oakland in the Rickey Henderson trade the following year. He developed into a competitive pitcher only after another move to Cincinnati in 1988. He has won at least 14 games for the Reds each year since 1990. Rijo is a free spirit on and off the field.

Ripken, Jr., Cal

1960–

Baltimore (AL 1981–93 Active)   SS   BR/TR

1,962 games	.275 ba
2,087 hits	297 hr
1,104 rbi	33 sb

Sometime in July 1995, Ripken will break Lou Gehrig's remarkable record of playing in 2,130 consecutive games. Some critics have claimed that his pursuit of the record has come at the expense of the Orioles' success, but Ripken feels that he can play every day and is the best man available for his position. In the field, he is extremely intelligent and makes the most difficult plays look easy. At bat, his offensive numbers have been inconsistent in recent years, but he has won two AL MVP awards (1983, 1991). In 1983, he led the AL in runs scored (121), hits (211), and doubles (47), and batted .318 with 27 home runs and 102 RBI.

Rivers, Mickey (Mick the Quick)

1948–
California (AL 1970–75), New York (AL 1976–79),
Texas (AL 1979–84) OF BL/TL

1,468 games	.295 ba
1,660 hits	61 hr
499 rbi	267 sb

When Rivers hobbled to the plate taking tiny, delicate steps, you'd think he could never run out a base hit, but nothing could be further from the truth. He could fly. After leading the AL in stolen bases in 1975 (70), he was dealt to the Yankees, where he proceeded to spark New York to its first pennant in 12 years. He batted .312 and .326 his first two years in the Bronx, but a series of minor injuries led to his departure. Off the field, Rivers loved to play the horses and frequently found himself short of funds.

Rixey, Eppa (Eppa Jephtha)

1891–1963
Philadelphia (NL 1912–17, 1919–20), Cincinnati
(NL 1921–33) P BR/LHP

692 games	4,494 innings
266-251 W–L	3.15 ERA
1,350 k's	14 saves

At 6 feet, 5 inches, Rixey was an imposing figure on the mound. Although he spent most of his years on losing teams, he was the winningest left-hander in NL history prior to Warren Spahn. His career high was 25 games in 1922. A control artist, Rixey forced batters to hit his pitch. He was elected to the Hall of Fame in 1963.

Rizzuto, Phil (Scooter)

1917–

New York (AL 1941–42, 1946–56)   SS

BR/TR

1,661 games	.273 ba
1,588 hits	38 hr
563 rbi	149 sb

Told by Brooklyn manager Casey Stengel to find a job shining shoes rather than attempt a career playing baseball, Rizzuto overcame the skeptics and his own phobias to enjoy a career that many baseball experts think warrant his induction into the Hall of Fame. Fast afield, with a quick release, Rizzuto was the glue of the Yankees defense during nine pennant-winning seasons. At the plate, he was a smart slap hitter and perhaps the best bunter the game has ever seen. In 1950, Rizzuto won the AL MVP award when he hit .324 with 200 hits and 125 runs scored. The Yankees retired his uniform number 10. Rizzuto stepped directly from the playing field to the broadcast booth, where his unique style has thrilled Yankees fans for over 30 years.

Roberts, Robin

1926–

Philadelphia (NL 1948–61), Baltimore (AL 1962–65), Houston (NL 1965–66), Chicago (NL 1966)   P   BB/RHP

676 games	4,688 innings
286-245 W–L	3.41 ERA
2,357 k's	25 saves

Roberts was the most consistent hurler in the NL during the fifties. Pitching on three days' rest, he led the league in innings pitched in 1951–55, games won in 1952–55, and complete games in 1952–56. His best success came in 1952, when he went 28-7 with a 2.59

ERA. Throwing directly overhead, Roberts had a great fastball and superb control, and he challenged batters to hit his pitch. As a result, he surrendered a major league high of 505 home runs in his career. The Phillies retired his uniform number 36, and he was inducted into the Hall of Fame in 1976.

Robinson, Brooks

1938–
Baltimore (AL 1955–77)   3B   BR/TR

2,896 games	.267 ba
2,848 hits	268 hr
1,357 rbi	28 sb

The most popular player in modern Baltimore history, Robinson resembled a human vacuum cleaner at third base, devouring grounders, charging in to field bunts, and rifling accurate throws to first. Robinson set major league career records for games, put-outs, assists, chances, double plays, and fielding percentage for third basemen. His 16 Gold Glove awards rank number one among nonpitchers. A clutch hitter, he held the record for most homers by an AL third baseman at his retirement (268). Robinson won the AL MVP award in 1964 and the World Series MVP award in 1970 for his dazzling performance at third.

Robinson, Frank

1935–
Cincinnati (NL 1956–65), Baltimore (AL 1966–71), Los Angeles (NL 1972), California (AL 1973–74), Cleveland (AL 1974–76); Mgr—Cleveland (AL 1975–77), San Francisco (NL 1981–84), Baltimore (AL 1988–91)   OF, DH, 1B, MGR   BR/TR

2,808 games	.294 ba
2,943 hits	586 hr
1,812 rbi	204 sb

One of the greatest players ever to appear on a big league diamond, Robinson holds a series of records for his accomplishments in both the AL and the NL. Traded by Cincinnati prior to the 1966 season because the Reds considered him an "old" 30, he went on to several outstanding seasons with the Orioles. Robinson remains the only player to hit more than 200 home runs in each league, and he earned MVP honors in both leagues as well. An aggressive batter, he stood erect only inches off the plate and dared pitchers to come inside with their best stuff, because he was a pull hitter who would smash those offerings over the left-field wall. A leader on the field, he became the first black manager in major league history, taking control of Cleveland in 1975. Robinson retired fourth on the all-time list for hitting home runs. He was inducted into the Hall of Fame in 1982.

Robinson, Jackie

1919–1972
Kansas City Monarchs (1945), Brooklyn (NL 1947–56)   2B, 3B   BR/TR

1,382 games	.311 ba
1,518 hits	137 hr
734 rbi	197 sb

Jackie Robinson was the first black player in modern major league history. An exceptional player who withstood the racist taunts of opponents, his hitting, running, and fielding skills thrilled fans across the nation. No one was a more intense competitor than Robinson. In 1949, he won the NL MVP award when he led the league with a .342 batting average and 37 stolen bases. On the bases, he intimidated pitchers and fielders like no player before him. The Dodgers retired his uniform number 42, and he was elected to the Hall of Fame in 1962.

Robinson, Wilbert (Uncle Robbie)

1863–1934

Philadelphia (AA 1886–90), Baltimore (AA
1890–91), Baltimore (NL 1892–99), St. Louis (NL
1900), Baltimore (AL 1901–02); Mgr—Baltimore
(AL 1902), Brooklyn (NL 1914–31)   C, MGR
BR/TR

1,371 games	.273 ba
1,388 hits	18 hr
622 rbi	163 sb

An outstanding catcher on the champion Baltimore
squads of the 1890s, Robinson knocked in 11 runs in a
single game in 1892—a major league record that remained unbroken until 1924. After a dispute with his
longtime boss, John McGraw, Robinson left his job as
Giants coach to manage the arch rival Brooklyn Dodgers. An affable man with a reputation for developing
fine pitching staffs, Robinson won pennants for Brooklyn in 1916 and 1920, but his later teams were known
for their daffy play. He was inducted into the Hall of
Fame in 1945.

Roe, Elwin (Preacher)

1915–

St. Louis (NL 1938), Pittsburgh (NL 1944–47),
Brooklyn (NL 1948–54)   P   BR/LHP

333 games	1,914 innings
127-84 W–L	3.43 ERA
956 k's	10 saves

When the Dodgers obtained Preacher Roe and Billy
Cox in the same trade from the Pirates in exchange for
Dixie Walker, they solidified an already strong team.
Roe had led the NL in strikeouts in 1945 but was coming off a 4-15 season in 1947. After joining the Dodgers, he reeled off 90 wins against only 33 losses in
1948–53. Roe threw a variety of junk, and he would
self-effacingly say that his curves went slow, slower,
and slowest.

Rogan, Wilber (Bullet Joe)
1889–1967

Kansas City Monarchs (1920–38); Mgr—Kansas City Monarchs (1926–31, 1933–34, 1936) P, MGR BR/RHP

1,337 innings	113-45 W–L
677 k's	15 saves

Most experts agree that Rogan was the best pitcher in the history of the Negro Leagues. A moving fastball, great breaking curve ball, and excellent control made him nearly unhittable. He was a smart pitcher who also fielded his position brilliantly. Rogan utilized a no-windup delivery. His batting style is sometimes compared to that of Cubs' Hall of Famer Ernie Banks.

Rogers, Steve
1949–

Montreal (NL 1973–85) P BR/RHP

399 games	2,837 innings
158-152 W–L	3.17 ERA
1,621 k's	2 saves

Rogers was the greatest pitcher in Montreal history. Joining the Expos midway through the 1973 season, he won 10 games and compiled a minuscule 1.54 ERA. After three successive losing seasons, he reeled off seven consecutive winning records. Between 1974 and 1983, Rogers pitched at least 200 innings in every year except for the strike-shortened 1981 season. His best season was 1982, when he led the NL in ERA (2.40) and went 19-8.

Rolfe, Robert (Red)
1908–1969

New York (AL 1931, 1934–42); Mgr—Detroit (AL 1949–52) 3B, MGR BL/TR

1,175 games	.289 ba
1,394 hits	69 hr
497 rbi	44 sb

The third baseman on two of baseball's greatest teams, the 1936 and 1939 Yankees, Rolfe led the AL in hits (213), runs scored (139), and doubles (46) while batting a robust .329 for the 1939 squad. He was a great fielder as well and led the AL in fielding percentage twice. Rolfe consistently posted lofty numbers despite being troubled by chronic stomach ulcers.

Rommel, Eddie

1897–1970

Philadelphia (AL 1920–32)   P   BR/RHP

500 games	2,556 innings
171-119 W–L	3.54 ERA
599 k's	29 saves

Rommel was one of the first pitchers to rely heavily on the knuckle ball. While pitching for some horrible Athletics teams in the twenties, he nonetheless led the AL in victories in 1922 (27) and 1925 (21). His 27 triumphs in 1922 represented more than 40 percent of his team's wins. After 1926, Rommel spent most of his time as a reliever, and he went 12-2 for the pennant-winning 1929 Athletics. He was an excellent fielding pitcher. Following his playing days, Rommel umpired in the AL from 1938 to 1959.

Root, Charlie (Chinski)

1899–1970

St. Louis (AL 1923), Chicago (NL 1926–41)   P
BR/RHP

632 games	3,197 innings
201-160 W–L	3.59 ERA
1,459 k's	40 saves

On the mound, Root was a mean customer who would throw at batters if the situation warranted it. In 1927, he led the NL in wins (26) and innings pitched (309), and he copped at least 14 triumphs each year from 1926 to 1933. In the 1932 World Series against the

Yankees, he delivered the home run pitch that Babe Ruth "called" by pointing to the center-field bleachers.

Rose, Pete (Charley Hustle)

1941–

Cincinnati (NL 1963–78, 1984–86), Philadelphia (NL 1979–83), Montreal (NL 1984);
Mgr—Cincinnati (NL 1984–89)   OF, 1B, 3B, 2B, MGR   BB/TR

3,562 games	.303 ba
4,256 hits	160 hr
1,314 rbi	198 sb

First nicknamed "Charley Hustle" by the Yankees during spring training in 1963, Rose never stopped hustling throughout his career. In 1985, he broke a record that most experts thought would last forever—Ty Cobb's mark of 4,192 career hits. Rose led the NL in batting three times and in base hits seven times. He was not a power hitter and established a record by driving in the most career runs without knocking in 100 runs in any one season. Rose excelled by hitting the ball where it was pitched and by studying each pitcher's tendencies. In the field, he moved from position to position to accommodate his team's needs. Rose was one ballplayer who truly loved the game and knew its history. Unfortunately, he believed he knew so much about the game that he channeled his competitive urges into gambling on baseball. As a result, Commissioner Giamatti banned Rose from baseball.

Roseboro, Johnny

1933–

Brooklyn (NL 1957), Los Angeles (NL 1958–67), Minnesota (NL 1968–69), Washington (AL 1970)
C   BL/TR

1,585 games	.249 ba
1,206 hits	104 hr
548 rbi	67 sb

Roseboro was a fine defensive catcher for the Dodgers during their first decade in Los Angeles. At the bat, he chipped in the occasional long ball, such as the clutch home run in game one of the 1963 World Series. Roseboro was involved in one of the most frightening brawls in major league history, when Giants pitcher Juan Marichal clubbed him over the head with his bat in a 1965 game.

Rosen, Al (Flip)

1924–
Cleveland (AL 1947–56)   **3B**   **BR/TR**

1,044 games	.285 ba
1,063 hits	192 hr
717 rbi	39 sb

A strong pull hitter who stood on top of the plate, Rosen was one of the American League's top sluggers of the fifties. He suffered from asthma as a youth and began playing sports as a means of getting fresh air. Once he became an Indians regular in 1950, he led the AL with 37 home runs and won Rookie of the Year honors. In 1953, he was the league's unanimous MVP; that year, he led in slugging percentage (.613), homers (43), runs scored (115), and RBI (145). Rosen later served as general manager for the Yankees, Astros, and Giants.

Roush, Edd (Eddie)

1893–1988
Chicago (AL 1913), Indianapolis (FL 1914), Newark (FL 1915), New York (NL 1916, 1927–29), Cincinnati (NL 1916–26, 1931)   **OF**   **BL/TL**

1,967 games	.323 ba
2,376 hits	68 hr
981 rbi	268 sb

As independent a man as ever played major league baseball, Roush abhorred training camp and engaged in yearly holdouts before signing his contract. In 1930, he skipped the entire campaign due to a squabble. Perhaps the top defensive center fielder of his generation, Roush swung a 48-ounce piece of lumber and led the NL in batting in both 1917 (.341) and 1919 (.321). He was elected to the Hall of Fame in 1962.

Rowe, Lynwood (Schoolboy)

1910–1961
Detroit (AL 1933–42), Brooklyn (NL 1942),
Philadelphia (NL 1943, 1946–49)   P   BR/RHP

382 games	2,219 innings
158-101 W–L	3.87 ERA
913 k's	12 saves

If a team was going to get to Rowe, it would have to be early, for he improved as the game progressed. Few squads could touch him between 1934 and 1936, when he won 62 games and helped the Tigers to two pennants. In 1934, Rowe won 16 consecutive games. Arm miseries sidelined him for much of the next two years, but he rebounded to go 16-3 for the 1940 flag winners. Rowe was also a fine batsman and frequently pinch-hit.

Rucker, George Napoleon (Nap)

1884–1970
Brooklyn (NL 1907–16)   P   BR/LHP

336 games	2,375 innings
134-134 W–L	2.42 ERA
1,217 k's	14 saves

Rucker was an outstanding hurler on some very weak-hitting Brooklyn teams. Over a seven-year span from 1907 to 1913, his ERA never went over 2.87, yet he amassed a won-lost record of only 116-123. A smart pitcher, he threw an assortment of pitches, including a knuckle ball. Rucker won a career-best 22 games in 1911.

Rudi, Joe

1946–

Kansas City (AL 1967), Oakland (AL 1968–76, 1982), California (AL 1977–80), Boston (AL 1981)

OF, 1B   BR/TR

1,547 games	.264 ba
1,468 hits	179 hr
810 rbi	25 sb

It took only one great catch against the left-field wall in Cincinnati during the 1972 World Series to put the baseball world on alert that Joe Rudi was no longer a hidden treasure. Coming off a season in which he batted .305 with a league-leading 181 hits, 19 homers, and 75 RBI, Rudi had nevertheless been overshadowed by Reggie Jackson and Vida Blue on the Athletics. A steady although not flashy performer, Rudi was a winning player.

Rudolph, Dick (Baldy)

1887–1949

New York (NL 1910–11), Boston (NL 1913–23, 1927)   P   BB/RHP

279 games	2,049 innings
121-108 W–L	2.66 ERA
786 k's	8 saves

Rudolph was the leading hurler for the 1914 Miracle Braves. That year, the Boston team won the pennant and swept the Athletics in the World Series after rebounding from last place in July. He went 26-10 in 1914 and followed it up with 19 wins the following year. Rudolph was one of the legal spitballers who continued to throw the wet one after 1920.

Ruel, Herold (Muddy)

1896–1963

St. Louis (AL 1915, 1933), New York (AL 1917–20),
Boston (AL 1921–22, 1931), Washington (AL
1923–30), Detroit (AL 1931–32), Chicago (AL
1934); Mgr—St. Louis (AL 1947)   **C, MGR**
BR/TR

1,468 games	.275 ba
1,242 hits	4 hr
534 rbi	61 sb

One of the leading catchers of the twenties, Ruel was
an eyewitness to one of baseball's most shocking events
of the decade. He was behind the plate when a Carl
Mays fastball struck Cleveland shortstop Ray Chapman in the head, killing him. In addition, Ruel scored
the winning run in the seventh game of the 1924
World Series. After his career ended, he obtained a law
degree from Washington University.

Ruether, Walter (Dutch)

1893–1970

Chicago (NL 1917), Cincinnati (NL 1917–20),
Brooklyn (NL 1921–24), Washington (AL
1925–26), New York (AL 1926–27)   **P**
BL/LHP

309 games	2,124 innings
137-95 W–L	3.50 ERA
708 k's	8 saves

Ruether won game one of the scandal-tainted 1919
World Series, but all anyone remembers about the
match is that Eddie Cicotte deliberately lost it as part
of the fix. That was Ruether's best season—he went
19-6 to lead the NL in winning percentage (.760).
Traded to Brooklyn, he won 21 times for "Uncle Rob-
bie" Robinson in 1922; but when the Dodgers battled
for the pennant in 1924, he was of little help, going
8-13 for the season.

Ruffing, Charles (Red)

1904–1986

Boston (AL 1924–30), New York (AL 1930–42, 1945–46), Chicago (AL 1947)   P   BR/RHP

624 games	4,344 innings
273-225 W–L	3.80 ERA
1,987 k's	16 saves

Ruffing was a tireless worker who thrived once he arrived in New York in 1930. After leading the AL in losses in 1928–29 for some poor Red Sox teams, Red became a big winner in pinstripes. He won 20 games in four consecutive years (1936–39) and was victorious in seven of nine World Series decisions. Ruffing was also baseball's best-hitting pitcher. He was inducted into the Hall of Fame in 1967.

Runnels, James (Pete)

1928–1991

Washington (AL 1951–57), Boston (AL 1958–62), Houston (NL 1963–64); Mgr—Boston (AL 1966)
1B, 2B, SS, MGR   BL/TR

1,799 games	.291 ba
1,854 hits	49 hr
630 rbi	37 sb

Dependable in the field at a variety of positions and reliable at the plate, Runnels was one of the AL's best batsmen in the late fifties and early sixties. After hitting his stride as a line-drive specialist in 1956, he rattled off six seasons of over-.300 swatting, leading the AL in 1960 (.320) and 1962 (.326).

Rush, Bob

1925–

Chicago (NL 1948–57), Milwaukee (NL 1958–60), Chicago (AL 1960)   P   BR/RHP

417 games	2,410 innings
127-152 W–L	3.65 ERA
1,244 k's	8 saves

Though he was stuck on a losing Cubs outfit for most of his career, Rush won 17 games in 1952 with a nifty 2.70 ERA. Traded to Milwaukee in 1958, he pitched on a pennant winner his first season there, earning 10 victories as a spot starter.

Rusie, Amos (The Hoosier Thunderbolt)

1871–1942

Indianapolis (NL 1889), New York (NL 1890–95, 1897–98), Cincinnati (NL 1901) P **BR/RHP**

462 games	3,769 innings
245-174 W–L	3.07 ERA
1,934 k's	5 saves

Rusie was probably the hardest thrower of the 19th century. After joining the Giants in the fallout from the Players League revolt in 1890, he won at least 20 games a season throughout his nine-year career in New York, surpassing 30 victories each year from 1891 to 1894. At 20 years and two months, Rusie was the youngest man to pitch a no-hitter in major league history. After leading the NL in both walks and strikeouts five times, Rusie sat out the entire 1896 season in a contract dispute with the Giants' parsimonious owner, Andrew Freedman. At the tail end of his career, Rusie was traded to the Reds for Christy Mathewson in a pre-arranged deal typical of syndicate ownership. He was inducted into the Hall of Fame in 1977.

Russell, Bill

1948–

Los Angeles (NL 1969–86) SS, OF **BR/TR**

2,181 games	.263 ba
1,926 hits	46 hr
627 rbi	167 sb

Russell appeared in more games than any other Los Angeles Dodger and trails only the legendary Zach Wheat in combined Dodger totals. He began his career in center field but switched to shortstop in 1971, where he became a dependable fielder. Although Russell was not a great hitter, he chipped in the occasional clutch hit and batted a career-high .286 in 1978.

Russell, Jeff

1961–

Cincinnati (NL 1983–84), Texas (AL 1985–92), Oakland (AL 1992), Boston (AL 1993 Active)   P
BR/RHP

455 games	970 innings
51-64 W–L	3.74 ERA
621 k's	146 saves

After five lackluster years in the majors, in 1988 Russell earned an All-Star berth while winning 10 games for the Rangers. The next year, he emerged as the best reliever in the AL, saving 38 games and compiling a 1.98 ERA. Russell saved 30 games in both 1991 and 1992. Signed as a free agent by the Red Sox in 1993, he continued to throw his 95-mile-an-hour fastball past batters, saving 33 games.

Ruth, George Herman (Babe, The Sultan of Swat, The Bambino)

1895–1948

Boston (AL 1914–19), New York (AL 1920–34), Boston (NL 1935)   OF, P   BL/TL

2,503 games	.342 ba
2,873 hits	714 hr
2,213 rbi	123 sb
1,221 innings	94-46 W–L
2.28 ERA	488 k's
4 saves	

Baseball pundits regard Ruth as the greatest baseball player of all time. On the mound, he led the Red Sox to their last World Series title in 1918. At the plate, Ruth swung from an exaggerated closed stance with his right shoulder nearly facing the catcher as he begun his swing. He had a tremendous ability to pull any pitch, and hurlers could not throw a fastball past him. His home runs were majestic, high-arcing drives that soared over the fence. Ruth swung for the fences in every at-bat, disdaining conventional baseball wisdom that said it was best to make contact and hit the ball through the infield. He still ranks first in lifetime slugging percentage and is second in home runs, runs scored, and RBI. The Yankees retired his uniform number 3, and he was an inaugural member of the Hall of Fame in 1936.

Ryan, Jimmy (Pony)
1863–1923
Chicago (NL 1885–89, 1891–1900), Chicago (PL 1890), Washington (NL 1902–03)   OF   BR/TL

2,012 games	.306 ba
2,502 hits	118 hr
1,093 rbi	418 sb

Consistency was the hallmark of Ryan's lengthy career. Primarily a leadoff batter for Chicago, he scored more than 100 runs eight times and batted at least .300 ten times. His best years were 1888, when he hit .332 with a league-best 182 hits, 33 doubles, and 16 homers, and 1894, when he batted .361.

Ryan, Nolan (The Express)
1947–
New York (NL 1966, 1968–71), California (AL 1972–79), Houston (NL 1980–88), Texas (AL 1989–93)   P   BR/RHP

807 games	5,387 innings
324-292 W–L	3.19 ERA
5,714 k's	3 saves

Nolan Ryan has had the last laugh on all the critics who claimed he was only a .500 pitcher. He pitched more seasons than any man in major league history (27); and in his final year, at the age of 46, he still threw the ball at 96 miles per hour. Ryan started his career with the Mets, saving game three of the 1969 World Series ultimately won by the Amazins'. Ironically, that was Ryan's only series appearance. Ryan established records for strikeouts and no-hitters that are unlikely ever to be broken. In 1973, he fanned a major league record 383 batters in a single season. His career total of 5,714 strikeouts is more than 1,500 higher than Steve Carlton's second-place mark. When it comes to no-hitters, no other pitcher approaches Ryan's seven gems. He even tossed one at the age of 44. In addition, Ryan has thrown a record 12 one-hitters. Besides his blazing fastball, Ryan also threw the sharpest-breaking curve ball in the majors, and later in his career, he developed a devastating change of pace. A native of Texas, he is probably the most popular man in the state today and will certainly enter the Hall of Fame in his first year of eligibility.

S

Saberhagen, Bret

1964–

Kansas City (AL 1984–91), New York (NL 1992–93 Active)   P   BR/RHP

288 games	1,897 innings
120-90 W–L	3.24 ERA
1,267 k's	1 save

A two-time AL Cy Young Award winner, Saberhagen alternated outstanding seasons with mediocre ones. In the odd-numbered years of 1985, 1987, 1989, and 1991, he won 74 games and lost only 30. He would rather forget the even-numbered seasons. At his best, Saberhagen throws a darting fastball, sharp slider, and change-up with precision, walking fewer than two men per nine innings. In 1989, he led the AL in wins (23), winning percentage (.793), complete games (12), innings pitched (262), and strikeouts (2.16).

Sadecki, Ray

1940–

St. Louis (NL 1960–66, 1975), San Francisco (NL 1966–69), New York (NL 1970–74, 1977), Atlanta (NL 1975), Kansas City (AL 1975–76), Milwaukee (AL 1976) **P** **BL/LHP**

563 games	2,500 innings
135-131 W–L	3.78 ERA
1,614 k's	7 saves

Sadecki won 20 games for the 1964 World Series champion Cardinals but could never match that performance again. Traded to the Giants for Orlando Cepeda, the San Francisco favorite, he struggled on the West Coast. Shuffled along to the Mets, he served as a useful spot starter and middle-inning reliever. Sadecki threw hard and had a big, breaking curve ball.

Sain, Johnny

1917–

Boston (NL 1942, 1946–51), New York (AL 1951–55), Kansas City (AL 1955) **P** **BR/RHP**

412 games	2,125 innings
139-116 W–L	3.49 ERA
910 k's	51 saves

"Spahn and Sain and pray for rain" went the refrain of Braves fans in the late forties. Indeed, Sain won at least 20 games in four of five seasons from 1946 to 1950, including an NL-high 24 triumphs in 1948. After Sain was traded to the Yankees, he starred in the bullpen, leading the AL in saves in 1954 (22). A longtime pitching coach, Sain advocated throwing the ball between starts as the pitcher's best strengthening exercise and he had many followers.

Sallee, Harry (Slim)

1885–1950

St. Louis (NL 1908–16), New York (NL 1916–18, 1920–21), Cincinnati (NL 1919–20)   P
BL/LHP

475 games	2,821 innings
173-143 W–L	2.56 ERA
835 k's	36 saves

Sallee was a control artist who walked only 20 men in 228 innings while going 21-7 in 1919 for the world champion Reds. He spent most of his career on losing Cardinals teams in the teens but recorded only one ERA above 3.00. Traded to the Giants, Sallee won 10 consecutive games for the 1917 pennant winners.

Sambito, Joe

1952–

Houston (NL 1976–84), New York (NL 1985), Boston (AL 1986–87)   P   BL/LHP

461 games	629 innings
37-38 W–L	3.03 ERA
489 k's	84 saves

Sambito was the NL's top lefty reliever in the late seventies and early eighties. In 1979–80, he won 16 games and saved 39 more while posting a stingy composite ERA below 2.00. Sambito's curve ball made him a nightmare for lefties, and he had the fastball to stifle right-handed swingers as well.

Sandberg, Ryne (Ryno)

1959–

Philadelphia (NL 1981), Chicago (NL 1982–93 Active)   2B   BR/TR

1,822 games	.290 ba
2,080 hits	241 hr
881 rbi	323 sb

The Phillies have long rued the day they included Sandberg as a throw-in a trade with the Cubs for

Ivan DeJesus. Sandberg quickly established himself as the NL's best-fielding second baseman, winning nine consecutive Gold Glove awards. His offensive achievements have been spectacular. Sandberg won the NL MVP award in 1984 when he batted .314 with 114 runs scored and 84 RBI. In his best season, 1990, he swatted .306 with a league-high 116 runs scored and 40 home runs, plus 100 RBI.

Sanderson, Scott

1956–

Montreal (NL 1978–83), Chicago (NL 1984–89), Oakland (AL 1990), New York (AL 1991–92), California (AL 1993), San Francisco (NL 1993 Active)   P   BR/RHP

442 games	2,411 innings
154-134 W–L	3.76 ERA
1,545 k's	5 saves

Sanderson made an effective adjustment from a hard thrower to a finesse pitcher. He won 16 games with the Expos in 1980 by relying on his hard stuff, but arm troubles cost him his fastball. Sanderson later resurfaced in the American League, where he tantalized batters with an assortment of curves, change-ups, and sliders. He won 17 games for Oakland in 1990 and 16 more the following year with the Yanks.

Sanford, Jack

1929–

Philadelphia (NL 1956–58), San Francisco (NL 1959–65), California (AL 1965–67), Kansas City (AL 1967)   P   BR/RHP

388 games	2,049 innings
137-101 W–L	3.69 ERA
1,182 k's	11 saves

The National League's Rookie of the Year in 1957, when he won 19 games and led the league with 188 strikeouts, the hard-working Sanford was traded to the

Giants after he failed to duplicate his early success. Since he went on to win 24 games in the Giants' pennant-winning season in 1962 and start another 42 games the following year, San Francisco considered the deal a steal.

Sanguillen, Manny

1944–

Pittsburgh (NL 1967, 1969–76, 1978–80), Oakland (AL 1977) C BR/TR

1,448 games	.296 ba
1,500 hits	65 hr
585 rbi	35 sb

A gregarious, sharp-fielding, strong-throwing backstop, Sanguillen was also a line-drive hitter with good speed who batted .318 in 1971 and .328 in 1975. When the Pirates wanted to hire Oakland manager Chuck Tanner, the Athletics wrested Sanguillen away from Pittsburgh in exchange.

Santo, Ron

1940–

Chicago (NL 1960–73), Chicago (AL 1974) 3B BR/TR

2,243 games	.277 ba
2,254 hits	342 hr
1,331 rbi	35 sb

A Cubs favorite for over a decade, Santo never received the recognition his talents warranted. He hit over .300, cracked 30 homers, and knocked in at least 100 runs four times each, plus leading the NL in walks four times. Defensively, he excelled. Santo was an emotional player who infuriated opposing fans by clicking his heels after each Cubs win in 1969. Santo played his entire career as a diabetic.

Santop, Louis (Top)

1890–1942

New York Lincoln Giants (1916–17), Philadelphia
Hilldales (1918–26) **C** **BL/TR**

162 games	.329 ba
168 hits	13 hr
15 sb	

A great slugger, Santop walloped home runs during the
dead ball era of the teens. He caught star hurlers "Cannonball" Redding and "Smokey Joe" Williams on the
Lincoln Giants.

Sauer, Hank

1917–

Cincinnati (NL 1941–42, 1945, 1948–49), Chicago
(NL 1949–55), St. Louis (NL 1956), New York (NL
1957), San Francisco (NL 1958–59) **OF**
BR/TR

1,399 games	.266 ba
1,278 hits	288 hr
876 rbi	11 sb

In 1952, Sauer swept the board, winning the NL MVP
award for his NL-leading 37 homers and 121 RBI for
the fifth-place Cubs. Not a regular until the age of 31,
Sauer belted at least 30 homers six times, including a
career-best 41 in 1954.

Sax, Steve

1960–

Los Angeles (NL 1981–88), New York (AL
1989–91), Chicago (AL 1992–93 Active) **2B**
BR/TR

1,762 games	.281 ba
1,943 hits	54 hr
549 rbi	444 sb

Sax was one in the long line of Dodgers who earned the
NL Rookie of the Year award. A durable, aggressive
player, he cracked over 200 hits for both the Dodgers

in 1986 and the Yankees in 1989. Early in his career, Sax suffered from an inability to make the routine throw to first base, but by the time he signed with New York as a free agent, that problem had vanished. Sax utilized his speed and base-running smarts to steal at least 27 bases every year between 1982 and 1992.

Schaefer, Herman (Germany)
1877–1919
Chicago (NL 1901–02), Detroit (AL 1905–09), Washington (AL 1909–14), Newark (FL 1915), New York (AL 1916), Cleveland (AL 1918)   **2B**
BR/TR

1,150 games	.257 ba
972 hits	9 hr
308 rbi	201 sb

The clown prince of baseball, Schaefer actually once stole first base in a game against Cleveland. On another occasion, after slamming a famous pinch-hit home run against Chisox star lefty Doc White, he slid into each base in grand style. He was a valuable utility player on the strong Tigers teams of the early years of the 20th century.

Schalk, Ray (Cracker)
1892–1970
Chicago (AL 1912–28), New York (NL 1929); Mgr—Chicago (AL 1927–28)   **C, MGR**
BR/TR

1,762 games	.253 ba
1,345 hits	11 hr
594 rbi	176 sb

Nimble behind the plate, Schalk was the leading defensive backstop of his era. He was the first catcher to hustle down to first base to provide backup for stray throws. Although he never batted more than .282 in a full season, the durable Schalk was inducted into the Hall of Fame in 1955.

Schang, Wally

1889–1965

Philadelphia (AL 1913–17, 1930), Boston (AL 1918–20), New York (AL 1921–25), St. Louis (AL 1926–29)   C   BB/TR

1,842 games	.284 ba
1,506 hits	59 hr
710 rbi	122 sb

A fine switch-hitter and sound defensive catcher, after Schang joined the Yankees on the shuttle from Boston in 1921, he played on pennant winners his first three years in New York. He batted .316 in 1921 and .319 in 1922. Fast afoot, his 122 career stolen bases rank with the best for catchers.

Schmidt, Michael (Mike)

1949–

Philadelphia (NL 1972–89)   3B   BR/TR

2,404 games	.267 ba
2,234 hits	548 hr
1,595 rbi	174 sb

Many experts regard Schmidt as the greatest third base-men ever to play in the major leagues. Superb defensively and a potent weapon at the plate, he led the NL in homers eight times and in RBI four times. He was a patient hitter who walked over 100 times in seven seasons. Early in his career, Schmidt hit for a low average; but after he learned to hit the ball up the middle, his average rose. A three-time winner of the NL MVP award, he hit .316 in the strike-shortened 1981 season. The Phillies retired his uniform number 20, and he is a certain first-ballot Hall of Famer when he becomes eligible in 1994.

Schoendienst, Albert (Red)
1923–

St. Louis (NL 1945–56, 1961–63), New York (NL 1956–57), Milwaukee (NL 1957–60); Mgr—St. Louis (NL 1965–76, 1980, 1990)   **2B, MGR**
BB/TR

2,216 games	.289 ba
2,449 hits	84 hr
773 rbi	89 sb

Schoendienst was a winner. A brilliant defensive second baseman and a smart switch-hitter, he sparkled on pennant winners in St. Louis and Milwaukee. He led NL second basemen in fielding percentage six times and hit over .300 in seven seasons. Schoendienst earned nine All-Star berths while a Cardinal and led the NL in hits in 1957 (200). He was inducted into the Hall of Fame in 1989.

Schumacher, Hal (Prince Hal)
1910–1993

New York (NL 1931–42, 1946)   **P**   **BR/RHP**

391 games	2,482 innings
158-121 W–L	3.36 ERA
906 k's	7 saves

Schumacher teamed with Carl Hubbell to form the best one-two staff in the NL. In 1933–35, he won 61 games and pitched in the 1933 and 1935 All-Star Games. In three World Series, he went 2-2. Schumacher threw an overhand curve ball that broke straight down as well as a sinker. He tended to give up a lot of hits, but he generally won the close games. Early control problems hindered his success, but he improved as his career progressed. After hurting his arm, Schumacher developed an effective palm ball.

Scioscia, Mike

1958–

Los Angeles (NL 1980–92), Texas (AL 1994 Active)

C   BL/TR

1,441 games	.259 ba
1,131 hits	68 hr
446 rbi	29 sb

Scioscia had a reputation as the best catcher in baseball when it came to blocking the plate and making the tag on runners attempting to score. Slow-footed and not really a power hitter, he nevertheless managed to deliver the clutch hit in key situations. In the 1988 NLCS, he homered off Dwight Gooden in the ninth inning of game four to propel the Dodgers to victory. Scioscia tore up his knee after signing with the Angels as a free agent, and he missed the entire 1993 season.

Score, Herb

1933–

Cleveland (AL 1955–59), Chicago (AL 1960–62)

P   BL/LHP

150 games	858 innings
55-46 W–L	3.36 ERA
837 k's	3 saves

Nearly 40 years later, Score's career remains one of the great mysteries of major league history. After breaking in with a 16-10 mark and a league-best 245 strikeouts in 1955, he went 20-9 with 263 K's in his second year, averaging more than one strikeout per inning each season. The following May, he was struck in the face by a line drive off the bat of Gil McDougald and suffered a serious eye injury. He didn't pitch again until the 1958 season, but he hurt his arm early in the year and never threw without pain again.

Scott, Everett (Deacon)

1892–1960

Boston (AL 1914–21), New York (AL 1922–25),
Washington (AL 1925), Chicago (AL 1926),
Cincinnati (NL 1926)   SS   BR/TR

1,654 games	.249 ba
1,455 hits	20 hr
551 rbi	69 sb

The AL's best shortstop in the teens and twenties,
Scott led the league in fielding percentage in eight consecutive seasons. In the course of his career, he played
in 1,307 consecutive games, a major league record
until it was surpassed by Lou Gehrig.

Scott, George (Boomer)

1944–

Boston (AL 1966–71, 1977–79), Milwaukee (AL
1972–76), Kansas City (AL 1979), New York (AL
1979)   1B, 3B   BR/TR

2,034 games	.268 ba
1,992 hits	271 hr
1,051 rbi	69 sb

One of the most popular players of his generation,
Scott looked the part of a slugger. Listed at 200
pounds, he weighed considerably more; but he was a
fine defensive first baseman who was particularly adept
at scooping the ball out of the dirt. As a youngster in
1967, he batted .303 with 19 home runs and 82 RBI
for the Red Sox in their Impossible Dream season. In
1975, "Boomer" enjoyed his best year, leading the AL
in homers (36) and RBI (109).

Scott, Jim (Death Valley Jim)

1888–1957

Chicago (AL 1909–17)   P   BR/RHP

317 games	1,892 innings
107-113 W–L	2.30 ERA
945 k's	9 saves

Pitching in the depths of the dead ball era, Scott retired with a minuscule ERA (2.30) and a losing record. Typical of his misfortunes was the 1913 season, when a scintillating ERA of 1.90 produced only a 20-20 record. Scott was also known as having one of the best pick-off moves of any right-hander.

Scott, Mike

1955–

New York (NL 1979–82), Houston (NL 1983–91)

P   BR/RHP

347 games	2,068 innings
124-108 W–L	3.54 ERA
1,469 k's	3 saves

Until he developed the splitter under the tutelage of Giants manager Roger Craig, Scott was an underachieving righty with a good fastball but little success. In 1986, he pitched a no-hitter to clinch the division title for Houston and was nearly unhittable in the NL championship series against the Mets, surrendering only one run in two complete game victories. He led the NL in ERA (2.22), strikeouts (306), and shutouts (5) on his way to winning the Cy Young Award. He won 20 games again in 1989 but hurt his arm the following year and was forced to retire. The Astros retired his uniform number 33.

Seaver, Tom (Tom Terrific)

1944–

New York (NL 1967–77, 1983), Cincinnati (NL 1977–82), Chicago (AL 1984–86), Boston (AL 1986)   P   BR/RHP

656 games	4,782 innings
311-205 W–L	2.86 ERA
3,640 k's	1 save

Seaver brought a professionalism to the mound that rubbed off on his Mets teammates. He had a healthy degree of arrogance and would not accept defeat. The modern-day equivalent of Christy Mathewson, Seaver also evoked comparisons with Robin Roberts for the similarities in their compact pitching deliveries. He had an explosive rising fastball that batters couldn't touch. Seaver won 25 games in 1969 when the Mets won their miraculous World Series, and he copped 20 victories four other times. A strikeout king, he fanned more than 200 batters in a record nine consecutive seasons. In a fitting irony, Seaver won his 300th game in New York as a member of the visiting White Sox. He was inducted into the Hall of Fame in 1992 with the highest percentage of votes in baseball history.

Selee, Frank
1859–1909
Mgr—Boston (NL 1890–1901), Chicago (NL 1902–05) **MGR**

Selee was a brilliant manager who guided the Boston Beaneaters to five pennants in the nineties and molded the powerful Cubs teams of the first decade of the 20th century. He innovated defensive alignments and promoted use of the hit-and-run on offense. Selee's teams compiled a winning percentage of .598, the fourth-highest mark in major league history.

Sewell, Joe
1898–1990
Cleveland (AL 1920–30), New York (AL 1931–33)
SS, 3B   BL/TR

1,903 games	.312 ba
2,226 hits	49 hr
1,055 rbi	74 sb

Sewell replaced Ray Chapman as the Indians' shortstop following his fatal beaning during the 1920 season. He went on to bat .300 in 10 of his 14 seasons, with a career high of .353 in 1923. He was extremely difficult to strike out, fanning only 114 times in his entire career.

A fast runner and a good fielder with outstanding range, Sewell was inducted into the Hall of Fame in 1977.

Sewell, Truett (Rip)

1907–1989

Detroit (AL 1932), Pittsburgh (NL 1938–49)   P
BR/RHP

390 games	2,119 innings
143-97 W-L	3.48 ERA
636 k's	15 saves

Sewell's trick pitch, the "Eephus ball," was the talk of baseball during the forties. Thrown with an easy motion, the ball followed a slow, high arc toward the batter before settling in the catcher's mitt. Sewell's bubble burst in the 1946 All-Star Game when Ted Williams sent his pitch soaring over the right-field fence at Fenway for a monstrous home run. He also had one of the best moves to first base of his era.

Seymour, James (Cy)

1872–1919

New York (NL 1896–1900, 1906–10), Baltimore (AL 1901–02), Cincinnati (NL 1902–06), Boston (NL 1913)   OF, P   BL/TL

1,528 games	.303 ba
1,723 hits	52 hr
799 rbi	222 sb
1,029 innings	61-56 W–L
3.76 ERA	584 k's

After winning 20 games twice in the nineties, Seymour converted to outfield duty to take advantage of his strong bat. Indeed, Seymour had a remarkable season in 1905, leading the NL in batting average (.377), hits (219), doubles (40), triples (21), and RBI (121).

Shantz, Bobby

1925–

Philadelphia (AL 1949–54), Kansas City (AL 1955–56), New York (AL 1957–60), Pittsburgh (NL 1961), Houston (NL 1962), St. Louis (NL 1962–64), Chicago (NL 1964), Philadelphia (NL 1964)   P   BR/LHP

537 games	1,935 innings
119-99 W–L	3.38 ERA
1,072 k's	48 saves

A diminutive left-hander, Shantz generated a good fastball from his 5-foot, 6-inch and 140-pound frame. Pitching for Philadelphia in 1952, he won 24 games with a nifty 2.48 ERA and 27 complete games in 33 starts. As a reliever and spot starter for the Yankees, Shantz went 30-18. He led the AL in ERA in 1957 (2.45). Schantz was also a great fielder.

Shawkey, Bob

1890–1980

Philadelphia (AL 1913–15), New York (AL 1915–27); Mgr—New York (AL 1930)   P, MGR BR/RHP

488 games	2,937 innings
196-150 W–L	3.09 ERA
1,360 k's	28 saves

Between 1914 and 1924, few pitchers had more success than did Bob Shawkey. Sold by Connie Mack during one of his economy drives, he left Philadelphia for greater glory in New York, where he won at least 20 games four times. Shawkey pitched and won the first game ever played in Yankee Stadium in 1923. In 1920, he won 20 games and led the AL in ERA (2.45).

Sheckard, Jimmy

1878–1947

Brooklyn (NL 1897–98, 1900–01, 1902–05),
Baltimore (NL 1899), Baltimore (AL 1902), Chicago
(NL 1906–12), St. Louis (NL 1913), Cincinnati (NL
1913)   **OF**   **BL/TR**

2,122 games	.274 ba
2,084 hits	56 hr
813 rbi	465 sb

The fleet-footed Sheckard was a hard-nosed player
who was not above brawling with teammate Heinie
Zimmerman. He was a dynamic base stealer who led
the NL twice and consistently ranked among the leaders in triples. Sheckard's best season came in 1901,
when he batted .354 with 11 homers, 19 triples, and
104 RBI. Traded to the Cubs after the 1905 season, he
played on four Cubs pennant winners but went hitless
in 21 at-bats in the 1906 debacle against the White
Sox.

Sheffield, Gary

1968–

Milwaukee (AL 1988–91), San Diego (NL
1992–93), Florida (NL 1993 Active)   **3B**
BR/TR

580 games	.285 ba
616 hits	74 hr
306 rbi	65 sb

Sheffield may have entered baseball as Dwight
Gooden's nephew, but he is likely to leave it as a major
star in his own right. A quick stroke at the plate and
tremendous strength make him a dangerous hitter with
power to all fields. Sheffield blossomed in 1992, nar-
rowly missing the NL triple crown. That year, he led
the league in batting (.330) and stroked 33 homers and
100 RBI.

Sherdel, Bill (Wee Willie)

1896–1968

St. Louis (NL 1918–30, 1932), Boston (NL
1930–32)   P   BL/LHP

514 games	2,708 innings
165-146 W–L	3.72 ERA
839 k's	26 saves

The slender Sherdel was the Cardinals' top lefty hurler
during the twenties. Unflappable on the mound, he
teased batters with an assortment of slow pitches. Sherdel won at least 15 games six times and topped the circuit in winning percentage in 1925 (.714). When the
Cardinals won the 1928 pennant, he chipped in 21
victories.

Sherry, Larry

1935–

Los Angeles (NL 1958–63), Detroit (AL 1964–67),
Houston (AL 1967), California (AL 1968)   P
BR/RHP

416 games	799 innings
53-44 W–L	3.67 ERA
606 k's	82 saves

Sherry was born with two club feet but he overcame his
handicap to become an outstanding relief pitcher for
the Dodgers. In 1959, he unexpectedly became the
World Series hero for Los Angeles. He won two games
and saved the other two, earning the Babe Ruth Award
as the series MVP. The following year, he won 14
games and saved seven more. Sherry's best pitches were
his fastball and slider.

Shocker, Urban

1890–1928

New York (AL 1916–17, 1925–28), St. Louis (AL
1918–24)   P   BR/RHP

412 games	2,681 innings
187-117 W–L	3.17 ERA
983 k's	25 saves

One of the AL's top hurlers in the twenties, Shocker won 20 games in four consecutive seasons for the Browns (1920–23). He was an intelligent pitcher who threw a variety of pitches, including the spitter. Traded to the Yankees, he copped 19 victories in 1926 and 18 more in 1927. Shocker died tragically during the 1928 season due to heart disease and pneumonia.

Short, Chris

1937–1991

Philadelphia (NL 1959–72), Milwaukee (AL 1973)

P   BR/LHP

501 games	2,325 innings
135-132 W–L	3.43 ERA
1,629 k's	18 saves

A crafty pitcher, Short was one of the finest lefties in Philadelphia's history. He won at least 17 games four times, including 20 triumphs in 1966. In 1964, he snared 17 victories, but he could not stop the Phillies' collapse in the final two weeks of the season despite pitching on two days' rest. A serious back injury hastened his decline after 1968.

Siebern, Norm

1933–

New York (AL 1956, 1958–59), Kansas City (AL 1960–63), Baltimore (AL 1964–65), California (AL 1966), San Francisco (NL 1967), Boston (AL 1967–68)   1B, OF   BL/TR

1,406 games	.272 ba
1,217 hits	132 hr
636 rbi	18 sb

It was difficult to break into the Yankees' starting outfield in the late fifties, but Siebern hit .300 in 1958 to earn a regular spot. Unfortunately, he lost two fly balls in Yankee Stadium's sunny left field in game four of the 1958 World Series, and his career with the Yankees was effectively finished. Traded to Kansas City prior to the 1960 season, he became one of the AL's most dangerous batters, hitting .308 in 1962 with 25 home runs and 117 RBI.

Siebert, Wilfred (Sonny)

1937–
Cleveland (AL 1964–69), Boston (AL 1969–73), Texas (AL 1973), St. Louis (NL 1974), San Diego (NL 1975), Oakland (AL 1975)   P   BR/RHP

399 games	2,152 innings
140-114 W–L	3.21 ERA
1,512 k's	16 saves

Siebert was a hard-throwing righty with a sharp-breaking curve ball who teamed with "Sudden Sam" McDowell and Luis Tiant to form the best trio of strikeout pitchers in the AL in the late sixties. He went 16-8 in consecutive seasons (1965–66), fanning a total of 354 batters.

Sierra, Ruben

1965–
Texas (AL 1986–92), Oakland (AL 1992–93 Active)
OF   BB/TR

1,218 games	.274 ba
1,307 hits	178 hr
774 rbi	113 sb

Sierra has a world of talent but it appears he will never develop into the league's outstanding player, as was once predicted. A notorious low-ball hitter, he swatted .306 with 14 triples, 29 homers, and 119 RBI in his best year, 1989. Sierra was traded in 1992 to Oakland in exchange for Jose Canseco, a reflection of both teams' unwillingness to pay huge salaries to underachieving superstars.

Sievers, Roy (Squirrel)

1926–

St. Louis (AL 1949–53), Washington (AL 1954–59, 1964–65), Chicago (AL 1960–61), Philadelphia (NL 1962–64) 1B, OF BR/TR

1,887 games	.267 ba
1,703 hits	318 hr
1,147 rbi	14 sb

A fan favorite in Washington, Sievers was one of the leading AL sluggers in the fifties. He won the AL Rookie of the Year award in 1949, batting .306 with 16 home runs and 91 RBI for the punchless Browns. After scrapping his open stance at the plate and recovering from a serious shoulder injury, Sievers slammed more than 20 home runs in nine consecutive years (1954–62). He hit a league-leading 42 homers in 1957, when he also topped the junior circuit with 114 RBI.

Simmons, Al (Bucketfoot Al)

1902–1956

Philadelphia (AL 1924–32, 1940–41, 1944), Chicago (AL 1933–35), Detroit (AL 1936), Washington (AL 1937–38), Boston (AL 1939, 1943), Cincinnati (NL 1939) OF BR/TR

2,215 games	.334 ba
2,927 hits	307 hr
1,827 rbi	87 sb

Simmons's unorthodox batting stance—he stepped in the bucket and away from the pitch—belied his ability to sting the ball. He batted over .300 and drove in more than 100 runs in 11 consecutive seasons from 1924 to 1934. He also held the AL record for base hits by a righty until it was broken by Al Kaline. Simmons was inducted into the Hall of Fame in 1953.

Simmons, Curt

1929–

Philadelphia (NL 1947–60), St. Louis (NL 1960–66), Chicago (NL 1966–67), California (AL 1967)   P   BL/LHP

569 games	3,348 innings
193-183 W–L	3.54 ERA
1,697 k's	5 saves

The Phillies signed Simmons as a bonus baby in 1947, and he lived up to their expectations. A hard thrower, he won 17 games for the pennant-winning 1950 squad and topped double digits in seven seasons for the Phillies. After hurting his arm, Simmons was shipped to St. Louis; there he became a finesse pitcher, going 18-9 for the 1964 world champions.

Simmons, Ted

1949–

St. Louis (NL 1968–80), Milwaukee (AL 1981–85), Atlanta (NL 1986–88)   C, DH   BB/TR

2,456 games	.285 ba
2,472 hits	248 hr
1,389 rbi	21 sb

Simmons was one of the best-hitting catchers in the history of the game. In 1975, he banged out 193 hits—the most ever by a catcher in a single season. He also holds the career record for most doubles by a backstop (477). Simmons batted over .300 seven times and knocked in over 100 runs in three seasons. His 182 home runs in the NL rank him number one among switch-hitters. Defensively, he was only average, and he frequently served as the designated hitter in the AL.

Singer, Bill (The Singer Throwing Machine)

1944–

Los Angeles (NL 1964–72), California (AL 1973–75), Texas (AL 1976), Minnesota (AL 1976), Toronto (AL 1977)   P   BR/RHP

322 games	2,174 innings
118-127 W–L	3.39 ERA
1,515 k's	2 saves

Singer's career was a puzzle. How could a pitcher with his stuff win 20 games twice yet suffer through four simply awful seasons to wind up as a below-.500 pitcher? A fastball pitcher, he threw a no-hitter in 1970 against Philadelphia and struck out at least 225 men in three seasons.

Singleton, Ken

1947–

New York (NL 1970–71), Montreal (NL 1972–74), Baltimore (AL 1975–84)   OF, DH   BB/TR

2,082 games	.282 ba
2,029 hits	246 hr
1,065 rbi	21 sb

Singleton's limited appearances with the Mets in 1970 and 1971 offered glimpses of his enormous talent, but the pennant-hungry Mets could not wait for him to mature. They shipped him off to Montreal in exchange for Rusty Staub. With the Expos and later the Orioles, Singleton emerged as a tremendous hitter, particularly in the clutch. His most productive year came in 1977, when he batted .328 with 24 homers and 99 RBI. He knocked out at least 20 dingers four times and chased home over 100 runs in three seasons.

Sisler, George (Gorgeous George)

1893–1973

St. Louis (AL 1915–27), Washington (AL 1928), Boston (NL 1928–30); Mgr—St. Louis (AL 1924–26) **1B, MGR**   **BL/TL**

2,055 games	.340 ba
2,812 hits	102 hr
1,175 rbi	375 sb

Sisler was a gentleman both on and off the field. Graceful in the field, he twice batted over .400 and smacked a major league record 257 hits in 1920. In 1922, Sisler hit safely in 41 consecutive games. A speedy base runner and excellent bunter, he did not swing for the fences. Sisler was inducted into the Hall of Fame in 1939.

Skowron, Bill (Moose)

1930–

New York (AL 1954–62), Los Angeles (NL 1963), Washington (AL 1964), Chicago (AL 1964–67), California (AL 1967) **1B**   **BR/TR**

1,658 games	.282 ba
1,566 hits	211 hr
888 rbi	16 sb

The Yankees' slugging first baseman on seven pennant-winning teams, Skowron took one look at Yankee Stadium's distant fence in left and center field and its short right-field porch, and adopted a closed batting stance to smack long drives to the opposite field. After incurring several injuries early in his career, he played a full season in 1960 and racked up a .309 average, 26 home runs, and 91 RBI. Traded to the Dodgers after the 1962 season to make way for Joe Pepitone, Skowron came back in 1963 to haunt his former teammates by batting .385 in the World Series.

Slaughter, Enos (Country)

1916–

St. Louis (NL 1938–42, 1946–53), New York (AL 1954–55, 1956–59), Kansas City (AL 1955–56), Milwaukee (NL 1959)   OF   BL/TR

2,380 games	.300 ba
2,383 hits	169 hr
1,304 rbi	71 sb

Slaughter was a hard-nosed player and a great hustler on the diamond. Consistent, if not spectacular, he batted over .300 in eight seasons with St. Louis. His aggressive base running won the 1946 World Series when he scored the winning run from first base on a single to left-center in the seventh game. Embroiled in controversy whenever the Cardinals played the Dodgers, he steadfastly denied deliberately spiking Jackie Robinson in a 1947 game, although few of his contemporaries believed him. Traded to the Yankees in 1954, he appeared in three World Series for New York, sparking the Yanks to victory in 1956. He was inducted into the Hall of Fame in 1985.

Smalley, Roy

1952–

Texas (AL 1975–76), Minnesota (AL 1976–82, 1985–87), New York (AL 1982–84), Chicago (AL 1984)   SS, DH   BB/TR

1,653 games	.257 ba
1,454 hits	163 hr
694 rbi	27 sb

Before hurting his back in 1981, Smalley was a productive power-hitting shortstop with good range in the field. In 1979, his best year, he batted .271 with 24 home runs and 95 RBI. Traded to the Yankees in 1982, he did not produce as expected and endured two tempestuous seasons.

Smith, Al (Fuzzy)

1928–

Cleveland (AL 1953–57, 1964), Chicago (AL 1958–62), Baltimore (AL 1963), Boston (AL 1964)

OF, 3B   BR/TR

1,517 games	.272 ba
1,458 hits	164 hr
676 rbi	67 sb

Smith became the unwitting subject of one of the most widely recognized photographs in baseball history, snapped as Charley Neal's home run at Comiskey Park in the 1959 World Series sailed into the left-field bleachers. Unfortunately for Smith, a full cup of beer fell onto his head as he leaned in disgust against the left-field wall. In 1960, Smith batted .315 and finished second in the AL in batting. He played on AL pennant winners under Al Lopez in Cleveland and Chicago.

Smith, Frank (Piano Mover)

1879–1952

Chicago (AL 1904–10), Boston (AL 1910–11), Cincinnati (NL 1911–12), Baltimore (FL 1914–15), Brooklyn (FL 1915)   P   BR/RHP

354 games	2,273 innings
139-111 W–L	2.59 ERA
1,051 k's	6 saves

Smith hurled no-hitters in 1905 and 1908 and won over 20 games in both 1907 and 1909, but he didn't see eye to eye with White Sox owner Charles Comiskey. He went 25-17 with a tidy 1.80 ERA in 1909, leading the AL in complete games (37), innings pitched (365), and strikeouts (177), but when he started slowly in 1910, Comiskey sent him packing to the Red Sox.

Smith, Hilton

1912–1983

New Orleans Black Creoles (1933), Kansas City
Monarchs (1937–48)   **P, OF   BR/RHP**

787 innings	72-32 W–L
354 k's	16 saves

Smith both started and relieved throughout his career.
Known as "Satchel's caddy" for his relief efforts on
Paige's behalf, he went undefeated in 1938. Smith later
roomed with Jackie Robinson on the Kansas City
Monarchs. College-educated, he taught school after
retiring from baseball.

Smith, Lee

1957–

Chicago (NL 1980–87), Boston (AL 1988–90), St.
Louis (NL 1990–93), New York (AL 1993)   **P**
BR/RHP

850 games	1,125 innings
67-78 W–L	2.91 ERA
1,110 k's	401 saves

The all-time major league leader in career saves, Smith
also ranks as the lifetime club leader in saves for both
the Cubs and Cards. When he first appeared on the
major league scene for the Cubs, he relied on a blazing
fastball and his intimidating mound presence to record
outs. Years later, he still throws hard, but he also utilizes an effective slider and pinpoint accuracy to stifle
opposition rallies. He led the NL in saves in 1983 (29),
1991 (47), and 1992 (43).

Smith, Lonnie (Skates)

1955–

Philadelphia (NL 1978–81), St. Louis (NL
1982–85), Kansas City (AL 1985–87), Atlanta (NL
1988–92), Pittsburgh (NL 1993), Baltimore (AL
1993 Active)   **OF   BR/TR**

1,578 games	.289 ba
1,476 hits	98 hr
531 rbi	369 sb

A fine, line-drive hitter with good speed, Smith earned his nickname, "Skates," for his adventures in the outfield. He played on five pennant winners for four different teams, winning titles in Philadelphia, St. Louis, and Kansas City. Smith batted over .300 six times, including .339 as a rookie. In the 1991 World Series, his base-running blunder cost the Braves a possible victory in game seven.

Smith, Ozzie (The Wizard)
1954–

San Diego (NL 1978–81), St. Louis (NL 1982–93 Active)   SS   BB/TR

2,349 games	.262 ba
2,265 hits	23 hr
734 rbi	563 sb

The acrobat of the infield, Smith is unquestionably the greatest fielding shortstop in the history of the game. Tremendous range, soft hands, and a quick release that compensates for an average arm all make him a fan favorite throughout the league. He led NL shortstops in fielding percentage seven times and set a record with 621 assists in 1980, but statistics alone can't describe his incredible feats. At the plate, Smith has improved dramatically and is now extremely tough in the clutch. Always a base-running threat, he stole at least 30 bases in 11 seasons. Smith is a certain Hall of Fame inductee.

Smith, Reggie
1945–

Boston (AL 1966–73), St. Louis (NL 1974–76), Los Angeles (NL 1976–81), San Francisco (NL 1982)
OF   BB/TR

1,987 games	.287 ba
2,020 hits	314 hr
1,092 rbi	137 sb

Possibly the greatest power-hitting switch-hitter since Mickey Mantle, Smith proved remarkably consistent throughout his career. He batted over .300 seven times and belted at least 20 homers eight times. Smith played on four pennant winners, including the world champion 1981 Dodgers. At the plate, he was a great fastball hitter from either side. In the field, he had the strongest throwing arm of his generation and was a fine outfielder.

Smith, Sherrod (Sherry)

1891–1949

Pittsburgh (NL 1911–12), Brooklyn (NL 1915–22), Cleveland (AL 1922–27)   P   BR/LHP

373 games	2,052 innings
114-118 W-L	3.32 ERA
428 k's	21 saves

Smith was a strapping left-hander who pitched Brooklyn to pennants in 1916 and 1920. Remembered today for his great pick-off move to first base, he also dueled Babe Ruth into the 14th inning in the second game of the 1916 World Series before losing 2-1. In 1920, he defeated Cleveland 2-1 in the third game of the World Series to put the Dodgers up two games to one, but it was the last game that Brooklyn won.

Smoltz, John

1967–

Atlanta (NL 1988–93 Active)   P   BR/RHP

181 games	1,220 innings
72-65 W-L	3.53 ERA
946 k's	

Few fans had heard of Smoltz when the Tigers, desperate for pitching help in 1987, traded the Detroit native to Atlanta for veteran Doyle Alexander. Rebuilding for the future, the Braves secured the best pitching prospect in the minor leagues. Smoltz has lived up to all the expectations, winning at least 12 games each year from 1989 to 1993. He blanked the Pirates in game seven to win the NL pennant in 1991, won twice more in the 1992 NLCS, and went 1-0 in the 1992 World Series. Smoltz throws a great fastball and slider and can spot his pitches with accuracy.

Snider, Edwin (Duke)

1926–

Brooklyn (NL 1947–57), Los Angeles (NL 1958–62), New York (NL 1963), San Francisco (NL 1964)   OF   BL/TR

2,143 games	.295 ba
2,116 hits	407 hr
1,333 rbi	99 sb

The Duke of Flatbush was a graceful fielder with good speed and a sweet swing at the plate. An intense, sensitive player, Snider belted 40 or more homers in five consecutive seasons. His 11 homers and 26 RBI are NL World Series records. The all-time Dodger leader in home runs, his uniform number 4 has been retired. Snider entered the Hall of Fame in 1980.

Snodgrass, Fred (Snow)

1887–1974

New York (NL 1908–15), Boston (NL 1915–16)
OF   BR/TR

923 games	.275 ba
852 hits	11 hr
351 rbi	215 sb

Snodgrass was unjustly maligned for losing the 1912 World Series by misplaying a fly ball to lead off the 10th inning. Actually, he made a great play on a long drive over his head later in that inning, and the Giants botched up a sure out on a foul pop that gave Tris Speaker another chance. Speaker doubled in the tying run, and the Red Sox won the series when Larry Gardner hit a sacrifice fly.

Sockalexis, Lou (Chief)
1871–1913
Cleveland (NL 1897–99)   OF   BL/TR

94 games	.313 ba
115 hits	3 hr
55 rbi	16 sb

The first recognized Native American in the major leagues, Sockalexis was a Penobscot from Maine who enjoyed a brief period of glory for Cleveland. A powerful batter and fine outfielder, he hit .338 as a rookie. In his memory, the team adopted the nickname "Indians" in 1915.

Soto, Mario
1956–
Cincinnati (NL 1977–88)   P   BR/RHP

297 games	1,730 innings
100-92 W–L	3.47 ERA
1,449 k's	4 saves

A big, hard-throwing righty, Soto relied on a fastball, slider, and possibly the best change-up in the NL to retire batters. He established a Cincinnati record by striking out 274 batters in 1982, a year in which he won 14 games. The following two seasons, Soto went 35-20 and led the NL in complete games. A serious shoulder injury limited his success thereafter.

Southworth, Billy
1893–1969
Cleveland (AL 1913, 1915), Pittsburgh (NL 1918–20), Boston (NL 1921–23), New York (NL 1924–26), St. Louis (NL 1926–27, 1929), Mgr—St. Louis (NL 1929, 1940–45), Boston (NL 1946–51)
OF, MGR   BL/TR

1,192 games	.297 ba
1,296 hits	52 hr
561 rbi	138 sb

A fine right fielder in his day, Southworth batted over .300 five times. He was instrumental in the Cardinals' capturing their first pennant in 1926 after his mid-season arrival in a trade. However, he made his real mark as a manager of first-place teams in St. Louis and Boston. A hard drinker and a strict disciplinarian, he won two World Series in St. Louis (1942, 1944).

Spahn, Warren

1921–
Boston (NL 1942, 1946–52), Milwaukee (NL 1953–64), New York (NL 1965), San Francisco (NL 1965)   **P**   **BL/LHP**

750 games	5,243 innings
363-245 W–L	3.09 ERA
2,583 k's	29 saves

The winningest left-hander in major league history, Spahn won 20 games 13 times. He used an assortment of pitches, including a screwball, and relied on pinpoint control for his success. Also an excellent fielder, he had one of the best pick-off moves to first base of all time. Winner of the 1957 Cy Young Award, he holds the NL lifetime record for games started and innings pitched. Spahn was inducted into the Hall of Fame in 1973.

Spalding, Albert

1850–1915
Chicago (NL 1876–77); Mgr—Chicago (NL 1876–77)   **P, MGR**   **BR/RHP**

48 games	539 innings
48-12 W–L	1.78 ERA
41 k's	1 save

One of the leading figures in 19th-century baseball, Spalding starred as a pitcher for the Boston Red Stockings in the National Association in 1871–75. He led the league in games won each year before signing on for the inaugural season of the Chicago White Stockings in 1876. He continued his outstanding hurling in 1876, winning 47 games. That year, he also opened a sporting goods establishment, A. G. Spalding and Brothers, that quickly became the leading purveyor of athletic equipment in the nation. In 1888–89, Spalding organized a world tour of baseball players that garnered great publicity for the game. He was inducted into the Hall of Fame in 1939.

Speaker, Tristram (Tris, the Gray Eagle)

1888–1958

Boston (AL 1907–15), Cleveland (AL 1916–26), Washington (AL 1927), Philadelphia (AL 1928); Mgr—Cleveland (AL 1919–26)   OF, MGR
BL/TL

2,789 games	.345 ba
3,514 hits	117 hr
1,529 rbi	433 sb

A magician in center field, Speaker played shallow to cut off short bloops but also had sufficient speed to race back and snare long drives. To this day, he leads all outfielders in career assists and chances. A brilliant, line-drive hitter, Speaker led the AL in batting in 1916 (.386), hit over .300 in 18 seasons, and slammed a major league record 792 doubles. He was inducted into the Hall of Fame in 1937.

Speier, Chris

1950–

San Francisco (NL 1971–77, 1987–89), Montreal (NL 1977–84), St. Louis (NL 1984), Minnesota (AL 1984), Chicago (NL 1985–86)   SS   BR/TR

2,260 games	.246 ba
1,759 hits	112 hr
720 rbi	42 sb

Speier was a strong-armed shortstop who solidified the Giants infield upon his arrival as a fresh-faced 21-year old in 1971. San Francisco won the division that year but fell short in the NLCS. Speier earned three consecutive All-Star selections (1972–74), but a shrinking batting average got him traded to Montreal. His best year came in 1975, when he led NL shortstops in fielding and drove home 69 runs.

Splittorff, Paul

1946–

Kansas City (AL 1970–84)   P   BL/LHP

429 games	2,554 innings
166-143 W–L	3.81 ERA
1,057 k's	1 save

The Royals' career leader in most pitching categories, including wins, losses, and innings pitched, Splittorff also became the first KC hurler to win 20 games (1973). In 1976–80, he went 75-55 as the Royals won four division titles and one pennant.

Stahl, Charles (Chick)

1873–1907

Boston (NL 1897–1900), Boston (AL 1901–06);
Mgr—Boston (AL 1906)   OF, MGR   BL/TL

1,304 games	.305 ba
1,546 hits	36 hr
622 rbi	189 sb

Stahl batted .354 as a Boston rookie in 1897. He hit at least .300 in five of his first six seasons and led the AL in triples in 1904 (19). Named as manager of the Red Sox late in the 1906 season, he committed suicide in spring training the following year, a victim of a love affair gone bad.

Staley, Gerry

1920–

St. Louis (NL 1947–54), Cincinnati (NL 1955), New York (AL 1955–56), Chicago (AL 1956–61), Kansas City (AL 1961), Detroit (AL 1961)   P   BR/RHP

640 games	1,981 innings
134-111 W–L	3.70 ERA
727 k's	61 saves

A sinker ball specialist, Staley was successful both as a starter in St. Louis, where he won 54 games in three years (1951–53), and in the bullpen for the White Sox as the stopper of the pennant-winning 1959 team. He appeared in a league-high 67 games in 1959 and saved a career-best 14 games.

Stanky, Eddie (The Brat, Muggsy)

1916–

Chicago (NL 1943–44), Brooklyn (NL 1944–47), Boston (NL 1948–49), New York (NL 1950–51), St. Louis (NL 1952–53); Mgr—St. Louis (NL 1952–55), Chicago (AL 1966–68), Texas (AL 1977)
2B, MGR   BR/TR

1,259 games	.268 ba
1,154 hits	29 hr
364 rbi	48 sb

Stanky's aggressive, win-at-all-costs attitude has come to define a hard-nosed ballplayer of limited skills who makes the most of his ability. He specialized in getting on base—whether by a hit, a walk, or getting hit by a pitch. Stanky led the NL in bases on balls three times and surpassed the century mark in six seasons. A winner, he played in three World Series for three different teams—the Dodgers, Braves, and Giants. As a manager, Stanky lost none of his hot-headed irascibility.

Stanley, Bob (Steamer)

1954–

Boston (AL 1977–89)   P   BR/RHP

637 games	1,707 innings
115-97 W–L	3.64 ERA
693 k's	132 saves

A natural sinker made Stanley an effective reliever and spot starter for the Red Sox for over a decade, but it also led to one of the most ignominious episodes in team history. Brought into game six of the 1986 World Series when Boston was only one out short of securing its first title since 1918, he threw a wild pitch with Mookie Wilson at the plate to let the tying run score. Stanley won 16 games in 1979 and saved 33 in 1983.

Stargell, Willie (Pops)

1940–

Pittsburgh (NL 1962–82)   OF, 1B   BL/TL

2,360 games	.282 ba
2,232 hits	475 hr
1,540 rbi	17 sb

Stargell ranks with Wagner and Kiner as the greatest sluggers in Pittsburgh history. An exemplary team leader on two Pirates title teams (1971 and 1979) he led the NL in homers in 1971 (48) and in 1973 (44). At the age of 39 in 1979, Stargell won the MVP Award—the oldest man ever to do so. He hit the first home run at New York's Shea Stadium in 1964 and is the only man ever to hit a fair ball out of Dodger Stadium. The Pirates retired his uniform number eight, and he was inducted into the Hall of Fame in 1988.

Staub, Daniel (Rusty, Le Grand Orange)

1944–

Houston (NL 1963–68), Montreal (NL 1969–71, 1979), New York (NL 1972–75, 1981–85), Detroit (AL 1976–79), Texas (AL 1980)   OF, DH, 1B   BL/TR

2,951 games	.279 ba
2,716 hits	292 hr
1,466 rbi	47 sb

Rushed to the majors by the fledgling Houston franchise in 1963, Staub was overmatched early in his career, but he worked hard to become one of the smartest hitters of his generation. Superb in the clutch, he knocked in more than 90 runs six times. Staub batted as high as .333 in 1967 by hitting the ball to all fields. In the field, he compensated for his lack of speed with smart positioning and a strong throwing arm, aggressively charging base hits to the outfield. Late in his career, Staub became the best pinch hitter in the league, stroking 24 hits in 1983. A popular player wherever he performed, his uniform number 10 has been retired by the Expos.

Stearnes, Norman (Turkey)
1901–1979
Detroit Stars (1923–31, 1937), New York Lincoln Giants (1930), Kansas City Monarchs (1931, 1938–40), Chicago American Giants (1932–35, 1937–38), Philadelphia Stars (1936)   **OF**
BL/TL

905 games	.359 ba
1,186 hits	185 hr
93 sb	

A four-time All-Star, Stearnes was one of the greatest power hitters in baseball history. He led the Negro National League in homers at least five times.

Steinbach, Terry
1962–
Oakland (AL 1986–93 Active)   **C**   **BR/TR**

837 games	.274 ba
786 hits	71 hr
373 rbi	12 sb

A two-time AL All-Star, Steinbach caught for four Oakland division winners. Fine defensively, he has improved at the plate each year. In 1992, he hit .279 and slammed 12 homers.

Steinbrenner, George (The Boss)

1930–

New York (AL 1973–91, 1993 Active)   **OWNER**

Few people have ever been neutral on the subject of George Steinbrenner. Since taking over the Yankees franchise in 1973, he has gone on a roller coaster ride from the great joys of consecutive World Series titles in 1977–78 to the despair of expulsion from the game for a total of three years on two separate occasions. A master manipulator, Steinbrenner uses the carrot-and-stick approach on his players, talent evaluators, and the fans. He is currently trying to persuade either New York City or New Jersey to build him a new stadium.

Steinfeldt, Harry

1877–1914

Cincinnati (NL 1898–1905), Chicago (NL 1906–10), Boston (NL 1911)   **3B**   **BR/TR**

1,646 games	.267 ba
1,576 hits	27 hr
762 rbi	194 sb

The forgotten man of the famed infield of Tinkers, Evers, and Chance, Steinfeldt patrolled third base for the greatest teams in Chicago history. A pretty fair hitter who peaked in 1906 with a .327 average and an NL-leading 83 RBI, Steinfeldt was a strong fielder with the most powerful throwing arm in the major leagues.

Stengel, Casey (The Old Professor)
1890–1975

Brooklyn (NL 1912–17), Pittsburgh (NL 1918–19), Philadelphia (NL 1920–21), New York (NL 1921–23), Boston (NL 1924–25); Mgr—Brooklyn (NL 1934–36), Boston (NL 1938–43), New York (AL 1949–60), New York (NL 1962–65)   OF, MGR   BL/TL

1,277 games	.284 ba
1,219 hits	60 hr
535 rbi	131 sb

One of the most beloved figures in baseball history, Stengel was a terrific raconteur and a tireless promoter of the game. As a player, he smacked line drives to all fields and was a smart outfielder, particularly in playing the right-field wall at Ebbets Field. He starred in the 1923 World Series for the Giants. Stengel piloted bad ball clubs in Brooklyn and Boston before joining the Yankees in 1949. A master at platooning his talented players, he won 10 pennants and seven world titles in a 12-year span in New York before being forced to resign at the age of 70. Casey returned to manage the expansion Mets in 1962 and made a 120-loss season bearable for New York fans. Stengel was inducted into the Hall of Fame in 1966.

Stephens, Vern (Junior)
1920–1968

St. Louis (AL 1941–47, 1953), Boston (AL 1948–52), Chicago (AL 1953, 1955), Baltimore (AL 1954–55)   SS, 3B   BR/TR

1,720 games	.286 ba
1,859 hits	247 hr
1,174 rbi	25 sb

An outstanding hitting shortstop, Stephens led the AL in RBI three times and in 1949 established a record for the position by knocking in 159 runs. That year, he also slammed 39 roundtrippers. A model of consistency, he batted between .285 and .295 seven times.

Stephenson, Riggs (Old Hoss)

1898–1985

Cleveland (AL 1921–25), Chicago (NL 1926–34)

OF, 2B   BR/TR

1,310 games	.336 ba
1,515 hits	63 hr
773 rbi	54 sb

Stephenson was one of the game's best batsmen in the twenties and thirties, hitting for a career-high .367 average in 1930. A liability in the field with one of the poorest throwing arms ever seen on an outfielder, he rarely played a full season.

Stewart, Dave (Smoke)

1957–

Los Angeles (NL 1978, 1981–83), Texas (AL 1983–85), Philadelphia (NL 1985–86), Oakland (AL 1986–92), Toronto (AL 1993 Active)   P

BR/RHP

485 games	2,415 innings
158-114 W–L	3.75 ERA
1,572 k's	19 saves

Stewart struggled in his first six years in the majors, but he blossomed after he joined his hometown Oakland team. Anchoring the staff, Stewart won at least 20 games each year from 1987 to 1990 after he began throwing a forkball to complement his fastball and slider. In 1989, he won two games in both the ALCS and the World Series and was named series MVP. On the mound, Stewart never loses his game face, a mean stare directed right at the batter.

Stieb, Dave

1957–

Toronto (AL 1979–92), Chicago (AL 1993)   P

RHP

424 games	2,845 innings
175-135 W-L	3.41 ERA
1,642 k's	1 save

Stieb threw the most wicked slider in the AL during the eighties. As ace of the Blue Jays staff, he won at least 16 games six times but never reached the 20-win level. Stieb had the reputation of being a difficult teammate, often criticizing his fielders after errors. After coming within one out of pitching a no-hitter on several occasions, he finally accomplished the feat in 1990 against Cleveland.

Stivetts, Jack (Happy Jack)

1868–1930
St. Louis (AA 1889–91), Boston (NL 1892–98), Cleveland (NL 1899)   P   BR/RHP

388 games	2,887 innings
203-132 W-L	3.74 ERA
1,223 k's	4 saves

A fine-hitting pitcher, Stivetts was the workhorse of staffs in St. Louis and Boston. After starring for the Browns in 1890–91, he had a dispute with team owner Chris Von der Ahe and jumped to the strongest squad in the rival NL, the Boston Beaneaters. In 1892, Stivetts won 35 games for Boston, and he later secured at least 20 victories three times in his career.

Stone, George

1877–1945
Boston (AL 1903), St. Louis (AL 1905–10)   OF
BL/TL

848 games	.301 ba
984 hits	23 hr
268 rbi	132 sb

A left-handed batter who stroked nearly all of his hits to the opposite field, Stone led the AL in hits as a rookie in 1905 (187) and won the batting title (.358) and slugging crown (.501) in his second year. After injuring his ankle in 1909, he was never the same player; he retired the following season. Stone was one of the first Jewish stars in baseball.

Stone, Steve

1947–

San Francisco (NL 1971–72), Chicago (AL 1973, 1977–78), Chicago (NL 1974–76), Baltimore (AL 1979–81)   P   BR/RHP

320 games	1,788 innings
107-93 W–L	3.97 ERA
1,065 k's	1 save

Stone always appeared to be on the brink of stardom, but he spent the first nine years of his career fighting injuries and inconsistency. In 1980, he stopped dawdling between throws and began using his best pitch, a curve ball, more frequently. As a result, Stone had a dream season, winning 25 games and the AL Cy Young Award. The next year, he hurt his arm and his career was over.

Stottlemyre, Mel

1941–

New York (AL 1964–74)   P   BR/RHP

360 games	2,661 innings
164-139 W–L	2.97 ERA
1,257 k's	1 save

Brought up to the major leagues by the Yankees midway through the 1964 season, Stottlemyre went 9-3 to rally New York to the pennant. A sinker, slider pitcher, he won 20 games on three occasions, but he played on some of the worst teams in Yankees history. Stottlemyre led the AL in complete games in 1965 (18) and 1969 (24). He pitched at least 250 innings for nine consecutive seasons. A torn rotator cuff ended his career prematurely.

Stovey, George
?

Jersey City (IL), Newark (IL), Cuban Giants, New York Gothams, Cuban X-Giants   P   LHP

An outstanding pitcher, Stovey formed a black battery with Moses Walker for Newark in 1887—the first such tandem in professional ball. In July 1887, the two men were scheduled to play with their Newark teammates in an exhibition game against Cap Anson's Chicago White Stockings of the NL. Anson refused to play the game if Stovey and Walker appeared on the field, and his threat carried the day. Thereafter, the International League banned black players on the grounds that whites refused to play with them.

Stovey, Harry
1856–1937

Worcester (NL 1880–82), Philadelphia (NL 1883–89), Boston (PL 1890), Boston (NL 1891–92), Baltimore (NL 1892–93), Brooklyn (NL 1893); Mgr—Worcester (NL 1881), Philadelphia (AA 1885) OF, 1B, MGR   BR/TR

1,486 games	.288 ba
1,769 hits	122 hr
549 rbi	500 sb

One of the top sluggers of the 1880s and the first man to reach 100 career home runs, Stovey led his league in homers five times and scored at least 115 runs in nine consecutive seasons (1883–91). An excellent fielder and smart base runner, he is one of the 19th-century stars most deserving of induction into the Hall of Fame.

Strawberry, Darryl (The Straw Man)
1962–

New York (NL 1983–91), Los Angeles (NL 1992–93 Active)   OF   BL/TL

1,323 games	.259 ba
1,210 hits	290 hr
869 rbi	205 sb

Strawberry felt that no matter what he accomplished in New York, he would never receive the credit or adulation that his feats warranted. Unfortunately, he was labeled "the black Ted Williams" when he signed with the Mets as the number-one draft pick in the nation. His long swing precluded him from hitting for a high average, although he generated tremendous power to all fields. Defensively, Strawberry was inconsistent at best. A fast runner, he stole at least 26 bases each year from 1984 to 1988. In Strawberry's best year, 1988, he led the NL in homers (39) and slugging percentage (.545) while driving home 101 runs but nonetheless failed to win the MVP award. After signing a free-agent contract with the Dodgers, he suffered a back injury and his run production fell dramatically.

Stuart, Dick (Dr. Strangeglove)

1932–

Pittsburgh (NL 1958–62), Boston (AL 1963–64), Philadelphia (NL 1965), New York (NL 1966), Los Angeles (NL 1966), California (AL 1969)   **1B**

BR/TR

1,112 games	.264 ba
1,055 hits	228 hr
743 rbi	2 sb

Stuart perfected "the matador defense"—waving at ground balls as they sped past his position at first base. He took his fielding troubles in stride because he was really paid to sock home runs. He became the first player in major league history to hit 30 home runs in both the National and American Leagues, slamming 35 roundtrippers for the Pirates in 1961 and 42 taters for the Red Sox in 1963. Stuart led the AL in RBI in 1963 (118).

Sunday, Billy (The Evangelist)

1862–1935

Chicago (NL 1883–87), Pittsburgh (NL 1888–90),
Philadelphia (NL 1890)   OF   BL/TR

499 games	.248 ba
498 hits	12 hr
170 rbi	246 sb

Baseball's original evangelist, Sunday was the fastest
man in the NL during his diamond career. In 1887, he
became a born-again Christian. Thereafter, he refused
to play games on Sunday and devoted his spare time to
speaking before YMCA groups. After retiring from the
game, he toured the country preaching the gospel
before adoring crowds. A colorful and energetic
speaker who sprinkled his sermons with baseball imag-
ery, Sunday gained nationwide fame as a preacher in
the 1910s.

Sundberg, Jim

1951–

Texas (AL 1974–83, 1988–89), Milwaukee (AL
1984), Kansas City (AL 1985–86), Chicago (NL
1987–88)   C   BR/TR

1,962 games	.248 ba
1,493 hits	95 hr
624 rbi	20 sb

Few AL catchers were better defensively in the seventies and eighties than Jim Sundberg. Although he never
batted over .291, his services were always in demand.
Great at blocking pitches in the dirt and throwing out
attempted base stealers, Sundberg delivered a clutch hit
to win the 1985 ALCS for the Royals.

Sutcliffe, Rick

1956–

Los Angeles (NL 1976, 1978–81), Cleveland (AL
1982–84), Chicago (NL 1984–91), Baltimore (AL
1992–93 Active)   P   BR/RHP

441 games	2,630 innings
165-135 W–L	4.02 ERA
1,653 k's	6 saves

Grit and determination were the hallmark's of Sutcliffe's career. He was named the NL Rookie of the Year in 1979, when he went 17-10, but he fell into disfavor and was sent packing to Cleveland. Midway in the 1984 season, the Cubs traded their best prospect, Joe Carter, to the Indians to acquire Sutcliffe. He didn't disappoint, going 16-1 and winning the NL CY Young Award. For a while, Sutcliffe appeared to be finished as a pitcher due to arm miseries, but he resurfaced in Baltimore in 1992 to win 16 games.

Sutter, Bruce

1953–

Chicago (NL 1976–80), St. Louis (NL 1981–84), Atlanta (NL 1985–86, 1988)   P   BR/RHP

661 games	1,042 innings
68-71 W–L	2.83 ERA
861 k's	300 saves

The first pitcher to master the split-fingered fastball, Sutter proved to be nearly unhittable upon arriving in Chicago in 1976. In 1977, he won seven games, saved 31 others, and compiled a minuscule 1.34 ERA. In 107 innings, he surrendered only 69 hits and fanned 129 men. Sutter led the NL in saves each year from 1979 to 1982 and again in 1984, when he saved a career-high 45 games for the Cardinals.

Suttles, George (Mule)

1901–1968

Birmingham Black Barons (1923–25), St. Louis Stars (1926–31), Baltimore Black Sox (1930), Washington Black Senators (1931), Detroit Wolves (1932), Washington Pilots (1932), Chicago American Giants (1933–35), Newark Eagles (1936–40, 1944), Indianapolis ABC's (1939), New York Black Yankees (1941–42)   1B   BR/TR

830 games	.338 ba
1,001 hits	183 hr
38 sb	

Suttles was born to hit. Fans paid attention when he approached the plate in anticipation of a long ball. He played defense indifferently. Suttles appeared in five East-West Negro League All-Star Games

Sutton, Don

1945–

Los Angeles (NL 1966–80, 1988), Houston (NL 1981–82), Milwaukee (AL 1982–84), Oakland (AL 1985), California (AL 1985–87)   P   BR/RHP

774 games	5,282 innings
324–256 W–L	3.26 ERA
3,574 k's	5 saves

Sutton received few accolades during his lengthy career; instead, critics harped on his inability to win 20 games in a season. He reached the 20-game level only once, in 1976, when he went 21-10. Yet that makes his 324 lifetime victories all the more remarkable. Sutton was a smart hurler whose pinpoint control of his fastball and curve kept opposition batters off-stride. Some claimed that Sutton's best pitch was illegal, but he was never caught using a foreign substance. On one occasion, he threatened to sue baseball if the umpires searched him on the mound, and that put an end to the controversy. He currently holds the Dodger career pitching records for games started (533), wins (233), strikeouts (2,696), and shutouts (52).

Swift, Bill

1961–

Seattle (AL 1985–86, 1988–91), San Francisco (NL 1992–93 Active)   P   BR/RHP

317 games	1,156 innings
61-52 W–L	3.52 ERA
526 k's	25 saves

Beset by arm injuries during his years in Seattle, Swift could never stay healthy long enough to pitch an entire season. Shifted to the bullpen in 1991, he saved 17 games while compiling a 1.99 ERA. Swift became a Giant in 1992 in a major trade for Kevin Mitchell. There he pitched brilliantly in a starting role, going 10-4 with an NL-best 2.08 ERA. Unfortunately, his arm gave out midway through the season. In 1993, he went 21-8 with a 2.82 ERA. Swift has an excellent slider and pinpoint control. His pick-off move to first ranks with the best in the game.

T

Tanana, Frank

1953–

California (AL 1973–80), Boston (AL 1981), Texas (AL 1982–85), Detroit (AL 1985–92), New York (NL 1993), New York (AL 1993)   P   BL/LHP

638 games	4,186 innings
240-236 W–L	3.66 ERA
2,773 k's	1 save

An apt description of Tanana's career is that he threw 90 miles an hour in the seventies and 70 miles an hour in the nineties. Before hurting his arm in 1979, he struck out at least 200 men from 1975 to 1977, including a league-best 269 in 1975. He went 82-59 when he had his hard stuff, but thereafter set out on a journey to three cities before he perfected his new style of pitching. Landing in his hometown of Detroit, Tanana became the master of the slow curve and a fastball that just nicked the outside corner. In 1987, he won the Eastern Division title for the Tigers by blanking the Blue Jays on the final day of the season.

Tannehill, Jesse (Tanny)
1874–1956
Cincinnati (NL 1894, 1911), Pittsburgh (NL 1897–1902), New York (AL 1903), Boston (AL 1904–08), Washington (AL 1908–09)   P
BB/LHP

358 games	2,750 innings
197-116 W–L	2.79 ERA
940 k's	7 saves

An outstanding pitcher for two dominant franchises in the first decade of the century, Pittsburgh and Boston, Tannehill had the misfortune to miss all of the World Series involving these teams. He won twenty or more games six times in his career—four times for the Pirates and twice for Boston. His career winning percentage of .667 (116-58) for the Pirates ranks first in the team's history.

Tanner, Charles (Chuck)
1929–
Milwaukee (NL 1955–57), Chicago (NL 1957–58), Cleveland (AL 1959–60), Los Angeles (AL 1961–62); MGR—Chicago (AL 1970–75), Oakland (AL 1976), Pittsburgh (NL 1977–85), Atlanta (NL 1986–88)   **OF, MGR**   BL/TL

396 games	.261 ba
231 hits	21 hr
105 rbi	2 sb

As a manager, Tanner was an eternal optimist who saw the game through rose-colored glasses. He piloted the White Sox to a second-place finish in 1972 by pampering slugger Dick Allen, who produced an outstanding season. He later managed a mature, fun-loving Pittsburgh team to victory in the 1979 World Series.

Tartabull, Danny

1962–

Seattle (AL 1984–86), Kansas City (AL 1987–91), New York (AL 1992–93 Active)   **OF, DH**

BR/TR

1,084 games	.280 ba
1,078 hits	208 hr
722 rbi	35 sb

Tartabull defies easy predictions about his talents. Those who thought that Danny would follow in the footsteps of his father Jose, who hit a grand total of two career home runs, were proven wrong after his first week in the majors. Hispanic players have a reputation for being aggressive swingers who abhor bases on ball; Tartabull, however, walked 103 times in 1988—a record for Latin players—and has drawn over 100 walks in three seasons. At the plate, Tartabull likes the pitch out over the plate so he can drive the ball to the opposite field, where he slams the majority of his home runs. He is a streaky hitter, but when he is in a groove, he can carry a team for weeks. Tartabull has been injury-prone throughout his career and has not played more than 138 games in any season since 1988.

Taylor, Charles (C. I.)

1875–1922

MGR—Birmingham Giants, West Baden Sprudels, Indianapolis ABC's   **MGR**

Considered by many of his contemporaries to be the best manager in the Negro Leagues, Taylor managed in Birmingham and Indianapolis with great success. His Indianapolis nine was sponsored by the American Brewing Company.

Taylor, Jack
1874–1938

Chicago (NL 1898–1903, 1906–07), St. Louis (NL 1904–06)   **P**   **BR/TR**

310 games	2,617 innings
152-139 W–L	2.66 ERA
657 k's	5 saves

Taylor packed a lot of excitement into his 10-year big league career. A man who liked to finish what he started, he recorded 188 consecutive complete games between 1901 and 1906. In 1902, he posted an ERA of 1.33—the ninth best in NL 20th-century history. Taylor also became involved in several on-field scandals. After being accused of dishonest play in the 1903 Chicago inter-city championship, he was traded in the off-season to St. Louis for "Three Finger" Brown. In 1904, Taylor was mired in controversy again when he was accused of fixing a game against Pittsburgh after a bout of heavy drinking. In both instances, he was acquitted even though most of his contemporaries believed he had acted improperly.

Taylor, Tony
1935–

Chicago (NL 1958–60), Philadelphia (NL 1960–71, 1974–76), Detroit (AL 1971–73)   **2B, 3B**   **BR/TR**

2,195 games	.261 ba
2,007 hits	75 hr
598 rbi	234 sb

One of the most popular players ever to wear a Phillies uniform, Taylor played a smart game at a variety of infield positions and chipped in with clutch hits while at bat. He hit .301 in 1970 and .287 in 1960, when he made the NL All-Star team.

Tebeau, Oliver (Patsy)

1864–1918

Chicago (NL 1887), Cleveland (NL 1889, 1891–98), Cleveland (PL 1890), St. Louis (NL 1899–1900); MGR—Cleveland (PL 1890), Cleveland (NL 1891–98), St. Louis (NL 1899–1900)   **1B, 3B, MGR**   **BR/TR**

1,167 games	.280 ba
1,291 hits	27 hr
735 rbi	164 sb

Tebeau was only an average batter and fielder, but he became an outstanding manager who piloted his Cleveland team to success in the 1890s. His best season at the plate was 1893, when he batted .329 with 102 RBI. Tebeau's Cleveland team won the Temple Cup in 1895, upsetting the heavily favored Baltimore Orioles. Like John McGraw, he had an aggressive style that included vituperative umpire-baiting. He committed suicide in 1918.

Tekulve, Kent

1947–

Pittsburgh (NL 1974–85), Philadelphia (NL 1985–88), Cincinnati (NL 1989)   **P**   **BR/RHP**

1,050 games	1,436 innings
94-90 W–L	2.85 ERA
779 k's	184 saves

This skinny, sidearming right-hander appeared in the second-most games by a pitcher in big league history. Tekulve relied on a sinking fastball and a slider. He led the NL in game appearances four times and saved 31 games in both 1978 and 1979.

Templeton, Garry (Jump Steady)

1956–

St. Louis (NL 1976–81), San Diego (NL 1982–91), New York (NL 1991)   **SS**   **BB/TR**

2,079 games	.271 ba
2,096 hits	70 hr
728 rbi	242 sb

Traded by the Cardinals to the Padres in exchange for Ozzie Smith, Templeton made San Diego fans long for the Wizard. He started his career with a big splash, but after six seasons, his indifferent play betrayed a lack of interest in the game. Relying on his great speed and power to the gaps, he led the NL in triples from 1977 to 1979. In 1979, he became the first major leaguer to collect more than 100 hits from each side of the plate in the same season. After Templeton made an obscene gesture to the fans in St. Louis, he was traded to San Diego and his career went into a downward spiral.

Tenney, Fred
1871–1952
Boston (NL 1894–1907, 1911), New York (NL 1908–09); MGR—Boston (AL 1905–07, 1911)
1B, MGR   BL/TL

1,994 games	.294 ba
2,231 hits	22 hr
688 rbi	285 sb

Tenney, who attended Brown University, was the first college graduate to become a major league star. He began his career as a left-handed catcher but later switched to first base, where he specialized in the 3-6-3 double play. His fielding wowed league observers. A patient hitter, Tenney batted more than .318 each year from 1896 to 1899. As manager in Boston, he acquired a reputation for a reserved, dour personality.

Terry, Bill (Memphis Bill)
1898–1989
New York (NL 1923–36); MGR—New York (NL 1932–41)   1B, MGR   BL/TL

1,721 games	.341 ba
2,193 hits	154 hr
1,078 rbi	56 sb

The last NL player to bat .400, Terry hit a high of .401 in 1930. His lifetime .341 average is also a modern NL record for left-handed batters. An excellent fielder with soft hands, he also had a good arm. Terry was not an easy man to deal with, for he didn't seek popular approval. In 1934, he quipped, "Are the Dodgers still in the league?" when reporters asked him for a pre-season pennant prediction. Of course, the Dodgers beat the Giants in the final two games that season, depriving them of the pennant. The Giants retired his uniform number 3, and he was inducted into the Hall of Fame in 1954.

Terry, Bill (Adonis)

1864–1915
Brooklyn (AA 1884–89), Brooklyn (NL 1890–91), Baltimore (NL 1892), Pittsburgh (NL 1892–94), Chicago (NL 1894–97)   **P, OF   BR/RHP**

667 games	.249 ba
594 hits	15 hr
163 rbi	106 sb
3,514 innings	197-196 W–L
3.73 ERA	1,552 k's
6 saves	

Terry's record in his rookie season with the Trolley Dodgers in 1884 was a dismal 19-35, but his 230 strikeouts and 476 innings pitched gave the fans hope for better results in the future. His record improved each year, and when Brooklyn won the 1889 AA pennant, he went 22-15. When the team entered the NL in 1890, the Dodgers won another pennant with the aid of Terry's 26 victories. Terry had two more big years left—he won 18 games in 1892 and 21 in 1895. Terry was an outstanding hitter and frequently played the outfield to get his bat into the lineup.

Terry, Ralph
1936–

New York (AL 1956–57, 1959–64), Kansas City (AL 1957–59, 1966), Cleveland (AL 1965), New York (NL 1966–67)   P   BR/RHP

338 games	1,849 innings
107-99 W–L	3.62 ERA
1,000 k's	11 saves

When Terry threw a high slider to Bill Mazeroski in the bottom of the ninth during the seventh game of the 1960 World Series, he served up the most famous home run in series history. Little did he know that two years later, he would retire Giants slugger Willie McCovey with the tying and winning runs in scoring position in the bottom of the ninth to win the decisive seventh game of the 1962 World Series 1-0. Terry threw a crackling fastball but had a tendency to surrender the long ball throughout his career. He went 16-3 in 1961 and 23-12 in 1962 for the Yanks.

Tesreau, Jeff (Big Jeff)
1889–1946

New York (NL 1912–18)   P   BR/RHP

247 games	1,679 innings
115-72 W–L	2.43 ERA
880 k's	9 saves

Nicknamed for his resemblance to heavyweight boxing champion Jim Jeffries, Tesreau threw a spitball upon his arrival as a rookie in 1912. An immediate success, he won 17 games and led the NL in ERA (1.96). In the World Series that fall, he started three games and went 1-2. Tesreau won 67 games in 1913–15, but his career lasted only three more years.

Tettleton, Mickey
1960–

Oakland (AL 1984–87), Baltimore (AL 1988–90), Detroit (AL 1991–93 Active)   C, 1B   BB/TR

1,084 games	.242 ba
821 hits	169 hr
516 rbi	21 sb

Tettleton's obsession with Froot Loops captured national attention after he claimed the cereal transformed him from a mediocre player in Oakland to a home-run slugger in Baltimore. Tettleton cracked 26 homers in 1989, but his career really took off after he arrived in Detroit. He socked 95 homers in 1991–93 and led the AL in walks in 1992 (122). When batting left-handed, Tettleton is a dead low-ball hitter. Defensively, he shuttles between catcher and first base, but he is most at ease with a bat in his hand.

Tewksbury, Bob

1960–

New York (AL 1986–87), Chicago (NL 1987–88), St. Louis (NL 1989–93 Active)   **P**   **BR/RHP**

169 games	998 innings
65-49 W–L	3.35 ERA
402 k's	1 save

A late bloomer, Tewksbury was found wanting by both the Yankees and the Cubs before earning his spurs with the Cardinals. He barely throws hard enough to break a pane of glass, but his accurate control makes him a difficult man to beat. He led the NL in winning percentage in 1992, going 16-5 for .762, when he walked only 20 batters in 233 innings.

Thigpen, Bobby

1963–

Chicago (AL 1986–93), Philadelphia (NL 1993 Active)   **P**   **RHP**

441 games	561 innings
31-34 W–L	3.35 ERA
372 k's	201 saves

In 1990, when he set a major league record with 57 saves, Thigpen threw his fastball at 90 to 95 miles an hour. Mechanical problems in his delivery have led to a loss in velocity and control since then, and he is no longer in the stopper's role.

Thomas, Clint (Hawk)

1896–1990

Columbus Buckeyes (1921), Detroit Stars (1922), Philadelphia Hilldales (1923–1928), Atlantic City Bacharach Giants (1928–1929), New York Lincoln Giants (1928, 1930), New York Harlem Stars (1931), Indianapolis ABC's (1932), New York Black Yankees (1933–1934, 1937–1938), New York Cubans (1936), Newark Eagles (1936)   OF   BR/TR

656 games	.305 ba
729 hits	51 hr
98 sb	

Thomas did his best work for the Philadelphia Hilldales squad, starring on their three consecutive championship seasons in the Eastern Colored League (1923–25). He went on to excel for the New York Black Yankees in the thirties.

Thomas, Frank (Donkey)

1929–

Pittsburgh (NL 1951–58), Cincinnati (NL 1959), Chicago (NL 1960–61, 1966), Milwaukee (NL 1961, 1965), New York (NL 1962–64), Philadelphia (NL 1964–65), Houston (NL 1965)   OF, 3B, 1B
BR/TR

1,766 games	.266 ba
1,671 hits	286 hr
962 rbi	15 sb

One of the leading sluggers in the NL in the fifties, Thomas slammed at least 20 homers six times. His best year came in 1958, when he batted .281 with 35 dingers and 109 RBI. Picked up by the Mets in the 1962 expansion draft, he poked 34 home runs playing in the

cozy Polo Grounds. That mark remained the Mets'
single-season record for 15 years.

Thomas, Frank (The Big Hurt)
1968–
Chicago (AL 1990–93 Active)   **1B**   **BR/TR**

531 games	.321 ba
600 hits	104 hr
383 rbi	11 sb

A can't-miss prospect after a standout career at Au-
burn, Thomas has surpassed even the grandest expectations. Patient at the plate, he hits for a high average,
draws a high number of walks, and hits the ball with
tremendous power. In 1991–92, he led the AL in
walks and on-base percentage, while slamming a total
of 56 homers and driving in 224 runs. In 1993 he
belted 41 home runs and knocked in 128 runs. If he
improves his defensive work at first base, Thomas will
be rated as the game's top player.

Thomas, Gorman (Stormin' Gorman)
1950–
Milwaukee (AL 1973–83, 1986), Cleveland (AL
1983), Seattle (AL 1984–86)   **OF, DH**   **BR/TR**

1,435 games	.225 ba
1,051 hits	268 hr
782 rbi	50 sb

Few players wore their hair longer than Thomas, but it
didn't hurt his popularity in Milwaukee. One of the
most popular men in Brewers history, he twice led the
AL in home runs, crushing 45 in 1979 and 39 in 1982.
Although he didn't hit for a high average, Thomas was
a major run producer. A big man physically, he covered
a lot of ground in center field.

Thomas, Roy
1874–1959
Philadelphia (NL 1899–1908, 1910–11), Pittsburgh
(NL 1908), Boston (NL 1909)   **OF**   **BL/TL**

1,470 games	.290 ba
1,537 hits	7 hr
299 rbi	244 sb

The NL's walk king, Thomas led the circuit seven times in the first decade of the 20th century. A singles hitter who could also steal bases, he scored over 100 runs in four seasons. Defensively, he ranked with the best in the league.

Thompson, Robby

1962–
San Francisco (NL 1986–93 Active)   2B   BR/TR

1,111 games	.265 ba
1,037 hits	104 hr
407 rbi	97 sb

Though he is not the ideal number-two hitter, given his good power and inability to make consistent contact, Thompson nevertheless still works as a catalyst in the Giants' attack. In 1993, he had his best season, batting .312 with 19 home runs.

Thompson, Sam (Big Sam)

1860–1922
Detroit (NL 1885–88), Philadelphia (NL 1889–1898), Detroit (AL 1906)   OF   BL/TL

1,407 games	.331 ba
1,979 hits	127 hr
1,299 rbi	229 sb

One of the leading sluggers of the 19th century, Thompson had an unusual half-slouch batting stance. He hit .407 in 1894 and led the NL in RBI in 1887 (166) and 1895 (165). Thompson had the second-highest slugging percentage and third-highest RBI total among 19th-century players. Thompson was inducted into the Hall of Fame in 1974.

Thomson, Bobby (The Flying Scot)

1923–

New York (NL 1946–53, 1957), Milwaukee (NL 1954–57), Chicago (NL 1958–59), Boston (AL 1960), Baltimore (AL 1960)   OF   BR/TR

1,779 games	.270 ba
1,705 hits	264 hr
1,026 rbi	38 sb

Thomson was immortalized on October 3, 1951, when he hit the most famous home run in major league history. His three-run clout in the bottom of the ninth inning won the pennant for the Giants in the most miraculous of comebacks. However, that one home run should not obscure his other accomplishments in the majors, including eight seasons with more than 20 homers and four years with at least 100 RBI.

Thornton, Andre

1949–

Chicago (NL 1973–76), Montreal (NL 1976), Cleveland (AL 1977–87)   DH, 1B   BR/TR

1,565 games	.254 ba
1,342 hits	253 hr
895 rbi	48 sb

One of the most popular players to wear a Cleveland uniform in the past 40 years, Thornton was a deeply religious man who overcame personal tragedy to star on the diamond. Thornton ranks second in career home runs for Cleveland. He belted 33 roundtrippers in 1978 and 1984 and 32 in 1982.

Tiant, Jr., Luis (El Tiante)

1940–

Cleveland (AL 1964–69), Minnesota (AL 1970), Boston (AL 1971–78), New York (AL 1979–80), Pittsburgh (NL 1981), California (AL 1982)   P   BR/RHP

573 games	3,486 innings
229-172 W–L	3.30 ERA
2,416 k's	15 saves

Tiant borrowed his unusual, peek-a-boo delivery from his father, a famous pitcher in the Negro Leagues. Before throwing each pitch, he spun around until his back faced the batter; then he wheeled, threw his head skyward, and released the ball. Any batters who weren't fooled by Tiant's style still had to contend with his 90-plus-mile-an-hour fastball and sharp-breaking curve ball. As a rookie, he went 10-4 after a mid-season recall from the minors. In 1968, the year of the pitcher, Tiant went 21-9 and led the AL in ERA (1.60) and shutouts (nine). Arm injuries led to his move first to Minnesota and then to Boston, where he resurrected his career. Tiant won at least 20 games three times for the Red Sox and became a favorite with the Boston fans.

Tiernan, Mike (Silent Mike)
1867–1918

New York (NL 1887–99)   OF   BL/TL

1,476 games	.311 ba
1,834 hits	106 hr
851 rbi	428 sb

Tiernan was one of the 19th century's greatest sluggers. A fixture at the Polo Grounds, he didn't jump to the Players League in 1890 and he played on some terrible Giants teams during the 1890s. He led the NL in homers in 1890 (13) and 1891 (16) and batted a career-high .369 in 1896. Tiernan earned his nickname, "Silent Mike," for his sober demeanor on the ballfield.

Tinker, Joe
1880–1948

Chicago (NL 1902–12, 1916), Cincinnati (NL 1913), Chicago (FL 1914–15); MGR—Cincinnati (NL 1913), Chicago (FL 1914–15), Chicago (NL 1916)　SS, MGR　　BR/TR

1,804 games	.262 ba
1,687 hits	31 hr
782 rbi	336 sb

Joe Tinker was the defensive glue of the Cubs' excellent teams in the early years of the 20th century. The shortstop in the Tinker-to-Evers-to-Chance double-play combination, he led Chicago to four pennants and two World Series titles. Only an average hitter, Tinker's cracked the .300 barrier just once in his career—he hit .317 in 1913. He was inducted into the Hall of Fame in 1946.

Toney, Fred
1888–1953

Chicago (NL 1911–13), Cincinnati (NL 1915–18), New York (NL 1918–22), St. Louis (NL 1923)　P
BR/RHP

336 games	2,206 innings
139-102 W–L	2.69 ERA
718 k's	12 saves

Toney engaged in one of the greatest mound duels in major league history in 1917 when he and Cubs hurler Jim Vaughn each hurled no-hit ball for nine innings. He pitched a hitless 10 inning and his Reds won the game 1-0. Toney won 24 games that season and 21 more while pitching for the Giants in 1920. In 1921, he won 18 times for the first-place Giants but was badly knocked around in the World Series.

Torre, Joe

1940–

Milwaukee (NL 1960–65), Atlanta (NL 1966–68),
St. Louis (NL 1969–74), New York (NL 1975–77);
MGR—New York (NL 1977–81), Atlanta (NL
1982–84), St. Louis (NL 1990–93 Active)   **C, 1B,
3B, MGR   BR/TR**

2,209 games	.297 ba
2,342 hits	252 hr
1,185 rbi	23 sb

An All-Star at three positions, Torre was a power hitter
who maintained a high batting average throughout his
career. Slow of foot, he rarely beat out infield hits,
making his .363 career-high mark in 1971 all the more
remarkable. That year, he also led the NL in hits (230)
and RBI (137). Torre liked the ball out over the plate,
and his best power was to right- and left-center. Patience is his foremost virtue as a manager. He piloted
the Braves to a division title in 1982.

Torrez, Mike

1946–

St. Louis (NL 1967–71), Montreal (NL 1971–74),
Baltimore (AL 1975), Oakland (AL 1976–77, 1984),
New York (AL 1977), Boston (AL 1978–82), New
York (NL 1983–84)   **P   BR/RHP**

494 games	3,044 innings
185-160 W–L	3.96 ERA
1,404 k's	

A big bear of a man, Torrez was the workhorse on several staffs. He worked quickly, and when his fastball
and slider found the right spots, he was hard to beat. In
12 seasons between 1972 and 1983, Torrez started at
least 31 games in every year except for the abbreviated
1981 season. He won 20 games for Baltimore in 1975
and two games for the Yankees in the 1977 World Series, but he will always be remembered for serving up
the pitch that Bucky Dent swatted into the screen atop

the Green Monster in the 1978 playoff game for the AL Eastern Division title.

Torriente, Christobel
1895–1938
Chicago American Giants (1914, 1920–25), New York Cubans (1915), Kansas City Monarchs (1926), Detroit Stars (1927–28), Cleveland Cubs (1932)

OF	BL/TL	
562 games		.334 ba
648 hits		44 hr
56 sb		

Torriente was one of the best ballplayers to come out of Cuba, yet he was barred from playing in the major leagues. Standing only 5 feet, 9 inches, he generated tremendous power, swinging at any pitch near the plate. In the outfield, Torriente had great range and a powerful throwing arm. He produced his best years for the Chicago American Giants, leading them to pennants in 1920–22. He batted a robust .396 in 1920.

Trammell, Alan
1958–
Detroit (AL 1977–93 Active)   SS   BR/TR

2,077 games	.288 ba
2,182 hits	174 hr
936 rbi	224 sb

The trouble with Trammell is that he makes every thing look so easy. The greatest shortstop in Tigers history, he teamed with second baseman Lou Whitaker for over 15 years in the best keystone duo in the league. He showed surprising power in 1987, when he cracked 28 homers, drove home 105 runs, and batted .343. Trammell is a possible Hall of Fame candidate.

Travis, Cecil

1913–
Washington (AL 1933–41, 1945–47)   SS, 3B
BL/TR

1,328 games	.314 ba
1,544 hits	27 hr
657 rbi	23 sb

Some baseball fans question Travis's exclusion from the Hall of Fame. He had a very fast bat at the plate and rarely struck out. His 218 hits in 1941 represent the highest total by a shortstop in a single season, and he hit over .300 in seven seasons. During WW II, Travis fought in the Battle of Bulge and suffered frostbite. When he returned to play major league ball, he could not perform at his previous level.

Traynor, Harold (Pie)

1899–1972
Pittsburgh (NL 1920–35, 1937); MGR—Pittsburgh (NL 1934–39)   3B, MGR   BR/TR

1,941 games	.320 ba
2,416 hits	58 hr
1,273 rbi	158 sb

The self-effacing Traynor was the greatest third baseman of the first half of the 20th century. Superb defensively, he had the strongest arm of his generation. At the plate, he rapped the ball to all fields, although he was not a slugger. Nevertheless, he knocked in over 100 runs seven times in his career. The Pirates retired his uniform number 20, and he was inducted into the Hall of Fame in 1948.

Trosky, Harold (Hal)

1912–1979
Cleveland (AL 1933–41), Chicago (AL 1944, 1946)
1B   BL/TR

1,347 games	.302 ba
1,561 hits	228 hr
1,012 rbi	28 sb

Trosky is the greatest home-run hitter in Cleveland history. As a rookie in 1934, he established a record for extra-base hits with 45 doubles, nine triples, and 35 home runs. He also batted .330 with 142 RBI that year. Trosky drove home at least 100 runs in six straight seasons, including a mammoth league-leading 162 in 1936. Since he played first base in the AL at the same time as Lou Gehrig and Hank Greenberg, Trosky rarely received the attention his numbers warranted.

Trout, Paul (Dizzy)
1915–1972
Detroit (AL 1939–52), Boston (AL 1952), Baltimore (AL 1957)   P   BR/RHP

521 games	2,725 innings
170-161 W–L	3.23 ERA
1,256 k's	35 saves

This flaky right-hander enjoyed his greatest seasons during World War II, winning 20 games in 1943 and 27 in 1944, and leading the AL both years in shutouts. Proving that those seasons were not a fluke, Trout won 17 games with a nifty 2.34 ERA after the veterans returned in 1946. He still ranks in the top 10 in all major pitching categories for the Tigers.

Trucks, Virgil (Fire)
1919–
Detroit (AL 1941–43, 1945–52, 1956), St. Louis (AL 1953), Chicago (AL 1953–55), Kansas City (AL 1957–58), New York (AL 1958)   P   BR/RHP

517 games	2,682 innings
177-135 W–L	3.39 ERA
1,534 k's	30 saves

A winning pitcher throughout most of his big league career, Trucks suffered through an inglorious 5-19 season for the last-place Tigers in 1952, but remarkably pitched two no-hitters that year. The next year, he won 20 games, and in 1954, he won another 19.

Tudor, John

1954—

Boston (AL 1979–83), Pittsburgh (NL 1984), St. Louis (NL 1985–88, 1990), Los Angeles (NL 1988–89) **P** **BL/LHP**

281 games	1,797 innings
117-72 W–L	3.12 ERA
988 k's	1 save

Few pitchers knew more about the craft than John Tudor. He changed speeds on all his pitches and placed them exactly where he wanted. Although Tudor never threw more than 90 miles an hour, he completely baffled hitters. He learned his art by pitching in cozy Fenway Park but had his greatest seasons in St. Louis. In 1985, he won 20 of his final 21 decisions to finish 21-8 with a league-best 10 shutouts. Arm injuries severely limited him thereafter, but when he was healthy, Tudor was hard to beat.

Turley, Bob (Bullet Bob)

1930—

St. Louis (AL 1951, 1953), Baltimore (AL 1954), New York (AL 1955–62), Los Angeles (AL 1963), Boston (AL 1963) **P** **BR/RHP**

310 games	1,712 innings
101-85 W–L	3.64 ERA
1,265 k's	12 saves

The Yankees rescued Turley from the obscurity of pitching for last-place teams in St. Louis and Baltimore in a mammoth 17-player trade in 1954. He immediately won 17 games in his first year in the Bronx. Control was always a problem for the fireballing Turley, and he had the reputation of being a thrower rather than a pitcher until he developed a no-windup delivery. In 1958, he won the AL Cy Young Award, going 21-7 with six shutouts plus two victories in the Yanks' World Series triumph. An intelligent man, Turley developed a multimillion-dollar insurance business after retiring from baseball.

U

Uhle, George (The Bull)
1898–1985
Cleveland (AL 1919–28, 1936), Detroit (AL 1929–33), New York (NL 1933), New York (AL 1933–34)   P   BR/RHP

513 games	3,119 innings
200-166 W–L	3.99 ERA
1,135 k's	25 saves

One of the best pitchers not inducted into the Hall of Fame, Uhle threw a full assortment of fastballs, curves, and change-ups. Three times a 20-game winner, he led the AL in wins in 1923 (26) and 1926 (27). Also an outstanding hitter, he batted .361 in 1923. Arm trouble limited Uhle's effectiveness during the last five years of his career.

V

Valenzuela, Fernando
1960–
Los Angeles (NL 1980–90), California (AL 1991), Baltimore (AL 1993 Active)   P   BL/LHP

365 games	2,534 innings
149-128 W–L	3.45 ERA
1,842 k's	2 saves

Fernando-mania swept Southern California in the early eighties, when the Mexican-born Valenzuela stifled NL batters with style. An instant success in the majors, he earned both the Rookie of the Year and Cy Young Awards in 1981, winning 13 games and leading the league in complete games (11), shutouts (eight), innings pitched (192), and strikeouts (180). Excellent control of his fastball and curve plus a tantalizing screwball made Valenzuela the best in the game. He won 21 games in 1986 but his arm gave out soon thereafter, and he has been on the comeback trail in the past two seasons.

Van Haltren, George (Rip)
1866–1945

Chicago (NL 1887–89), Brooklyn (PL 1890), Baltimore (AA 1891), Baltimore (NL 1892), Pittsburgh (NL 1892–93), New York (NL 1894–1903); MGR—Baltimore (AA 1891), Baltimore (NL 1892)   OF, P, MGR   BL/TL

1,984 games	.316 ba
2,532 hits	69 hr
1,014 rbi	583 sb
689 innings	40-31 W–L
4.05 ERA	281 k's
4 saves	

A fine pitcher and an outstanding hitter, Van Haltren had his greatest seasons for the Giants, batting well over .300 each year from 1894 to 1901. In 1896, he swatted a league-high 21 triples while hitting .351.

Van Slyke, Andy (Slick)
1960–

St. Louis (NL 1983–86), Pittsburgh (NL 1987–93 Active)   OF   BL/TR

1,473 games	.278 ba
1,408 hits	152 hr
738 rbi	231 sb

Excellent defensively and steadily improving at the plate, he hit a career-high .324 in 1992 with an NL-leading 199 hits and 45 doubles. Previously inept against left-handed pitchers, Van Slyke now handles them well.

Vance, Clarence (Dazzy)

1891–1961

Pittsburgh (NL 1915), New York (AL 1915, 1918), Brooklyn (NL 1922–32, 1935), St. Louis (NL 1933–34), Cincinnati (NL 1934)   P   BR/RHP

442 games	2,967 innings
197-140 W–L	3.24 ERA
2,045 k's	11 saves

Vance was the greatest pitcher in Brooklyn Dodgers history, yet he didn't win his first major league game until the age of 31. Though he was fond of pitching with a torn undershirt to distract batters, he didn't really need any help. Once he developed control of his superior fastball and great hook, he led the NL in strikeouts from 1922 to 1928. He earned the NL MVP award in 1925, when he won 15 consecutive games and hurled a no-hitter against the Phillies. A witty storyteller, Vance was inducted into the Hall of Fame in 1955.

Vander Meer, Johnny (The Dutch Master)

1914–

Cincinnati (NL 1937–43, 1946–49), Chicago (NL 1950), Cleveland (AL 1951)   P   BB/LHP

346 games	2,104 innings
119-121 W–L	3.44 ERA
1,294 k's	2 saves

Though he was otherwise hindered by poor control throughout his career, Vander Meer had no such problem on two consecutive starts in 1938, when he became the first and only pitcher to throw back-to-back no-hitters. The second gem took place at Ebbets Field, in the first night game ever played in Brooklyn. A hard thrower, Vander Meer led the NL in strikeouts from

1941 to 1943; he also won a total of 49 games in that span.

Vaughan, Joseph (Arky)
1912–1952
Pittsburgh (NL 1932–41), Brooklyn (NL 1942–43, 1947–48)   SS   BL/TR

1,817 games	.318 ba
2,103 hits	96 hr
926 rbi	118 sb

A nine-time All-Star, Vaughan was a first-ball, fastball hitter with great running speed who rarely struck out. He batted .385 in 1935; no NL'er has bettered that mark since. Vaughan led the NL in runs scored, doubles, and walks three times. In the field, he was superb. Soon after retiring from the game, Vaughan drowned while trying to save a friend. He was inducted into the Hall of Fame in 1985.

Vaughn, James (Hippo)
1888–1966
New York (AL 1908, 1910–12), Washington (AL 1912), Chicago (NL 1913–21)   P   BB/LHP

390 games	2,730 innings
178-137 W–L	2.49 ERA
1,416 k's	5 saves

Vaughn compressed his best years into his time in Chicago, winning at least 20 games five times in six seasons. In 1917, he won 23 games. In one game that year, Vaughn and Cincinnati's Fred Toney both pitched no-hit ball for nine innings. Vaughn surrendered a 10th-inning run and lost the game. The following year, he led the NL in wins (22), innings pitched (290), strikeouts (148), and ERA (1.74).

Veach, Bobby

1888–1945

Detroit (AL 1912–23), Boston (AL 1924–25), New York (AL 1925), Washington (AL 1925)   OF
BL/TR

1,821 games	.310 ba
2,063 hits	64 hr
1,166 rbi	195 sb

Veach was overshadowed on the Tigers by teammates like Ty Cobb and Sam Crawford, but he drove home over 100 runs six times in his career. He led the league in 1915 (112), 1917 (103), and 1918 (78), despite belting a total of only 14 homers in those seasons. His best year came in 1919, when he hit .355 while leading the AL in hits (191), doubles (45), and triples (17).

Veale, Bob

1935–

Pittsburgh (NL 1962–72), Boston (AL 1972–74)   P
BB/LHP

397 games	1,926 innings
120-95 W–L	3.07 ERA
1,703 k's	21 saves

National League batters in the sixties had to stay alert in the batter's box when Veale was on the mound. A hard and sometimes wild thrower, he would occasionally take off his glasses and clean them with a handkerchief, leading hitters to hope that he cleaned them well. At 6 feet, 6 inches, he intimidated batters. Veale led NL hurlers in strikeouts in 1964 (250) and fanned at least 200 men four times. He won in double figures and threw at least 200 innings each year from 1964 to 1970.

Veeck, Bill

1914–1987

Cleveland (AL 1946–49), St. Louis (AL 1951–53), Chicago (AL 1959–61, 1976–80)   OWNER

The iconoclastic and innovative owner of three different major league franchises, Veeck enjoyed tweaking the noses of baseball's establishment. In 1943, he nearly bought the Philadelphia Phillies and had plans to integrate the team. When he did purchase the Cleveland Indians in 1946, he transformed a moribund team into baseball's attendance leader, drawing a then-record 2.6 million fans in the pennant-winning 1948 season. When he ran the Browns, he hired a midget, Eddie Gaedel, to appear as a pinch hitter. Veeck could do little to boost attendance in St. Louis, but he got another chance in Chicago. After he purchased the club in 1959, the White Sox won their first pennant in 40 years. Always looking to entertain the fans, Veeck introduced the first exploding scoreboard at Comiskey Park in 1960. Fireworks erupted whenever a White Sox player cracked a home run. He wrote a well-received autobiography, *Veeck as in Wreck*.

Ventura, Robin

1967–

Chicago (AL 1989–93 Active)　　3B　　BL/TR

637 games	.269 ba
615 hits	66 hr
348 rbi	6 sb

A standout college player at Oklahoma State, Ventura arrived in the majors with great fanfare and he has not disappointed. As a rookie in 1990, he got off to a horrible start but recovered to hit .249. The following year, he batted .284 with 23 homers and 100 RBI to launch his career.

Vernon, James (Mickey)

1918–

Washington (AL 1939–43, 1946–48, 1950–55), Cleveland (AL 1949–50, 1958), Boston (AL 1956–57), Milwaukee (NL 1959), Pittsburgh (NL 1960); MGR—Washington (AL 1961–63)   1B, MGR   BL/TL

2,409 games	.286 ba
2,495 hits	172 hr
1,311 rbi	137 sb

The soft-spoken Vernon remains one of the best players not elected to the Hall of Fame. Though he played most of his career on second-division Washington teams, he led the AL in batting in 1946 (.353) and 1953 (.337). Vernon was not a home-run hitter, but he had good extra-base power. He smacked more than 30 doubles six times, hitting league-high marks in 1946 (51), 1953 (43), and 1954 (33). He was a smooth-fielding first baseman with good range.

Viola, Frank (Sweet Music)

1960–

Minnesota (AL 1982–89), New York (AL 1989–91), Boston (AL 1992–93 Active)   P   BL/LHP

406 games	2,760 innings
174-145 W–L	3.66 ERA
1,813 k's	

A hard thrower with a good curve, Viola did not become a big winner in the majors until Johnny Podres taught him how to throw the change-up. He has won at least 13 games each year since 1984, but his best success came in Minnesota in 1988. Following his two victories in the 1987 World Series, Viola won 24 games in 1988 and earned the AL Cy Young Award. Contract problems led to his departure from Minnesota, but after winning 20 games in 1990 for the Mets, his career declined. For the past five seasons,

Viola has started the season well only to falter after the All-Star break.

Vuckovich, Pete

1952–

Chicago (AL 1975–76), Toronto (AL 1977), St. Louis (NL 1978–80), Milwaukee (AL 1981–86)   **P**

BR/RHP

286 games	1,455 innings
93-69 W–L	3.66 ERA
882 k's	10 saves

Vuckovich never looked pretty on the mound, pitching with a full day's growth of beard and long, unruly hair, but no one ever complained about his effort. He won 15 games for the 1979 Cards, and after a trade to Milwaukee, led the AL in winning percentage in 1981 (.778) and 1982 (.750). In the latter year, he earned the Cy Young Award despite a high 3.34 ERA. Vuckovich's career fizzled due to a torn rotator cuff suffered in 1983.

W

Waddell, George (Rube)

1876–1914

Louisville (NL 1897, 1899), Pittsburgh (NL 1900–01), Chicago (NL 1902), Philadelphia (AL 1902–07), St. Louis (AL 1908–10)   **P**

BR/LHP

407 games	2,961 innings
193-143 W–L	2.16 ERA
2,316 k's	5 saves

Baseball was truly a game to "Rube," who amused fans and players alike with his eccentric personality. Waddell prospered under the gentle tutelage of Athletics manager Connie Mack, winning more than 20 games in his first four seasons in Philadelphia and leading the

AL in strikeouts for six consecutive seasons (1902–07). He whipped his overpowering fastball past batters with alacrity. Waddell entered the Hall of Fame in 1946.

Wagner, John (Honus, The Flying Dutchman)

1874–1955

Louisville (NL 1897–99), Pittsburgh (NL 1900–17); MGR—Pittsburgh (NL 1917) **SS, OF, 1B, 3B, MGR** **BR/TR**

2,792 games	.327 ba
3,415 hits	101 hr
1,732 rbi	722 sb

Many experts regard Wagner as the greatest player in the history of the game. Barrel-chested and bowlegged, Wagner was extremely strong and very fast. A quiet player who didn't seek the limelight, he hit .300 or better for 17 consecutive seasons. He led the NL in batting eight times and in stolen bases five times. Popular in cities around the National League, Wagner was cheered by large groups of German immigrants in Cincinnati and New York in particular. The Pirates later retired his uniform number 33 (worn as a coach). Wagner was an inaugural member of the Hall of Fame in 1936.

Wagner, Leon (Daddy Wags)

1934–

San Francisco (NL 1958–59, 1969), St. Louis (NL 1960), Los Angeles (AL 1961–63), Cleveland (AL 1964–68), Chicago (AL 1968) **OF** **BL/TR**

1,352 games	.272 ba
1,202 hits	211 hr
669 rbi	54 sb

There was no room in the San Francisco outfield for the colorful Wagner so he made his way to other teams, eventually landing with the expansion Angels in 1961. A strong wrist hitter, his sweet swing produced 91 home runs for the team in three years. Wagner was an indifferent fielder.

Walberg, George (Rube)

1896–1978

New York (NL 1923), Philadelphia (AL 1923–33), Boston (AL 1934–37)   P   BL/LHP

544 games	2,644 innings
155-141 W–L	4.16 ERA
1,085 k's	32 saves

Nothing seemed to bother Walberg on the mound. He won at least 12 games for seven consecutive seasons in Philadelphia despite walking nearly as many men as he fanned. Walberg's best year came in 1931, the last of the Athletics' three successive pennant-winning seasons, when he won 20 games and led the AL in innings pitched (291).

Walker, Moses (Fleet)

1856–1924

Toledo (AA 1884), Newark (IL 1887), Syracuse (IL 1888–89)   C   BR/TR

42 games	.263 ba
40 hits	

Walker was the first black player in major league ball, joining Toledo after attending Oberlin College. A fine bare-handed catcher, he endured racial prejudice throughout his one season in the majors. He later became a leading proponent of black emigration to Africa.

Walker, Fred (Dixie, The People's Cherce)

1910–1982

New York (AL 1931, 1933–36), Chicago (AL 1936–37), Detroit (AL 1938–39), Brooklyn (NL 1939–47), Pittsburgh (NL 1948–49)   OF
BL/TR

1,905 games	.306 ba
2,064 hits	105 hr
1,023 rbi	59 sb

Brooklyn took a liking to Dixie Walker and, in their distinctive accent, labeled him their "cherce." A fine hitter, he blossomed once given steady duty in Ebbets Field, batting an NL-high .357 in 1944. The following year, he led the league in RBI with 124.

Walker, Larry

1966–

Montreal (NL 1989–93 Active)   **OF**   **BL/TR**

571 games	.273 ba
539 hits	80 hr
298 rbi	83 sb

Born and raised in British Columbia, Walker is the Expos' best Canadian-bred star. He raised his batting average from .241 to .301 between 1990 and 1992 and hit 23 homers with 93 RBI in 1992. Walker excels in the outfield and has one of the strongest arms in the majors.

Wallace, Rhoderick (Bobby)

1873–1960

Cleveland (NL 1894–98), St. Louis (NL 1899–1901, 1917–18), St. Louis (AL 1902–16)   **SS, 3B, P**
BR/TR

2,383 games	.266 ba
2,303 hits	34 hr
1,121 rbi	201 sb
402 innings	24-22 W–L
3.87 ERA	120 k's
1 save	

Wallace entered the big show as a pitcher before moving to the infield in 1897. Known as the most effective shortstop of his era, he played 25 years in the majors without winning a pennant. Wallace entered the Hall of Fame in 1953.

Wallach, Tim

1957–

Montreal (NL 1980–92), Los Angeles (NL 1993
Active)   **3B**   **BR/TR**

1,900 games	.257 ba
1,800 hits	216 hr
967 rbi	50 sb

Wallach is an excellent low-ball hitter who never appears ruffled on the field. He drove home between 69 and 98 runs each year from 1982 to 1991 except for 1987, when he exploded with 123 RBI. At third base, Wallach makes all the plays with understated grace.

Walsh, Ed (Big Ed)

1881–1959

Chicago (AL 1904–16), Boston (NL 1917);
MGR—Chicago (AL 1924)   **P, MGR**
BR/RHP

430 games	2,964 innings
195-126 W–L	1.82 ERA
1,736 k's	34 saves

This stingy spitballer compiled the lowest career ERA among pitchers hurling more than 1,500 innings. Walsh averaged 25 victories from 1907 to 1912, and his 464 innings pitched in 1908 are a 20th-century high. He was inducted into the Hall of Fame in 1946.

Walters, William (Bucky)

1909–1991

Boston (NL 1931–32, 1950), Boston (AL 1933–34),
Philadelphia (NL 1934–38), Cincinnati (NL
1939–48); MGR—Cincinnati (NL 1948–49)   **P,
MGR**   **BR/RHP**

428 games	3,104 innings
198-160 W–L	3.30 ERA
1,107 k's	4 saves

In 1935, during his second year in the majors, Walters switched from third base to the pitcher's mound and

he never looked back. He threw a natural sinker as well
as a good curve. Walters was a great competitor. After
he improved his control, he formed a great one two
combo with Paul Derringer for the Reds. Walters led
the NL in wins three times, including a career high of
27 wins in 1939. That year, he finished first in complete games (31), innings pitched (319), strikeouts
(137), and ERA (2.29).

Waner, Lloyd (Little Poison)
1906–1982
Pittsburgh (NL 1927–41, 1944–45), Boston (NL
1941), Cincinnati (NL 1941), Philadelphia (NL
1942), Brooklyn (NL 1944)   **OF**   **BL/TR**

1,993 games	.316 ba
2,459 hits	27 hr
598 rbi	67 sb

A slap hitter whose tremendous speed enabled him to
beat out many infield hits, Waner's slight size belied his
success on the diamond. He and his big brother Paul
combined for 5,611 hits in the majors. "Little Poison"
hit over .300 10 times. He was inducted into the Hall
of Fame in 1967.

Waner, Paul (Big Poison)
1903–1965
Pittsburgh (NL 1926–40), Brooklyn (N 1941,
1943–44), Boston (NL 1941–42), New York (AL
1944–45)   **OF**   **BL/TL**

2,549 games	.333 ba
3,152 hits	113 hr
1,309 rbi	104 sb

"Big Poison" wasn't much bigger than his little brother
Lloyd, but he was a strong, line-drive hitter who won
the NL batting title three times. The MVP award winner in 1927 when he sparked the Pirates to the pennant, he led the league in batting (.380), hits (237),
triples (17), and RBI (131). Waner was the second

NL'er to reach 3,000 hits. He was inducted into the Hall of Fame in 1952.

Ward, John (Monte)
1860–1925

Providence (NL 1878–82), New York (NL 1883–89, 1893–94), Brooklyn (PL 1890), Brooklyn (NL 1891–92); MGR—Providence (NL 1880), New York (NL 1884, 1893–94), Brooklyn (PL 1890), Brooklyn (NL 1891–92)   **SS, 2B, P, OF, MGR BL/TR**

1,825 games	.275 ba
2,105 hits	26 hr
867 rbi	540 sb
2,461 innings	164-102 W–L
2.10 ERA	920 k's
3 saves	

The Renaissance man of the diamond, Monte Ward starred in his many roles as a pitcher, infielder, manager, team owner, and labor leader. A graduate of Columbia Law School, Ward pitched Providence to the National League pennant in 1879 and hurled a perfect game the following year. He organized the Brotherhood of Baseball Players in 1885 and formed the Players League that operated in 1890. Later, he owned the Boston Braves. Ward entered the Hall of Fame in 1964.

Warneke, Lon (The Arkansas Hummingbird)
1909–1976

Chicago (NL 1930–36, 1942–43, 1945), St. Louis (NL 1937–42)   **P   BR/RHP**

445 games	2,782 innings
192-121 W–L	3.18 ERA
1,140 k's	13 saves

A tough customer who wouldn't hesitate to knock down an opponent in the clutch, Warneke earned five

All-Star spots in his lengthy career. He won at least 20 games three times, including a league-high 22 wins for the pennant-winning Cubs in 1932. That year, he also led the league in shutouts (four) and ERA (2.37). Warneke, who liked to sing, also performed with the Cardinals' Mudcat Band.

Watson, Bob (Bull)
1946–

Houston (NL 1966–79), Boston (AL 1979), New York (AL 1980–82), Atlanta (NL 1982–84)   1B, OF   BR/TR

1,832 games	.295 ba
1,826 hits	184 hr
989 rbi	27 sb

Watson could flat-out hit. Feared by opposing pitchers, if unrecognized by fans around the league, Watson gained his greatest publicity by scoring the one-millionth run in major league history in 1976. He batted over .300 in six seasons and knocked in over 100 runs in both 1976 and 1977. Watson became the first African-American general manager in baseball history when he was hired by the Astros in 1993.

Weaver, Earl
1930–

Baltimore (AL 1968–82, 1985–86)   **MGR**

An umpire's nightmare, Weaver knew the rule book inside out and aggressively fought baseball's arbiters for every possible advantage. Sound defensively, his Baltimore teams understood the game's fundamentals and rarely beat themselves. Weaver disliked the sacrifice and played for the big inning, but when you had sluggers like Frank Robinson and Boog Powell you could afford to wait for the three-run homer. His Baltimore teams compiled a 1,480-1,060 record and won the 1970 World Series.

Weiss, George
1894–1972

Executive New York (AL 1932–60), New York (NL 1962–66)   **EXECUTIVE**

The mastermind behind the Yankees dynasty, Weiss won 19 pennants in 29 seasons at the helm. Personally, players felt that Weiss treated them shabbily, but no one questioned his administrative skill. He built up the Yankees' farm system to include 20 clubs, and the flow of talent remained constant throughout his tenure. He was inducted into the Hall of Fame in 1971.

Welch, Bob
1956–

Los Angeles (NL 1978–87), Oakland (AL 1988–93) Active)   **P**   **BR/RHP**

481 games	3,022 innings
208-140 W–L	3.39 ERA
1,925 k's	8 saves

As a Dodgers rookie, this fastballing righty struck out Reggie Jackson to win game two of the 1978 World Series, thereby making himself a household name. Moved into the starting rotation in 1980, he won at least 13 games in six of the next eight years. Traded to the Athletics, he put together a dream season in 1990, going 27-6 to win the AL Cy Young Award.

Welch, Mickey (Smiling Mickey)
1859–1941

Troy (NL 1880–82), New York (NL 1883–92)   **P** **BR/RHP**

564 games	4,802 innings
307-210 W–L	2.71 ERA
1,850 k's	4 saves

Welch starred in the era of two-man pitching staffs when starters were expected to go nine innings. The good-natured hurler threw complete games in all of his first 105 starts—a remarkable achievement in any age.

In 1885, he went 44-11 with a scintillating 1.66 ERA. Welch was the third man to accumulate 300 wins. He was inducted into the Hall of Fame in 1973.

Wells, Willie (Devil)

1908–1989

St. Louis Stars (1924–31), Kansas City Monarchs (1932), Detroit Wolves (1932), Homestead Grays (1932), Chicago American Giants (1933–35), Newark Eagles (1936–39, 1942, 1945), New York Black Yankees (1945–46), Baltimore Elite Giants (1946), Memphis Red Sox (1948)   SS   BR/TR

909 games	.331 ba
1,139 hits	123 hr
91 sb	

No shortstop covered more ground than Wells. He starred in the thirties for the Chicago American Giants and later anchored Newark's million-dollar infield.

Werber, Bill

1908–

New York (AL 1930, 1933), Boston (AL 1933–36), Philadelphia (AL 1937–38), Cincinnati (NL 1939–41), New York (NL 1942)   3B   BR/TR

1,295 games	.271 ba
1,363 hits	78 hr
539 rbi	215 sb

A scrappy hustler, Werber applied his great speed to swipe the most bases in the NL three times in his career. Traded to Cincinnati in 1939, he sparked the Reds to their first pennant since 1919, leading the league in runs scored (115).

Wertz, Vic

1925–1983

Detroit (AL 1947–52, 1961–63), St. Louis (AL 1952–53), Baltimore (AL 1954), Cleveland (AL 1954–58), Boston (AL 1959–61), Minnesota (AL 1963)   OF, 1B   BL/TR

1,862 games	.277 ba
1,692 hits	266 hr
1,178 rbi	9 sb

In game one of the 1954 World Series, Wertz smashed the 460-foot drive to center field that Willie Mays caught in one of the greatest defensive plays in baseball history. A lumbering power hitter, he socked at least 20 homers six times and knocked home over 100 runs five times in his career.

West, Sammy

1904–1985

Washington (AL 1927–32, 1938–41), St. Louis (AL 1933–38), Chicago (AL 1942)   OF   BL/TL

1,753 games	.299 ba
1,838 hits	75 hr
838 rbi	53 sb

West was an outstanding defensive center fielder who also wielded a strong bat throughout his career. He batted .328 and .333 for solid Washington teams in 1930 and 1931, but he was traded to the Browns for future Hall of Famer Goose Goslin prior to the 1933 season and missed playing in that fall's World Series.

Weyhing, Gus (Rubber Arm Gus)

1866–1955

Philadelphia (AA 1887–89, 1891), Brooklyn (PL 1890), Philadelphia (NL 1892–95), Pittsburgh (NL 1895), Louisville (NL 1895–96), Washington (NL 1898–99), St. Louis (NL 1900), Brooklyn (NL 1900), Cleveland (AL 1901), Cincinnati (NL 1901)   P   BR/RHP

538 games	4,324 innings
264-232 W–L	3.89 ERA
1,665 k's	4 saves

A veteran of 10 major league franchises, Weyhing won at least 20 games in each of his first seven years in the bigs, including 30 or more between 1889 and 1892. Regrettably, he toiled on mostly second-division teams and never received proper recognition during his career.

Wheat, Zach (Buck)

1888–1972

Brooklyn (NL 1909–26), Philadelphia (AL 1927)

OF   BL/TR

2,410 games	.317 ba
2,884 hits	132 hr
1,248 rbi	205 sb

Wheat was a quiet man beloved by his Brooklyn teammates and fans alike. Branch Rickey called him the greatest outfielder in Brooklyn Dodgers history. He was a line-drive hitter and a sure fielder with a strong, accurate arm. At his retirement, he held nearly every offensive record in Brooklyn. A great curve-ball hitter, Wheat improved with age, batting .375 twice and .359 after the age of 35. He entered the Hall of Fame in 1959.

Whitaker, Lou (Sweet Lou)

1957–

Detroit (AL 1977–93 Active)   **2B   BL/TR**

2,214 games	.275 ba
2,199 hits	218 hr
997 rbi	137 sb

Few second basemen have played the position as well and packed as much power as Whitaker. For most of his career, he teamed with shortstop Alan Trammell to form the best duo in the AL. Whitaker smacked at least 20 homers four times and drove in a career-high 85 runs in 1989. He has a sharp eye at the plate and has drawn at least 80 walks four times.

White, Bill

1934–

New York (NL 1956), San Francisco (NL 1958), St. Louis (NL 1959–65, 1969), Philadelphia (NL 1966–68)   **1B   BL/TL**

1,673 games	.286 ba
1,706 hits	202 hr
870 rbi	103 sb

White has had a varied career in baseball as a star first baseman, longtime announcer, and since 1988, the first black president of the National League. He broke in with 22 home runs as a rookie for the Giants in 1956; but he hit his stride after a trade to St. Louis, batting .302 in his first year with the Cardinals. Three more .300-plus seasons followed, along with five All-Star berths and three seasons with more than 100 RBI. In addition, he was a first-rate defensive player. Inexplicably, the Cardinals traded him to Philadelphia, where he had one more big season in 1966 with 103 RBI.

White, Devon (Devo)

1962–

California (AL 1985–90), Toronto (AL 1991–93 Active)   **OF   BB/TR**

1,067 games	.256 ba
1,054 hits	108 hr
413 rbi	234 sb

A great defensive outfielder, White has also matured into a dangerous hitter since his arrival in Toronto. As an Angels rookie, he posted good numbers in 1987 (24 homers and 87 RBI) when run production around the majors soared, but his average steadily dropped to as low as .217 prior to his trade to the Blue Jays. Great speed and a strong throwing arm make him valuable in the field at nearly any average.

White, Frank

1950–

Kansas City (AL 1973–90)   **2B**   **BR/TR**

2,324 games	.255 ba
2,006 hits	160 hr
886 rbi	178 sb

White was a sterling defensive second baseman with great range, sharp reflexes, and the quick hands and feet needed to turn the double play. At the plate, he showed surprising power, crunching 22 home runs in consecutive seasons (1985–86). An aggressive swinger, he rarely walked and his on-base percentage never topped .326.

White, Guy (Doc)

1879–1969

Philadelphia (NL 1901–02), Chicago (AL 1903–13)
P   **BL/LHP**

427 games	3,041 innings
189-156 W–L	2.39 ERA
1,384 k's	5 saves

The ace of the 1906 White Sox Hitless Wonders pitching staff, White went 18-6 that season with a league-low 1.52 ERA. Four times he compiled a season ERA below 2.00—a remarkable accomplishment even in the dead ball era. White rarely walked a batter; in one stretch, he pitched 65 consecutive innings without allowing a single base on balls.

White, James (Deacon)

1847–1939

Chicago (NL 1876), Boston (NL 1877), Cincinnati (NL 1878–80), Buffalo (1881–85), Detroit (NL 1886–88), Pittsburgh (NL 1889), Buffalo (PL 1890); MGR—Cincinnati (NL 1879)   **3B, C, MGR**
BL/TR

1,299 games	.303 ba
1,619 hits	18 hr
756 rbi	46 sb

Deacon White's moral rectitude stood in sharp contrast to the general character of the league. He was one of the Big Four sold by Buffalo to Detroit in 1885 when the Bisons were strapped for cash. Along with Buffalo teammate Jack Rowe, White threatened to invoke the NL's reserve clause, but he backed away from a full confrontation. An innovator on the field, he helped develop the first catcher's chest protector. He was the brother of hurler Will White.

White, Roy

1943–

New York (AL 1965–79)   OF   BB/TR

1,881 games	.271 ba
1,803 hits	160 hr
758 rbi	233 sb

A latter-day "Old Reliable," White produced consistent numbers throughout his career. Not a power hitter, he nevertheless had good extra-base pop in his bat and drove home over 80 runs twice. He seemed to specialize in hitting sacrifice flies. When batting left-handed, White had an unusual pigeon-toed stance and swung from a deep crouch. Fast afield, he stole at least 10 bases in each of his seasons as a regular. His only weakness was a poor throwing arm.

White, Solomon (Sol)

1868–1948?

Philadelphia Giants   2B, MGR   BR/TR

The acknowledged father of black baseball, White chronicled the game in a famous work published in 1907, *Sol White's Official Base Ball Guide: History of Colored Base Ball.* He played in the 1890s for the leading black teams and founded the Philadelphia Giants in 1902.

White, Will (Whoop-La)

1854–1911

Boston (NL 1877), Cincinnati (NL 1878–80),
Detroit (NL 1881), Cincinnati (AA 1882–86);
MGR—Cincinnati (AA 1884)   P, MGR
BB/RHP

403 games	3,542 innings
229-166 W–L	2.28 ERA
1,041 k's	

White was one of the first players to sign with the new
American Association in 1882. He pitched Cincinnati
to the pennant by winning a league-high 40 games
against only 12 losses. A deeply religious man, he was
the brother of "Deacon" White. He was also the first
bespectacled player in the National League. White still
ranks 10th on the all-time ERA list.

Whitehill, Earl

1900–1954

Detroit (AL 1923–32), Washington (AL 1933–36),
Cleveland (AL 1937–38), Chicago (NL 1939)   P
BL/LHP

541 games	3,564 innings
218-185 W–L	4.36 ERA
1,350 k's	11 saves

Whitehill was one tough customer on the mound—he
could blast teammates and foes alike. In modern par-
lance, he played with a lit fuse. Whitehill always
seemed to pitch with men on base, but he knew how to
wiggle out of jams. He won at least 11 games in 13
straight seasons (1924–36), although his lifetime ERA
is the highest ever recorded by a career 200-game winner.

Whitney, Jim (Grasshopper Jim)

1857–1891

Boston (NL 1881–85), Kansas City (NL 1886),
Washington (NL 1887–88), Indianapolis (NL 1889),
Philadelphia (AA 1890)   P   BL/RHP

413 games	3,496 innings
191-204 W–L	2.97 ERA
1,571 k's	2 saves

A blazing fastball and excellent control were the chief
attributes of Whitney, one of the 19th century's top
hurlers. Known for his combativeness on the mound
and his constant complaining to umpires, he went
31-33 as a rookie. Whitney is one of only three pitchers
in major league history to lose more than 200 games
without winning 200. In sharp contrast to other pitchers of his era, he produced a remarkable walk-strikeout
ratio of nearly 1:4.

Whitson, Ed

1955–

Pittsburgh (NL 1977–79), San Francisco (NL
1979–81), Cleveland (AL 1982), San Diego (NL
1983–84, 1986–91), New York (AL 1985–86)   P
BR/RHP

452 games	2,240 innings
126-123 W–L	3.79 ERA
1,266 k's	8 saves

Whitson was the prime example of a modern-day ballplayer who could not play in the charged atmosphere
of New York. On the verge of a nervous breakdown
following threats against his life, he pitched only on the
road. In the course of his adventures in New York, he
roughed up manager Billy Martin in a fistfight in a Baltimore hotel. On the mound, Whitson had a moving
fastball, a sharp breaking ball, and excellent control.
His best years came in San Diego, where he won in
double figures five times, including 16 triumphs in
1989.

Wilcox, Milt

1950–

Cincinnati (NL 1970–71), Cleveland (AL 1972–74),
Chicago (NL 1975), Detroit (AL 1977–85), Seattle
(AL 1986)   P   BR/RHP

394 games	2,016 innings
119-113 W–L	4.07 ERA
1,137 k's	6 saves

Though he was not overpowering on the mound, Wilcox knew how to keep batters off-stride with an assortment of pitches at a variety of speeds. He spent his best years in Detroit, winning at least 11 games in seven straight seasons (1978–84), including 17 in 1984.

Wilhelm, Hoyt

1923–

New York (NL 1952–56), St. Louis (NL 1957),
Cleveland (AL 1957–58), Baltimore (AL 1958–62),
Chicago (AL 1963–68), California (AL 1969),
Atlanta (NL 1969–70, 1971), Chicago (NL 1970),
Los Angeles (NL 1971–72)   P   BR/RHP

1,070 games	2,254 innings
143-122 W–L	2.52 ERA
1,610 k's	227 saves

The greatest knuckleballer in baseball, Wilhelm pitched in the most games in major league history, 1,070. His first year in the majors included many highlights—he hit a home run in his first at-bat and led the NL in winning percentage (.833), game appearances (71), and ERA (2.43), plus he won 15 games. Although Wilhelm spent most of his career in the bullpen, he pitched a no-hitter against the Yankees in 1958, the last time New York has been held without a hit. For five straight seasons, he recorded an ERA below 2.00. Wilhelm was inducted into the Hall of Fame in 1985.

Williams, Billy

1938–

Chicago (NL 1959–74), Oakland (AL 1975) **OF, DH BL/TR**

2,488 games	.290 ba
2,711 hits	426 hr
1,475 rbi	90 sb

Williams had one of the sweetest swings in baseball history. A quiet player on and off the field, he rarely received the attention his performance warranted. As a Cubs regular, he never had a poor season, batting at least .275 each year. Named the NL Rookie of the Year in 1961 and NL batting champion in 1972 (.333), Williams held the NL record for consecutive games played (1,117) at his retirement and still ranks 21st on the career home-run list. The Cubs retired his uniform number 26, and he was inducted into the Hall of Fame in 1987.

Williams, Dick

1928–

Brooklyn (NL 1951–54, 1956), Baltimore (AL 1956–57, 1958, 1961–62), Cleveland (AL 1957), Kansas City (AL 1959–60), Boston (AL 1963–64); MGR—Boston (AL 1967–69), Oakland (AL 1971–73), California (AL 1974–76), Montreal (NL 1977–81), San Diego (NL 1982–85), Seattle (AL 1986–88) **OF, 3B, MGR BR/TR**

1,023 games	.260 ba
768 hits	70 hr
331 rbi	12 sb

Raised in the Dodgers' system, Williams was a mediocre player who became an outstanding manager. He won pennants in Boston, Oakland, and San Diego on teams that played hard, disciplined baseball. The improbable yet exhilarating rise of the 1967 Red Sox to first place stamped Williams as a sound handler of young talent—a label that proved apt given his later success with the boisterous Athletics teams of the early seventies. In all, his teams won 1,571 games.

Williams, Fred (Cy)
1887–1974
Chicago (NL 1912–17), Philadelphia (NL 1918–30)
OF   BL/TL

2,002 games	.292 ba
1,981 hits	251 hr
1,005 rbi	115 sb

Williams made a fine adjustment from the dead ball era to the free-swinging days of the twenties, winning home-run titles in both periods. His 12 homers topped the NL in 1916, and he swatted 41 long balls in 1923 and 30 more in 1927. Williams was a dead-pull hitter who benefited from the short right-field fence at Philadelphia's home park, Baker Bowl.

Williams, Joe (Smokey Joe, Cyclone)
1886–1946
San Antonio Broncos, Chicago Leland Giants
(1910–1911), New York Lincoln Giants
(1912–1915, 1916–1921, 1923), Chicago American
Giants (1915), Brooklyn Royal Giants (1916,
1924–1926), Atlantic City Bacharach Giants (1921),
Homestead Grays (1927–1931), Detroit Wolves
(1932)   P   BR/RHP

144 games	917 innings
78-47 W–L	341 k's

A huge, intimidating presence on the mound, the 6-foot, 5-inch fireballing righty is regarded as the greatest black pitcher of the early 20th century. In 1914, he won 41 games while pitching in assorted leagues. In one memorable game against the pennant-winning Phillies, he shut the team out on only three hits and fanned 10 men.

Williams, Ken

1890–1959

Cincinnati (NL 1915–16), St. Louis (AL 1918–27), Boston (AL 1928–29) **OF** **BL/TR**

1,397 games	.319 ba
1,552 hits	196 hr
913 rbi	154 sb

In the early twenties, the Brownies' potent offense featured George Sisler, Baby Doll Jacobson, and Ken Williams. Williams had a career year in 1922, batting .332 and leading the AL in homers (39) and RBI (155). In all, he batted over .300 ten times in his career.

Williams, Matt

1965–

San Francisco (NL 1987–93 Active) **3B** **BR/TR**

827 games	.251 ba
756 hits	159 hr
486 rbi	25 sb

The Giants never wavered in their belief that Williams was star material, even after three aborted attempts at a regular position on the team. In 1990, he exploded for 33 home runs, a league-leading 122 RBI, and a respectable .277 batting average. At the plate, he is a strict pull hitter. In the field, his quick reflexes and strong throwing arm make him one of the game's best defensive players.

Williams, Mitch (Wild Thing)

1964–

Texas (AL 1986–88), Chicago (NL 1989–90), Philadelphia (NL 1991–93), Houston (NL 1994 Active) **P** **BL/LHP**

567 games	654 innings
43-51 W–L	3.39 ERA
620 k's	186 saves

It seems that Williams takes every batter to a full count, but he somehow wriggles out of jams, both those of his own creation and those he walks into. Sometimes it takes just a single blazing fastball or sharp slider to make up for pitch after pitch that misses the strike zone. Williams's high-water mark for saves came in 1989, with 36. After starring in the Phillies' upset of Atlanta in the 1993 NLCS, he surrendered the series-winning home run to Toronto's Joe Carter in the sixth game of the World Series.

Williams, Ted (The Splendid Splinter, Teddy Ballgame)

1918–
Boston (AL 1939–42, 1946–60);
MGR—Washington (AL 1969–71), Texas (AL 1972)   OF, MGR   BL/TR

2,292 games	.344 ba
2,654 hits	521 hr
1,839 rbi	24 sb

Unquestionably the greatest hitter of his era, Williams took a scientific approach to batting, utilizing his exceptional vision, great reflexes, and studied analysis of opposing pitchers to lead the AL in batting six times. Patient at the plate, he refused to swing at pitches out of the strike zone. He stood deep in the batter's box, and his quick wrists allowed him to wait until the last moment before uncoiling his swing. Williams won two triple crowns and two MVP awards, although he might well have won more awards had it not been for his thorny relationship with the sportswriters. He was the last man to hit over .400, reaching .406 in 1941. Williams lifetime stats also reflect nearly five full seasons missed due to military service and injuries. He was inducted into the Hall of Fame in 1966.

Willis, Vic

1876–1947

Boston (NL 1898–1905), Pittsburgh (NL 1906–09),
St. Louis (NL 1910)   P   **BR/RHP**

513 games	3,996 innings
249-205 W–L	2.63 ERA
1,651 k's	11 saves

Some of the best pitchers in the history of the game
endured terrible seasons. One such hurler was Willis,
who lost a combined total of 54 games in 1904–05, a
20th-century record. A curve-ball artist, he also won 20
games eight times. His 45 complete games (in 46
starts) are a post-1900 NL record. In his last big year,
while pitching for the 1909 Pirates, Willis won 10 consecutive games.

Wills, Maury

1932–

Los Angeles (NL 1959–66, 1969–72), Pittsburgh
(NL 1967–68), Montreal (NL 1969); MGR—Seattle
(AL 1980–81)   SS, 3B, MGR   **BB/TR**

1,942 games	.281 ba
2,134 hits	20 hr
458 rbi	586 sb

Many experts look back on Wills's play in 1962 and
conclude that he revolutionized baseball. In 1962, the
third of six consecutive years of leading the NL in stolen bases, Wills broke Ty Cobb's sacrosanct record of
96 steals by swiping 104, thus proving that you could
scratch out one run at a time and win games, even in
the age of the long ball. Of course it helped to have the
Dodgers' pitching staff. Stressing pitching, speed, and
defense, the Dodgers won pennants in 1963, 1965,
and 1966, after just missing in 1962. Wills was a brilliant base runner who analyzed each pitcher's delivery
to home plate in order to get the best possible jump.

Wilson, Don
1945–1975
Houston (NL 1966–74) P BR/RHP

266 games	1,748 innings
104-92 W–L	3.15 ERA
1,283 k's	2 saves

Wilson was a big, fireballing righty who teamed with Larry Dierker as a great pitching duo for Houston. He won 15 or more games three times and struck out a career-high 235 batters in 1969. Wilson pitched a no-hitter in 1967 against Atlanta and struck out 18 men in a 1968 game. He died accidentally from carbon monoxide asphyxiation after the 1974 season. The Astros later retired his uniform number 40.

Wilson, Earl
1934–
Boston (AL 1959–66), Detroit (AL 1966–70), San Diego (NL 1970) P BR/RHP

338 games	2,051 innings
121-109 W–L	3.69 ERA
1,452 k's	

After being traded from the Red Sox to the Tigers during the 1966 season, Wilson turned his career around. A strapping right-handed pitcher with a rising fastball but poor control, he led the AL by throwing 21 wild pitches in 1963. But he went on to win 18 games in 1966, a league-best 22 in 1967, and 13 in 1968, when the Tigers won the World Series.

Wilson, Lewis (Hack)
1900–1948
New York (NL 1923–25), Chicago (NL 1926–31), Brooklyn (NL 1932–34), Philadelphia (NL 1934)
OF BR/TR

1,348 games	.307 ba
1,461 hits	244 hr
1,062 rbi	52 sb

At 5 feet, 6 inches and 190 pounds, Wilson made an odd figure on the field. He was built like a fireplug, with short arms, short legs, and a ruddy face that took on more color due to his fondness for alcohol. He took a great deal of abuse from opponents around the NL, but they all respected his ability to belt the ball over the fence. In 1930, he crushed an NL-record 56 home runs and chased home a major league-best 190 runs. Strong in the clutch, Wilson surpassed 100 RBI six times. He was inducted into the Hall of Fame in 1979.

Wilson, William (Mookie)

1956–
New York (NL 1980–89), Toronto (AL 1989–91)
OF   BB/TR

1,403 games	.274 ba
1,397 hits	67 hr
438 rbi	327 sb

Wilson exuded a love for the game every day he stepped on the field. A fan favorite in New York and during his brief stay in Toronto, he ran the bases aggressively and was one of the smartest base runners of his generation. At the plate, Mookie was an undisciplined batsman who swung at any pitch within reach—curves in the dirt, fastballs over his shoulders. A streak hitter, he carried the Mets for weeks at a time. Wilson batted a career-high .299 in 1987 but will be remembered forever for jumping out of the way of Bob Stanley's wild pitch and hitting the famous ground ball booted by Bill Buckner in the 10th inning of the sixth game of the 1986 World Series.

Wilson, Willie

1955–
Kansas City (AL 1976–90), Oakland (AL 1991–92), Chicago (NL 1993 Active)   **OF   BB/TR**

2,137 games	.286 ba
2,202 hits	41 hr
585 rbi	669 sb

One of the fastest men to play major league baseball in the past 50 years, Wilson was built to play on a fast artificial surface like Kansas City's. His grounders found holes in the infield and his gap hits became triples; however, as a leadoff hitter, he drew far too few walks and struck out too frequently. Wilson's speed enabled him to outrun the ball in center field. His best year led to the Royals' first appearance in the World Series in 1980, when he batted .326 with a league-leading 133 runs scored, 230 hits, 15 triples, and 79 stolen bases.

Wiltse, George (Hooks, Snake)
1880–1959
New York (NL 1904–14), Brooklyn (FL 1915)   P
BR/LHP

357 games	2,112 innings
139-90 W–L	2.47 ERA
965 k's	34 saves

Wiltse burst upon the majors like a meteor, winning his first 13 decisions as a rookie in 1904. Proving that his debut was no fluke, he never had a losing season for the Giants. He won 23 games in 1908 and 20 the following year.

Winfield, Dave (Winny, Big Dave)
1951–
San Diego (NL 1973–80), New York (AL 1981–88, 1990), California (AL 1990–91), Toronto (AL 1992), Minnesota (AL 1993 Active)   OF
BR/TR

2,850 games	.285 ba
3,014 hits	453 hr
1,786 rbi	220 sb

It was only toward the end of Winfield's career that people took notice of just how great a player he was. Consistently excellent at bat and in the field, he knocked in over 100 runs eight times, including five consecutive seasons (1982–86), and he batted over .300 four times. At bat, Winfield's strength generated tremendous bat speed that overcame the hitch in his long swing. Defensively, he had great range. In addition, his leaping ability and 6-foot, 6-inch frame allowed him to literally climb the outfield wall to snare potential home runs. Winfield is a definite future Hall of Famer.

Wise, Rick

1945–

Philadelphia (NL 1964–71), St. Louis (NL 1972–73), Boston (AL 1974–77), Cleveland (AL 1978–79), San Diego (NL 1980–82)   P

BR/RHP

506 games	3,127 innings
188–181 W–L	3.69 ERA
1,647 k's	

It was Rick Wise's misfortune to be traded for future Hall of Famer Steve Carlton at a stage in both players' careers when they were rated evenly. Carlton's career took off in Philadelphia, while Wise's continued at the same pace in St. Louis and Boston. He won at least 15 games in five different seasons, including a career-high 19 wins for Boston's pennant-winning 1975 team. One area where Wise had it all over Carlton was at the plate, where he was the best-hitting pitcher of his generation. In Wise's no-hitter in 1971 against Cincinnati, for instance, he smacked two home runs.

Wood, Joe (Smokey Joe)

1889–1985

Boston (AL 1908–15), Cleveland (AL 1917–22)   P, OF   BR/TR

695 games	.283 ba
553 hits	24 hr
325 rbi	23 sb
1,436 innings	116-57 W-L
2.03 ERA	989 k's
11 saves	

In 1912, Smokey Joe Wood dominated baseball. Pitching for the world champion Red Sox, he won an AL-best 34 games against only five losses and hurled 10 shutouts. Unfortunately, he hurt his arm the following spring and never could cut loose on the mound again. Undaunted, he became an outfielder for Cleveland and batted .366 in limited duty in 1921.

Wood, Wilbur

1941–
Boston (AL 1961–64), Pittsburgh (NL 1964–65), Chicago (AL 1967–78)   **P**   **BR/LHP**

651 games	2,684 innings
164-156 W-L	3.24 ERA
1,411 k's	57 saves

In 1972 and 1973, it seemed that Wood started every other day for the White Sox. Relying exclusively on a knuckle ball, he started 49 games in 1972 and 48 the following year. In 1972, he pitched 377 innings—the most in the American League since 1912. On one memorable day in 1973, he started—and lost—both games of a doubleheader against the Yankees.

Woodling, Gene

1922–
Cleveland (AL 1943, 1946, 1955–57), Pittsburgh (NL 1947), New York (AL 1949–54), Baltimore (AL 1955, 1958–60), Washington (AL 1961–62), New York (NL 1962)   **OF**   **BL/TR**

1,796 games	.284 ba
1,585 hits	147 hr
830 rbi	29 sb

Hot-tempered on the field and determined to succeed, Woodling fought a running battle with manager Casey Stengel to gain more playing time in the crowded Yankees outfield. At bat, he swung from a deep crouch and made consistent contact, rarely striking out. A fine ball hawk, Woodling could not accept part-time duty. Thriving on a steady diet of right-handed pitchers, he batted .309 in 1952 and .306 in 1953. In five World Series appearances—all Yankees' victories—he hit .318.

Wright, George

1847–1937

Boston (NL 1876–78, 1880–81), Providence (NL 1879, 1882); MGR—Providence (NL 1879)   SS, MGR   BR/TR

329 games	.256 ba
383 hits	2 hr
132 rbi	

Wright was the star shortstop on the Cincinnati Red Stockings squad that started pro ball in 1869. He later sparked the Boston team in the National Association and also led Providence to the NL flag in 1879 as player-manager. Wright was inducted into the Hall of Fame in 1937.

Wright, Harry

1835–1895

Boston (NL 1876–81), Providence (NL 1882–83), Philadelphia (NL 1884–93)   MGR

In 1869, Wright organized, managed, and played center field for the Cincinnati Red Stockings—America's first professional team. He later managed Boston's initial squads in the National Association and the National League, winning a total of 1,225 games as a skipper. He was inducted into the Hall of Fame in 1953.

Wyatt, Whit

1907–

Detroit (AL 1929–33), Chicago (AL 1933–36),
Cleveland (AL 1937), Brooklyn (NL 1939–44),
Philadelphia (NL 1945)   P   BR/RHP

360 games	1,761 innings
106-95 W–L	3.79 ERA
872 k's	13 saves

Though he had been a spot starter and reliever for
much of his career, Wyatt became a key member of the
Brooklyn starting staff soon after his arrival in Flatbush
in 1939. Two years later, his 22 victories and seven
shutouts led the Dodgers to the pennant. The next two
seasons, he went 33-14. On the mound, Wyatt earned
a reputation as a mean-spirited competitor who never
hesitated to knock down a batter.

Wynn, Early (Gus)

1920–

Washington (AL 1939, 1941–44, 1946–48),
Cleveland (AL 1949–57, 1963), Chicago (AL
1958–62)   P   BB/RHP

691 games	4,564 innings
300-244 W–L	3.54 ERA
2,334 k's	15 saves

A hard-nosed competitor who owned the inside corner
of the plate, Wynn relished his reputation as a pitcher
so tough that he would knock down his own mother if
she crowded the dish. He won 20 or more games five
times and earned the Cy Young Award in 1959, when
his 22 victories led the Chisox to their first pennant
since the White Sox scandal in 1919. Wynn hung on
until he won his 300th game with Cleveland in 1963.
He was inducted into the Hall of Fame in 1972.

Wynn, Jim (The Toy Cannon)

1942–

Houston (NL 1963–73), Los Angeles (NL 1974–75), Atlanta (NL 1976), New York (AL 1977), Milwaukee (AL 1977)   OF   BR/TR

1,920 games	.250 ba
1,665 hits	291 hr
964 rbi	225 sb

A powerful right-handed slugger, Wynn's small stature belied his ability to reach the seats. Playing in the cavernous Astrodome, he belted more than 20 home runs in seven seasons. Wynn was a patient hitter who drew more than 100 walks six times, including a league-best 148 in 1969.

Y

Yastrzemski, Carl (Yaz)

1939–

Boston (AL 1961–83)   OF, 1B, DH   BL/TR

3,308 games	.285 ba
3,419 hits	452 hr
1,844 rbi	168 sb

Yastrzemski could never satisfy the Boston fans', thirst for perfection, but to fans around the league, he was the most dangerous hitter of his generation. Heralded as the next Ted Williams, Yastrzemski was a great fastball hitter with a flair for the dramatic. He cemented his claim to superstar status in 1967, when he single-handedly led Boston to an improbable pennant, winning the triple crown with a .326 average, 44 home runs, and 121 RBI. That year, he also led the AL in hits (189) and runs scored (112). Yaz led the league in batting three times, and he cracked at least 40 homers in three seasons. Defensively, he mastered the caroms of balls hit against Fenway Park's Green Monster. Perhaps the only blemish on his career was his pop-up for the final out in the 1978 playoff game against the Yankees.

Yawkey, Thomas
1903–1976
Boston (AL 1933–76)   OWNER

Elected to the Hall of Fame in 1980, Yawkey was one of baseball's most beloved owners. No franchise treated its players better; indeed, some skeptics believed that the team's so-called country-club atmosphere prevented it from being truly successful on the field. Boston won three pennants under his aegis, but the World Series title eluded them each time.

York, Rudolph (Rudy)
1913–1970
Detroit (AL 1934, 1937–45), Boston (AL 1946–47), Chicago (AL 1947), Philadelphia (AL 1948)   1B, C
BR/TR

1,603 games	.275 ba
1,621 hits	277 hr
1,152 rbi	38 sb

York's arrival in Detroit prompted Hank Greenberg's shift from first base to left field because York could not play another position and the team needed his bat in the lineup. Indeed, his big bat slammed 35 homers as a Tigers rookie, and he reached the seats no fewer than 20 times each year from 1937 to 1943. York played on three pennant winners, going to the World Series twice with Detroit and once with the Red Sox.

Yost, Eddie (The Walking Man)
1926–
Washington (AL 1944, 1946–58), Detroit (AL 1959–60), Los Angeles (AL 1961–62)   3B
BR/TR

2,109 games	.254 ba
1,863 hits	139 hr
683 rbi	72 sb

A walk was certainly as good as a hit for Yost, who led the AL in bases on balls six times, including 151 in 1956. He ended his career ranked seventh all-time in garnering walks—a notable achievement on his weak-hitting Washington teams. A durable player, Yost also retired having played more games at third base than any other man in major league history. His best year was probably the first he spent in Detroit, 1959, when he batted .278 with 21 home runs and a league-best 115 runs scored.

Young, Denton (Cy)

1867–1955
Cleveland (NL 1890–98), St. Louis (NL 1899–1900), Boston (AL 1901–08), Cleveland (AL 1909–11), Boston (NL 1911); MGR—Boston (AL 1907)   P, MGR   BR/RHP

906 games	7,354 innings
511-316 W–L	2.63 ERA
2,800 k's	17 saves

The indestructible Cy Young is the winningest pitcher in major league history. He won more than 20 games 15 times and more than 30 games five times. At the age of 34 in 1901, Young jumped to the upstart American League and revived his career with Boston, where he pitched a perfect game three years later. He was inducted into the Hall of Fame in 1937.

Youngs, Royce (Ross, Pep)

1897–1927
New York (NL 1917–26)   OF   BL/TR

1,211 games	.322 ba
1,491 hits	42 hr
592 rbi	153 sb

One of McGraw's favorite Giants in the 1920s, Youngs was an aggressive, hard-nosed player with a powerful throwing arm and great speed. He hit better than .300 in seven consecutive seasons and led NL outfielders in assists three times. Youngs died tragically of Bright's disease at the age of 30. He was inducted into the Hall of Fame in 1972.

Yount, Robin
1955–
Milwaukee (AL 1974–93 Active)   SS, OF
BR/TR

2,856 games	.285 ba
3,142 hits	251 hr
1,406 rbi	271 sb

Yount knows only one way to play the game—he gives his best whether it's April or September, whether his team is in a pennant race or 20 games out. A precocious shortstop at 18, he matured into the best player in Brewers history. Although he is not a slugger, Yount has exceptional strength to the opposite field. He earned the AL MVP award in 1982, batting .331 with 29 homers, 114 RBI, and a league-best 210 hits and 46 doubles. After being switched to the outfield, Yount continued his fine defensive play. In 1992, he connected for his 3,000th career hit.

Z

Zachary, Tom
1896–1969
Philadelphia (AL 1918), Washington (AL 1919–25, 1927–28), St. Louis (AL 1926–27), New York (AL 1928–30), Boston (NL 1930–34), Brooklyn (NL 1934–36), Philadelphia (NL 1936)   P   BL/LHP

533 games	3,126 innings
186-191 W–L	3.73 ERA
720 k's	22 saves

Most fans remember Zachary only as the man who surrendered Babe Ruth's 60th home run in 1927. However, he also won three World Series games and went
undefeated in 1929, going 12-0 for the Yankees.

Zernial, Gus (Ozark Ike)
1923–
Chicago (AL 1949–51), Philadelphia (AL 1951–54),
Kansas City (AL 1955–57), Detroit (AL 1958–59)
OF   BR/TR

1,234 games	.265 ba
1,093 hits	237 hr
776 rbi	15 sb

Strong as an ox, Zernial was one of the AL's most
feared sluggers in the fifties. He led the circuit in home
runs (33) and RBI (129) in 1951 and slugged 42
roundtrippers in 1952.

Zisk, Richie
1949–
Pittsburgh (NL 1971–76), Chicago (AL 1977), Texas
(AL 1978–80), Seattle (AL 1981–83)   **OF, DH**
BR/TR

1,453 games	.287 ba
1,477 hits	207 hr
792 rbi	8 sb

When the Pittsburgh Lumber Company flexed its
muscles around the NL in the seventies, one of its leading strongmen was Richie Zisk. He batted .324 and
.313 for the Pirates in his first two seasons as a regular
(1973–74). Traded to the White Sox, he took part in
the glorious summer of 1977 on the South Side, batting .290 with 30 homers and 101 RBI. Weak defensively, he was best suited to be a designated hitter.

About the Author

A lifetime baseball fanatic, Stephen Weinstein received his Ph.D. in American History from Columbia University for a social history of Coney Island. He wrote the *Random House Pro Football Dictionary* and has contributed essays to the forthcoming *Encyclopedia of New York City* and the *Dictionary of American Biography*.